Lecture Notes in Artificial Intelligence  3176

Edited by J. G. Carbonell and J. Siekm

Subseries of Lecture Notes in Computer Science

Olivier Bousquet   Ulrike von Luxburg
Gunnar Rätsch (Eds.)

Advanced Lectures on Machine Learning

ML Summer Schools 2003
Canberra, Australia, February 2-14, 2003
Tübingen, Germany, August 4-16, 2003
Revised Lectures

 Springer

Series Editors

Jaime G. Carbonell, Carnegie Mellon University, Pittsburgh, PA, USA
Jörg Siekmann, University of Saarland, Saarbrücken, Germany

Volume Editors

Olivier Bousquet
Ulrike von Luxburg
Max Planck Institute for Biological Cybernetics
Spemannstr. 38, 72076 Tübingen, Germany
E-mail: {bousquet, ule}@tuebingen.mpg.de

Gunnar Rätsch
Fraunhofer FIRST
Kekuléstr. 7, 10245 Berlin, Germany
and Max Planck Institute for Biological Cybernetics
Spemannstr. 38, 72076 Tübingen, Germany
E-mail: Gunnar.Raetsch@tuebingen.mpg.de

Library of Congress Control Number: 2004111357

CR Subject Classification (1998): I.2.6, I.2, F.1, F.2, I.5

ISSN 0302-9743
ISBN 3-540-23122-6 Springer Berlin Heidelberg New York

Springer is a part of Springer Science+Business Media

springeronline.com

© Springer-Verlag Berlin Heidelberg 2004
Printed in Germany

Typesetting: Camera-ready by author, data conversion by Scientific Publishing Services, Chennai, India
Printed on acid-free paper   SPIN: 11322894   06/3142   5 4 3 2 1 0

Preface

Machine Learning has become a key enabling technology for many engineering applications, investigating scientific questions and theoretical problems alike. To stimulate discussions and to disseminate new results, a series of summer schools was started in February 2002. One year later two more such summer schools were held, one at the Australian National University in Canberra, Australia, and the other one at the Max Planck Institute for Biological Cybernetics, in Tübingen, Germany.

The current book contains a collection of the main talks held during those two summer schools, presented as tutorial chapters on topics such as pattern recognition, Bayesian inference, unsupervised learning and statistical learning theory. The papers provide an in-depth overview of these exciting new areas, contain a large set of references, and thereby provide the interested readers with further information to start or to pursue their own research in these directions.

Complementary to the book, photos and slides of the presentations can be obtained at

http://mlg.anu.edu.au/summer2003

and

http://www.irccyn.ec-nantes.fr/mlschool/mlss03/home03.php.

The general entry point for past and future Machine Learning Summer Schools is

http://www.mlss.cc

It is our hope that graduate students, lecturers, and researchers alike will find this book useful in learning and teaching machine learning, thereby continuing the mission of the Machine Learning Summer Schools.

.Tübingen, June 2004

Olivier Bousquet
Ulrike von Luxburg
Gunnar Rätsch

Empirical Inference for Machine Learning and Perception
Max Planck Institute for Biological Cybernetics

Acknowledgments

We gratefully thank all the individuals and organizations responsible for the success of the summer schools.

Local Arrangements

Canberra

Special thanks go to Michelle Moravec and Heather Slater for all their support during the preparations, to Joe Elso, Kim Holburn, and Fergus McKenzie-Kay for IT support, to Cheng Soon-Ong, Kristy Sim, Edward Harrington, Evan Greensmith, and the students at the Computer Sciences Laboratory for their help throughout the course of the Summer School.

Tübingen

Special thanks go to Sabrina Nielebock for all her work during the preparation and on the site, to Dorothea Epting and the staff of the Max Planck Guest House, to Sebastian Stark for IT support, and to all the students and administration of the Max Planck Institute for Biological Cybernetics for their help throughout the Summer School.

Sponsoring Institutions

Canberra

- Research School of Information Sciences and Engineering, Australia
- National Institute of Engineering and Information Science, Australia

Tübingen

- Centre National de la Recherche Scientifique, France
- French-German University
- Max Planck Institute for Biological Cybernetics, Germany

Speakers

Canberra

Shun-Ichi Amari	Gabor Lugosi	Petra Phillips
Eleazar Eskin	Jyrki Kivinen	Gunnar Rätsch
Zoubin Ghahramani	John Lloyd	Alex Smola
Peter Hall	Shahar Mendelson	S.V.N. Vishwanathan
Markus Hegland	Mike Osborne	Robert C. Williamson

Tübingen

Christophe Andrieu	André Elisseeff	Steve Smale
Pierre Baldi	Arthur Gretton	Alex Smola
Léon Bottou	Peter Grünwald	Vladimir Vapnik
Stéphane Boucheron	Thorsten Joachims	Jason Weston
Olivier Bousquet	Massimiliano Pontil	Elad Yom-Tov
Chris Burges	Carl Rasmussen	Ding-Xuan Zhou
Jean-François Cardoso	Mike Tipping	
Manuel Davy	Bernhard Schölkopf	

Organization Committees

Canberra: Gunnar Rätsch and Alex Smola
Tübingen: Olivier Bousquet, Manuel Davy, Frédéric Desobry,
        Ulrike von Luxburg and Bernhard Schölkopf

Table of Contents

An Introduction to Pattern Classification

Elad Yom-Tov

IBM Haifa Research Labs, University Campus, Haifa 31905, Israel
yomtov@il.ibm.com

1 Introduction

Pattern classification is the field devoted to the study of methods designed to categorize data into distinct classes. This categorization can be either distinct labeling of the data (supervised learning), division of the data into classes (unsupervised learning), selection of the most significant features of the data (feature selection), or a combination of more than one of these tasks.

Pattern classification is one of a class of problems that humans (under most circumstances) are able to accomplish extremely well, but are difficult for computers to perform. This subject has been under extensive study for many years. However during the past decade, with the introduction of several new classes of pattern classification algorithms this field seems to achieve performance much better than previously attained.

The goal of the following article is to give the reader a broad overview of the field. As such, it attempts to introduce the reader to important aspects of pattern classification, without delving deeply into any of the subject matters. The exceptions to this rule are those points deemed especially important or those that are of special interest. Finally, we note that the focus of this article are statistical methods for pattern recognition. Thus, methods such as fuzzy logic and rule-based methods are outside the scope of this article.

2 What Is Pattern Classification?

Pattern classification, also referred to as pattern recognition, attempts to build algorithms capable of automatically constructing methods for distinguishing between different exemplars, based on their differentiating patterns.

Watanabe [53] described a pattern as "the opposite of chaos; it is an entity, vaguely defined, that could be given a name." Examples of patterns are human faces, handwritten letters, and the DNA sequences that may cause a certain disease. More formally, the goal of a (supervised) pattern classification task is to find a functional mapping between the input data X, used to describe an input pattern, to a class label Y so that $Y = f(X)$. Construction of the mapping is based on **training data** supplied to the pattern classification algorithm. The mapping f should give the smallest possible error in the mapping, i.e. the minimum number of examples where Y will be the wrong label, especially on **test data** not seen by the algorithm during the learning phase.

O. Bousquet et al. (Eds.): Machine Learning 2003, LNAI 3176, pp. 1–20, 2004.

An important division of pattern classification tasks are **supervised** as opposed to **unsupervised** classification. In supervised tasks the training data consists of training patterns, as well as their required labeling. An example are DNA sequences labeled to show which examples are known to harbor a genetic trait and which ones do not. In unsupervised classification tasks the labels are not provided, and the task of the algorithm is to find a "good" partition of the data into clusters. Examples for this kind of task are grouping of Web pages into sets so that each set is concerned with a single subject matter.

A pattern is described by its **features**. These are the characteristics of the examples for a given problem. For example, in a face recognition task some features could be the color of the eyes or the distance between the eyes. Thus, the input to a pattern recognition task can be viewed as a two-dimensional matrix, whose axes are the examples and the features.

Pattern classification tasks are customarily divided into several distinct blocks. These are:

1. Data collection and representation.
2. Feature selection and/or feature reduction.
3. Clustering.
4. Classification.

Data collection and representation are mostly problem-specific. Therefore it is difficult to give general statements about this step of the process. In broad terms, one should try to find invariant features, that describe the differences in classes as best as possible.

Feature selection and feature reduction attempt to reduce the dimensionality (i.e. the number of features) for the remaining steps of the task. Clustering methods are used in order to reduce the number of training examples to the task. Finally, the classification phase of the process finds the actual mapping between patterns and labels (or targets). In many applications not all steps are needed. Indeed, as computational power grows, the need to reduce the number of patterns used as input to the classification task decreases, and may therefore make the clustering stage superfluous for many applications.

In the following pages we describe feature selection and reduction, clustering, and classification.

3   Feature Selection and Feature Reduction: Removing Excess Data

When data is collected for later classification, it may seem reasonable to assume that if more features describing the data are collected it will be easier to classify these data correctly. In fact, as Trunk [50] demonstrated, more data may be detrimental to classification, especially if the additional data is highly correlated with previous data. Furthermore, noisy and irrelevant features are detrimental to classification as they are known to cause the classifier to have poor generalization, increase the computational complexity, and require many training samples to reach a given accuracy [4].

Conversely, selecting too few features will lead to the ugly duckling theorem [53], that is, it will be impossible to distinguish between the classes because there is too little data to differentiate the classes. For example, suppose we wish to classify a vertebrated animal into one of the vertebra classes (Mammals, Birds, Fish, Reptiles, or Amphibians). A feature that will tell us if the animal has skin is superfluous, since all vertebrates have skins. However, a feature that measures if the animal has warm blood is highly significant for the classification. A feature selection algorithm should be able to identify and remove the former feature, while preserving the latter.

Hence the goal of this stage in the processing is to choose a subset of features or some combination of the input features that will best represent the data. We refer to the process of choosing a subset of the features as **feature selection**, and to finding a good combination of the features as **feature reduction**.

Feature selection is a difficult combinatorial optimization problem. Finding the best subset of features by testing all possible combinations is practically impossible even when the number of input features is modest. For example, attempting to test all possible combinations of 100 input features will require testing 10^{30} combinations. It is not uncommon for text classification problems to have 10^4 to 10^7 features [27]. Consequently numerous methods have been proposed for finding a (suboptimal) solution by testing a fraction of the possible combinations.

Feature selection methods can be divided into three main types [4]:

1. Wrapper methods: The feature selection is performed around (and with) a given classification algorithm. The classification algorithm is used for ranking possible feature combinations.
2. Embedded methods: The feature selection is embedded within the classification algorithm.
3. Filter methods: Features are selected for classification independently of the classification algorithm.

Most feature selection methods are of the wrapper type. The simplest algorithms in this category are the exhaustive search, which is practical only when the number of features is small, **sequential forward feature selection (SFFS)** and **sequential backward feature selection (SBFS)**. In sequential forward feature selection the feature with which the lowest classification error is reached is selected. Then, the feature that, when added, causes the largest reduction in error is added to the set of selected features. This process is continued iteratively until the maximum number of features needed are found or until the classification error starts to increase. Although sequential feature selection does not assume dependence between features, it usually attains surprisingly reasonable results. There are several minor modifications to SFFS and SBFS, such as Sequential Floating Search [41] or the "Plus n, take away m" features.

One of the major drawbacks of methods that select and add a single feature at each step is that they might not find combinations of features that perform well together, but are poor predictors individually. More sophisticated methods for feature selection use simulated annealing or genetic algorithms [56] for solving the optimization problem of feature selection. The latter approach has shown promise in solving problems where the number of input features is extremely large.

An interesting approach to feature selection is based in information theoretic considerations [25]. This algorithm estimates the cross-entropy between every pair of features, and discards those features that have a large cross-entropy with other features, thus removing features that add little additional classification information. This is because the cross-entropy estimates the amount of knowledge that one feature provides on other features. The algorithm is appealing in that it is independent of the classification algorithm, i.e. it is a filter algorithm. However, the need to estimate the cross entropy between features limits its use to applications where the datasets are large or to cases where features are discrete.

As mentioned above, a second approach to reducing the dimension of the features is to find a lower-dimensional combination (linear or non-linear) of the features which represent the data as well as possible in the required dimension.

The most commonly used technique for feature reduction is **principal component analysis (PCA)**, also known as the Karhunen-Loeve Transform (KLT). PCA reshapes the data along the directions of maximal variance. PCA works by computing the eigenvectors corresponding to the largest eigenvalues of the covariance matrix of the data, and returning the projection of the data on these eigenvectors. An example of feature reduction using PCA is given in Figure 1.

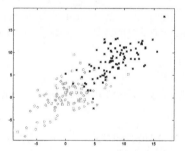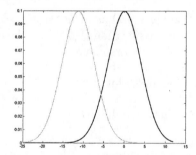

Fig. 1. Feature reduction using principle component analysis. The figure on the left shows the original data. Note that most of the variance in the data is along a single direction. The figure on the right shows probability density function of the same data after feature reduction to a dimension of 1 using PCA

Principle component analysis does not take into account the labels of the data. As such, it is an unsupervised method. A somewhat similar, albeit supervised, linear method is the **Fisher Discriminant Analysis (FDA)**. This method projects the data on a single dimension, while maximizing the separation between the classes of the data.

A more sophisticated projection method is **Independent Component Analysis (ICA)**[8]. This method finds a linear mixture of the data, in the same dimension of the data or lower. ICA attempts to find a mixture matrix such that each of the projections will be as independent as possible from the other projections.

Instead of finding a linear mixture of the feature, it is also possible to find a nonlinear mixture of the data. This is usually done through modifications of the above-mentioned linear methods. Examples of such methods are nonlinear component analysis [33], nonlinear FDA [32], and Kernel PCA[46]. The latter method works by remapping data by way of a kernel function into feature space where the principle components of the data are found.

As a final note on feature selection and feature reduction, one should note that as the ratio between the number of features and the number of training examples increases, it becomes likelier for a noisy and irrelevant feature to seem relevant for the specific set of examples. Indeed, feature selection is sometimes viewed as an ill-posed problem [52], which is why application of such methods should be performed with care. For example, if possible, the feature selection algorithm should be run several times, and the results tested for consistency.

4   Clustering

The second stage of the classification process endeavors to reduce the number of data points by clustering the data and finding representative data points (for example, cluster centers), or by removing superfluous data points. This stage is usually performed using unsupervised methods.

A cluster of points is not a well-defined object. Instead, clusters are defined based on their environment and the scale at which the data is examined. Figure 2 demonstrates the nature of the problem. Two possible definitions for clusters[23] are: (I) Patterns within a cluster are more similar to each other than are patterns belonging to other clusters. (II) A cluster is a volume of high-density points separated from other clusters by a relatively low density volumes. Both these definitions do not suggest a practical solution to the problem of finding clusters. In practice one usually specifies a criterion for joining points into clusters or the number of clusters to be found, and these are used by the clustering algorithm in place of a definition of a cluster. This practicality results in a major drawback of clustering algorithms: A clustering algorithm will find clusters even if there are no clusters in the data.

Returning to the vertebrate classification problem discussed earlier, if we are given data on all vertebrate species, we may find that this comprises of too many training examples. It may be enough to find a representative sample for each of the classes and use it to build the classifier. Clustering algorithms attempt to find such representatives. Note that representative samples can be either actual samples drawn from the data (for example, a human as an example for a mammal) or an average of several samples (i.e. an animal with some given percentage of hair on its body as a representative mammal).

The computational cost of finding an optimal partition of a dataset into a given number of clusters is usually prohibitively high. Therefore, in most cases

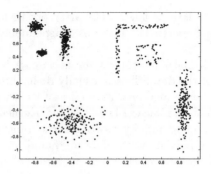

Fig. 2. An example of data points for clustering. Many possible clustering configurations can be made for this data, based on the scale at which the data is examined, the shape of the clusters, etc

clustering algorithms attempt to find a suboptimal partition in a reasonable number of computations. Clustering algorithms can be divided into Top-Down (or partitional) algorithms and Bottom-Up (or hierarchical) algorithms.

A simple example for Bottom-Up algorithms is the **Agglomerative Hierarchical Clustering Algorithm (AGHC)**. This algorithm is an iterative algorithm, which starts by assuming that each data point is a cluster. At each iteration two clusters are merged until a preset number of clusters is reached. The decision on which clusters are to be merged can be done using one of several functions, i.e. distance between cluster centers, distance between the two nearest points in different clusters, etc. AGHC is a very simple, intuitive scheme. However, it is computationally intensive and thus impractical for medium and large datasets.

Top-Down methods are the type more frequently used for clustering due to their lower computational cost, despite the fact that they usually find an inferior solution compared to Bottom-Up algorithms. Probably the most popular amongst Top-Down clustering algorithms in the **K-means algorithm** [28], a pseudo-code of which is given in figure 3. K-means is usually reasonably fast, but care should be taken in the initial setting of the cluster centers so as to attain a good partition of the data. There are probably hundreds of Top-Down clustering algorithms, but popular algorithms include fuzzy k-means [3], Kohonen maps [24], and competitive learning [44].

Recently, with the advent of kernel-based methods several algorithms for clustering using kernels have been suggested (e.g. [2]). The basic idea behind these algorithms is to map the data into a higher dimension using a non-linear function of the input features, and to cluster the data using simple clustering algorithms at the higher dimension. More details regarding kernels are given in the Classification section of this paper. One of the main advantages of kernel methods is that simple clusters (for example, ellipsoid clusters) formed in a higher dimension correspond to complex clusters in the input space. These methods seem to provide excellent clustering results, with reasonable computational costs.

A related class of clustering algorithms are the **Spectral Clustering** methods [37, 11]. These methods first map the data into a matrix representing the distance between the input patterns. The matrix is then projected onto its k largest eigenvectors, and the clustering is performed on this projection. These methods demonstrated impressive results on several datasets, with computational costs slightly higher than those of kernel-based algorithms.

The K-means clustering algorithm

1. Begin initialize N random cluster centers.
2. Assign each of the data points the nearest of the N cluster centers.
3. Recompute the cluster centers by averaging the points assigned to each cluster.
4. Repeat steps 2-4 until the there is no change in the location of the cluster centers.
5. Return the cluster centers.

Fig. 3. Pseudo-code of the K-means clustering algorithm

5   Classification

Classification, the final stage of a pattern classifier, is the process of assigning labels to test patterns, based on previously labeled training patterns. This process is commonly divided into a learning phase, where the classification algorithm is trained, and a classification phase, where the algorithm labels new data.

The general model for statistical pattern classification is one where patterns are drawn from an unknown distribution P, which depends on the label of the data (i.e., $P(x|\omega_i)$ $i = 1, \ldots, N$, where N is the number of labels in the data). During the learning phase the classification algorithm is trained with the goal of minimizing the error that will be obtained when classifying some test data. This error is known as the **risk** or the **expected loss**.

When discussing the pros and cons of classification algorithms, it is important to set criteria for assessing these algorithms. In the following pages we describe several classification algorithms and later summarize (in table 1) their strong and weak points with regard to the following points:

- How small are the classification errors reached by the algorithm?
- What is the computational cost and the memory requirements for both training and testing?
- How difficult is it for a novice user to build and train an efficient classifier?
- Is the algorithm able to learn on-line (i.e. as the data appears, allowing each data point to be addressed only once)?
- Can one gain insight about the problem from examining the trained classifier?

It is important to note that when discussing the classification errors of classifiers one is usually interested in the errors obtained when classifying test data. Many classifiers can be trained to classify all the training data correctly. This does not imply that they will perform well on unseen test data. In fact, it is more often the case that if a classification algorithm reduces the training set error to zeros it has been **over-fitted** to the training data. Section 6 discusses methods that can be applied in order to avoid over-fitting. A good classifier should be able to generalize from the training data, i.e. learn a set of rules from the training data that will then be used to classify the test data.

The first question one should address in the context of classification is, is there an optimal classification rule (with regard to the classification error)? Surprisingly, such a rule exists, but in practice one can rarely use it. The optimal classification rule is the Bayes rule. Suppose that we wish to minimize the expected loss function: $R\left(\omega_i | x\right) = \sum L\left(\omega_i, \omega_j\right) P\left(\omega_j | x\right)$ where L is the loss function for deciding on class i given that the correct class is class j. If the zero/one loss is used (i.e. a wrong decision entails a loss of one, and a correct decision results in a loss of zero) the Bayes rule simplifies to the **Maximum Aposteriory (MAP)** rule, which requires that we label an input sample x with the label i if $P\left(\omega_i | x\right) > P\left(\omega_j | x\right)$ for all $j \neq i$.

As mentioned above, it is usually impossible to use the Bayes rule because it requires full knowledge of the class-conditional densities of the data. Thus, one is frequently left with one of two options. If a model for the class-conditional densities is known (for example, if it is known that the data consists of two Gaussians for one class and a single uniform distribution for the other class), one can use **plug-in** rules to build a classifier. Here, given the model, its parameters are estimated, and then the MAP rule can be used. If a model for the data cannot be provided, classifiers can proceed by estimating the density of the data or the decision boundaries between the different classes.

The simplest plug-in model for data is to assume that each class of data is drawn from a single Gaussian. Under this assumption, the mean and variance of each class is estimated, and the labeling of test points is achieved through the MAP rule. If the data is known to contain more than one variate (e.g. Gaussian or uniform) distribution, the parameters of these distributions can be computed through algorithms such as Expectation-Maximization (EM) [12] algorithm. In order to operate the EM algorithm, the number of components in each class must be known in advance. This is not always simple, and an incorrect number might result in an erroneous solution. It is possible to alleviate this effect by estimating the number of components in the data using ML-II [29] or MDL [1].

Most classification algorithms do not attempt to find or even to approximate the Bayes decision region. Instead, these algorithms classify points by estimating decision regions or through estimation of densities. Arguably the simplest of these methods is the **k-Nearest Neighbor** classifier. Here the k points of the training data closest to the test point are found, and a label is given to the test point by a majority vote between the k points. This method is highly intuitive and attains a remarkably low classification errors, but it is computationally intensive and requires a large memory to store the training data.

Another intuitive class of classification algorithms are **decision trees**. These algorithms solve the classification problem by repeatedly partitioning the input

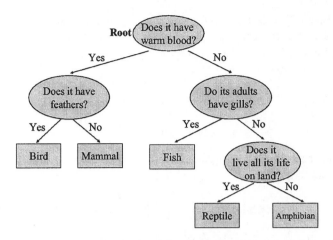

Fig. 4. An example a decision tree. Classification of a new test point is achieved by moving from top to bottom along the branches of the tree, starting from the root node, until a terminal node (square) is reached

space, so as to build a tree whose nodes are as pure as possible (that is, they contain points of a single class). An example of a tree for classifying vertebrates into classes is shown in 4. Classification of a new test point is achieved by moving from top to bottom along the branches of the tree, starting from the root node, until a terminal node is reached. Decision trees are simple yet effective classification schemes for small datasets. Large datasets tend to result in complicated trees, which in turn require a large memory for storage. There is considerable literature on methods for simplifying and pruning decision trees (for example [30]). Another drawback of decision trees is their relative sensitivity to noise, especially if the size of the training data is small. The most commonly used algorithms for building decision trees, all developed by Quinlan, are CART [6], ID3 [42], and C4.5 [43].

An important approach to classification is through estimation of the density of data for each of the classes and classifying test points according to the maximum posterior probability. A useful algorithm for density estimation is the **Parzen windows** estimation[39]. Parzen windows estimate the probability of a point in the input space by weighing training points using a Gaussian window function (the farther a training sample is from the test sample, the lower its weight). This method is, however, expensive both computationally and memory wise. Furthermore, many training points are required for correct estimation of the class densities.

Another approach for classification is to optimize a functional mapping from input patterns to output labels so that the training error will be as small as possible. If, for example, we assume a linear mapping (i.e. that the classifier takes the form of a weighted sum of the input patterns), it is possible to find a closed-form solution to the optimization (under a least-squares criterion) through the Moore-Penrose pseudo-inverse. Suppose the training patterns are placed in a matrix of size $N \times D$ where D is the input dimension and N the number of examples, and that the corresponding labels are placed in a $N \times 1$ vector T. We wish to find a weight vector w so that:

$$P \cdot w = T$$

The least-squares (LS) solution to this problem is:

$$w = \left(P^T \cdot P\right)^{-1} \cdot P^T \cdot T$$

Assuming that the labels of the data are either -1 or $+1$, the labeling of a new test point x will be:

$$\hat{t} = sign\left(w^T \cdot x\right) = \begin{cases} +1 & if \ \ w^T \cdot x > 0 \\ -1 & if \ \ w^T \cdot x < 0 \end{cases}$$

LS is extremely efficient in both memory requirement and computational effort, but it is usually too simplistic a model to obtain sufficiently good results for the data.

The optimization approach to pattern classification has been utilized in numerous other algorithms. An interesting example is the use of Genetic Programming (GP) for classification. Genetic algorithms are computational models inspired by evolution [55]. As such, they encode potential solutions to an optimization problem as a chromosome-like data structure and apply recombination operators on these structures. These recombination operators are designed so as to gradually improve the solutions, much like evolution improves individuals in a population. In genetic programming the encoded solution is a function, and the goal is to search in function space for a mapping of inputs to labels that will reduce the training error. GP can sometimes find a very good solution with both a low error and small computational and memory requirements, but there is no proof that it will converge (At all or to a good solution) and thus it is not a popular algorithm.

Perhaps one of the commonly used approaches to classification that solves an optimization problem are Neural Networks (NN). Neural networks (suggested first by Alan Turing [51]) are a computational model inspired by the connectivity of neurons in animate nervous systems. A further boost to their popularity came with the proof that they can approximate any function mapping via the Universal Approximation Theorem [22]. A simple scheme for a neural network is shown in 5. Each circle denotes a computational element referred to as a neuron. A neuron computes a weighted sum of its inputs, and possibly performs a nonlinear function on this sum. If certain classes of nonlinear functions are used, the function computed by the network can approximate any function (specifically a mapping from the training patterns to the training targets), provided enough neurons exist in the network. Common nonlinear functions are the sign function and the hyperbolic tangent.

The architecture of neural networks is not limited to the feed-forward structure shown in Figure 5. Many other structures have been suggested, such as recurrent NN, where the output is fed back as an input to the net, networks

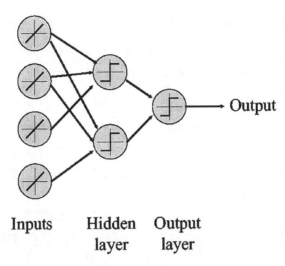

Inputs   Hidden   Output
          layer   layer

Fig. 5. A schematic diagram of a neural network. Each circle in the hidden and output layer is a computational element known as a neuron

with multiple outputs, and networks where each of the neurons activates only if the input pattern is in a certain region of the input space (an example of which are radial-basis function (RBF) networks).

If a single neuron exists in a network, it is usually referred to as a perceptron. Perceptrons find a linear separating hyperplane and proof can be given to show that it will converge to a solution, if one exists. There are many algorithms for training (i.e. finding the weight vector for the perceptron): Batch and stochastic, on-line and off-line, with and without memory [15]. The perceptron is a good choice for an on-line linear classifier. It shares the same pros and cons as the LS classifier, with the additional drawback that it might not converge if no linear separation exists. However, for off-line applications it is usually simpler to use the LS algorithm.

Multiple-layered NNs are far more difficult to train. Indeed this was a major obstacle in the development of NNs until an efficient algorithm for training was developed. This algorithm is known as the backpropagation algorithm, so-called because the errors that are the driving force in the training (if there is no error, there is no need to change the weights of the NN) are propagated from the output layer, through the hidden layers, to the input layer. This algorithm, whether in batch or stochastic mode, enables the network to be trained according to the need. Further advancement was attained through second-order methods for training, which achieve faster convergence. Among these we note the conjugate-gradient descent (CGD) algorithm [36] and Quickprop [18], both of which significantly accelerate network training.

NNs have significant advantages in memory requirements and classification speed, and have shown excellent results on real-world problems [26]. Nevertheless, they suffer from major drawbacks. Among these are the difficulty in deciding

Table 1. Comparison of the reviewed classification algorithms

Algorithm	Classification error	Computational cost	Memory requirements	Difficulty to Implement	On-line	Insight from the classifier
Expectation-Maximization (EM)	Low	Medium	Small	Low	No	Yes
Nearest neighbor	Medium-low	High	High	Low	No	No
Decision trees	Medium	Medium	Medium	Low	No	Yes
Parzen windows	Low	High	High	Low	No	No
Linear least squares (LS)	High	Low	Low	Low	Yes	Yes
Genetic programming	Medium-low	Medium	Low	Low	No	Some
Neural Networks	Low	Medium	Low	High	Yes	No
Ada-Boost	Low	Medium	Medium	Medium	No	No
Support vector machines (SVM)	Low	Medium	Low	Medium	Yes	Some

on network architecture as well as several other network parameters, and that the resulting classifier is a "black box", where it is difficult to understand why the network training resulted in a certain set of weights. Finally, contrary to other classification algorithms, efficient training of NNs is also dependent on several "tricks of the trade" such as normalizing the inputs, setting the initial weight values, etc. This makes it difficult for the novice to use NN effectively.

An interesting and extremely useful approach to classification is to use simple classifiers as building blocks for constructing complicated decision regions. This approach is known as **Boosting**. Schematically, we first train a simple (or weak) classifier for the data. Then, those points of the train-set that are incorrectly classified are located and another weak classifier is trained so as to improve the classification of these incorrectly labeled points. This process is repeated until a sufficiently low training error is reached.

The training of the weak classifiers can be performed by either drawing points from the training data with a probability inversely proportional to the distance of the points from the decision region or by selecting a cluster of the incorrectly trained points. In the first case, the algorithm is known as AdaBoost [19], which is the most popular boosting algorithm. In the second case, the algorithm is the Local Boosting algorithm [31].

Boosting has been shown to give very results on many data-sets. Its computational cost is reasonably low, as are its memory requirements. Thus, boosting is one of the most useful classification algorithms.

The last type of classification algorithm we discuss in this introduction is the **Support Vector Machine (SVM)** classifier. This classifier is the result of seminal work by Boser, Guyon, and Vapnik [5] and later others. SVM draws on two main practical observations:

1. At a sufficiently high dimension, patterns are orthogonal to each other, and thus it is easier to find a separating hyperplane for data in a high dimension.
2. Not all patterns are necessary for finding a separating hyperplane. In fact, it is sufficient to use only those points that are near the boundary between groups for constructing the boundary.

An SVM classifier is a linear classifier which finds the hyperplane that separates the data with the largest **margin**(i.e. the distance between the hyperplane and the closest data point) possible, built after transforming the data into a high dimension (known as the feature space). Let us begin with the second part of the process - the separating hyperplane. A linear separating hyperplane is a decision function in the form

$$f\left(x\right) = sign\left(\langle w, x \rangle + b\right)$$

where x is the input pattern, w is the weight vector, b is a bias term, and $\langle \cdot, \cdot \rangle$ denotes the inner product.

If the data is to be classified correctly, this hyperplane should ensure that

$$y_i \cdot \left(\langle w, x_i \rangle + b\right) > 0 \quad for \ all \ i = 1, \dots, m$$

assuming that $y \in \{-1, +1\}$.

There is one separating hyperplane that maximizes the margin separating the data, which is attractive since this hyperplane gives good generalization performance[46]. In order to find this hyperplane we need to minimize $\|w\|^2$.

Thus the SVM problem can be written as:

$$minimize \ \tfrac{1}{2} \|w\|^2$$
$$subject \ to \ y_i \cdot \left(\langle w, x_i \rangle + b\right) \geq 1 \quad for \ all \ i = 1, \dots, m$$

(The right hand side of the bottom equation was changed to one instead of zero otherwise the minimum of w would be the trivial solution. In fact, any positive number would suffice)

This constrained minimization problem is solved using Lagrange multipliers, which results in a dual optimization problem:

$$maximize \ W\left(\alpha\right) = \sum_{i=1}^{m} \alpha_i - \tfrac{1}{2} \sum_{i,j=1}^{m} \alpha_i \alpha_j y_i y_j \langle x_i, x_j \rangle$$
$$s.t. \ \alpha_i \geq 0, \sum_{i=1}^{m} \alpha_i y_i = 0$$

The coefficients of a corresponding to input patterns that are not used for construction of the class boundary should be zero. The remaining coefficients are known as the **support vectors**. The above optimization problem can be solved in several ways, for example: Through a perceptron, which finds the largest margin hyperplane separating the data[15]; By use of quadratic programming optimization algorithms, which solve the optimization problem [15]; or through other efficient optimization algorithms such as the sequential minimal optimization (SMO) algorithm [40].

Classification of new samples is performed using the equation

$$y = sign \left(\sum_{i=1}^{m} y_i \alpha_i \langle x, x_i \rangle + b \right)$$

As noted above, it is useful to map the input patterns into a high dimensional space. This could be done by mapping each input pattern through a function so that $\tilde{x} = \varphi(x)$. However, in practice, if the function maps the data into a very high dimension, it would be problematic to compute and to store the results of the mapping. If the mapping is done into an infinite dimensional space this would be impossible. Fortunately, this problem can be avoided through a substitute known as the kernel trick[5]. Note that in the optimization problem above, the input patterns only appear in an inner product of pairs of patterns. Thus, instead of mapping each sample to a higher dimension and then performing the inner product, it is possible (for certain classes of kernels) to first compute the inner product between patterns and only then compute the mapping on a scalar. Thus, in the equations above we now replace the inner products $\langle x, x' \rangle$ with $k(x, x')$ where k is the kernel function. The kernel function used for mapping should conform to conditions known as the Mercer conditions [22]. Examples of such functions are polynomials, radial basis functions (Gaussian functions), and hyperbolic tangents.

SVMs have been studied extensively[46]. They have been extended in many directions. Some notable examples include:

1. Cases where the optimal hyperplane does not exist, through the introduction of a penalty term which allows some training patterns to be incorrectly classified [10].
2. Single class learning (outlier detection) [45].
3. Online learning [17].
4. Feature selection [20, 54].
5. Incremental classification so as to reduce the computational cost of SVMs[7].

It is difficult to find thorough comparative studies of classification algorithms. Several such studies (for example [33, 46]) point to the conclusion that a few classification algorithms, namely SVM, AdaBoost, Kernel Fisher discriminant, and Neural networks achieve similar results with regard to error rates. Lately, the Relevance Vector Machine [49], a kernel method stemming from Bayesian learning, has also joined this group of algorithms. However, these algorithm differ greatly in the other factors outlined at the beginning of this chapter.

Finally, we note several practical points of importance which one should take into account when designing classifiers:

1. In order to reduce the likelihood of over-fitting the classifier to the training data, the ratio of the number of training examples to the number of features should be at least 10:1. For the same reason the ratio of the number of training examples to the number of unknown parameters should be at least 10:1.
2. It is important to use proper error-estimation methods (see next section), especially when selecting parameters for the classifier.

3. Some algorithms require the input features to be scaled to similar ranges. This is especially evident those that use some kind of a weighted average of the inputs such as neural networks, SVM, etc.
4. There is no single best classification algorithm!

Thus far we have implicitly only discussed problems where there are two classes of data, i.e. the labels can take one of two values. In many applications it is necessary to distinguish between more than two classes. Some classifiers are suitable for such applications with only minor changes. Examples of such classifiers are the LS classifier, the Nearest Neighbor classifier, and decision trees. Neural networks require a minor modification to work with multiclass problems. Instead of having a single output neuron there should be as many output neurons as labels. Each of the output neurons is trained to respond to data of one class, and the strongest activated neuron is taken to be the predicted class label. SVMs have been modified to solve multiclass problems through a slight change in the objective function to the minimization procedure [46].

Not all classifiers are readily modifiable to multiclass applications. The strategy for solution of such cases is to train several classifiers and add a gating network that decides on the predicted label based on the output of these classifiers. The simplest example of such a strategy is to train as many classifiers as classes where each classifier is trained to respond to one class of data. The gating network then outputs the number of the classifier that responded to a given input. This type of solution is called a one-against-all solution. The main drawbacks of this solution are that it is heuristic, that the classifiers are solving problems that are very different in their difficulty, and that, if the output of the classifiers is binary, there might be more than one possible class for each output. A variation on the one-against-all solution is to train classifiers to distinguish between each pair of classes[21]. This solution has the advantage that the individual classifiers are trained on smaller datasets. The main drawback of this solution is the large number of classifiers that are needed to be trained $((N-1)N/2)$.

An elegant solution to multiclass problems was suggested in [13]. That article showed the parallel between multiclass problems and the study of error-correcting codes for communication applications. In the latter, bits of data are sent over a noisy channel. At the receiver, the data is reconstructed through thresholding of the received bit. In order to reduce the probability of error, additional bits of data are sent to the receiver. These bits are a function of the data bits, and are designed so that they can correct errors that occurred during transmission (if only a small numbers of error appeared). The functions by which these extra bits are computed are known as error-correcting codes. The application of error-correcting codes to multiclass problems is straightforward. Classifiers are trained according to an error-correcting code, and their output to test patterns is interpreted as though they were the received bits of information. This solution requires the addition of classifiers according to the specific error-correcting code (for example, the simple Hamming code requires $2^N - N - 1$

classifiers for N classes of data), but if a few of the classifiers are in error, the total output would still be correct.

In practice, the one-against-all method is usually not much worse than the more sophisticated approaches described above. When selecting the solution, one should consider training times and the available memory, in addition to the overall accuracy of the system.

The last topic we address in the context of classification is one-class learning. This is an interesting philosophical subject, as well as an extremely practical one. We usually learn by observing different examples (Car vs. Plane, Cat vs. Dog, etc). Is it possible to learn by observing examples of only a single class? (e.g. would a child who only saw cats be able to say that a dog, first seen, is not a cat?). In the framework of classification, the object of single-class learning is to distinguish between objects of one kind (the target object) and all other possible objects)[48], where the latter are not seen during training. Single-class learning has been applied to problems such as image retrieval[9], typist identification[38], and character recognition[46].

The idea behind single-class learning is to identify areas where the data representing the target object is of high density. If a test sample appears close to (or inside) such a high-density area, it would be classified as a target object. If it is in a low-density area of the input space, it would be classified as a different object.

The simplest type of single-class algorithm describes the data by a single Gaussian (with a mean and a covariance matrix). The probability estimate that a test sample is drawn from this Gaussian is computed, and this measure is reported to the user. A more sophisticated measure is the Parzen windows estimation of density, or through the use of a multi-Gaussian model, with EM used for training. Neural networks have also been used for this task training the network to form closed decision surfaces, and labeling points outside these surfaces as non-target-class data [34].

More recently, single-class SVMs were developed[47]. These are a modification of the two-class SVM described above, with the SVM attempting to enclose the data with a sphere in feature space. Any data falling outside this sphere is deemed not to be of the target class.

6   Error Estimation Techniques

As noted above, the most important factor in the performance of a classifier is its error rate. This measure is important for assessing if the classifier is useful, for tuning its parameters[35], and in order to compare it to other classifiers. It is often difficult to estimate the error rate of a given classifier even if there is full knowledge of the underlying distribution is available.

In practice, it is desirable to estimate the error rate given a sample data set. This problem is aggravated if the dataset is small[23]. If the whole dataset is used to both training the classifier and for estimating its error, there is a serious danger of over-fitting the classifier to the training data (in the extreme case, consider a 1-Nearest Neighbor classifier). Therefore, the data should be split into training data and testing data.

There are three main methods for splitting the data:

1. Resubstitution: Here the whole dataset is used for both training and testing. As noted above this method is extremely optimistic. In practice, for small datasets error estimation obtained using this method is erroneous.
2. Holdout: Part of the data (for example, 80%) is used for training, and the remaining is used for testing. This method is pessimistically biased, and different splits of the data will result of different error rates.
3. Cross-validation: The data is divided into N equal sub-sets. The data is trained using (N-1) sub-sets, and tested on the N-th subset. The process is repeated until each of the N sub-sets is used as a test set. The error rate is the average of the N resulting errors. The resulting error rate has a lower bias than the holdout method. An extreme form of cross-validation is known as leave-one-out, where the sub-sets contain a single point. The estimate of leave-one-out is unbiased but it has a large variance and is computationally expensive to compute.

After computing the error rate of a classifier, we have an estimation of how well the algorithm will perform on new data. The algorithm should then be trained using the whole dataset, in preparation of new data.

Although it is desirable to use the error rate as a way to compare the performance of different classification algorithms, this is (surprisingly) still an open issue for future research. Some researchers have used the Wilcoxon signed-rank tests for such comparison, although the underlying assumptions of this test are violated when it is used for such a comparison[14].

7   Summary

The purpose of pattern classification algorithms is to automatically construct methods for distinguishing between different exemplars, based on their differentiating patterns.

The goal of completely automated learning algorithms is yet to be attained. Most pattern classification algorithms need some manual parameter tuning to achieve the best possible performance. More importantly, in most practical applications, domain knowledge remains crucial for the successful operation of Pattern Classification algorithms.

Pattern classification has been an object of research for several decades. In the past decade this research resulted in a multitude of new algorithms, better theoretic understanding of previous ideas, as well as many successful practical applications.

Pattern classification remains an exciting domain for theoretic research, as well as for application of its' tools to practical problems. Some of the problems yet to be solved were outlined in previous paragraphs, and a more detailed list appears in [16].

References

1. A.R. Barron and T.M. Cover. Minimum complexity density estimation. *IEEE Transactions on information theory*, IT-37(4):1034–1054, 1991.
2. A. Ben-Hur, D. Horn, H.T. Siegelmann, and V. Vapnik. Support vector clustering. *Journal of Machine Learning Research*, 2:125–137, 2001.
3. J.C. Bezdek. *Fuzzy mathematics in pattern classification*. PhD thesis, Cornell University, Applied mathematics center, Ithaka, NY, 1973.
4. A.L. Blum and P. Langley. Selection of relevant features and examples in machine learning. *Artificial Intelligence*, 97:245–271, 1997.
5. B.E. Boser, I.M. Guyon, and V. Vapnik. A training algorithm for optimal margin classifiers. In D. Haussler, editor, *Proceedings of the 5th annual ACM workshop on computational learning theory*, pages 144–152, Pittsburgh, PA, USA, 1992. ACM Press.
6. L. Breiman, J.H. Friedman, R.A. Olshen, and C.J. Stone. *Classification and regression trees*. Chapman and Hall, New York, USA, 1993.
7. C.J.C. Burges and B. Schölkopf. Improving the accuracy and speed of support vector machines. In M.C. Mozer, M.I. Jordan, and T. Petsche, editors, *Advances in Neural Information Processing Systems*, volume 9, page 375, Cambridge, MA, USA, 1997. The MIT Press.
8. J-F Cardoso. Blind signal separation: Statistical principles. *Proceedings of the IEEE*, 9(10):2009–2025, 1998.
9. Y. Chen, X.S. Zhou, and T.S. Huang. One-class svm for learning in image retrieval. In *Proceedings of the international conference on image processing*, volume 1, pages 34–37. IEEE, 2001.
10. C. Cortes and V. Vapnik. Support vector networks. *Machine learning*, 20:273–297, 1995.
11. N. Cristianini, J. Shawe-Taylor, and J. Kandola. Spectral kernel methods for clustering. In T.G. Dietterich, S. Becker, and Z. Ghahramani, editors, *Advances in Neural Information Processing Systems*, volume 14, pages 649–655, Cambridge, MA, USA, 2002. The MIT Press.
12. A.P. Dempster, N.M. Laird, and D.B. Rubin. Maximum-likelihood from incomplete data via the em algorithm (with discussion). *Journal of the royal statistical society, Series B*, 39:1–38, 1977.
13. T.G. Dietrich and G. Bakiri. Solving multi-class learning problems via error-correcting output codes. *Journal of artificial intelligence research*, 2:263–286, 1995.
14. T.G. Dietterich. Approximate statistical tests for comparing supervised classification learning algorithms. *Neural Computation*, 10(7):1895–1923, 1998.
15. R.O. Duda, P.E. Hart, and D.G. Stork. *Pattern classification*. John Wiley and Sons, Inc, New-York, USA, 2001.
16. R.P.W. Duin, F. Roli, and D. de Ridder. A note on core research issues for statistical pattern recognition. *Pattern recognition letters*, 23:493–499, 2002.
17. Y. Engel, S. Mannor, and R. Meir. The kernel recursive least squares algorithm. Technion CCIT Report number 446, Technion, Haifa, Israel, 2003.
18. S.E. Fahlman. Faster-learning variations on back-propagation: An empirical study. In T.J. Sejnowski, G.E. Hinton, and D.S. Touretzky, editors, *Connectionist Models Summer School*, San Mateo, CA, USA, 1988. Morgan Kaufmann.
19. Y. Freund and R.E. Schapire. A decision-theoretic generalization of online learning and an application to boosting. *Journal of Computer and System Sciences*, 55:119–139, 1995.

20. I. Guyon, J. Weston, S. Barnhill, and V. Vapnik. Gene selection for cancer classification using support vector machines. *Machine learning*, 46(1-3):389–422, 2002.

21. T.J. Hastie and R.J. Tibshirani. Classification by pairwise coupling. In M.I. Jordan, M.J. Kearns, and S.A. Solla, editors, *Advances in Neural Information Processing Systems*, volume 10, Cambridge, MA, USA, 1998. The MIT Press.

22. S. Haykin. *Neural Networks: A comprehensive foundation, 2nd Ed.* Prentice-Hall, 1999.

23. A.K. Jain, R.P.W. Duin, and J. Mao. Statistical pattern recognition: A review. *IEEE Transactions on pattern analysis and machine intelligence*, 22(1):4–37, 1999.

24. T. Kohonen. Self-organization and associative memory. *Biological Cybernetics*, 43(1):59–69, 1982.

25. D. Koller and M. Sahami. Toward optimal feature selection. In *Proceedings of the 13th International Conference on Machine Learning*, pages 284–292, Bari, Italy, 1996. Morgan Kaufmann.

26. Y. LeCun, L. Bottou, Y. Bengio, and P. Haffner. Gradient-based learning applied to document recognition. *Proceedings of IEEE*, 86(11):2278–2324, 1998.

27. D.D. Lewis. Feature selection and feature extraction for text categorization. In *Proceedings of speech and natural language workshop*, pages 212–217, San Francisco, USA, 1992. Morgan Kaufmann.

28. S.P. Lloyd. Least squares quantization in pcm. *IEEE Transactions on Information Theory*, IT-2:129–137, 1982.

29. D.J. MacKay. Bayesian model comparison and backprop nets. In J.E. Moody, S.J. Hanson, and R.P. Lippmann, editors, *Neural Networks for Signal Processing 4*, pages 839–846, San Mateo, CA, USA, 1992. Morgan Kaufmann.

30. M. Mehta, J. Rissanen, and R. Agrawal. Mdl-based decision tree pruning. In *Proceedings of the first international conference on knowledge discovery and data mining*, pages 216–221, 1995.

31. R. Meir, R. El-Yaniv, and S. Ben-David. Localized boosting. In *Proceedings of the 13th Annual Conference on Computer Learning Theory*, pages 190–199, San Francisco, 2000. Morgan Kaufmann.

32. S. Mika, G. Rätsch, J. Weston, B. Schölkopf, and K.-R. Müller. Fisher discriminant analysis with kernels. In Y.-H. Hu, J. Larsen, E. Wilson, and S. Douglas, editors, *Neural Networks for Signal Processing IX*, pages 41–48. IEEE, 1999.

33. S. Mika, B. Schölkopf, A. J. Smola, K.-R. Müller, M. Scholz, and G. Rätsch. Kernel pca and de–noising in feature spaces. In M.S. Kearns, S.A. Solla, and D.A. Cohn, editors, *Advances in Neural Information Processing Systems 11*, Cambridge, MA, USA, 1999. MIT Press.

34. M.R. Moya, M.W. Koch, and L.D. Hostetler. One-class classifier networks for target recognition applications. In *Proceedings of the world congress on neural networks*, Portland, OR, USA, 1993. International neural networks society.

35. K.-R. Müller, S. Mika, G. Rätsch, K. Tsuda, and B. Schölkopf. An introduction to kernel-based learning algorithms," ieee transactions on neural networks. *IEEE Transactions on Neural Networks*, 12(2):181–201, 2001.

36. M. Muller. A scaled conjugate gradient algorithm for fast supervised learning. *Neural Networks*, 6:525–533, 1993.

37. A.Y. Ng, M.I. Jordan, and Y. Weiss. On spectral clustering: Analysis and an algorithm. In T.G. Dietterich, S. Becker, and Z. Ghahramani, editors, *Advances in Neural Information Processing Systems*, volume 14, pages 849–856, Cambridge, MA, USA, 2002. The MIT Press.

38. M. Nisenson, I. Yariv, R. El-Yaniv, and R. Meir. Towards behaviometric security systems: Learning to identify a typist. In *Proceedings of the 7th European Conference on Principles and Practice of Knowledge Discovery in Databases (ECML/PKDD)*, 2003.

39. E. Parzen. On estimation of a probability density function and mode. *Annals of mathematical statistics*, 33(3):1065–1076, 1962.

40. J. Platt. Fast training of support vector machines using sequential minimal optimization. In A.J. Smola, P.L. Bartlett, B. Schölkopf, and D. Schuurmans, editors, *Advances in kernel methods - Support vector learning*, pages 185–208, Cambridge, MA, USA, 1999. MIT Press.

41. P. Pudil, J. Novovicova, and J. Kittler. Floating search methods in feature selection. *Pattern recognition letters*, 15(11):1119–1125, 1994.

42. J.R. Quinlan. Learning efficient classification procedures and their application to chess end games. In R.S. Michalski, J.G. Carbonell, and T.M. Mitchell, editors, *Machine learning: An artificial intelligence approach*, pages 463–482, San Francisco, CA, USA, 1983. Morgan Kaufmann.

43. J.R. Quinlan. *C4.5: Programs for machine learning*. Morgan Kaufmann, San Francisco, CA, USA, 1993.

44. D.E. Rumelhart and D. Zipser. Feature discovery by competitive learning. *Parallel Distributed Processing*, pages 151–193, 1986.

45. B. Schölkopf, J. Platt, J. Share-Taylor, A.J. Smola, and R.C. Williamson. Estimating the support of a high-dimensional distribution. TR87, Microsoft Research, Redmond, WA, USA, 1999.

46. B. Schölkopf and A.J. Smola. *Leaning with kernels: Support vector machines, regularization, optimization, and beyond*. MIT Press, Cambridge, MA, USA, 2002.

47. D.M.J. Tax and R.P.W. Duin. Data domain description by support vectors. In M. Verleysen, editor, *Proceedings of the European symposium on artificial neural networks*, pages 251–256, Brussel, 1999.

48. D.M.J. Tax and R.P.W. Duin. Combining one-class classifiers. In J. Kittler and F. Roli, editors, *Proceedings of the Second International Workshop on Multiple Classifier Systems, MCS 2001*, Heidelberg, Germany, 2001. Springer-Verlag.

49. M. Tipping. The relevance vector machine. *Journal of machine learning research*, 1:211–244, 2001.

50. G.V. Trunk. A problem of dimensionality: A simple example. *IEEE Transactions on pattern analysis and machine intelligence*, 1(3):306–307, 1979.

51. A.M. Turing. Intelligent machinery. In D.C. Ince, editor, *Collected works of A.M. Turing: Mechanical Intelligence*, Amsterdam, The Netherlands, 1992. Elsevier Science Publishers.

52. V.N. Vapnik. Personal communication, 2003.

53. W. Watanabe. *Pattern recognition: Human and mechanical*. Wiley, 1985.

54. J. Weston, A. Elisseeff, B. Schölkopf, and M. Tipping. Use of the zero-norm with linear models and kernel methods. *Journal of machine learning research*, 3:1439–1461, 2003.

55. D. Whitley. A genetic algorithm tutorial. *Statistics and Computing*, 4(2):65–85, 6 1994.

56. E. Yom-Tov and G.F. Inbar. Feature selection for the classification of movements from single movement-related potentials. *IEEE Transactions on Neural Systems and Rehabilitation Engineering*, 10(3):170–177, 2001.

Some Notes on Applied Mathematics for Machine Learning

Christopher J.C. Burges

Microsoft Research, One Microsoft Way, Redmond, WA 98052-6399, USA
cburges@microsoft.com
http://research.microsoft.com/~cburges

Abstract. This chapter describes Lagrange multipliers and some selected subtopics from matrix analysis from a machine learning perspective. The goal is to give a detailed description of a number of mathematical constructions that are widely used in applied machine learning.

1   Introduction

The topics discussed in this chapter are ones that I felt are often assumed in applied machine learning (and elsewhere), but that are seldom explained in detail. This work is aimed at the student who's taken some coursework in linear methods and analysis, but who'd like to see some of the tricks used by researchers discussed in a little more detail. The mathematics described here is a small fraction of that used in machine learning in general (a treatment of machine learning theory would include the mathematics underlying generalization error bounds, for example)[1], although it's a largely self-contained selection, in that derived results are often used downstream. I include two kinds of homework, 'exercises' and 'puzzles'. Exercises start out easy, and are otherwise as you'd expect; the puzzles are exercises with an added dose of mildly Machiavellian mischief.

Notation: vectors appear in bold font, and vector components and matrices in normal font, so that for example $v_i^{(a)}$ denotes the i'th component of the a'th vector $\mathbf{v}^{(a)}$. The symbol $A \succ 0$ ($\succeq$) means that the matrix A is positive (semi)definite. The transpose of the matrix A is denoted A^T, while that of the vector $\mathbf{x}$ is denoted $\mathbf{x}'$.

2   Lagrange Multipliers

Lagrange multipliers are a mathematical incarnation of one of the pillars of diplomacy (see the historical notes at the end of this section): sometimes an indirect approach will work beautifully when the direct approach fails.

---

[1] My original lectures also contained material on functional analysis and convex optimization, which is not included here.

O. Bousquet et al. (Eds.): Machine Learning 2003, LNAI 3176, pp. 21–40, 2004.

2.1   One Equality Constraint

Suppose that you wish to minimize some function $f(\mathbf{x})$, $\mathbf{x} \in \mathcal{R}^d$, subject to the constraint $c(\mathbf{x}) = 0$. A direct approach is to find a parameterization of the constraint such that f, expressed in terms of those parameters, becomes an unconstrained function. For example, if $c(\mathbf{x}) = \mathbf{x}'A\mathbf{x} - 1$, $\mathbf{x} \in \mathcal{R}^d$, and if $A \succ 0$, you could rotate to a coordinate system and rescale to diagonalize the constraints to the form $\mathbf{y}'\mathbf{y} = 1$, and then substitute with a parameterization that encodes the constraint that $\mathbf{y}$ lives on the $(d-1)$-sphere, for example

$$
\begin{aligned}
y_1 &= \sin\theta_1 \sin\theta_2 \cdots \sin\theta_{d-2} \sin\theta_{d-1} \\
y_2 &= \sin\theta_1 \sin\theta_2 \cdots \sin\theta_{d-2} \cos\theta_{d-1} \\
y_3 &= \sin\theta_1 \sin\theta_2 \cdots \cos\theta_{d-2}
\end{aligned}
$$
$$\cdots$$

Unfortunately, for general constraints (for example, when c is a general polynomial in the d variables) this is not possible, and even when it is, the above example shows that things can get complicated quickly. The geometry of the general situation is shown schematically in Figure 1.

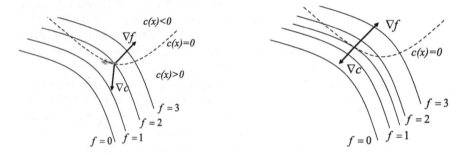

Fig. 1. At the constrained optimum, the gradient of the constraint must be parallel to that of the function

On the left, the gradient of the constraint is not parallel to that of the function; it's therefore possible to move along the constraint surface (thick arrow) so as to further reduce f. On the right, the two gradients are parallel, and any motion along $c(x) = 0$ will increase f, or leave it unchanged. Hence, at the solution, we must have $\nabla f = \lambda \nabla c$ for some constant λ; λ is called an *(undetermined) Lagrange multiplier*, where 'undetermined' arises from the fact that for some problems, the value of λ itself need never be computed.

2.2   Multiple Equality Constraints

How does this extend to multiple equality constraints, $c_i(x) = 0$, $i = 1, \ldots, n$? Let $\mathbf{g}_i \equiv \nabla c_i$. At any solution $\mathbf{x}_*$, it must be true that the gradient of f has no components that are perpendicular to all of the $\mathbf{g}_i$, because otherwise you could move $\mathbf{x}_*$ a little in that direction (or in the opposite direction) to increase (decrease) f without changing any of the c_i, i.e. without violating any constraints. Hence for multiple equality constraints, it must be true that at the solution $\mathbf{x}_*$, the space spanned by the $\mathbf{g}_i$ contains the vector ∇f, i.e. there are some constants λ_i such that $\nabla f(\mathbf{x}_*) = \sum_i \lambda_i \mathbf{g}_i(\mathbf{x}_*)$. Note that this is not sufficient, however - we also need to impose that the solution is on the correct constraint surface (i.e. $c_i = 0 \ \forall i$). A neat way to encapsulate this is to introduce the Lagrangian $L \equiv f(\mathbf{x}) - \sum_i \lambda_i c_i(\mathbf{x})$, whose gradient with respect to the $\mathbf{x}$, and with respect to all the λ_i, vanishes at the solution.

Puzzle 1: *A single constraint gave us one Lagrangian; more constraints must give us more information about the solution; so why don't multiple constraints give us multiple Lagrangians?*

Exercise 1. *Suppose you are given a parallelogram whose side lengths you can choose but whose perimeter is fixed. What shaped parallelogram gives the largest area? (This is a case where the Lagrange multiplier can remain undetermined.) Now, your enterprising uncle has a business proposition: to provide cheap storage in floating containers that are moored at sea. He wants to build a given storage facility out of a fixed area of sheet metal which he can shape as necessary. He wants to keep construction simple and so desires that the facility be a closed parallelepiped (it has to be protected from the rain and from the occasional wave). What dimensions should you choose in order to maximize the weight that can be stored without sinking?*

Exercise 2. *Prove that the distance between two points that are constrained to lie on the n-sphere is extremized when they are either antipodal, or equal.*

2.3   Inequality Constraints

Suppose that instead of the constraint $c(\mathbf{x}) = 0$ we have the single constraint $c(\mathbf{x}) \leq 0$. Now the entire region labeled $c(\mathbf{x}) < 0$ in Figure 1 has become feasible. At the solution, if the constraint is active ($c(\mathbf{x}) = 0$), we again must have that ∇f is parallel to ∇c, by the same argument. In fact we have a stronger condition, namely that if the Lagrangian is written $L = f + \lambda c$, then since we are minimizing f, we must have $\lambda \geq 0$, since the two gradients must point in opposite directions (otherwise a move away from the surface $c = 0$ and into the feasible region would further reduce f). Thus for an inequality constraint, the sign of λ matters, and so here $\lambda \geq 0$ itself becomes a constraint (it's useful to remember that if you're minimizing, and you write your Lagrangian with the multiplier appearing with a positive coefficient, then the constraint is $\lambda \geq 0$). If the constraint is *not* active, then at the solution $\nabla f(\mathbf{x}_*) = 0$, and if $\nabla c(\mathbf{x}_*) \neq 0$, then in order that $\nabla L(\mathbf{x}_*) = 0$ we must set $\lambda = 0$ (and if in fact if $\nabla c(x_*) = 0$, we can still set $\lambda = 0$). Thus in either case (active or inactive), we can find the solution by requiring that the gradients of the Lagrangian vanish, and we also have $\lambda c(\mathbf{x}_*) = 0$. This latter condition is one of the important Karush-Kuhn-Tucker conditions of convex optimization theory [15, 4], and can facilitate the search for the solution, as the next exercise shows.

For multiple inequality constraints, again at the solution ∇f must lie in the space spanned by the ∇c_i, and again if the Lagrangian is $L = f + \sum_i \lambda_i c_i$, then we must in addition have $\lambda_i \geq 0\ \forall i$ (since otherwise f could be reduced by moving into the feasible region); and for inactive constraints, again we (can, usually must, and so might as well) set $\lambda_i = 0$. Thus the above KKT condition generalizes to $\lambda_i c_i(\mathbf{x}_*) = 0\ \forall i$. Finally, a simple and often useful trick is to solve ignoring one or more of the constraints, and then check that the solution satisfies those constraints, in which case you have solved the problem; we'll call this the *free constraint gambit* below.

Exercise 3. *Find the $\mathbf{x} \in \mathcal{R}^d$ that minimizes $\sum_i x_i^2$ subject to $\sum_i x_i = 1$. Find the $\mathbf{x} \in \mathcal{R}^d$ that maximizes $\sum_i x_i^2$ subject to $\sum_i x_i = 1$ and $x_i \geq 0$ (hint: use $\lambda_i x_{*i} = 0$).*

2.4   Cost Benefit Curves

Here's an example from channel coding. Suppose that you are in charge of four fiber optic communications systems. As you pump more bits down a given channel, the error rate increases for that channel, but this behavior is slightly different for each channel. Figure 2 show a graph of the bit rate for each channel versus the 'distortion' (error rate). Your goal is to send the maximum possible number of bits per second at a given, fixed total distortion rate D. Let D_i be the number

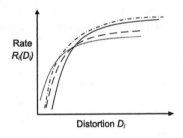

Fig. 2. Total bit rate versus distortion for each system

of errored bits sent down the i'th channel. Given a particular error rate, we'd like to find the maximum overall bit rate; that is, we must maximize the total rate $R \equiv \sum_{i=1} R_i$ subject to the constraint $D = \sum_{i=1} D_i$. Introducing a Lagrange multiplier λ, we wish to maximize the objective function

$$L = \sum_{i=1}^{4} R_i(D_i) + \lambda(D - \sum_{i=1}^{4} D_i) \tag{1}$$

Setting $\partial L/\partial D_i = 0$ gives $\partial R_i/\partial D_i = \lambda$, that is, each fiber should be operated at a point on its rate/distortion curve such that its slope is the same for all fibers. Thus we've found the general rule for resource allocation, for benefit/cost curves like those shown[2] in Figure 2: whatever operating point is chosen for each system, in order to maximize the benefit at a given cost, the slope of the graph at that point should be the same for each curve. For the example shown, the slope of each graph decreases monotonically, and we can start by choosing a single large value of the slope λ for all curves, and decrease it until the condition $\sum_{i=1} D_i = D$ is met, so in general for m fibers, an m dimensional search problem has been reduced to a one dimensional search problem. We can get the same result informally as follows: suppose you had just two fibers, and were at an operating point where the slope s_1 of the rate/distortion graph for fiber 1 was greater than the slope s_2 for fiber 2. Suppose you then adjusted things so that fiber 1 sent one more errored bit every second, and fiber 2 sent one fewer. The extra number of bits you can now send down fiber 1 more than offsets the fewer number of bits you must send down fiber 2. This will hold whenever the slopes are different. For an arbitrary number of fibers, we can apply this argument to any pair of fibers, so the optimal point is for all fibers to be operating at the same slope.

Puzzle 2: *Suppose that instead of fibers, you have four factories making widgets, that the y-axis in Figure 2 represents the total cost for making n_i widgets, and that the x-axis represents the number n_i of widgets made by the i'th factory. The curves have the same shape (they drop off at larger n_i due to the economies of scale). Does the above argument mean that, to produce a total, fixed number of widgets, in order to minimize the cost, each factory should be operated at the same slope on its curve as all the other factories?*

2.5   An Isoperimetric Problem

Isoperimetric problems - problems for which a quantity is extremized while a perimeter is held fixed - were considered in ancient times, but serious work on them began only towards the end of the seventeenth century, with a minor battle between the Bernoulli brothers [14]. It is a fitting example for us, since the general isoperimetric problem had been discussed for fifty years before Lagrange solved it in his first venture into mathematics [1], and it provides an introduction to functional derivatives, which we'll need. Let's consider a classic isoperimetric problem: to find the plane figure with maximum area, given fixed perimeter. Consider a curve with fixed endpoints $\{x = 0, y = 0\}$ and $\{x = 1, y = 0\}$, and fixed length ρ. We will assume that the curve defines a function, that is, that for a given $x \in [0, 1]$, there corresponds just one y. We wish to maximize the area between the curve and the x axis, $A = \int_0^1 y dx$, subject to the constraint that the length, $\rho = \int_0^1 \sqrt{1 + y'^2} dx$, is fixed (here, prime denotes differentiation with respect to x). The Lagrangian is therefore

$$L = \int_0^1 y dx + \lambda \left(\int_0^1 \sqrt{1 + y'^2} dx - \rho \right) \tag{2}$$

---

[2] This seemingly innocuous statement is actually a hint for the puzzle that follows.

Two new properties of the problem appear here: first, integrals appear in the Lagrangian, and second, we are looking for a solution which is a function, not a point. To solve this we will use the calculus of variations, introduced by Lagrange and Euler. Denote a small variation of a function[3] f by δf: that is, replace $f(x)$ by $f(x) + \delta f(x)$ everywhere, where δf is chosen to vanish at the boundaries, that is, $\delta f(0) = \delta f(1) = 0$ (note that δf is also a function of x). Here, y is the variable function, so the change in L is

$$\delta L = \int_0^1 \delta y dx + \lambda \int_0^1 (1 + y'^2)^{-1/2} y' \delta y' dx$$

By using the facts that $\delta y' = \delta \frac{dy}{dx} = \frac{d}{dx} \delta y$ and that the variation in y vanishes at the endpoints, integrating by parts then gives:

$$\delta L = \int_0^1 \left(1 - \lambda y''(1 + y'^2)^{-3/2}\right) \delta y dx$$
$$\Rightarrow \quad 1 - \lambda y''(1 + y'^2)^{-3/2} \equiv 1 - \lambda \kappa = 0$$

where κ is the local curvature, and where the second step results from our being able to choose δy arbitrarily on $(0,1)$, so the quantity multiplying δy in the integrand must vanish (imagine choosing δy to be zero everywhere except over an arbitrarily small interval around some point $x \in [0,1]$). Since the only plane curves with constant curvature are the straight line and the arc of circle, we find the result (which holds even if the diameter of the circle is greater than one). Note that, as often happens in physical problems, λ here has a physical interpretation (as the inverse curvature); λ is always the ratio of the norms of ∇f and ∇c at the solution, and in this sense the size of λ measures the influence of the constraint on the solution.

2.6   Which Univariate Distribution has Maximum Entropy?

Here we use differential entropy, with the understanding that the bin width is sufficiently small that the usual sums can be approximated by integrals, but fixed, so that comparing the differential entropy of two distributions is equivalent to comparing their entropies. We wish to find the function f that minimizes

$$\int_{-\infty}^{\infty} f(x) \log_2 f(x) dx, \quad x \in \mathcal{R} \tag{3}$$

subject to the four constraints

$$f(x) \geq 0 \; \forall x, \quad \int_{-\infty}^{\infty} f(x) = 1, \quad \int_{-\infty}^{\infty} x f(x) = c_1 \quad \int_{-\infty}^{\infty} x^2 f(x) = c_2$$

---

[3] In fact Lagrange first suggested the use of the symbol δ to denote the variation of a whole function, rather than that at a point, in 1755 [14].

Note that the last two constraints, which specify the first and second moments, is equivalent to specifying the mean and variance. Our Lagrangian is therefore:

$$\mathcal{L} = \int_{-\infty}^{\infty} f(x) \log_2 f(x) dx + \lambda \left(1 - \int_{-\infty}^{\infty} f(x) \right) + \beta_1 \left(c_1 - \int_{-\infty}^{\infty} x f(x) dx \right)$$
$$+ \beta_2 \left(c_2 - \int_{-\infty}^{\infty} x^2 f(x) dx \right)$$

where we'll try the free constraint gambit and skip the positivity constraint. In this problem we again need the calculus of variations. In modern terms we use the *functional derivative*, which is just a shorthand for capturing the rules of the calculus of variations, one of which is:

$$\frac{\delta g(x)}{\delta g(y)} = \delta(x - y) \tag{4}$$

where the right hand side is the Dirac delta function. Taking the functional derivative of the Lagrangian with respect to $f(y)$ and integrating with respect to x then gives

$$\log_2 f(y) + \log_2(e) - \lambda - \beta_1 y - \beta_2 y^2 = 0 \tag{5}$$

which shows that f must have the functional form

$$f(y) = C \exp^{(\lambda + \beta_1 y + \beta_2 y^2)} \tag{6}$$

where C is a constant. The values for the Lagrange multipliers λ, β_1 and β_2 then follow from the three equality constraints above, giving the result that the Gaussian is the desired distribution. Finally, choosing $C > 0$ makes the result positive everywhere, so the free constraint gambit worked.

Puzzle 3: *For a given event space, say with N possible outcomes, the maximum entropy is attained when $p_i = 1/N \; \forall i$, that is, by the uniform distribution. That doesn't look very Gaussian. What gives?*

Exercise 4. *What distribution maximizes the entropy for the class of univariate distributions whose argument is assumed to be positive, if only the mean is fixed? How about univariate distributions whose argument is arbitrary, but which have specified, finite support, and where no constraints are imposed on the mean or the variance?*

Puzzle 4: *The differential entropy for a uniform distribution with support in $[-C, C]$ is*

$$h(P_U) = - \int_{-C}^{C} (1/2C) \log_2(1/2C) dx$$
$$= - \log_2(1/2C) \tag{7}$$

This tends to ∞ as $C \to \infty$. How should we interpret this? Find the variance for any fixed C, and show that the univariate Gaussian with that variance has differential entropy greater than h.

2.7   Maximum Entropy with Linear Constraints

Suppose that you have a discrete probability distribution P_i, $\sum_i^n P_i = 1$, and suppose further that the only information that you have about the distribution is that it must satisfy a set of linear constraints:

$$\sum_i \alpha_{ji} P_i = C_j, \; j = 1, \ldots, m \tag{8}$$

The *maximum entropy* approach (see [5], for example) posits that, subject to the known constraints, our uncertainty about the set of events described by the distribution should be as large as possible, or specifically, that the mean number of bits required to describe an event generated from the constrained probability distribution be as large as possible. Maximum entropy provides a principled way to encode our uncertainty in a model, and it is the precursor to modern Bayesian techniques [13]. Since the mean number of bits is just the entropy of the distribution, we wish to find that distribution that maximizes[4]

$$-\sum_i P_i \log P_i + \sum_j \lambda_j (C_j - \sum_i \alpha_{ji} P_i) + \mu(\sum_i P_i - 1) - \sum_i \delta_i P_i \tag{9}$$

where the sum constraint on the P_i is imposed with μ, and the positivity of each P_i with δ_i (so $\delta_i \geq 0$ and at the maximum, $\delta_i P_i = 0 \; \forall i$)[5]. Differentiating with respect to P_k gives

$$P_k = \exp(-1 + \mu - \delta_k - \sum_j \lambda_j \alpha_{jk}) \tag{10}$$

Since this is guaranteed to be positive we have $\delta_k = 0 \; \forall k$. Imposing the sum constraint then gives $P_k = \frac{1}{Z} \exp(-\sum_j \lambda_j \alpha_{jk})$ where the "partition function" Z is just a normalizing factor. Note that the Lagrange multipliers have shown us the form that the solution must take, but that form does not automatically satisfy the constraints - they must still be imposed as a condition on the solution. The problem of maximizing the entropy subject to linear constraints therefore gives the widely used logistic regression model, where the parameters of the model are the Lagrange multipliers λ_i, which are themselves constrained by Eq. (8). For an example from the document classification task of how imposing linear constraints on the probabilities can arise in practice, see [16].

2.8   Some Algorithm Examples

Lagrange multipliers are ubiquitous for imposing constraints in algorithms. Here we list their use in a few modern machine learning algorithms; in all of these applications, the free constraint gambit proves useful. For support vector machines, the Lagrange multipliers have a physical force interpretation, and can be used to

---

[4] The factor $\log_2 e$ can be absorbed into the Lagrange multipliers.
[5] Actually the free constraint gambit would work here, too.

find the exact solution to the problem of separating points in a symmetric simplex in arbitrary dimensions [6]. For the remaining algorithms mentioned here, see [7] for details on the underlying mathematics. In showing that the principal PCA directions give minimal reconstruction error, one requires that the projection directions being sought after are orthogonal, and this can be imposed by introducing a matrix of multipliers. In locally linear embedding [17], the translation invariance constraint is imposed for each local patch by a multiplier, and the constraint that a solution matrix in the reconstruction algorithm be orthogonal is again imposed by a matrix of multipliers. In the Laplacian eigenmaps dimensional reduction algorithm [2], in order to prevent the collapse to trivial solutions, the dimension of the target space is enforced to be $d > 0$ by requiring that the rank of the projected data matrix be d, and again this imposed using a matrix of Lagrange multipliers.

Historical Notes. Joseph Louis Lagrange was born in 1736 in Turin. He was one of only two of eleven siblings to survive infancy; he spent most of his life in Turin, Berlin and Paris. He started teaching in Turin, where he organized a research society, and was apparently responsible for much fine mathematics that was published from that society under the names of other mathematicians [3, 1]. He *'believed that a mathematician has not thoroughly understood his own work till he has made it so clear that he can go out and explain it effectively to the first man he meets on the street'* [3][6]. His contributions lay in the subjects of mechanics, calculus[7], the calculus of variations[8], astronomy, probability, group theory, and number theory [14]. Lagrange is at least partly responsible for the choice of base 10 for the metric system, rather than 12. He was supported academically by Euler and d'Alembert, financed by Frederick and Louis XIV, and was close to Lavoisier (who saved him from being arrested and having his property confiscated, as a foreigner living in Paris during the Revolution), Marie Antoinette and the Abbé Marie. He survived the Revolution, although Lavoisier did not. His work continued to be fruitful until his death in 1813, in Paris.

3   Some Notes on Matrices

This section touches on some useful results in the theory of matrices that are rarely emphasized in coursework. For a complete treatment, see for example [12] and [11]. Following [12], the set of p by q matrices is denoted M_{pq}, the set of (square) p by p matrices by M_p, and the set of symmetric p by p matrices by S_p. We work only with real matrices - the generalization of the results to the complex field is straightforward. In this section only, we will use the notation in which repeated indices are assumed to be summed over, so that for example

---

[6] Sadly, at that time there were very few female mathematicians.

[7] For example he was the first to state Taylor's theorem with a remainder [14].

[8] ... with which he started his career, in a letter to Euler, who then generously delayed publication of some similar work so that Lagrange could have time to finish his work [1].

$A_{ij}B_{jk}C_{kl}$ is written as shorthand for $\sum_{j,k} A_{ij}B_{jk}C_{kl}$. Let's warm up with some basic facts.

3.1   A Dual Basis

Suppose you are given a basis of d orthonormal vectors $\mathbf{e}^{(a)} \in \mathcal{R}^d$, $a = 1, \ldots, d$, and you construct a matrix $E \in M_d$ whose columns are those vectors. It is a striking fact that the rows of E then also always form an orthonormal basis. We can see this as follows. Let the $\mathbf{e}^{(a)}$ have components $e_i^{(a)}$, $i = 1, \ldots, d$. Let's write the vectors constructed from the rows of E as $\hat{\mathbf{e}}$ so that $\hat{\mathbf{e}}_i^{(a)} \equiv e_a^{(i)}$. Then orthonormality of the columns can be encapsulated as $E^T E = \mathbf{1}$. However since E has full rank, it has an inverse, and $E^T E E^{-1} = E^{-1} = E^T$, so $E E^T = \mathbf{1}$ (using the fundamental fact that the left and right inverses of any square matrix are the same) which shows that the rows of E are also orthonormal. The vectors $\hat{\mathbf{e}}^{(a)}$ are called the dual basis to the $\mathbf{e}^{(a)}$. This result is sometimes useful in simplifying expressions: for example $\sum_a e_i^{(a)} e_j^{(a)} \Lambda(i,j)$, where Λ is some function, can be replaced by $\Lambda(i,i)\delta_{ij}$.

3.2   Other Ways to Think About Matrix Multiplication

Suppose you have matrices $X \in M_{mn}$ and $Y \in M_{np}$ so that $XY \in M_{mp}$. The familiar way to represent matrix multiplication is $(XY)_{ab} = \sum_{i=1}^n X_{ai}Y_{ib}$, where the summands are just products of numbers. However an alternative representation is $XY = \sum_{i=1}^n \mathbf{x}_i \mathbf{y}_i'$, where $\mathbf{x}_i$ $(\mathbf{y}_i')$ is the i'th column (row) of X (Y), and where the summands are outer products of matrices. For example, we can write the product of a 2×3 and a 3×2 matrix as

$$\begin{bmatrix} a\,b\,c \\ d\,e\,f \end{bmatrix} \begin{bmatrix} g\,h \\ i\,j \\ k\,l \end{bmatrix} = \begin{bmatrix} a \\ d \end{bmatrix} \begin{bmatrix} g\,h \end{bmatrix} + \begin{bmatrix} b \\ e \end{bmatrix} \begin{bmatrix} i\,j \end{bmatrix} + \begin{bmatrix} c \\ f \end{bmatrix} \begin{bmatrix} k\,l \end{bmatrix}$$

One immediate consequence (which we'll use in our description of singular value decomposition below) is that you can always add columns at the right of X, and rows at the bottom of Y, and get the same product XY, provided either the extra columns, or the extra rows, contain only zeros. To see why this expansion works it's helpful to expand the outer products into standard matrix form: the matrix multiplication is just

$$\left\{ \begin{pmatrix} a\,0\,0 \\ d\,0\,0 \end{pmatrix} + \begin{pmatrix} 0\,b\,0 \\ 0\,e\,0 \end{pmatrix} + \begin{pmatrix} 0\,0\,c \\ 0\,0\,f \end{pmatrix} + \right\} \times \left\{ \begin{pmatrix} g\,h \\ 0\,0 \\ 0\,0 \end{pmatrix} + \begin{pmatrix} 0\,0 \\ i\,j \\ 0\,0 \end{pmatrix} + \begin{pmatrix} 0\,0 \\ 0\,0 \\ k\,l \end{pmatrix} \right\}$$

Along a similar vein, the usual way to view matrix-vector multiplication is as an operation that maps a vector $\mathbf{z} \in \mathcal{R}^n$ to another vector $\mathbf{z}' \in \mathcal{R}^m$: $\mathbf{z}' = X\mathbf{z}$. However you can also view the product as a linear combination of the columns of X: $\mathbf{z}' = \sum_{i=1}^n z_i \mathbf{x}_i$. With this view it's easy to see why the result must lie in the span of the columns of X.

3.3   The Levi-Civita Symbol

The Levi-Civita symbol[9] in d dimensions is denoted $\epsilon_{ij\ldots k}$ and takes the value 1 if its d indices are an even permutation of $1, 2, 3, \cdots, d$, the value -1 if an odd permutation, and 0 otherwise. The 3-dimensional version of this is the fastest way I know to derive vector identities in three dimensions, using the identity $\epsilon_{ijk}\epsilon_{imn} = \delta_{jm}\delta_{kn} - \delta_{jn}\delta_{km}$ (recall that repeated indices are summed).

Exercise 5. *Use the fact that* $\mathbf{a} = \mathbf{b} \wedge \mathbf{c}$ *can be written in component form as* $a_i = \epsilon_{ijk}b_j c_k$ *to derive, in one satisfying line, the vector identity in three dimensions:* $(\mathbf{a} \wedge \mathbf{b}) \cdot (\mathbf{c} \wedge \mathbf{d}) = (\mathbf{a} \cdot \mathbf{c})(\mathbf{b} \cdot \mathbf{d}) - (\mathbf{a} \cdot \mathbf{d})(\mathbf{b} \cdot \mathbf{c}).$

3.4   Characterizing the Determinant and Inverse

The determinant of a matrix $A \in M_n$ can be defined as

$$|A| \equiv \frac{1}{n!}\epsilon_{\alpha_1\alpha_2\cdots\alpha_n}\epsilon_{\beta_1\beta_2\cdots\beta_n}A_{\alpha_1\beta_1}A_{\alpha_2\beta_2}\cdots A_{\alpha_n\beta_n} \qquad (11)$$

Exercise 6. *Show that also,*

$$|A| = \epsilon_{\alpha_1\alpha_2\cdots\alpha_n}A_{1\alpha_1}A_{2\alpha_2}\cdots A_{n\alpha_n} \qquad (12)$$

We can use this to prove an interesting theorem linking the determinant, derivatives, and the inverse:

Lemma 1. *For any square nonsingular matrix A,*

$$\frac{\partial|A|}{\partial A_{ij}} = A_{ji}^{-1} \qquad (13)$$

Proof.

$$\frac{\partial|A|}{\partial A_{ij}} = \epsilon_{j\alpha_2\cdots\alpha_n}\delta_{i1}A_{2\alpha_2}\cdots A_{n\alpha_n} + \epsilon_{\alpha_1 j\cdots\alpha_n}A_{1\alpha_1}\delta_{i2}A_{3\alpha_3}\cdots A_{n\alpha_n} + \cdots$$

so

$$A_{kj}\frac{\partial|A|}{\partial A_{ij}} = \epsilon_{\alpha_1\alpha_2\cdots\alpha_n}(A_{k\alpha_1}\delta_{i1}A_{2\alpha_2}\cdots A_{n\alpha_n} + A_{1\alpha_1}A_{k\alpha_2}\delta_{i2}A_{3\alpha_3}\cdots+\cdots)$$

For any value of i, one and only one term in the sum on the right survives, and for that term, we must have $k = i$ by antisymmetry of the ϵ. Thus the right hand side is just $|A|\delta_{ki}$. Multiplying both sides on the right by $(A^T)^{-1}$ gives the result. $\qquad\square$

---

[9] The name 'tensor' is sometimes incorrectly applied to arbitrary objects with more than one index. In factor a tensor is a generalization of the notion of a vector and is a geometrical object (has meaning independent of the choice of coordinate system); ϵ is a pseudo-tensor (transforms as a tensor, but changes sign upon inversion).

We can also use this to write the following closed form for the inverse:

$$A_{ij}^{-1} = \frac{1}{|A|(n-1)!} \epsilon_{j\alpha_1\alpha_2\cdots\alpha_{n-1}} \epsilon_{i\beta_1\beta_2\cdots\beta_{n-1}} A_{\alpha_1\beta_1} A_{\alpha_2\beta_2} \cdots A_{\alpha_{n-1}\beta_{n-1}} \qquad (14)$$

Exercise 7. *Prove this, using Eqs. (11) and (13).*

Exercise 8. *Show that, for an arbitrary non-singular square matrix A,*
$\frac{\partial A_{ij}^{-1}}{\partial A_{\alpha\beta}} = -A_{i\alpha}^{-1} A_{\beta j}^{-1}$. *(Hint: take derivatives of $A^{-1}A = \mathbf{1}$).*

Exercise 9. *The density $p(\mathbf{x})$ for a multivariate Gaussian is proportional to $|\Sigma|^{-1/2} \exp\left(-\frac{1}{2}(\mathbf{x}-\boldsymbol{\mu})'\Sigma^{-1}(\mathbf{x}-\boldsymbol{\mu})\right)$. For n independent and identically distributed points, the density is $p(\mathbf{x}_1, \mathbf{x}_2, \cdots, \mathbf{x}_n | \boldsymbol{\mu}, \Sigma) = \prod_i p(\mathbf{x}_i | \boldsymbol{\mu}, \Sigma)$. By taking derivatives with respect to $\boldsymbol{\mu}$ and Σ and using the above results, show that the maximum likelihood values for the mean and covariance matrix are just their sample estimates.*

Puzzle 5: *Suppose that in Exercise 9, $n = 2$, and that $\mathbf{x}_1 = -\mathbf{x}_2$, so that the maximum likelihood estimate for the mean is zero. Suppose that Σ is chosen to have positive determinant but such that $\mathbf{x}$ is an eigenvector with negative eigenvalue. Then the likelihood can be made as large as you like by just scaling Σ with a positive scale factor, which appears to contradict the results of Exercise 9. What's going on?*

3.5   SVD in Seven Steps

Singular value decomposition is a generalization of eigenvalue decomposition. While eigenvalue decomposition applies only to square matrices, SVD applies to rectangular; and while not all square matrices are diagonalizable, every matrix has an SVD. SVD is perhaps less familiar, but it plays important roles in everything from theorem proving to algorithm design (for example, for a classic result on applying SVD to document categorization, see [10]). The key observation is that, given $A \in M_{mn}$, although we cannot perform an eigendecomposition of A, we can do so for the two matrices $AA^T \in S_m$ and $A^TA \in S_n$. Since both of these are positive semidefinite, their eigenvalues are non-negative; if AA^T has rank k, define the 'singular values' σ_i^2 to be its k positive eigenvalues. Below we will use 'nonzero eigenvector' to mean an eigenvector with nonzero eigenvalue, will denote the diagonal matrix whose i'th diagonal component is σ_i by $\mathrm{diag}(\sigma_i)$, and will assume without loss of generality that $m \le n$. Note that we repeatedly use the tricks mentioned in Section (3.2). Let's derive the SVD.

1. AA^T *has the same nonzero eigenvalues as* A^TA. Let $\mathbf{x}_i \in \mathcal{R}^m$ be an eigenvector of AA^T with positive eigenvalue σ_i^2, and let $\mathbf{y}_i \equiv (1/\sigma_i)(A^T\mathbf{x}_i)$, $\mathbf{y} \in \mathcal{R}^n$. Then $A^TA\mathbf{y}_i = (1/\sigma_i)A^TAA^T\mathbf{x}_i = \sigma_i A^T\mathbf{x}_i = \sigma_i^2\mathbf{y}_i$. Similarly let $\mathbf{y}_i \in \mathcal{R}^n$ be an eigenvector of A^TA with eigenvalue $\sigma_i'^2$, and let $\mathbf{z}_i \equiv (1/\sigma_i')(A\mathbf{y}_i)$. Then $AA^T\mathbf{z}_i = (1/\sigma_i')AA^TA\mathbf{y}_i = \sigma_i'A\mathbf{y}_i = \sigma_i'^2\mathbf{z}_i$. Thus there is a 1-1 correspondence between nonzero eigenvectors for the matrices A^TA and AA^T, and the corresponding eigenvalues are shared.

2. *The $\mathbf{x}_i$ can be chosen to be orthonormal, in which case so also are the $\mathbf{y}_i$.* The $\mathbf{x}_i$ are orthonormal, or can be so chosen, since they are eigenvectors of a symmetric matrix. Then $\mathbf{y}_i \cdot \mathbf{y}_j \propto \mathbf{x}'_i AA^T \mathbf{x}_j \propto \mathbf{x}_i \cdot \mathbf{x}_j \propto \delta_{ij}$.

3. $\mathrm{rank}(A) = \mathrm{rank}(A^T) = \mathrm{rank}(AA^T) = \mathrm{rank}(A^T A) \equiv k$ [12].

4. Let the $\mathbf{x}_i$ be the nonzero eigenvectors of AA^T and the $\mathbf{y}_i$ those of $A^T A$. Let $X \in M_{mk}$ ($Y \in M_{nk}$) be the matrix whose columns are the $\mathbf{x}_i$ ($\mathbf{y}_i$). Then $Y = A^T X \mathrm{diag}(1/\sigma_i) \Rightarrow \mathrm{diag}(\sigma_i) Y^T = X^T A$. Note that $m \geq k$; if $m = k$, then $A = X \mathrm{diag}(\sigma_i) Y^T$.

5. If $m > k$, add $m - k$ rows of orthonormal null vectors of A^T to the bottom of X^T, and add $m - k$ zero rows to the bottom of $\mathrm{diag}(\sigma_i)$; defining the latter to be $\mathrm{diag}(\sigma_i, 0)$, then X is orthogonal and $A = X \mathrm{diag}(\sigma_i, 0) Y^T$. Note that here, $X \in M_m$, $\mathrm{diag}(\sigma_i, 0) \in M_{mk}$ and $Y \in M_{nk}$.

6. To get something that looks more like an eigendecomposition, add $n - k$ rows of vectors that, together with the $\mathbf{y}_i$ form an orthonormal set, to the bottom of Y^T, and add $n - k$ columns of zeros to the right of $\mathrm{diag}(\sigma_i, 0)$; defining the latter to be $\mathrm{diag}(\sigma_i, 0, 0)$, then the Y are also orthogonal and $A = X \mathrm{diag}(\sigma_i, 0, 0) Y^T$. Note that here, $X \in M_m$, $\mathrm{diag}(\sigma_i, 0, 0) \in M_{mn}$, and $Y \in M_n$.

7. To get something that looks more like a sum of outer products, just write A in step (4) as $A = \sum_{i=1}^{k} \sigma_i \mathbf{x}_i \mathbf{y}'_i$.

Let's put the singular value decomposition to work.

3.6   The Moore-Penrose Generalized Inverse

Suppose $B \in S_m$ has eigendecomposition $B = E\Lambda E^T$, where Λ is diagonal and E is the orthogonal matrix of column eigenvectors. Suppose further that B is non-singular, so that $B^{-1} = E\Lambda^{-1}E^T = \sum_i (1/\lambda_i) \mathbf{e}_i \mathbf{e}'_i$. This suggests that, since SVD generalizes eigendecomposition, perhaps we can also use SVD to generalize the notion of matrix inverse to non-square matrices $A \in M_{mn}$. The Moore-Penrose generalized inverse (often called just the generalized inverse) does exactly this[10]. In outer product form, it's the SVD analog of the ordinary inverse, with the latter written in terms of outer products of eigenvectors: $A^\dagger = \sum_{i=1}^{k} (1/\sigma_i) \mathbf{y}_i \mathbf{x}'_i \in M_{nm}$. The generalized inverse has several special properties:

1. $AA^\dagger$ and $A^\dagger A$ are Hermitian;
2. $AA^\dagger A = A$;
3. $A^\dagger AA^\dagger = A^\dagger$.

In fact, $A^\dagger$ is uniquely determined by conditions (1), (2) and (3). Also, if A is square and nonsingular, then $A^\dagger = A^{-1}$, and more generally, if $(A^T A)^{-1}$ exists, then $A^\dagger = (A^T A)^{-1} A^T$, and if $(AA^T)^{-1}$ exists, then $A^\dagger = A^T (AA^T)^{-1}$. The generalized inverse comes in handy, for example, in characterizing the general solution to linear equations, as we'll now see.

---

[10] The Moore-Penrose generalized inverse is one of many pseudo inverses.

3.7   SVD, Linear Maps, Range and Null Space

If $A \in M_{mn}$, the *range* of A, $\mathcal{R}(A)$, is defined as that subspace spanned by $\mathbf{y} = A\mathbf{x}$ for all $\mathbf{x} \in \mathcal{R}^n$. A's *null space* $\mathcal{N}(A)$, on the other hand, is that subspace spanned by those $\mathbf{x} \in \mathcal{R}^n$ for which $A\mathbf{x} = 0$. Letting $A_{|i}$ denote the columns of A, recall that $A\mathbf{x} = x_1 A_{|1} + x_2 A_{|2} + \cdots + x_n A_{|n}$, so that the dimension of $\mathcal{R}(A)$ is the rank k of A, and $\mathcal{R}(A)$ is spanned by the columns of A. Also, $\mathcal{N}(A^T)$ is spanned by those vectors which are orthogonal to every row of A^T (or every column of A), so $\mathcal{R}(A)$ is the orthogonal complement of $\mathcal{N}(A^T)$. The notions of range and null space are simply expressed in terms of the SVD, $A = \sum_{i=1}^{k} \sigma_i \mathbf{x}_i \mathbf{y}_i'$, $\mathbf{x} \in \mathcal{R}^m$, $\mathbf{y} \in \mathcal{R}^n$. The null space of A is the subspace orthogonal to the k $\mathbf{y}_i$, so $\dim(\mathcal{N}(A)) = n - k$. The range of A is spanned by the $\mathbf{x}_i$, so $\dim(\mathcal{R}(A)) = k$. Thus in particular, we have $\dim(\mathcal{R}(A)) + \dim(\mathcal{N}(A)) = n$.

The SVD provides a handy way to characterize the solutions to linear systems of equations. In general the system $A\mathbf{z} = \mathbf{b}$, $A \in M_{mn}$, $\mathbf{z} \in \mathcal{R}^n$, $\mathbf{b} \in \mathcal{R}^m$ has 0, 1 or ∞ solutions (if $\mathbf{z}_1$ and $\mathbf{z}_2$ are solutions, then so is $\alpha \mathbf{z}_1 + \beta \mathbf{z}_2$, $\alpha, \beta \in \mathcal{R}$). When does a solution exist? Since $A\mathbf{z}$ is a linear combination of the columns of A, $\mathbf{b}$ must lie in the span of those columns. In fact, if $\mathbf{b} \in \mathcal{R}(A)$, then $\mathbf{z}_0 = A^\dagger \mathbf{b}$ is a solution, since $A\mathbf{z}_0 = \sum_{i=1}^{k} \sigma_i \mathbf{x}_i \mathbf{y}_i' \sum_{j=1}^{k} (1/\sigma_i) \mathbf{y}_j \mathbf{x}_j' \mathbf{b} = \sum_{i=1}^{k} \mathbf{x}_i \mathbf{x}_i' \mathbf{b} = \mathbf{b}$, and the general solution is therefore $\mathbf{z} = A^\dagger \mathbf{b} + \mathcal{N}(A)$.

Puzzle 6: *How does this argument break down if* $\mathbf{b} \notin \mathcal{R}(A)$*?*

What if $\mathbf{b} \notin \mathcal{R}(A)$, i.e. $A\mathbf{z} = \mathbf{b}$ has no solution? One reasonable step would be to find that $\mathbf{z}$ that minimizes the Euclidean norm $\|A\mathbf{z} - \mathbf{b}\|$. However, adding any vector in $\mathcal{N}(A)$ to a solution $\mathbf{z}$ would also give a solution, so a reasonable second step is to require in addition that $\|\mathbf{z}\|$ is minimized. The general solution to this is again $\mathbf{z} = A^\dagger \mathbf{b}$. This is closely related to the following unconstrained quadratic programming problem: minimize $f(\mathbf{z}) = \frac{1}{2} \mathbf{z}' A \mathbf{z} + b\mathbf{z}$, $\mathbf{x} \in \mathcal{R}^n$, $A \succeq 0$. (We need the extra condition on A since otherwise f can be made arbitrarily negative). The solution to this is at $\nabla f = 0 \rightarrow A\mathbf{z} + \mathbf{b} = 0$, so the general solution is again $\mathbf{z} = A^\dagger \mathbf{b} + \mathcal{N}(A)$.

Puzzle 7: *If* $\mathbf{b} \notin \mathcal{R}(A)$*, there is again no solution, even though* $A \succeq 0$*. What happens if you go ahead and try to minimize* f *anyway?*

3.8   Matrix Norms

A function $\|\cdot\| : M_{mn} \rightarrow \mathcal{R}$ is a *matrix norm* over a field $\mathcal{F}$ if for all $A, B \in M_{mn}$,

1. $\|A\| \geq 0$
2. $\|A\| = 0 \Leftrightarrow A = 0$
3. $\|cA\| = |c| \|A\|$ for all scalars $c \in \mathcal{F}$
4. $\|A + B\| \leq \|A\| + \|B\|$

The Frobenius norm, $\|A\|_F = \sqrt{\sum_{ij} |A_{ij}|^2}$, is often used to represent the distance between matrices A and B as $\|A - B\|_F^2$, when for example one is searching for that matrix which is as close as possible to a given matrix, given some constraints. For example, the closest positive semidefinite matrix, in Frobenius norm, to a given symmetric matrix A, is $\hat{A} \equiv \sum_{i:\lambda_i>0} \lambda_i \mathbf{e}^{(i)} \mathbf{e}'^{(i)}$ where the λ_i, $\mathbf{e}^{(i)}$ are the eigenvalues and eigenvectors of A, respectively. The Minkowski vector p-norm also has a matrix analog: $\|A\|_p \equiv \max_{\|\mathbf{x}\|=1} \|A\mathbf{x}\|_p$. There are three interesting special cases of this which are easy to compute: the maximum absolute column norm, $\|A\|_1 \equiv \max_j \sum_i^n |A_{ij}|$, the maximum absolute row norm, $\|A\|_\infty \equiv \max_i \sum_j^n |A_{ij}|$, and the spectral norm, $\|A\|_2$. Both the Frobenius and spectral norms can be written in terms of the singular values: assuming the ordering $\sigma_1 \geq \sigma_2 \cdots \geq \sigma_k$, then $\|A\|_2 = \sigma_1$ and $\|A\|_F = \sqrt{\sum_{i=1}^k \sigma_i^2}$.

Exercise 10. *Let U and W be orthogonal matrices. Show that $\|UAW\|_F = \|A\|_F$.*

Exercise 11. *The **submultiplicative property**, $\|AB\| \leq \|A\|\|B\|$, is an additional property that some matrix norms satisfy [11][11]. Prove that, if $A \in M_m$ and if a submultiplicative norm exists for which $\|A\| < 1$, then $(1+A)^{-1} = 1 - A + A^2 - A^3 + \cdots$, and if A is nonsingular and a submultiplicative norm exists for which $\|A^{-1}\| < 1$, then $(1+A)^{-1} = A^{-1}(1-A^{-1}+A^{-2}-A^{-3}+\cdots)$. Show that for any rectangular matrix W, $W(1+W'W)^{-1}W' = (1+WW')^{-1}WW' = WW'(1+WW')^{-1}$. (This is used, for example, in the derivation of the conditional distribution of the latent variables given the observed variables, in probabilistic PCA [19].)*

The Minkowski p norm has the important property that $\|A\mathbf{x}\|_p \leq \|A\|_p \|\mathbf{x}\|_p$. Let's use this, and the L_1 and L_∞ matrix norms, to prove a basic fact about stochastic matrices. A matrix P is stochastic if its elements can be interpreted as probabilities, that is, if all elements are real and non-negative, and each row sums to one (row-stochastic), or each column sums to one (column-stochastic), or both (doubly stochastic).

Theorem 1. *If P is a square stochastic matrix, then P has eigenvalues whose absolute values lie in the range $[0,1]$.*

Proof. For any $p \geq 1$, and $\mathbf{x}$ any eigenvector of P, $\|P\mathbf{x}\|_p = |\lambda| \|\mathbf{x}\|_p \leq \|P\|_p \|\mathbf{x}\|_p$ so $|\lambda| \leq \|P\|_p$. Suppose that P is row-stochastic; then choose the L_∞ norm, which is the maximum absolute row norm $\|P\|_\infty = \max_i \sum_j |P_{ij}| = 1$; so $|\lambda| \leq 1$. If P is column-stochastic, choosing the 1-norm (the maximum absolute column norm) gives the same result. □

Note that stochastic matrices, if not symmetric, can have complex eigenvalues, so in this case $\mathcal{F}$ is the field of complex numbers.

3.9 Positive Semidefinite Matrices

Positive semidefinite matrices are ubiquitous in machine learning theory and algorithms (for example, every kernel matrix is positive semidefinite, for Mercer

---

[11] Some authors include this in the definition of matrix norm [12].

kernels). Again we restrict ourselves to real matrices. A matrix $A \in S_n$ is positive definite iff for every $\mathbf{x} \in \mathcal{R}^n$, $\mathbf{x}'A\mathbf{x} > 0$; it is positive semidefinite iff for every $\mathbf{x} \in \mathcal{R}^n$, $\mathbf{x}'A\mathbf{x} \geq 0$, and some $\mathbf{x}$ exists for which the equality is met. Recall that we denote the property of positive definiteness of a matrix A by $A \succ 0$, and positive semidefiniteness by $A \succeq 0$. Let's start by listing a few properties, the first of which relate to what positive semidefinite matrices look like (here, repeated indices are not summed):

1. If $A \succ 0$, then $A_{ii} > 0\ \forall i$;
2. If $A \succeq 0$, then $A_{ii} \geq 0\ \forall i$;
3. If $A \succeq 0$, then $A_{ii} = 1\ \forall i \Rightarrow |A_{ij}| \leq 1\ \forall i,j$;
4. If $A \in S_n$ is strictly diagonally dominant, that is, $A_{ii} > \sum_{j \neq i} |A_{ij}|\ \forall i$, then it is also positive definite;
5. If $A \succeq 0$ and $A_{ii} = 0$ for some i, then $A_{ij} = A_{ji} = 0\ \forall j$;
6. If $A \succeq 0$ then $A_{ii}A_{jj} \geq |A_{ij}|^2\ \forall i,j$;
7. If $A \in S_n \succeq 0$ and $B \in S_n \succeq 0$ then $AB \succeq 0$;
8. $A \in S_n$ is positive semidefinite and of rank one iff $A = \mathbf{xx}'$ for some $\mathbf{x} \in \mathcal{R}^n$;
9. $A \succ 0 \Leftrightarrow A$ all of the leading minors of A are positive.

A very useful way to think of positive semidefinite matrices is in terms of Gram matrices. Let V be a vector space over some field $\mathcal{F}$, with inner product $\langle \cdot, \cdot \rangle$. The *Gram matrix* G of a set of vectors $\mathbf{v}_i \in V$ is defined by $G_{ij} \equiv \langle \mathbf{v}_i, \mathbf{v}_j \rangle$. Now let V be Euclidean space and let $\mathcal{F}$ be the reals. The key result is the following: let $A \in S_n$. Then A is positive semidefinite with rank r if and only if there exists a set of vectors $\{\mathbf{v}_1, \ldots, \mathbf{v}_n\}$, $\mathbf{v}_i \in V$, containing exactly r linearly independent vectors, such that $A_{ij} = \mathbf{v}_i \cdot \mathbf{v}_j$.

Note in particular that the vectors $\mathbf{v}$ can always be chosen to have dimension $r \leq n$.

Puzzle 8: *A kernel matrix $K \in S_n$ is a matrix whose elements take the form $K_{ij} \equiv k(\mathbf{x}_i, \mathbf{x}_j)$ for some $\mathbf{x}_i, \mathbf{x}_j \in \mathcal{R}^d$, $i,j = 1, \ldots, n$ for some d, where k is a symmetric function which satisfies Mercer's condition (see e.g. [6]). For any such function k, there exists an inner product space $\mathcal{H}$ and a map $\Phi : \mathcal{R}^d \mapsto \mathcal{H}$ such that $k(\mathbf{x}_i, \mathbf{x}_j) = \Phi(\mathbf{x}_i) \cdot \Phi(\mathbf{x}_j)$. The dimension of $\mathcal{H}$ can be large, or even infinite (an example of the latter is $k(\mathbf{x}_i, \mathbf{x}_j) = \exp^{-(1/\sigma^2)\|\mathbf{x}_i - \mathbf{x}_j\|^2}$). In particular, the dimension of the dot product space can be larger than n. How does this square with the claim just made about the maximum necessary dimension of the Gram vectors?*

Some properties of positive semidefinite matrices that might otherwise seem mysterious become obvious, when they are viewed as Gram matrices, as I hope the following exercise helps demonstrate.

Exercise 12. *Use the fact that every positive semidefinite matrix is a Gram matrix to prove items (2), (3), (5), and (6) in the list above. Use the definition of a positive (semi)definite matrix to prove (1), (4), (7) and (8).*

If the Gram representation is so useful, the question naturally arises: given a positive semidefinite matrix, how can you extract a set of Gram vectors for it? (Note that the set of Gram vectors is never unique; for example, globally rotating them gives the same matrix). Let $A \in S_n \succeq 0$ and write the eigendecomposition of A in outer product form: $A = \sum_{a=1}^{n} \lambda_a \mathbf{e}^{(a)} \mathbf{e}'^{(a)}$ or $A_{ij} = \sum_{a=1}^{n} \lambda_a e_i^{(a)} e_j^{(a)}$. Written in terms of the dual eigenvectors (see Section 3.1): $A_{ij} = \sum_{a=1}^{n} \lambda_a \hat{e}_a^{(i)} \hat{e}_a^{(j)}$, the summand has become a weighted dot product; we can therefore take the set of Gram vectors to be $v_a^{(i)} = \sqrt{\lambda_a} \hat{e}_a^{(i)}$. The Gram vectors therefore are the dual basis to the scaled eigenvectors.

3.10   Distance Matrices

One well-known use of the Gram vector decomposition of positive semidefinite matrices is the following. Define a 'distance matrix' to be any matrix of the form $D_{ij} \in S_n \equiv \|\mathbf{x}_i - \mathbf{x}_j\|^2$, where $\| \cdot \|$ is the Euclidean norm (note that the entries are actually squared distances). A central goal of multidimensional scaling is the following: given a matrix which is a distance matrix, or which is approximately a distance matrix, or which can be mapped to an approximate distance matrix, find the underlying vectors $\mathbf{x}_i \in \mathcal{R}^d$, where d is chosen to be as small as possible, given the constraint that the distance matrix reconstructed from the $\mathbf{x}_i$ approximates D with acceptable accuracy [8]. d is chosen to be small essentially to remove unimportant variance from the problem (or, if sufficiently small, for data visualization). Now let $\mathbf{e}$ be the column vector of n ones, and introduce the 'centering' projection matrix $P^e \equiv 1 - \frac{1}{n} \mathbf{e} \mathbf{e}'$.

Exercise 13. *Prove the following: (1) for any* $\mathbf{x} \in \mathcal{R}^n$, $P^e \mathbf{x}$ *subtracts the mean value of the components of* $\mathbf{x}$ *from each component of* $\mathbf{x}$, *(2)* $P^e \mathbf{e} = 0$, *(3)* $\mathbf{e}$ *is the only eigenvector of* P^e *with eigenvalue zero, and (4) for any dot product matrix* $A_{ij} \in S_m \equiv \mathbf{x}_i \cdot \mathbf{x}_j$, $i, j = 1, \ldots, m$, $\mathbf{x}_i \in \mathcal{R}^n$, *then* $(P^e A P^e)_{ij} = (\mathbf{x}_i - \boldsymbol{\mu}) \cdot (\mathbf{x}_j - \boldsymbol{\mu})$, *where* $\boldsymbol{\mu}$ *is the mean of the* $\mathbf{x}_i$.

The earliest form of the following theorem is due to Schoenberg [18]. For a proof of this version, see [7].

Theorem 2. *Consider the class of symmetric matrices* $A \in S_n$ *such that* $A_{ij} \geq 0$ *and* $A_{ii} = 0$ $\forall i, j$. *Then* $\bar{A} \equiv -P^e A P^e$ *is positive semidefinite if and only if* A *is a distance matrix, with embedding space* $\mathcal{R}^d$ *for some d. Given that* A *is a distance matrix, the minimal embedding dimension d is the rank of* $\bar{A}$, *and the embedding vectors are any set of Gram vectors of* $\bar{A}$, *scaled by a factor of* $\frac{1}{\sqrt{2}}$.

3.11   Computing the Inverse of an Enlarged Matrix

We end our excursion with a look at a trick for efficiently computing inverses. Suppose you have a symmetric matrix $K \in S_{n-1}$, and suppose you form a new symmetric matrix by adding a number $u \equiv K_{nn}$ and a column $\mathbf{v}$, $v_i \equiv K_{in}$ (and a corresponding row $K_{ni} \equiv K_{in}$). Denote the enlarged matrix by

$$K_+ = \begin{pmatrix} K & \mathbf{v} \\ \mathbf{v}' & u \end{pmatrix} \tag{15}$$

Now consider the inverse

$$K_+^{-1} \equiv \begin{pmatrix} A & \mathbf{b} \\ \mathbf{b}' & c \end{pmatrix} \tag{16}$$

where again $\mathbf{b}$ is a column vector and c is a scalar. It turns out that it is straight-forward to compute A, $\mathbf{b}$ and c in terms of K^{-1}, $\mathbf{v}$ and u. Why is this useful? In any machine learning algorithm where the dependence on all the data is captured by a symmetric matrix $K(\mathbf{x}_i, \mathbf{x}_j)$, then in test phase, when a prediction is being made for a single point $\mathbf{x}$, the dependence on all the data is captured by K_+, where $v_i = K(\mathbf{x}_i, \mathbf{x})$ and $u = K(\mathbf{x}, \mathbf{x})$. If that algorithm in addition requires that the quantities $\mathbf{b}$ and c be computed, it's much more efficient to compute them by using the following simple lemma (and computing K^{-1} just once, for the training data), rather than by computing K_+^{-1} for each $\mathbf{x}$. This is used, for example, in Gaussian process regression and Gaussian process classification, where in Gaussian process regression, c is needed to compute the variance in the estimate of the function value $f(\mathbf{x})$ at the test point $\mathbf{x}$, and $\mathbf{b}$ and c are needed to compute the mean of $f(\mathbf{x})$ [9, 20].

Lemma 2. *Given $K \in M_{n-1}$ and $K_+ \in M_n$ as defined above, then the elements of K_+ are given by:*

$$c = \frac{1}{u - \mathbf{v}'K^{-1}\mathbf{v}} \tag{17}$$

$$\mathbf{b} = -\frac{1}{u - \mathbf{v}'K^{-1}\mathbf{v}} \mathbf{v}'K^{-1} \tag{18}$$

$$A_{ij} = K_{ij}^{-1} + \frac{1}{u - \mathbf{v}'K^{-1}\mathbf{v}} (\mathbf{v}'K^{-1})_i (\mathbf{v}'K^{-1})_j \tag{19}$$

and furthermore,

$$\frac{\det(K)}{\det(K_+)} = \frac{1}{u - \mathbf{v}'K^{-1}\mathbf{v}} = c \tag{20}$$

Proof. Since the inverse of a symmetric matrix is symmetric, K_+^{-1} can be written in the form (16). Then requiring that $K_+^{-1}K_+ = \mathbf{1}$ gives (repeated indices are summed):

$$i < n, \; j < n: \quad A_{im}K_{mj} + b_i v_j = \delta_{ij} \tag{21}$$

$$i = n, \; j < n: \quad b_m K_{mj} + c v_j = 0 \tag{22}$$

$$i < n, \; j = n: \quad A_{im}v_m + b_i u = 0 \tag{23}$$

$$i = n, \; j = n: \quad b_m v_m + cu = 1 \tag{24}$$

Eq. (22) gives $b = -c\mathbf{v}'K^{-1}$. Substituting this in (24) gives Eq. (17), and substituting it in (21) gives Eq. (19). Finally the expression for the ratio of determinants follows from the expression for the elements of an inverse matrix in terms of ratios of its cofactors. $\square$

Exercise 14. *Verify formulae (17), (18), (19) and (20) for a matrix $K_+ \in S_2$ of your choice.*

Puzzle 9: *Why not use this result iteratively (starting at $n = 2$) to compute the inverse of an arbitrary symmetric matrix $A \in S_n$? How does the number of operations needed to do this compare with the number of operations needed by Gaussian elimination (as a function of n)? If, due to numerical problems, the first (top left) element of the first matrix is off by a factor $1 + \epsilon$, $\epsilon \ll 1$, what is the error (roughly) in the estimated value of the final (bottom right) element of S_n?*

References

1. W.W. Rouse Ball. *A Short Account of the History of Mathematics.* Dover, 4 edition, 1908.
2. M. Belkin and P. Niyogi. Laplacian eigenmaps for dimensionality reduction and data representation. In *Advances in Neural Information Processing Systems 14.* MIT Press, 2002.
3. E.T. Bell. *Men of Mathematics.* Simon and Schuster, Touchstone edition, 1986; first published 1937.
4. S. Boyd and L. Vandenberghe. *Convex Optimization.* Cambridge University Press, 2004.
5. B. Buck and V. Macaualay (editors). *Maximum Entropy in Action.* Clarendon Press, 1991.
6. C.J.C. Burges. A tutorial on support vector machines for pattern recognition. *Data Mining and Knowledge Discovery,* 2(2):121–167, 1998.
7. C.J.C. Burges. Geometric Methods for Feature Extraction and Dimensional Reduction. In L. Rokach and O. Maimon, editors, *Data Mining and Knowledge Discovery Handbook: A Complete Guide for Practitioners and Researchers.* Kluwer Academic, 2004, to appear.
8. T.F. Cox and M.A.A. Cox. *Multidimensional Scaling.* Chapman and Hall, 2001.
9. Noel A.C. Cressie. *Statistics for spatial data.* Wiley, revised edition, 1993.
10. S. Deerwester, S.T. Dumais, T.K. Landauer, G.W. Furnas, and R.A. Harshman. Indexing by Latent Semantic Analysis. *Journal of the Society for Information Science,* 41(6):391–407, 1990.
11. G.H. Golub and C.F. Van Loan. *Matrix Computations.* Johns Hopkins, third edition, 1996.
12. R.A. Horn and C.R. Johnson. *Matrix Analysis.* Cambridge University Press, 1985.
13. E.T. Jaynes. Bayesian methods: General background. In J.H. Justice, editor, *Maximum Entropy and Bayesian Methods in Applied Statistics,* pages 1–25. Cambridge University Press, 1985.
14. Morris Kline. *Mathematical Thought from Ancient to Modern Times, Vols. 1,2,3.* Oxford University Press, 1972.
15. O.L. Mangasarian. *Nonlinear Programming.* McGraw Hill, New York, 1969.
16. K. Nigam, J. Lafferty, and A. McCallum. Using maximum entropy for text classification. In *IJCAI-99 Workshop on Machine Learning for Information Filtering,* pages 61–67, 1999.
17. S.T. Roweis and L.K. Saul. Nonlinear dimensionality reduction by locally linear embedding. *Science,* 290(22):2323–2326, 2000.

18. I.J. Schoenberg. Remarks to maurice frechet's article *sur la définition axiomatique d'une classe d'espace distanciés vectoriellement applicable sur l'espace de Hilbert*. *Annals of Mathematics*, 36:724–732, 1935.
19. M.E. Tipping and C.M. Bishop. Probabilistic principal component analysis. *Journal of the Royal Statistical Society*, 61(3):611, 1999.
20. C.K.I. Williams. Prediction with gaussian processes: from linear regression to linear prediction and beyond. In Michael I. Jordan, editor, *Learning in Graphical Models*, pages 599–621. MIT Press, 1999.

Bayesian Inference: An Introduction to Principles and Practice in Machine Learning

Michael E. Tipping

Microsoft Research, 7 J J Thomson Avenue, Cambridge CB3 0FB, U.K.
mtipping@microsoft.com
http://www.research.microsoft.com/users/mtipping

Abstract. This article gives a basic introduction to the principles of Bayesian inference in a machine learning context, with an emphasis on the importance of marginalisation for dealing with uncertainty. We begin by illustrating concepts via a simple regression task before relating ideas to practical, contemporary, techniques with a description of 'sparse Bayesian' models and the 'relevance vector machine'.

1 Introduction

What is meant by "Bayesian inference" in the context of machine learning? To assist in answering that question, let's start by proposing a conceptual task: we wish to learn, from some given number of example instances of them, a model of the relationship between pairs of variables A and B. Indeed, many machine learning problems are of the type "given A, what is B?".[1]

Verbalising what we typically treat as a mathematical task raises an interesting question in itself. How do we answer "what is B?"? Within the appealingly well-defined and axiomatic framework of propositional logic, we 'answer' the question with complete certainty, but this logic is clearly too rigid to cope with the realities of real-world modelling, where uncertainty over 'truth' is ubiquitous. Our measurements of both the dependent (B) and independent (A) variables are inherently noisy and inexact, and the relationships between the two are invariably non-deterministic. This is where probability theory comes to our aid, as it furnishes us with a principled and consistent framework for meaningful reasoning in the presence of uncertainty.

We might think of probability theory, and in particular Bayes' rule, as providing us with a "logic of uncertainty" [1]. In our example, given A we would 'reason' about the likelihood of the truth of B (let's say B is binary for example) via its conditional probability $P(B|A)$: that is, "what is the probability of B given that A takes a particular value?". An appropriate answer might be "B is true with probability 0.6". One of the primary tasks of 'machine learning' is

---

[1] In this article we will focus exclusively on such 'supervised learning' tasks, although of course there are other modelling applications which are equally amenable to Bayesian inferential techniques.

O. Bousquet et al. (Eds.): Machine Learning 2003, LNAI 3176, pp. 41–62, 2004.

then to approximate $P(B|A)$ with some appropriately specified model based on a given set of corresponding examples of A and B.[2]

It is in the modelling procedure where Bayesian inference comes to the fore. We typically (though not exclusively) deploy some form of parameterised model for our conditional probability:

$$P(B|A) = f(A; \mathbf{w}),\qquad(1)$$

where $\mathbf{w}$ denotes a vector of all the 'adjustable' parameters in the model. Then, given a set $\mathcal{D}$ of N examples of our variables, $\mathcal{D} = \{A_n, B_n\}_{n=1}^{N}$, a conventional approach would involve the maximisation of some measure of 'accuracy' (or minimisation of some measure of 'loss') of our model for $\mathcal{D}$ with respect to the adjustable parameters. We then can make predictions, given A, for unknown B by evaluating $f(A; \mathbf{w})$ with parameters $\mathbf{w}$ set to their optimal values. Of course, if our model f is made too complex — perhaps there are many adjustable parameters $\mathbf{w}$ — we risk over-specialising to the observed data $\mathcal{D}$, and consequently realising a poor model of the true underlying distribution $P(B|A)$.

The first key element of the Bayesian inference paradigm is to treat parameters such as $\mathbf{w}$ as random variables, exactly the same as A and B. So the conditional probability now becomes $P(B|A, \mathbf{w})$, and the dependency of the probability of B on the parameter settings, as well as A, is made explicit. Rather than 'learning' comprising the optimisation of some quality measure, a *distribution* over the parameters $\mathbf{w}$ is inferred from Bayes' rule. We will demonstrate this concept by means of a simple example regression task in Section 2.

To obtain this 'posterior' distribution over $\mathbf{w}$ alluded to above, it is necessary to specify a 'prior' distribution $p(\mathbf{w})$ before we observe the data. This may be considered an inconvenience, but Bayesian inference treats all sources of uncertainty in the modelling process in a unified and consistent manner, and forces us to be explicit as regards our assumptions and constraints; this in itself is arguably a philosophically appealing feature of the paradigm.

However, the most attractive facet of a Bayesian approach is the manner in which "Ockham's Razor" is automatically implemented by 'integrating out' all irrelevant variables. That is, under the Bayesian framework there is an automatic preference for simple models that sufficiently explain the data without unnecessary complexity. We demonstrate this key feature in Section 3, and in particular underline the point that *this property holds even if the prior $p(\mathbf{w})$ is completely uninformative*. We show that, in practical terms, the concept of Ockham's Razor enables us to 'set' regularisation parameters and 'select' models without the need for any additional validation procedure.

The practical disadvantage of the Bayesian approach is that it requires us to perform integrations over variables, and many of these computations are analytically intractable. As a result, much contemporary research in Bayesian

---

[2] In many learning methods, this conditional probability approximation is not made explicit, though such an interpretation may exist. However, one might consider it a significant limitation if a particular machine learning procedure *cannot* be expressed coherently within a probabilistic framework.

approaches to machine learning relies on, or is directly concerned with, approximation techniques. However, we show in Section 4, where we describe the "sparse Bayesian" model, that a combination of analytic calculation and straightforward, practically efficient, approximation can offer state-of-the-art results.

2   From Least-Squares to Bayesian Inference

We introduce the methodology of Bayesian inference by considering an example prediction (regression) problem. Let us assume we are given a very simple data set (illustrated later within Figure 1) comprising $N = 15$ samples artificially generated from the function $y = \sin(x)$ with added Gaussian noise of variance 0.2. We will denote the 'input' variables in our example by x_n, $n = 1 \ldots N$. For each such x_n, there is an associated real-valued 'target' t_n, $n = 1 \ldots N$, and from these input-target pairs, we wish to 'learn' the underlying functional mapping.

2.1   Linear Models

We will model this data with some parameterised function $y(x; \mathbf{w})$, where $\mathbf{w} = (w_1, w_2, \ldots, w_M)$ is the vector of adjustable model parameters. Here, we consider linear models (strictly, "linear-in-the-parameter") models which are a linearly-weighted sum of M fixed (but potentially *non*linear) basis functions $\phi_m(x)$:

$$y(x; \mathbf{w}) = \sum_{m=1}^{M} w_m \phi_m(x). \tag{2}$$

For our purposes here, we make the common choice to utilise Gaussian data-centred basis functions $\phi_m(x) = \exp\left\{-(x - x_m)^2 / r^2\right\}$, which gives us a 'radial basis function' (RBF) type model.

"Least-Squares" Approximation. Our objective is to find values for $\mathbf{w}$ such that $y(x; \mathbf{w})$ makes good predictions for new data: *i.e.* it models the *underlying generative function*. A classic approach to estimating $y(x; \mathbf{w})$ is "least-squares", minimising the error measure:

$$E_{\mathcal{D}}(\mathbf{w}) = \frac{1}{2} \sum_{n=1}^{N} \left[t_n - \sum_{m=1}^{M} w_m \phi_m(x_n) \right]^2 . \tag{3}$$

If $\mathbf{t} = (t_1, \ldots, t_N)^{\mathrm{T}}$ and $\boldsymbol{\Phi}$ is the 'design matrix' such that $\boldsymbol{\Phi}_{nm} = \phi_m(x_n)$, then the minimiser of (3) is obtained in closed-form via linear algebra:

$$\mathbf{w}_{LS} = (\boldsymbol{\Phi}^{\mathrm{T}} \boldsymbol{\Phi})^{-1} \boldsymbol{\Phi}^{\mathrm{T}} \mathbf{t}. \tag{4}$$

However, with $M = 15$ basis functions and only $N = 15$ examples here, we know that minimisation of squared-error leads to a model which exactly interpolates the data samples, as shown in Figure 1.

Now, we may look at Figure 1 and exclaim "the function on the right is clearly over-fitting!". But, without prior knowledge of the 'truth', can we really

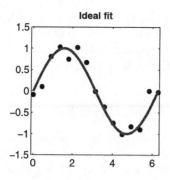
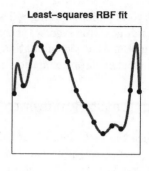

Fig. 1. Overfitting? The 'ideal fit' is shown on the left, while the least-squares fit using 15 basis functions is shown on the right and perfectly interpolates all the data points

judge which model is genuinely better? The answer is that we can't — in a real-world problem, the data could quite possibly have been generated by a complex function such as shown on the right. The only way that we can proceed to meaningfully learn from data such as this is by imposing some *a priori* prejudice on the nature of the complexity of functions we expect to elucidate. A common way of doing this is via 'regularisation'.

2.2   Complexity Control: Regularisation

A common, and generally very reasonable, assumption is that we typically expect that data is generated from smooth, rather than complex, functions. In a linear model framework, smoother functions typically have smaller weight magnitudes, so we can penalise complex functions by adding an appropriate penalty term to the cost function that we minimise:

$$\widehat{E}(\mathbf{w}) = E_{\mathcal{D}}(\mathbf{w}) + \lambda E_W(\mathbf{w}). \tag{5}$$

A standard choice is the squared-weight penalty, $E_W(\mathbf{w}) = \frac{1}{2}\sum_{m=1}^{M} w_m^2$, which conveniently gives the "penalised least-squares" (PLS) estimate for $\mathbf{w}$:

$$\mathbf{w}_{PLS} = (\boldsymbol{\Phi}^{\mathrm{T}}\boldsymbol{\Phi} + \lambda\mathbf{I})^{-1}\boldsymbol{\Phi}^{\mathrm{T}}\mathbf{t}. \tag{6}$$

The *hyperparameter* λ balances the trade-off between $E_{\mathcal{D}}(\mathbf{w})$ and $E_W(\mathbf{w})$ — *i.e.* between how well the function fits the data and how smooth it is. Given that we can compute the weights directly for a given λ, the learning problem is now transformed into one of finding an appropriate value for that hyperparameter. A very common approach is to assess potential values of λ according to the error calculated on a set of 'validation' data (*i.e.* data which is not used to estimate $\mathbf{w}$), and examples of fits for different values of λ and their associated validation errors are given in Figure 2.

In practice, we might evaluate a large number of models with different hyperparameter values and select the model with lowest validation error, as demonstrated in Figure 3. We would then hope that this would give us a model which

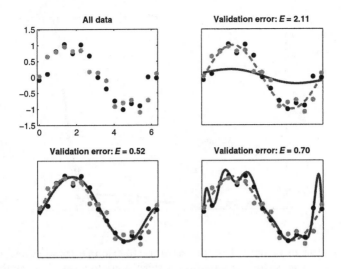

Fig. 2. Function estimates (solid line) and validation error for three different values of regularisation hyperparameter λ (the true function is shown dashed). The training data is plotted in black, and the validation set in green (gray)

was close to 'the truth'. In this artificial case where we know the generative function, the deviation from 'truth' is illustrated in the figure with the measurement of 'test error', the error on noise-free samples of $\sin(x)$. We can see that the minimum validation error does not quite localise the best test error, but it is arguably satisfactorily close. We'll come back to this graph in Section 3 when we look at marginalisation and how Bayesian inference can be exploited in order to estimate λ. For now, we look at how this regularisation approach can be initially reformulated within a Bayesian probabilistic framework.

2.3   A Probabilistic Regression Framework

We assume as before that the data is a noisy realisation of an underlying functional model: $t_n = y(x_n; \mathbf{w}) + \epsilon_n$. Applying least-squares resulted in us minimising $\sum_n \epsilon_n^2$, but here we first define an explicit probabilistic model over the noise component ϵ_n, chosen to be a Gaussian distribution with mean zero and variance σ^2. That is, $p(\epsilon_n | \sigma^2) = N(0, \sigma^2)$. Since $t_n = y(x_n; \mathbf{w}) + \epsilon_n$ it follows that $p(t_n | x_n, \mathbf{w}, \sigma^2) = N(y(x_n; \mathbf{w}), \sigma^2)$. Assuming that each example from the the data set has been generated independently (an often realistic assumption, although not always true), the *likelihood*[3] of all the data is given by the product:

---

[3] Although 'probability' and 'likelihood' functions may be identical, a common convention is to refer to "probability" when it is primarily interpreted as a function of the random variable **t**, and "likelihood" when interpreted as a function of the parameters **w**.

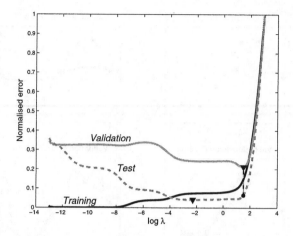

Fig. 3. Plots of error computed on the separate 15-example training and validation sets, along with 'test' error measured on a third noise-free set. The minimum test and validation errors are marked with a triangle, and the intersection of the best λ computed via validation is shown

$$p(\mathbf{t}|\mathbf{x},\mathbf{w},\sigma^2) = \prod_{n=1}^{N} p(t_n|x_n,\mathbf{w},\sigma^2), \tag{7}$$

$$= \prod_{n=1}^{N} (2\pi\sigma^2)^{-1/2} \exp\left[-\frac{\{t_n - y(x_n;\mathbf{w})\}^2}{2\sigma^2}\right]. \tag{8}$$

Note that, from now on, we will write terms such as $p(\mathbf{t}|\mathbf{x},\mathbf{w},\sigma^2)$ as $p(\mathbf{t}|\mathbf{w},\sigma^2)$, since we never seek to model the given input data $\mathbf{x}$. Omitting to include such conditioning variables is purely for notational convenience (it implies no further model assumptions) and is common practice.

2.4   Maximum Likelihood and Least-Squares

The 'maximum-likelihood' estimate for $\mathbf{w}$ is that value which maximises $p(\mathbf{t}|\mathbf{w}, \sigma^2)$. In fact, this is identical to the 'least-squares' solution, which we can see by noting that minimising squared-error is equivalent to minimising the negative logarithm of the likelihood which here is:

$$-\log p(\mathbf{t}|\mathbf{w},\sigma^2) = \frac{N}{2}\log(2\pi\sigma^2) + \frac{1}{2\sigma^2}\sum_{n=1}^{N}\{t_n - y(x_n;\mathbf{w})\}^2. \tag{9}$$

Since the first term on the right in (9) is independent of $\mathbf{w}$, this leaves only the second term which is proportional to the squared error.

2.5   Specifying a Bayesian Prior

Of course, giving an identical solution for $\mathbf{w}$ as least-squares, maximum likelihood estimation will also result in overfitting. To control the model complexity, instead of the earlier regularisation weight penalty $E_W(\mathbf{w})$, we now define a *prior distribution* which expresses our 'degree of belief' over values that $\mathbf{w}$ might take:

$$p(\mathbf{w}|\alpha) = \prod_{m=1}^{M} \left(\frac{\alpha}{2\pi}\right)^{1/2} \exp\left\{-\frac{\alpha}{2}w_m^2\right\}. \tag{10}$$

This (common) choice of a zero-mean Gaussian prior, expresses a preference for smoother models by declaring smaller weights to be *a priori* more probable. Though the prior is independent for each weight, there is a shared inverse variance hyperparameter α, analogous to λ earlier, which moderates the strength of our 'belief'.

2.6   Posterior Inference

Previously, given our error measure and regulariser, we computed a single *point estimate* $\mathbf{w}_{LS}$ for the weights. Now, given the likelihood and the prior, we compute the *posterior distribution* over $\mathbf{w}$ via Bayes' rule:

$$p(\mathbf{w}|\mathbf{t},\alpha,\sigma^2) = \frac{\text{likelihood} \times \text{prior}}{\text{normalising factor}} = \frac{p(\mathbf{t}|\mathbf{w},\sigma^2)p(\mathbf{w}|\alpha)}{p(\mathbf{t}|\alpha,\sigma^2)}. \tag{11}$$

As a consequence of combining a Gaussian prior and a linear model within a Gaussian likelihood, the posterior is also conveniently Gaussian: $p(\mathbf{w}|\mathbf{t},\alpha,\sigma^2) = N(\boldsymbol{\mu},\boldsymbol{\Sigma})$ with

$$\boldsymbol{\mu} = (\boldsymbol{\Phi}^{\mathrm{T}}\boldsymbol{\Phi} + \sigma^2\alpha\mathbf{I})^{-1}\boldsymbol{\Phi}^{\mathrm{T}}\mathbf{t}, \tag{12}$$

$$\boldsymbol{\Sigma} = \sigma^2(\boldsymbol{\Phi}^{\mathrm{T}}\boldsymbol{\Phi} + \sigma^2\alpha\mathbf{I})^{-1}. \tag{13}$$

So instead of 'learning' a single value for $\mathbf{w}$, we have inferred a distribution over all possible values. In effect, we have updated our prior 'belief' in the parameter values in light of the information provided by the data $\mathbf{t}$, with more posterior probability assigned to values which are both probable under the prior and which 'explain the data'.

MAP Estimation: A 'Bayesian' Short-Cut. The "maximum *a posteriori*" (MAP) estimate for $\mathbf{w}$ is the single most probable value under the posterior distribution $p(\mathbf{w}|\mathbf{t},\alpha,\sigma^2)$. Since the denominator in Bayes' rule (11) earlier is independent of $\mathbf{w}$, this is equivalent to maximising the numerator, or equivalently minimising $E_{MAP}(\mathbf{w}) = -\log p(\mathbf{t}|\mathbf{w},\sigma^2) - \log p(\mathbf{w}|\alpha)$. Retaining only those terms dependent on $\mathbf{w}$ gives:

$$E_{MAP}(\mathbf{w}) = \frac{1}{2\sigma^2}\sum_{n=1}^{N}\{t_n - y(x_n;\mathbf{w})\}^2 + \frac{\alpha}{2}\sum_{m=1}^{M}w_m^2. \tag{14}$$

The MAP estimate is therefore identical to the PLS estimate with $\lambda = \sigma^2\alpha$.

Illustration of Sequential Bayesian Inference. For our example problem, we'll end this section by looking at how the posterior $p(\mathbf{w}|\mathbf{t}, \alpha, \sigma^2)$ evolves as we observe increasingly more data points t_n. Before proceeding, we note that we can compute the posterior incrementally since here the data are assumed independent (conditioned on $\mathbf{w}$). *e.g.* for $\mathbf{t} = (t_1, t_2, t_3)$:

$$p(\mathbf{w}|t_1, t_2, t_3) \propto p(t_1, t_2, t_3|\mathbf{w}) \, p(\mathbf{w}),$$
$$= p(t_2, t_3|\mathbf{w}) \, p(t_1|\mathbf{w}) \, p(\mathbf{w}),$$
$$= \text{Likelihood of } (t_2, t_3) \times \text{posterior having observed } t_1.$$

So, more generally, we can treat the posterior having observed $(t_1, \ldots, t_K)$ as the 'prior' for the remaining data $(t_{K+1}, \ldots, t_N)$ and obtain the equivalent result to seeing all the data at once. We exploit this result in Figure 4 where we illustrate how the posterior distribution updates with increasing amounts of data.

The second row in Figure 4 illustrates some relevant points. First, because the data observed up to that point are not generally near the centres of the two basis functions visualised, those values of x are relatively uninformative regarding the associated weights and the posterior thereover has not deviated far from the prior. Second, on the far right in the second row, we can see that the function is fairly well determined in the vicinity of the observations, but at higher values of x, where data are yet to be observed, the MAP estimate of the function is not accurate and the posterior samples there exhibit high variance. On the third row we have observed all data, and notice that although the MAP predictor appears subjectively good, the posterior still seems quite diffuse and the variance in the samples is noticeable. We emphasise this point in the bottom row, where we have generated and observed an extra 200 data points and it can be seen how the posterior is now much more concentrated, and samples from it are now quite closely concentrated about the MAP value.

Note that this facility to sample from the prior or posterior is a very informative feature of the Bayesian paradigm. For the posterior, it is a helpful way of visualising the remaining uncertainty in parameter estimates in cases where the posterior distribution itself cannot be visualised. Furthermore, the ability to visualise samples from the prior alone is very advantageous, as it offers us evidence to judge the appropriateness of our prior assumptions. No equivalent facility exists within the regularisation or penalty function framework.

3   Marginalisation and Ockham's Razor

Since we have just seen that the *maximum a posteriori* (MAP) and penalised least-squares (PLS) estimates are equivalent, it might be tempting to assume that the Bayesian framework is simply a probabilistic re-interpretation of classical methods. This is certainly not the case! It is sometimes overlooked that the distinguishing element of Bayesian methods is really *marginalisation*, where instead of seeking to 'estimate' all 'nuisance' variables in our models, we attempt to integrate them out. As we will now see, this is a powerful component of the Bayesian framework.

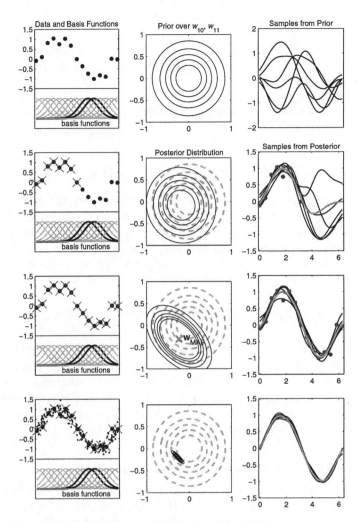

Fig. 4. Illustration of the evolution of the posterior distribution as data is sequentially 'absorbed'. The left column shows the data, with those points which have been observed so far crossed, along with a plot of the basis functions. The contour plots in the middle column show the prior/posterior over just two (for visualisation purposes) of the weights, w_{10} and w_{11}, corresponding to the highlighted basis functions on the left. The right hand column plots $y(x; \mathbf{w})$ from a number of samples of $\mathbf{w}$ from the full prior/posterior, along with the posterior mean, or MAP, estimator (in thicker green/gray). From top to bottom, the number of data is increasing. Row 1 shows the *a priori* case for no data, row 2 shows the model after 8 examples, and row 3 shows the model after all 15 data points have been observed. Finally, the bottom row shows the case when an additional 200 data points have been generated and absorbed in the posterior model

3.1   Making Predictions

First lets reiterate some of the previous section and consider how, having 'learned' from the training values $\mathbf{t}$, we make a prediction for the value of t_* given a new input datum x_*:

Framework	Learned Quantity	Prediction
Classical	$\mathbf{w}_{PLS}$	$y(x_*; \mathbf{w}_{PLS})$
MAP Bayesian	$p(\mathbf{w}|\mathbf{t}, \alpha, \sigma^2)$	$p(t_*|\mathbf{w}_{MAP}, \sigma^2)$
True Bayesian	$p(\mathbf{w}|\mathbf{t}, \alpha, \sigma^2)$	$p(t_*|\mathbf{t}, \alpha, \sigma^2)$

The first two approaches result in similar predictions, although the MAP Bayesian model does give a probability distribution for t_* (which can be sampled from, *e.g.* see Figure 4). The mean of this distribution is the same as that of the classical predictor $y(x_*; \mathbf{w}_{PLS})$, since $\mathbf{w}_{MAP} = \mathbf{w}_{PLS}$.

However, the 'true Bayesian' way is to *integrate out*, or *marginalise* over, the uncertain variables $\mathbf{w}$ in order to obtain the *predictive distribution*:

$$p(t_*|\mathbf{t}, \alpha, \sigma^2) = \int p(t_*|\mathbf{w}, \sigma^2) \, p(\mathbf{w}|\mathbf{t}, \alpha, \sigma^2) \, d\mathbf{w}. \qquad (15)$$

This distribution $p(t_*|\mathbf{t}, \alpha, \sigma^2)$ incorporates our uncertainty over the weights having seen $\mathbf{t}$, by averaging the model probability for t_* over all possible values of $\mathbf{w}$. If we are unsure about the parameter settings, for example if there were very few data points, then $p(\mathbf{w}|\mathbf{t}, \alpha, \sigma^2)$ and similarly $p(t_*|\mathbf{t}, \alpha, \sigma^2)$ will be appropriately diffuse. The classical, and even MAP Bayesian, predictions take no account of how well-determined our parameters $\mathbf{w}$ really are.

3.2   The General Bayesian Predictive Framework

You way well find the presence of α and σ^2 as conditioning variables in the predictive distribution, $p(t_*|\mathbf{t}, \alpha, \sigma^2)$, in (15) rather disconcerting, and indeed, for any general model, if we wish to predict t_* given some training data $\mathbf{t}$, what we really, really want is $p(t_*|\mathbf{t})$. That is, we wish to integrate out *all* variables not directly related to the task at hand. So far, we've only placed a prior over the weights $\mathbf{w}$ — to be truly, truly Bayesian, we should define $p(\alpha)$, a so-called *hyperprior*, along with a prior over the noise level $p(\sigma^2)$. Then the full posterior over 'nuisance' variables becomes:

$$p(\mathbf{w}, \alpha, \sigma^2|\mathbf{t}) = \frac{p(\mathbf{t}|\mathbf{w}, \sigma^2)p(\mathbf{w}|\alpha)p(\alpha)p(\sigma^2)}{p(\mathbf{t})}. \qquad (16)$$

The denominator, or normalising factor, in (16) is the *marginalised* probability of the data:

$$p(\mathbf{t}) = \int p(\mathbf{t}|\mathbf{w}, \sigma^2)p(\mathbf{w}|\alpha)p(\alpha)p(\sigma^2) \, d\mathbf{w} \, d\alpha \, d\sigma^2, \qquad (17)$$

and is nearly always analytically intractable to compute! Nevertheless, as we'll soon see, $p(\mathbf{t})$ is a very useful quantity and can be amenable to effective approximation.

3.3   Practical Bayesian Prediction

Given the full posterior (16), Bayesian inference in our example regression model would proceed with:

$$p(t_*|\mathbf{t}) = \int p(t_*|\mathbf{w}, \sigma^2) \, p(\mathbf{w}, \alpha, \sigma^2|\mathbf{t}) \, d\mathbf{w} \, d\alpha \, d\sigma^2, \qquad (18)$$

but as we indicated, we can't compute either $p(\mathbf{w}, \alpha, \sigma^2|\mathbf{t})$ or $p(t_*|\mathbf{t})$ analytically. If we wish to proceed, we must turn to some approximation strategy (and it is here that much of the Bayesian "voodoo" resides). A sensible approach might be to perform those integrations that are analytically computable, and then approximate remaining integrations, perhaps using one of a number of established methods:

- Type-II maximum likelihood (discussed shortly)
- Laplace's method (see, *e.g.*, [2])
- Variational techniques (see, *e.g.*, [3, 4])
- Sampling (*e.g.* [2, 5])

Much research in Bayesian inference has gone, and continues to go, into the development and assessment of approximation techniques, including those listed above. For the purposes of this article, we will primarily exploit the first of them.

3.4   A Type-II Maximum Likelihood Approximation

Here, using the product rule of probability, we can rewrite the ideal full posterior $p(\mathbf{w}, \alpha, \sigma^2|\mathbf{t})$ as:

$$p(\mathbf{w}, \alpha, \sigma^2|\mathbf{t}) \equiv p(\mathbf{w}|\mathbf{t}, \alpha, \sigma^2) \, p(\alpha, \sigma^2|\mathbf{t}). \qquad (19)$$

The first term is our earlier weight posterior which we have already computed: $p(\mathbf{w}|\mathbf{t}, \alpha, \sigma^2) \sim N(\boldsymbol{\mu}, \boldsymbol{\Sigma})$. The second term $p(\alpha, \sigma^2|\mathbf{t})$ we will approximate, admittedly crudely, by a δ-function at its mode. *i.e.* we find "most probable" values α_{MP} and σ^2_{MP} which maximise:

$$p(\alpha, \sigma^2|\mathbf{t}) = \frac{p(\mathbf{t}|\alpha, \sigma^2) \, p(\alpha) \, p(\sigma^2)}{p(\mathbf{t})}. \qquad (20)$$

Since the denominator is independent of α and σ^2, we only need maximise the numerator $p(\mathbf{t}|\alpha, \sigma^2)p(\alpha)p(\sigma^2)$. Furthermore, if we assume flat, *uninformative*, priors over $\log \alpha$ and $\log \sigma$, then we equivalently just need to find the maximum of $p(\mathbf{t}|\alpha, \sigma^2)$. Assuming a flat prior here may seem to be a computational convenience, but in fact it is arguably our prior of choice since our model will be invariant to the scale of the target data (and basis set), which is almost always an advantageous feature[4]. For example, our results won't change if we measure t in metres instead of miles. We'll return to the task of maximising $p(\mathbf{t}|\alpha, \sigma^2)$ in Section 3.6.

3.5   The Approximate Predictive Distribution

Having found α_{MP} and σ^2_{MP}, our approximation to the predictive distribution would be:

$$
\begin{aligned}
p(t_*|\mathbf{t}) &= \int p(t_*|\mathbf{w}, \sigma^2)\, p(\mathbf{w}|\mathbf{t}, \alpha, \sigma^2)\, p(\alpha, \sigma^2|\mathbf{t})\ d\mathbf{w}\ d\alpha\ d\sigma^2, \\
&\approx \int p(t_*|\mathbf{w}, \sigma^2)\, p(\mathbf{w}|\mathbf{t}, \alpha, \sigma^2)\, \delta(\alpha_{\text{MP}}, \sigma^2_{\text{MP}})\ d\mathbf{w}\ d\alpha\ d\sigma^2, \\
&= \int p(t_*|\mathbf{w}, \sigma^2_{\text{MP}})\, p(\mathbf{w}|\mathbf{t}, \alpha_{\text{MP}}, \sigma^2_{\text{MP}})\ d\mathbf{w}. \qquad (21)
\end{aligned}
$$

In our example earlier, recall that $p(\mathbf{w}|\mathbf{t}, \alpha_{\text{MP}}, \sigma^2_{\text{MP}}) \sim N(\boldsymbol{\mu}, \boldsymbol{\Sigma})$, from which the approximate predictive distribution can be finally written as:

$$
p(t_*|\mathbf{t}) \approx \int p(t_*|\mathbf{w}, \sigma^2_{\text{MP}})\, p(\mathbf{w}|\mathbf{t}, \alpha_{\text{MP}}, \sigma^2_{\text{MP}})\ d\mathbf{w}. \qquad (22)
$$

This is now computable and is Gaussian: $N(\mu_*, \sigma^2_*)$, with:

$$
\begin{aligned}
\mu_* &= y(x_*; \boldsymbol{\mu}), \\
\sigma^2_* &= \sigma^2_{\text{MP}} + \mathbf{f}^{\mathsf{T}} \boldsymbol{\Sigma} \mathbf{f},
\end{aligned}
$$

where $\mathbf{f} = [\phi_1(x_*), \dots, \phi_M(x_*)]^{\mathsf{T}}$. Intuitively, we see that

- the mean predictor μ_* is the model function evaluated with the posterior mean weights (the same as the MAP prediction),
- the predictive variance σ^2_* is the sum of variances associated with both the noise process and the uncertainty of the weight estimates. In particular, it can be clearly seen that when the posterior over $\mathbf{w}$ is more diffuse, and $\boldsymbol{\Sigma}$ is larger, σ^2_* is also increased.

3.6   Marginal Likelihood

Returning now to the question of finding α_{MP} and σ^2_{MP}, as noted earlier we find the maximising values of the 'marginal likelihood' $p(\mathbf{t}|\alpha, \sigma^2)$. This is given by:

---

[4] Note that for *scale* parameters such as α and σ^2, it can be shown that it is appropriate to define uninformative priors uniformly over a *logarithmic* scale [6]. While for brevity we will continue to denote parameters "α" and "σ", from now on we will work with the logarithms thereof, and in particular, will maximise distributions with respect to $\log \alpha$ and $\log \sigma$. In this respect, one must note with caution that finding the maximum of a distribution with respect to parameters is *not* invariant to transformations of those parameters, whereas the result of integration with respect to transformed distributions *is* invariant.

$$p(\mathbf{t}|\alpha, \sigma^2) = \int p(\mathbf{t}|\mathbf{w}, \sigma^2) \, p(\mathbf{w}|\alpha) \, d\mathbf{w},$$

$$= (2\pi)^{-N/2} |\sigma^2 \mathbf{I} + \alpha^{-1} \boldsymbol{\Phi}\boldsymbol{\Phi}^{\mathrm{T}}|^{-1/2} \exp\left\{ -\frac{1}{2}\mathbf{t}^{\mathrm{T}}(\sigma^2 \mathbf{I} + \alpha^{-1}\boldsymbol{\Phi}\boldsymbol{\Phi}^{\mathrm{T}})^{-1}\mathbf{t} \right\}. \tag{23}$$

This is a Gaussian distribution over the single N-dimensional dataset vector $\mathbf{t}$, and (23) is readily evaluated for arbitrary values of α (and σ^2). Note that here we can use *all the data* to directly determine α_{MP} and σ^2_{MP} — we don't need to reserve a separate data set to validate their values. We can use gradient-based techniques to maximise (23) (and we will do so for a similar quantity in Section 4), but here we choose to repeat the earlier experiment for the regularised linear model. While we fix σ^2 (though we could also experimentally evaluate it), in Figure 5 we have computed the marginal likelihood (in fact, its negative logarithm) at a number of different values of α (for just the 15-example training set, though we could also have made use of the validation set too) and compared with the training, validation and test errors of Figure 3 earlier.

It is quite striking that *using only 15 examples and no validation data*, the Bayesian approach for setting α (giving test error 1.66) finds a closer model to the 'truth' than the classical model with its validated value of λ (test error 2.33). It is also interesting to see, and is it not immediately obvious why, that the marginal likelihood measure, although only measured on the training data, is not monotonic (unlike training error) and exhibits a maximum at some intermediate complexity level. The marginal likelihood criterion appears to be successfully penalising *both* models that are too simple *and* too complex — this is "Ockham's Razor" at work.

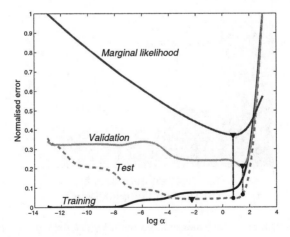

Fig. 5. Plots of the training, validation and test errors of the model as shown in Figure 3 (with the horizontal scale adjusted appropriately to convert from λ to α) along with the negative log marginal likelihood evaluated *on the training data alone* for that same model. The values of α and test error achieved by the model with highest marginal likelihood (smallest negative log) are indicated

3.7   Ockham's Razor

In the fourteenth century, William of Ockham proposed:

"Pluralitas non est ponenda sine neccesitate"

which literally translates as "entities should not be multiplied unnecessarily". Its original historic context was theological, but the concept remains relevant for machine learning today, where it might be translated as "models should be no more complex than is sufficient to explain the data". The Bayesian procedure is effectively implementing "Ockham's Razor" by assigning lower probability *both* to models that are too simple *and* too complex. We might ask: why is an intermediate value of α preferred? The schematic of Figure 6 shows how this can be the case, as a result of the marginal likelihood $p(\mathbf{t}|\alpha)$ being a normalised distribution over the space of all possible data sets $\mathbf{t}$. Models with high α only fit (assign significant marginal probability to) data from smooth functions. Models with low values of α can fit data generated from functions that are both smooth and complex. However, because of normalisation, the low-α model must generally assign lower probability to data from smooth functions, so the marginal likelihood naturally prefers the simpler model if the data is smooth, which is precisely the meaning of Ockham's Razor. Furthermore, one can see from Figure 6 that for a data set of 'intermediate' complexity, a 'medium' value of α can be preferred. This is qualitatively analogous to the case of our example set, where we indeed find that an intermediate value of α is optimal. Note, crucially, that this is achieved without any prior preference for any particular value of α as we originally assumed

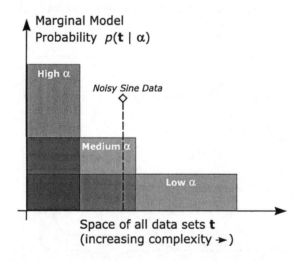

Fig. 6. A schematic plot of three marginal probability distributions for 'high', 'medium' and 'low' values of α. The figure is a simplification of the case for the actual distribution $p(\mathbf{t}|\alpha)$, where for illustrative purposes the N-dimensional space of $\mathbf{t}$ has been compressed onto a single axis and where, notionally, data sets (instances of $\mathbf{t}$) arising from simpler (smoother) functions lie towards the left-hand end of the horizontal scale, and data from complex functions to the right

a uniform hyperprior over its logarithm. The effect of Ockham's Razor is an automatic and pleasing consequence of applying the Bayesian framework.

3.8   Model Selection

While we have concentrated so far on the search for an appropriate value of hyperparameter α (and, to an extent, σ^2), our model is also conditioned on other variables we have up to now overlooked: the choice of basis set $\boldsymbol{\Phi}$ and, for our Gaussian basis, its width parameter r (as defined in Section 2.1). Ideally, we should define priors $P(\boldsymbol{\Phi})$ and $p(r)$, and integrate out those variables when making predictions. More practically, we could use $p(\mathbf{t}|\boldsymbol{\Phi}, r)$ as a criterion for *model selection* with the expectation that Ockham's Razor will assist us in selecting a model that is sufficient to explain the data but is not over-complex. In our example model, we previously optimised the marginal likelihood to find a value for α. In fact, as there are only two nuisance parameters here, it is feasible to integrate out α and σ^2 numerically.

In Figure 7 we evaluate several basis sets $\boldsymbol{\Phi}$ and width values r by computing the integral

$$p(\mathbf{t}|\boldsymbol{\Phi}, r) = \int p(\mathbf{t}|\alpha, \sigma^2, \boldsymbol{\Phi}, r) \, p(\alpha) \, p(\sigma^2) \, d\alpha \, d\sigma^2, \tag{24}$$

$$\approx \frac{1}{S} \sum_{s=1}^{S} p(\mathbf{t}|\alpha_s, \sigma_s^2, \boldsymbol{\Phi}, r), \tag{25}$$

with a Monte-Carlo average where we obtain S samples log-uniformly from $\alpha \in [10^{-12}, 10^{12}]$ and $\sigma \in [10^{-4}, 10^0]$.

The results of Figure 7 are quite compelling: with uniform priors over all nuisance variables —*i.e.* we have imposed *absolutely no prior knowledge* — we observe that test error appears very closely related to marginal likelihood. The qualitative shapes of the curves, and the relative merits, of Gaussian and Laplacian basis functions are also captured. For the Gaussian basis we are very close to obtaining the optimal value of r, in terms of test error, from just 15 examples and no validation data. Reassuringly, the simplest model that contains the 'truth', $y = w_1 \sin(x)$, is the most probable model here. We also show in the figure the model $y = w_1 \sin(x) + w_2 \cos(x)$ which is also an ideal fit for the data, but it is penalised in marginal probability terms since the addition of the $w_2 \cos(x)$ term allows it to explain more data sets, and normalisation thus requires it to assign less probability to our particular set. Nevertheless, it is still some orders of magnitude more probable than the Gaussian basis model.

3.9   Summary So Far...

Marginalisation is the key element of Bayesian inference, and hopefully some of the examples above have persuaded the reader that it can be an exceedingly powerful one. Problematically though, ideal Bayesian inference proceeds by integrating out all irrelevant variables, and we must concede that

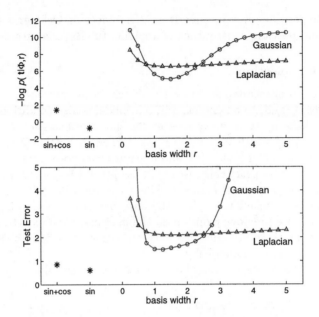

Fig. 7. Top: negative log model probability $-\log p(\mathbf{t}|\boldsymbol{\Phi}, r)$ for various basis sets, evaluated by analytic integration over $\mathbf{w}$ and Monte-Carlo averaging over α and σ^2. **Bottom:** corresponding test error for the posterior mean predictor. Basis sets examined were 'Gaussian', $\exp\left\{-|x - x_m|^2/r^2\right\}$, 'Laplacian', $\exp\left\{-|x - x_m|/r\right\}$, $\sin(x)$, $\sin(x)$ with $\cos(x)$. For the Gaussian and Laplacian basis, the horizontal axis denotes varying 'width' parameter r shown. For the sine/cosine bases, the horizontal axis has no significance and the values are placed to the left for convenience

- for practical purposes, it may be appropriate to require point estimates of some 'nuisance' variables, since it could easily be impractical to average over many parameters and particularly models every time we wish to make a prediction (imagine, for example, running a handwriting recogniser on a portable computing device),
- many of the desired integrations necessitate some form of approximation.

Nevertheless, regarding these points, we can still leverage Bayesian techniques to considerable benefit exploiting carefully-applied approximations. In particular, marginalised likelihoods within the Bayesian framework allow us to estimate fixed values of hyperparameters where desired and, most beneficially, choose between models and their varying parameterisations. This can all be done without the need to use validation data. Furthermore:

- it is straightforward to estimate other parameters in the model that may be of interest, *e.g.* the noise variance,
- we can sample from both prior and posterior models of the data,
- the exact parameterisation of the model is irrelevant when integrating out,
- we can incorporate other priors of interest in a principled manner.

We now further demonstrate these points, notably the last one, in the next section where we present a practical framework for the inference of 'sparse' models.

4 Sparse Bayesian Models

4.1 Bayes and Contemporary Machine Learning

In the previous section we saw that marginalisation is a valuable component of the Bayesian paradigm which offers a number of advantageous features applicable to many data modelling tasks. Disadvantageously, we also saw that the integrations required for full Bayesian inference can often be analytically intractable, although approximations for simple linear models could be very effective. Historically, interest in Bayesian "machine learning" (but not statistics!) has focused on approximations for *non-linear* models, *e.g.* for neural networks, the "evidence procedure" [7] and "hybrid Monte Carlo" sampling [5]. More recently, flexible (*i.e.* many-parameter) linear kernel methods have attracted much renewed interest, thanks mainly to the popularity of the "support vector machine". These kind of models, of course, are particularly amenable to Bayesian techniques.

Linear Models and Sparsity. Much interest in linear models has focused on *sparse* learning algorithms, which set many weights w_m to zero in the estimated predictor function $y(x) = \sum_m w_m \phi_m(x)$. Sparsity is an attractive concept; it offers elegant complexity control, feature extraction, the potential for elucidation of meaningful input variables along with the practical benefits of computational speed and compactness.

How do we impose a preference for sparsity in a model? The most common approach is via an appropriate regularisation term or prior. The most common regularisation term that we have already met, $E_W(\mathbf{w}) = \sum_{m=1}^{M} |w_m|^2$, of course corresponds to a Gaussian prior and is easy to work with, but while it is an effective way to control complexity, it does not promote sparsity. In the regularisation sense, the 'correct' term would be $E_W(\mathbf{w}) = \sum_m |w_m|^0$, but this, being discontinuous in w_m, is very difficult to work with. Instead, $E_W(\mathbf{w}) = \sum_m |w_m|^1$ is a workable compromise which gives reasonable sparsity and reasonable tractability, and is exploited in a number of methods, including as a Laplacian prior $p(\mathbf{w}) \propto \exp(-\sum_m |w_m|)$ [8]. However, there is an arguably more elegant way of obtaining sparsity within a Bayesian framework that builds effectively on the ideas outlined in the previous section and we conclude this article with a brief outline thereof.

4.2 A Sparse Bayesian Prior

In fact, we *can* obtain sparsity by retaining the traditional Gaussian prior, which is great news for tractability. The modification to our earlier Gaussian prior (10) is subtle:

$$p(\mathbf{w}|\alpha_1, \ldots, \alpha_M) = \prod_{m=1}^{M} \left[(2\pi)^{-1/2} \alpha_m^{1/2} \exp\left\{ -\frac{1}{2}\alpha_m w_m^2 \right\} \right]. \qquad (26)$$

In contrast to the model in Section 2, we now have M hyperparameters $\boldsymbol{\alpha} = (\alpha_1, \ldots, \alpha_M)$, one α_m independently controlling the (inverse) variance of each weight w_m.

A Hierarchical Prior. The prior $p(\mathbf{w}|\boldsymbol{\alpha})$ is nevertheless still Gaussian, and superficially seems to have little preference for sparsity. However, it remains conditioned on $\boldsymbol{\alpha}$, so for full Bayesian consistency we should now define hyperpriors over all α_m. Previously, we utilised a log-uniform hyperprior — this is a special case of a *Gamma* hyperprior, which we introduce for greater generality here. This combination of the prior over α_m controlling the prior over w_m gives us what is often referred to as a *hierarchical* prior. Now, if we have $p(w_m|\alpha_m)$ and $p(\alpha_m)$ and we want to know the 'true' $p(w_m)$ we already know what to do — we must marginalise:

$$p(w_m) = \int p(w_m|\alpha_m)\, p(\alpha_m)\, d\alpha_m. \tag{27}$$

For a Gamma $p(\alpha_m)$, this integral is computable and we find that $p(w_m)$ is a *Student-t* distribution illustrated as a function of two parameters in Figure 8; its equivalent as a regularising penalty function would be $\sum_m \log |w_m|$.

4.3   A Sparse Bayesian Model for Regression

We can develop a sparse regression model by following an identical methodology to the previous sections. Again, we assume independent Gaussian noise: $t_n \sim N(y(\mathbf{x}_n; \mathbf{w}), \sigma^2)$, which gives a corresponding likelihood:

$$p(\mathbf{t}|\mathbf{w}, \sigma^2) = (2\pi\sigma^2)^{-N/2} \exp\left\{ -\frac{1}{2\sigma^2} \|\mathbf{t} - \boldsymbol{\Phi}\mathbf{w}\|^2 \right\}, \tag{28}$$

where as before we denote $\mathbf{t} = (t_1 \ldots t_N)^{\mathrm{T}}$, $\mathbf{w} = (w_1 \ldots w_M)^{\mathrm{T}}$, and $\boldsymbol{\Phi}$ is the $N \times M$ 'design' matrix with $\boldsymbol{\Phi}_{nm} = \phi_m(\mathbf{x}_n)$.

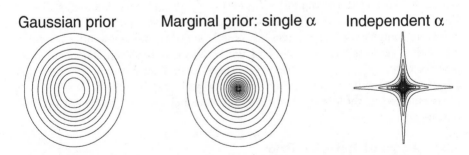

Gaussian prior   Marginal prior: single α   Independent α

Fig. 8. Contour plots of Gaussian and Student-t prior distributions over two parameters. While the marginal prior $p(w_1, w_2)$ for the 'single' hyperparameter model of Section 2 has a much sharper peak than the Gaussian at zero, it can be seen that it is not sparse unlike the multiple 'independent' hyperparameter prior, which as well as having a sharp peak at zero, places most of its probability mass along axial ridges where the magnitude of one of the two parameters is small

Following the Bayesian framework, we desire the posterior distribution over all unknowns:

$$p(\mathbf{w}, \boldsymbol{\alpha}, \sigma^2 | \mathbf{t}) = \frac{p(\mathbf{t}|\mathbf{w}, \boldsymbol{\alpha}, \sigma^2) p(\mathbf{w}, \boldsymbol{\alpha}, \sigma^2)}{p(\mathbf{t})}, \tag{29}$$

which we can't compute analytically. So as previously, we decompose this as:

$$p(\mathbf{w}, \boldsymbol{\alpha}, \sigma^2 | \mathbf{t}) \equiv p(\mathbf{w}|\mathbf{t}, \boldsymbol{\alpha}, \sigma^2) \; p(\boldsymbol{\alpha}, \sigma^2 | \mathbf{t}) \tag{30}$$

where $p(\mathbf{w}|\mathbf{t}, \boldsymbol{\alpha}, \sigma^2)$ is the 'weight posterior' distribution, and is tractable. This leaves $p(\boldsymbol{\alpha}, \sigma^2 | \mathbf{t})$ which must be approximated.

The Weight Posterior Term. Given the data, the posterior distribution over weights is Gaussian:

$$p(\mathbf{w}|\mathbf{t}, \boldsymbol{\alpha}, \sigma^2) = \frac{p(\mathbf{t}|\mathbf{w}, \sigma^2)\, p(\mathbf{w}|\boldsymbol{\alpha})}{p(\mathbf{t}|\boldsymbol{\alpha}, \sigma^2)},$$

$$= (2\pi)^{-(N+1)/2} |\boldsymbol{\Sigma}|^{-1/2} \exp\left\{ -\frac{1}{2}(\mathbf{w} - \boldsymbol{\mu})^{\mathrm{T}} \boldsymbol{\Sigma}^{-1}(\mathbf{w} - \boldsymbol{\mu}) \right\}, \tag{31}$$

with

$$\boldsymbol{\Sigma} = (\sigma^{-2}\boldsymbol{\Phi}^{\mathrm{T}}\boldsymbol{\Phi} + \mathbf{A})^{-1}, \tag{32}$$

$$\boldsymbol{\mu} = \sigma^{-2}\boldsymbol{\Sigma}\boldsymbol{\Phi}^{\mathrm{T}}\mathbf{t}, \tag{33}$$

and where we collect all the hyperparameters into a diagonal matrix: $\mathbf{A} = \mathrm{diag}(\alpha_1, \alpha_2, \ldots, \alpha_M)$. A key point to note from (31–33) is that if any $\alpha_m = \infty$, the corresponding $\mu_m = 0$.

The Hyperparameter Posterior Term. Again we will adopt the "type-II maximum likelihood" approximation where we maximise $p(\mathbf{t}|\boldsymbol{\alpha}, \sigma^2)$ to find $\boldsymbol{\alpha}_{\mathrm{MP}}$ and σ^2_{MP}. As before, for uniform hyperpriors over $\log \alpha$ and $\log \sigma$, $p(\boldsymbol{\alpha}, \sigma^2|\mathbf{t}) \propto p(\mathbf{t}|\boldsymbol{\alpha}, \sigma^2)$, where the *marginal likelihood* $p(\mathbf{t}|\boldsymbol{\alpha}, \sigma^2)$ is obtained by integrating out the weights:

$$p(\mathbf{t}|\boldsymbol{\alpha}, \sigma^2) = \int p(\mathbf{t}|\mathbf{w}, \sigma^2)\, p(\mathbf{w}|\boldsymbol{\alpha})\, d\mathbf{w},$$

$$= (2\pi)^{-N/2} |\sigma^2\mathbf{I} + \boldsymbol{\Phi}\mathbf{A}^{-1}\boldsymbol{\Phi}^{\mathrm{T}}|^{-1/2} \exp\left\{ -\frac{1}{2}\mathbf{t}^{\mathrm{T}}(\sigma^2\mathbf{I} + \boldsymbol{\Phi}\mathbf{A}^{-1}\boldsymbol{\Phi}^{\mathrm{T}})^{-1}\mathbf{t} \right\}. \tag{34}$$

In Section 2, we found the single α_{MP} empirically but here for multiple (in practice, perhaps thousands of) hyperparameters, we cannot experimentally explore the space of possible $\boldsymbol{\alpha}$ so we instead optimise $p(\mathbf{t}|\boldsymbol{\alpha}, \sigma^2)$ directly, via a gradient-based approach.

Hyperparameter Re-estimation. Differentiating $\log p(\mathbf{t}|\boldsymbol{\alpha}, \sigma^2)$ with respect to α and σ^2, setting to zero and rearranging (see [9]) ultimately gives iterative re-estimation formulae:

$$\alpha_i^{\text{new}} = \frac{\gamma_i}{\mu_i^2}, \tag{35}$$

$$(\sigma^2)^{\text{new}} = \frac{\|\mathbf{t} - \boldsymbol{\Phi}\boldsymbol{\mu}\|^2}{N - \sum_{i=1}^{M} \gamma_i}. \tag{36}$$

For convenience we have defined

$$\gamma_i = 1 - \alpha_i \boldsymbol{\Sigma}_{ii}, \tag{37}$$

where $\gamma_i \in [0, 1]$ is a measure of 'well-determinedness' of parameter w_i. This quantity effectively captures the influence of the likelihood (total when $\gamma \to 1$) and the prior (total when $\gamma \to 0$) on the value of each w_i. Note that the quantities on the right-hand-side of equations (35–37) are computed using the 'old' values of $\boldsymbol{\alpha}$ and σ^2.

Summary of Inference Procedure. We're now in a position to define a 'learning algorithm' for approximate Bayesian inference in this model:

1. Initialise all $\{\alpha_i\}$ and σ^2 (or fix latter if known)
2. Compute weight posterior sufficient statistics $\boldsymbol{\mu}$ and $\boldsymbol{\Sigma}$
3. Compute all $\{\gamma_i\}$, then re-estimate $\{\alpha_i\}$ (and σ^2 if desired)
4. Repeat from 2. until convergence
5. 'Delete' weights (and basis functions) for which optimal $\alpha_i = \infty$, since this implies $\mu_i = 0$
6. Make predictions for new data via the predictive distribution computed with the converged $\boldsymbol{\alpha}_{\text{MP}}$ and σ^2_{MP}:

$$p(t_*|\mathbf{t}) = \int p(t_*|\mathbf{w}, \sigma^2_{\text{MP}}) \, p(\mathbf{w}|\mathbf{t}, \boldsymbol{\alpha}_{\text{MP}}, \sigma^2_{\text{MP}}) \, d\mathbf{w} \tag{38}$$

the mean of which is $y(\mathbf{x}_*; \boldsymbol{\mu})$

Step 5. rather ideally assumes that we can reliably estimate such large values of α, whereas in reality limited computational precision implies that in this algorithm we have to place some finite upper limit on α (*e.g.* 10^{12} times the value of the smallest α). In many real-world tasks, we do indeed find that many α_i do tend towards infinity, and we converge toward a model that is very sparse, even if M is very large.

4.4   The "Relevance Vector Machine" (RVM)

To give an example of the potential of the above model, we briefly introduce here the "Relevance Vector Machine" (RVM), which is simply a specialisation of a sparse Bayesian model which utilises the same data-dependent kernel basis as the popular "support vector machine" (SVM):

$$y(\mathbf{x}; \mathbf{w}) = \sum_{n=1}^{N} w_n K(\mathbf{x}, \mathbf{x}_n) + w_0 \qquad (39)$$

This model is described, with a number of examples, in much more detail elsewhere [9]. For now, Figure 9 provides an illustration, on some noise-polluted synthetic data, of the potential of this Bayesian framework for effectively combining sparsity with predictive accuracy.

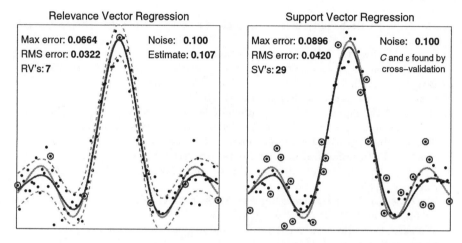

Fig. 9. The relevance vector and support vector machines applied to a regression problem using a Gaussian kernel, which demonstrates some of the advantages of the Bayesian approach. Of particular note is the sparsity of the final Bayesian model, which qualitatively appears near-optimal. It is also worth underlining that the 'nuisance' parameters C and ϵ for the SVM had to be found by a separate cross-validation procedure, whereas the RVM algorithm estimates them automatically, and arguably quite accurately in the case of the noise variance

5   Summary

While the tone of the first three sections of this article has been introductory and the models considered therein have been quite simplistic, the brief example of the 'sparse Bayesian' learning procedure given in Section 4 is intended to demonstrate that 'practical' Bayesian inference procedures have the potential to be highly effective in the context of modern machine learning. Readers who find this demonstration sufficiently convincing and who are interested specifically in the sparse Bayesian model framework can find further information (including some implementation code), and details of related approaches, at a web-page maintained by the author: http://www.research.microsoft.com/mlp/RVM. In particular, note that the algorithm for hyperparameter estimation of Section 4.3 was presented here as it has a certain intuitive simplicity, but in fact there is a much more efficient and practical approach to optimising $\log p(\mathbf{t}|\alpha, \sigma^2)$ which is detailed in [10].

We summarised some of the features, advantages and limitations of the general Bayesian framework earlier in Section 3.9, and so will not repeat them here. The reader interested in investigating further and in more depth on this general topic may find much helpful further material in the references [1, 5, 11, 12, 13, 14].

References

1. Jaynes, E.T.: Probability theory: the logic of science. Cambridge University Press (2003)
2. Evans, M., Swartz, T.B.: Methods for approximating integrals in statistics with special emphasis on Bayesian integration. Statistical Science **10** (1995) 254–272
3. Beal, M., Ghahramani, Z.: The Variational Bayes web site at http://www.variational-bayes.org/ (2003)
4. Bishop, C.M., Tipping, M.E.: Variational relevance vector machines. In Boutilier, C., Goldszmidt, M., eds.: Proceedings of the 16th Conference on Uncertainty in Artificial Intelligence, Morgan Kaufmann (2000) 46–53
5. Neal, R.M.: Bayesian Learning for Neural Networks. Springer (1996)
6. Berger, J.O.: Statistical decision theory and Bayesian analysis. Second edn. Springer (1985)
7. MacKay, D.J.C.: The evidence framework applied to classification networks. Neural Computation **4** (1992) 720–736
8. Williams, P.M.: Bayesian regularisation and pruning using a Laplace prior. Neural Computation **7** (1995) 117–143
9. Tipping, M.E.: Sparse Bayesian learning and the relevance vector machine. Journal of Machine Learing Research **1** (2001) 211–244
10. Tipping, M.E., Faul, A.C.: Fast marginal likelihood maximisation for sparse Bayesian models. In Bishop, C.M., Frey, B.J., eds.: Proceedings of the Ninth International Workshop on Artificial Intelligence and Statistics, Key West, FL, Jan 3-6. (2003)
11. MacKay, D.J.C.: Bayesian interpolation. Neural Computation **4** (1992) 415–447
12. Bishop, C.M.: Neural Networks for Pattern Recognition. Oxford University Press (1995)
13. Gelman, A., Carlin, J.B., Stern, H.S., Rubin, D.B.: Bayesian Data Analysis. Chapman & Hall (1995)
14. MacKay, D.J.C.: Information Theory, Inference and Learning Algorithms. Cambridge University Press (2003)

Gaussian Processes in Machine Learning

Carl Edward Rasmussen

Max Planck Institute for Biological Cybernetics, 72076 Tübingen, Germany
carl@tuebingen.mpg.de
http://www.tuebingen.mpg.de/~carl

Abstract. We give a basic introduction to Gaussian Process regression models. We focus on understanding the role of the stochastic process and how it is used to define a distribution over functions. We present the simple equations for incorporating training data and examine how to learn the hyperparameters using the marginal likelihood. We explain the practical advantages of Gaussian Process and end with conclusions and a look at the current trends in GP work.

Supervised learning in the form of regression (for continuous outputs) and classification (for discrete outputs) is an important constituent of statistics and machine learning, either for analysis of data sets, or as a subgoal of a more complex problem.

Traditionally parametric[1] models have been used for this purpose. These have a possible advantage in ease of interpretability, but for complex data sets, simple parametric models may lack expressive power, and their more complex counterparts (such as feed forward neural networks) may not be easy to work with in practice. The advent of kernel machines, such as Support Vector Machines and Gaussian Processes has opened the possibility of flexible models which are practical to work with.

In this short tutorial we present the basic idea on how Gaussian Process models can be used to formulate a Bayesian framework for regression. We will focus on understanding the stochastic process and how it is used in supervised learning. Secondly, we will discuss practical matters regarding the role of hyperparameters in the covariance function, the marginal likelihood and the automatic Occam's razor. For broader introductions to Gaussian processes, consult [1], [2].

1   Gaussian Processes

In this section we define Gaussian Processes and show how they can very naturally be used to define distributions over functions. In the following section we continue to show how this distribution is updated in the light of training examples.

---

[1] By a parametric model, we here mean a model which during training "absorbs" the information from the training data into the parameters; after training the data can be discarded.

O. Bousquet et al. (Eds.): Machine Learning 2003, LNAI 3176, pp. 63–71, 2004.

Definition 1. *A Gaussian Process is a collection of random variables, any finite number of which have (consistent) joint Gaussian distributions.*

A Gaussian *process* is fully specified by its mean function $m(x)$ and covariance function $k(x, x')$. This is a natural generalization of the Gaussian *distribution* whose mean and covariance is a vector and matrix, respectively. The Gaussian distribution is over vectors, whereas the Gaussian process is over functions. We will write:

$$f \sim \mathcal{GP}(m, k), \tag{1}$$

meaning: "the function f is distributed as a GP with mean function m and covariance function k".

Although the generalization from distribution to process is straight forward, we will be a bit more explicit about the details, because it may be unfamiliar to some readers. The individual random variables in a vector from a Gaussian distribution are indexed by their position in the vector. For the Gaussian process it is the argument x (of the random function $f(x)$) which plays the role of index set: for every input x there is an associated random variable $f(x)$, which is the value of the (stochastic) function f at that location. For reasons of notational convenience, we will enumerate the x values of interest by the natural numbers, and use these indexes as if they were the indexes of the process – don't let yourself be confused by this: the index to the process is x_i, which we have chosen to index by i.

Although working with infinite dimensional objects may seem unwieldy at first, it turns out that the quantities that we are interested in computing, require only working with finite dimensional objects. In fact, answering questions about the process reduces to computing with the related distribution. This is the key to why Gaussian processes are feasible. Let us look at an example. Consider the Gaussian process given by:

$$f \sim \mathcal{GP}(m, k), \quad \text{where} \quad m(x) = \tfrac{1}{4}x^2, \text{ and } k(x, x') = \exp(-\tfrac{1}{2}(x - x')^2). \tag{2}$$

In order to understand this process we can draw samples from the function f. In order to work only with finite quantities, we request only the value of f at a distinct finite number n of locations. How do we generate such samples? Given the x-values we can evaluate the vector of means and a covariance matrix using Eq. (2), which defines a regular Gaussian distribution:

$$
\begin{aligned}
\mu_i &= m(x_i) = \tfrac{1}{4}x_i^2, \quad i = 1, \ldots, n \text{ and} \\
\Sigma_{ij} &= k(x_i, x_j) = \exp(-\tfrac{1}{2}(x_i - x_j)^2), \quad i, j = 1, \ldots, n,
\end{aligned}
\tag{3}
$$

where to clarify the distinction between process and distribution we use m and k for the former and μ and Σ for the latter. We can now generate a random vector from this distribution. This vector will have as coordinates the function values $f(x)$ for the corresponding x's:

$$\mathbf{f} \sim \mathcal{N}(\mu, \Sigma). \tag{4}$$

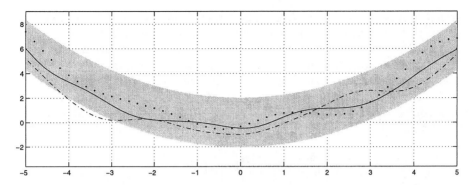

Fig. 1. Function values from three functions drawn at random from a GP as specified in Eq. (2). The dots are the values generated from Eq. (4), the two other curves have (less correctly) been drawn by connecting sampled points. The function values suggest a smooth underlying function; this is in fact a property of GPs with the squared exponential covariance function. The shaded grey area represent the 95% confidence intervals

We could now plot the values of f as a function of x, see Figure 1. How can we do this in practice? Below are a few lines of Matlab[2] used to create the plot:

```
xs = (-5:0.2:5)'; ns = size(xs,1); keps = 1e-9;
m = inline('0.25*x.^2');
K = inline('exp(-0.5*(repmat(p'',size(q))-repmat(q,size(p''))).^2)');
fs = m(xs) + chol(K(xs,xs)+keps*eye(ns))'*randn(ns,1);
plot(xs,fs,'.')
```

In the above example, m and k are mean and covariances; `chol` is a function to compute the Cholesky decomposition[3] of a matrix.

This example has illustrated how we move from process to distribution and also shown that the Gaussian process defines a distribution over functions. Up until now, we have only been concerned with random functions – in the next section we will see how to use the GP framework in a very simple way to make inferences about functions given some training examples.

2 Posterior Gaussian Process

In the previous section we saw how to define distributions over functions using GPs. This GP will be used as a *prior* for Bayesian inference. The prior does not depend on the training data, but specifies some properties of the functions; for

---

[2] Matlab is a trademark of The MathWorks Inc.

[3] We've also added a tiny `keps` multiple of the identity to the covariance matrix for numerical stability (to bound the eigenvalues numerically away from zero); see comments around Eq. (8) for a interpretation of this term as a tiny amount of noise.

example, in Figure 1 the function is smooth, and close to a quadratic. The goal of this section is to derive the simple rules of how to update this prior in the light of the training data. The goal of the next section is to attempt to learn about some properties of the prior[4] in the the light of the data.

One of the primary goals computing the posterior is that it can be used to make predictions for unseen test cases. Let $\mathbf{f}$ be the known function values of the training cases, and let $\mathbf{f}_*$ be a set of function values corresponding to the test set inputs, X_*. Again, we write out the joint distribution of everything we are interested in:

$$
\begin{bmatrix} \mathbf{f} \\ \mathbf{f}_* \end{bmatrix} \sim \mathcal{N}\left(\begin{bmatrix} \mu \\ \mu_* \end{bmatrix}, \begin{bmatrix} \Sigma & \Sigma_* \\ \Sigma_*^\top & \Sigma_{**} \end{bmatrix} \right),
\tag{5}
$$

where we've introduced the following shorthand: $\mu = m(x_i), i = 1, \ldots, n$ for the training means and analogously for the test means μ_*; for the covariance we use Σ for training set covariances, Σ_* for training-test set covariances and Σ_{**} for test set covariances. Since we know the values for the training set $\mathbf{f}$ we are interested in the conditional distribution of $\mathbf{f}_*$ given $\mathbf{f}$ which is expressed as[5]:

$$
\mathbf{f}_* | \mathbf{f} \sim \mathcal{N}\big(\mu_* + \Sigma_*^\top \Sigma^{-1} (\mathbf{f} - \mu), \ \Sigma_{**} - \Sigma_*^\top \Sigma^{-1} \Sigma_* \big).
\tag{6}
$$

This is the posterior distribution for a specific set of test cases. It is easy to verify (by inspection) that the corresponding posterior process is:

$$
\begin{aligned}
f | \mathcal{D} &\sim \mathcal{GP}(m_\mathcal{D}, k_\mathcal{D}), \\
m_\mathcal{D}(x) &= m(x) + \Sigma(X, x)^\top \Sigma^{-1} (\mathbf{f} - \mathbf{m}) \\
k_\mathcal{D}(x, x') &= k(x, x') - \Sigma(X, x)^\top \Sigma^{-1} \Sigma(X, x'),
\end{aligned}
\tag{7}
$$

where $\Sigma(X, x)$ is a vector of covariances between every training case and x. These are the central equations for Gaussian process predictions. Let's examine these equations for the posterior mean and covariance. Notice that the posterior variance $k_\mathcal{D}(x, x)$ is equal to the prior variance $k(x, x)$ minus a positive term, which depends on the training inputs; thus the posterior variance is always smaller than the prior variance, since the data has given us some additional information.

We need to address one final issue: noise in the training outputs. It is common to many applications of regression that there is noise in the observations[6]. The most common assumption is that of additive i.i.d. Gaussian noise in the outputs.

---

[4] By definition, the prior is independent of the data; here we'll be using a hierarchical prior with free parameters, and make inference about the parameters.

[5] the formula for conditioning a joint Gaussian distribution is:

$$
\begin{bmatrix} \mathbf{x} \\ \mathbf{y} \end{bmatrix} \sim \mathcal{N}\left(\begin{bmatrix} \mathbf{a} \\ \mathbf{b} \end{bmatrix}, \begin{bmatrix} A & C \\ C^\top & B \end{bmatrix} \right) \implies \mathbf{x} | \mathbf{y} \sim \mathcal{N}(a + CB^{-1}(\mathbf{y} - b), \ A - CB^{-1}C^\top).
$$

[6] However, it is perhaps interesting that the GP model works also in the noise-free case – this is in contrast to most parametric methods, since they often cannot model the data exactly.

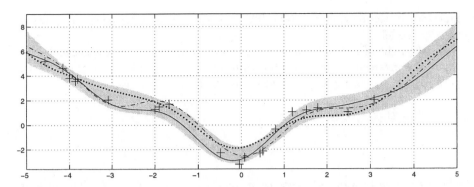

Fig. 2. Three functions drawn at random from the posterior, given 20 training data points, the $\mathcal{GP}$ as specified in Eq. (3) and a noise level of $\sigma_n = 0.7$. The shaded area gives the 95% confidence region. Compare with Figure 1 and note that the uncertainty goes down close to the observations

In the Gaussian process models, such noise is easily taken into account; the effect is that every $f(x)$ has a extra covariance with itself only (since the noise is assumed independent), with a magnitude equal to the noise variance:

$$
\begin{aligned}
y(x) &= f(x) + \varepsilon, \qquad \varepsilon \sim \mathcal{N}(0, \sigma_n^2), \\
f &\sim \mathcal{GP}(m, k), \qquad y \sim \mathcal{GP}(m, k + \sigma_n^2 \delta_{ii'}),
\end{aligned}
\tag{8}
$$

where $\delta_{ii'} = 1$ iff $i = i'$ is the Kronecker's delta. Notice, that the indexes to the Kronecker's delta is the identify of the cases, i, and not the inputs x_i; you may have several cases with identical inputs, but the noise on these cases is assumed to be independent. Thus, the covariance function for a noisy process is the sum of the signal covariance and the noise covariance.

Now, we can plug in the posterior covariance function into the little Matlab example on page 65 to draw samples from the posterior process, see Figure 2. In this section we have shown how simple manipulations with mean and covariance functions allow updates of the prior to the posterior in the light of the training data. However, we left some questions unanswered: How do we come up with mean and covariance functions in the first place? How could we estimate the noise level? This is the topic of the next section.

3 Training a Gaussian Process

In the previous section we saw how to update the prior Gaussian process in the light of training data. This is useful if we have enough prior information about a dataset at hand to confidently specify prior mean and covariance functions. However, the availability of such detailed prior information is not the typical case in machine learning applications. In order for the GP techniques to be of value in practice, we must be able to chose between different mean and covariance functions in the light of the data. This process will be referred to as *training*[7] the GP model.

In the light of typically vague prior information, we use a hierarchical prior, where the mean and covariance functions are parameterized in terms of hyper-parameters. For example, we could use a generalization of Eq. (2):

$$f \sim \mathcal{GP}(m, \ k),$$

$$m(x) = ax^2 + bx + c, \quad \text{and} \quad k(x, x') = \sigma_y^2 \exp\left(-\frac{(x - x')^2}{2\ell^2}\right) + \sigma_n^2 \delta_{ii'}, \tag{9}$$

where we have introduced *hyperparameters* $\theta = \{a, b, c, \sigma_y, \sigma_n, \ell\}$. The purpose of this hierarchical specification is that it allows us to specify vague prior information in a simple way. For example, we've stated that we believe the function to be close to a second order polynomial, but we haven't said exactly what the polynomial is, or exactly what is meant by "close". In fact the discrepancy between the polynomial and the data is a smooth function plus independent Gaussian noise, but again we're don't need exactly to specify the characteristic length scale ℓ or the magnitudes of the two contributions. We want to be able to make inferences about all of the hyperparameters in the light of the data.

In order to do this we compute the probability of the data given the hyperparameters. Fortunately, this is not difficult, since by assumption the distribution of the data is Gaussian:

$$L = \log p(\mathbf{y}|\mathbf{x}, \theta) = -\tfrac{1}{2}\log|\Sigma| - \tfrac{1}{2}(\mathbf{y} - \boldsymbol{\mu})^\top \Sigma^{-1}(\mathbf{y} - \boldsymbol{\mu}) - \tfrac{n}{2}\log(2\pi). \tag{10}$$

We will call this quantity the log *marginal likelihood*. We use the term "marginal" to emphasize that we are dealing with a non-parametric model. See e.g. [1] for the weight-space view of Gaussian processes which equivalently leads to Eq. (10) after marginalization over the weights.

We can now find the values of the hyperparameters which optimizes the marginal likelihood based on its partial derivatives which are easily evaluated:

$$\frac{\partial L}{\partial \theta_m} = -(\mathbf{y} - \boldsymbol{\mu})^\top \Sigma^{-1} \frac{\partial m}{\partial \theta_m},$$

$$\frac{\partial L}{\partial \theta_k} = \tfrac{1}{2}\operatorname{trace}\left(\Sigma^{-1}\frac{\partial \Sigma}{\partial \theta_k}\right) + \tfrac{1}{2}(\mathbf{y} - \boldsymbol{\mu})^\top \frac{\partial \Sigma}{\partial \theta_k}\Sigma^{-1}\frac{\partial \Sigma}{\partial \theta_k}(\mathbf{y} - \boldsymbol{\mu}), \tag{11}$$

where θ_m and θ_k are used to indicate hyperparameters of the mean and covariance functions respectively. Eq. (11) can conveniently be used in conjunction

---

[7] Training the GP model involves both model selection, or the discrete choice between different functional forms for mean and covariance functions as well as adaptation of the hyperparameters of these functions; for brevity we will only consider the latter here – the generalization is straightforward, in that marginal likelihoods can be compared.

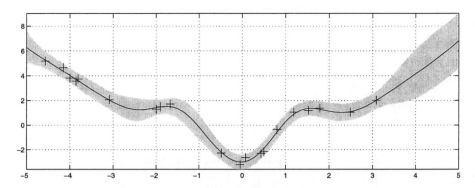

Fig. 3. Mean and 95% posterior confidence region with parameters learned by maximizing marginal likelihood, Eq. (10), for the Gaussian process specification in Eq. (9), for the same data as in Figure 2. The hyperparameters found were $a = 0.3, b = 0.03, c = -0.7, \ell = 0.7, \sigma_y = 1.1, \sigma_n = 0.25$. This example was constructed so that the approach without optimization of hyperparameters worked reasonably well (Figure 2), but there is of course no guarantee of this in a typical application

with a numerical optimization routine such as conjugate gradients to find good[8] hyperparameter settings.

Due to the fact that the Gaussian process is a non-parametric model, the marginal likelihood behaves somewhat differently to what one might expect from experience with parametric models. Note first, that it is in fact very easy for the model to fit the training data exactly: simply set the noise level σ_n^2 to zero, and the model produce a mean predictive function which agrees exactly with the training points. However, this is not the typical behavior when optimizing the marginal likelihood. Indeed, the log marginal likelihood from Eq. (10) consists of three terms: The first term, $-\frac{1}{2} \log |\Sigma|$ is a *complexity penalty term*, which measures and penalizes the complexity of the model. The second term a negative quadratic, and plays the role of a data-fit measure (it is the only term which depends on the training set output values **y**). The third term is a log normalization term, independent of the data, and not very interesting. Figure 3 illustrates the predictions of a model trained by maximizing the marginal likelihood.

Note that the tradeoff between penalty and data-fit in the GP model is automatic. There is no weighting parameter which needs to be set by some external method such as cross validation. This is a feature of great practical importance, since it simplifies training. Figure 4 illustrates how the automatic tradeoff comes about.

We've seen in this section how we, via a hierarchical specification of the prior, can express prior knowledge in a convenient way, and how we can learn values of hyperparameters via optimization of the marginal likelihood. This can be done using some gradient based optimization. Also, we've seen how the marginal

---

[8] Note, that for most non-trivial Gaussian processes, optimization over hyperparameters is not a convex problem, so the usual precautions against bad local minima should be taken.

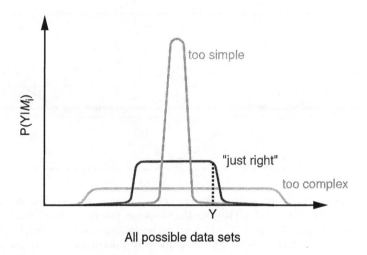

Fig. 4. Occam's razor is automatic. On the x-axis is an abstract representation of all possible datasets (of a particular size). On the y-axis the probability of the data given the model. Three different models are shown. A more complex model can account for many more data sets than a simple model, but since the probabilities have to integrate to unity, this means more complex models are automatically penalized more

likelihood automatically incorporates Occam's razor; this property of of great practical importance, since it simplifies training a lot.

4   Conclusions and Future Directions

We've seen how Gaussian processes can conveniently be used to specify very flexible non-linear regression. We only mentioned in passing one type of covariance function, but in fact any positive definite function[9] can be used as covariance function. Many such functions are known, and understanding the properties of functions drawn from GPs with particular covariance functions is an important ongoing research goal. When the properties of these functions are known, one will be able to chose covariance functions reflecting prior information, or alternatively, one will be able to interpret the covariance functions chosen by maximizing marginal likelihood, to get a better understanding of the data.

In this short tutorial, we have only treated the simplest possible case of regression with Gaussian noise. In the case of non-Gaussian likelihoods (such as e.g. needed for classification) training becomes more complicated. One can resort to approximations, such as the Laplace approximation [3], or approximations based on projecting the non-Gaussian posterior onto the closest Gaussian (in a KL sense) [4] or sampling techniques [5].

---

[9] The covariance function must be positive definite to ensure that the resulting covariance matrix is positive definite.

Another issue is the computational limitations. A straightforward implementation of the simple techniques explained here, requires inversion of the covariance matrix Σ, with a memory complexity of $\mathcal{O}(n^2)$ and a computational complexity of $\mathcal{O}(n^3)$. This is feasible on a desktop computer for dataset sizes of n up to a few thousands. Although there are many interesting machine learning problems with such relatively small datasets, a lot of current work is going into the development of approximate methods for larger datasets. A number of these methods rely on sparse approximations.

Acknowledgements

The author was supported by the German Research Council (DFG) through grant RA 1030/1.

References

1. Williams, C.K.I.: Prediction with Gaussian processes: From linear regression to linear prediction and beyond. In Jordan, M.I., ed.: Learning in Graphical Models. Kluwer Academic (1998) 599–621
2. MacKay, D.J.C.: Gaussian processes — a replacement for supervised neural networks? Tutorial lecture notes for NIPS 1997 (1997)
3. Williams, C.K.I., Barber, D.: Bayesian classification with Gaussian processes. IEEE Transactions on Pattern Analysis and Machine Intelligence **20(12)** (1998) 1342–1351
4. Csató, L., Opper, M.: Sparse on-line Gaussian processes. Neural Computation **14** (2002) 641–668
5. Neal, R.M.: Regression and classification using Gaussian process priors (with discussion). In Bernardo, J.M., et al., eds.: Bayesian statistics 6. Oxford University Press (1998) 475–501

Unsupervised Learning

Zoubin Ghahramani*

Gatsby Computational Neuroscience Unit, University College London, UK
zoubin@gatsby.ucl.ac.uk
http://www.gatsby.ucl.ac.uk/~zoubin

Abstract. We give a tutorial and overview of the field of unsupervised learning from the perspective of statistical modeling. Unsupervised learning can be motivated from information theoretic and Bayesian principles. We briefly review basic models in unsupervised learning, including factor analysis, PCA, mixtures of Gaussians, ICA, hidden Markov models, state-space models, and many variants and extensions. We derive the EM algorithm and give an overview of fundamental concepts in graphical models, and inference algorithms on graphs. This is followed by a quick tour of approximate Bayesian inference, including Markov chain Monte Carlo (MCMC), Laplace approximation, BIC, variational approximations, and expectation propagation (EP). The aim of this chapter is to provide a high-level view of the field. Along the way, many state-of-the-art ideas and future directions are also reviewed.

1   Introduction

Machine learning is the field of research devoted to the formal study of learning systems. This is a highly interdisciplinary field which borrows and builds upon ideas from statistics, computer science, engineering, cognitive science, optimization theory and many other disciplines of science and mathematics. The purpose of this chapter is to introduce in a fairly concise manner the key ideas underlying the sub-field of machine learning known as *unsupervised learning*. This introduction is necessarily incomplete given the enormous range of topics under the rubric of unsupervised learning. The hope is that interested readers can delve more deeply into the many topics covered here by following some of the cited references. The chapter starts at a highly tutorial level but will touch upon state-of-the-art research in later sections. It is assumed that the reader is familiar with elementary linear algebra, probability theory, and calculus, but not much else.

1.1   What Is Unsupervised Learning?

Consider a machine (or living organism) which receives some sequence of inputs $x_1, x_2, x_3, \ldots$, where x_t is the sensory input at time t. This input, which we will

---

* The author is also at the Center for Automated Learning and Discovery, Carnegie Mellon University, USA.

O. Bousquet et al. (Eds.): Machine Learning 2003, LNAI 3176, pp. 72–112, 2004.

often call the *data*, could correspond to an image on the retina, the pixels in a camera, or a sound waveform. It could also correspond to less obviously sensory data, for example the words in a news story, or the list of items in a supermarket shopping basket.

One can distinguish between four different kinds of machine learning. In *supervised learning* the machine[1] is also given a sequence of desired outputs $y_1, y_2, \ldots$, and the goal of the machine is to learn to produce the correct output given a new input. This output could be a class label (in classification) or a real number (in regression).

In *reinforcement learning* the machine interacts with its environment by producing actions $a_1, a_2, \ldots$. These actions affect the state of the environment, which in turn results in the machine receiving some scalar rewards (or punishments) $r_1, r_2, \ldots$. The goal of the machine is to learn to act in a way that maximizes the future rewards it receives (or minimizes the punishments) over its lifetime. Reinforcement learning is closely related to the fields of decision theory (in statistics and management science), and control theory (in engineering). The fundamental problems studied in these fields are often formally equivalent, and the solutions are the same, although different aspects of problem and solution are usually emphasized.

A third kind of machine learning is closely related to *game theory* and generalizes reinforcement learning. Here again the machine gets inputs, produces actions, and receives rewards. However, the environment the machine interacts with is not some static world, but rather it can contain other machines which can also sense, act, receive rewards, and learn. Thus the goal of the machine is to act so as to maximize rewards in light of the other machines' current and future actions. Although there is a great deal of work in game theory for simple systems, the dynamic case with multiple adapting machines remains an active and challenging area of research.

Finally, in *unsupervised learning* the machine simply receives inputs $x_1, x_2, \ldots$, but obtains neither supervised target outputs, nor rewards from its environment. It may seem somewhat mysterious to imagine what the machine could possibly learn given that it doesn't get any feedback from its environment. However, it is possible to develop of formal framework for unsupervised learning based on the notion that the machine's goal is to build representations of the input that can be used for decision making, predicting future inputs, efficiently communicating the inputs to another machine, etc. In a sense, unsupervised learning can be thought of as finding patterns in the data above and beyond what would be considered pure unstructured noise. Two very simple classic examples of unsupervised learning are clustering and dimensionality reduction. We discuss these in Section 2. The remainder of this chapter focuses on unsupervised learning,

---

[1] Henceforth, for succinctness I'll use the term machine to refer both to machines and living organisms. Some people prefer to call this a system or agent. The same mathematical theory of learning applies regardless of what we choose to call the learner, whether it is artificial or biological.

although many of the concepts discussed can be applied to supervised learning as well. But first, let us consider how unsupervised learning relates to statistics and information theory.

1.2   Machine Learning, Statistics, and Information Theory

Almost all work in unsupervised learning can be viewed in terms of learning a probabilistic model of the data. Even when the machine is given no supervision or reward, it may make sense for the machine to estimate a model that represents the probability distribution for a new input x_t given previous inputs $x_1, \ldots, x_{t-1}$ (consider the obviously useful examples of stock prices, or the weather). That is, the learner models $P(x_t|x_1, \ldots, x_{t-1})$. In simpler cases where the order in which the inputs arrive is irrelevant or unknown, the machine can build a model of the data which assumes that the data points $x_1, x_2, \ldots$ are independently and identically drawn from some distribution $P(x)^2$.

Such a model can be used for *outlier detection* or *monitoring*. Let x represent patterns of sensor readings from a nuclear power plant and assume that $P(x)$ is learned from data collected from a normally functioning plant. This model can be used to evaluate the probability of a new sensor reading; if this probability is abnormally low, then either the model is poor or the plant is behaving abnormally, in which case one may want to shut it down.

A probabilistic model can also be used for *classification*. Assume $P_1(x)$ is a model of the attributes of credit card holders who paid on time, and $P_2(x)$ is a model learned from credit card holders who defaulted on their payments. By evaluating the relative probabilities $P_1(x')$ and $P_2(x')$ on a new applicant x', the machine can decide to classify her into one of these two categories.

With a probabilistic model one can also achieve efficient *communication* and *data compression*. Imagine that we want to transmit, over a digital communication line, symbols x randomly drawn from $P(x)$. For example, x may be letters of the alphabet, or images, and the communication line may be the Internet. Intuitively, we should encode our data so that symbols which occur more frequently have code words with fewer bits in them, otherwise we are wasting bandwidth. Shannon's source coding theorem quantifies this by telling us that the optimal number of bits to use to encode a symbol with probability $P(x)$ is $-\log_2 P(x)$. Using these number of bits for each symbol, the expected coding cost is the entropy of the distribution P.

$$H(P) \stackrel{\text{def}}{=} -\sum_x P(x) \log_2 P(x) \qquad (1)$$

In general, the true distribution of the data is unknown, but we can learn a model of this distribution. Let's call this model $Q(x)$. The optimal code *with*

---

^{2} We will use both P and p to denote probability distributions and probability densities. The meaning should be clear depending on whether the argument is discrete or continuous.

respect to this model would use $-\log_2 Q(x)$ bits for each symbol x. The expected coding cost, taking expectations with respect to the true distribution, is

$$-\sum_x P(x)\log_2 Q(x) \tag{2}$$

The difference between these two coding costs is called the Kullback-Leibler (KL) divergence

$$\text{KL}(P\|Q) \overset{\text{def}}{=} \sum_x P(x)\log\frac{P(x)}{Q(x)} \tag{3}$$

The KL divergence is non-negative and zero if and only if P=Q. It measures the coding inefficiency in bits from using a model Q to compress data when the true data distribution is P. *Therefore, the better our model of the data, the more efficiently we can compress and communicate new data.* This is an important link between machine learning, statistics, and information theory. An excellent text which elaborates on these relationships and many of the topics in this chapter is [1].

1.3   Bayes Rule

Bayes rule,

$$P(y|x) = \frac{P(x|y)P(y)}{P(x)} \tag{4}$$

which follows from the equality $P(x,y) = P(x)P(y|x) = P(y)P(x|y)$, can be used to motivate a coherent statistical framework for machine learning. The basic idea is the following. Imagine we wish to design a machine which has beliefs about the world, and updates these beliefs on the basis of observed data. The machine must somehow represent the strengths of its beliefs numerically. It has been shown that if you accept certain axioms of coherent inference, known as the *Cox axioms*, then a remarkable result follows [2]: If the machine is to represent the strength of its beliefs by real numbers, then the only reasonable and coherent way of manipulating these beliefs is to have them satisfy the rules of probability, such as Bayes rule. Therefore, $P(X = x)$ can be used not only to represent the frequency with which the variable X takes on the value x (as in so-called frequentist statistics) but it can also be used to represent the degree of belief that $X = x$. Similarly, $P(X = x|Y = y)$ can be used to represent the degree of belief that $X = x$ given that one knows $Y = y$.[3]

---

[3] Another way to motivate the use of the rules of probability to encode degrees of belief comes from game-theoretic arguments in the form of the *Dutch Book Theorem*. This theorem states that if you are willing to accept bets with odds based on your degrees of beliefs, then unless your beliefs are coherent in the sense that they satisfy the rules of probability theory, there exists a set of simultaneous bets (called a "Dutch Book") which you will accept and which is guaranteed to lose you money, no matter what the outcome. The only way to ensure that Dutch Books don't exist against you, is to have degrees of belief that satisfy Bayes rule and the other rules of probability theory.

From Bayes rule we derive the following simple framework for machine learning. Assume a universe of models Ω; let $\Omega = \{1, \ldots, M\}$ although it need not be finite or even countable. The machines starts with some prior beliefs over models $m \in \Omega$ (we will see many examples of models later), such that $\sum_{m=1}^{M} P(m) = 1$. A model is simply some probability distribution over data points, i.e. $P(x|m)$. For simplicity, let us further assume that in all the models the data is taken to be independently and identically distributed (i.i.d.). After observing a data set $\mathcal{D} = \{x_1, \ldots, x_N\}$, the beliefs over models is given by:

$$P(m|\mathcal{D}) = \frac{P(m)P(\mathcal{D}|m)}{P(\mathcal{D})} \propto P(m) \prod_{n=1}^{N} P(x_n|m) \tag{5}$$

which we read as the *posterior over models* is the *prior* multiplied by the *likelihood*, normalized.

The *predictive distribution* over new data, which would be used to encode new data efficiently, is

$$P(x|\mathcal{D}) = \sum_{m=1}^{M} P(x|m)P(m|\mathcal{D}) \tag{6}$$

Again this follows from the rules of probability theory, and the fact that the models are assumed to produce i.i.d. data.

Often models are defined by writing down a parametric probability distribution (again, we'll see many examples below). Thus, the model m might have parameters θ, which are assumed to be unknown (this could in general be a vector of parameters). To be a well-defined model from the perspective of Bayesian learning, one has to define a prior over these model parameters $P(\theta|m)$ which naturally has to satisfy the following equality

$$P(x|m) = \int P(x|\theta, m)P(\theta|m)d\theta \tag{7}$$

Given the model m it is also possible to infer the posterior over the parameters of the model, i.e. $P(\theta|\mathcal{D}, m)$, and to compute the predictive distribution, $P(x|\mathcal{D}, m)$. These quantities are derived in exact analogy to equations (5) and (6), except that instead of summing over possible models, we integrate over parameters of a particular model. All the key quantities in Bayesian machine learning follow directly from the basic rules of probability theory.

Certain approximate forms of Bayesian learning are worth mentioning. Let's focus on a particular model m with parameters θ, and an observed data set $\mathcal{D}$. The predictive distribution averages over all possible parameters weighted by the posterior

$$P(x|\mathcal{D}, m) = \int P(x|\theta)P(\theta|\mathcal{D}, m)d\theta. \tag{8}$$

In certain cases, it may be cumbersome to represent the entire posterior distribution over parameters, so instead we will choose to find a *point-estimate* of the parameters $\hat{\theta}$. A natural choice is to pick the most probable parameter value given the data, which is known as the *maximum a posteriori* or MAP parameter estimate

$$\hat{\theta}_{\mathrm{MAP}} = \arg\max_\theta P(\theta|\mathcal{D}, m) = \arg\max_\theta \left[\log P(\theta|m) + \sum_n \log P(x_n|\theta, m)\right] \quad (9)$$

Another natural choice is the *maximum likelihood* or ML parameter estimate

$$\hat{\theta}_{\mathrm{ML}} = \arg\max_\theta P(\mathcal{D}|\theta, m) = \arg\max_\theta \sum_n \log P(x_n|\theta, m) \quad (10)$$

Many learning algorithms can be seen as finding ML parameter estimates. The ML parameter estimate is also acceptable from a frequentist statistical modeling perspective since it does not require deciding on a prior over parameters. However, ML estimation does not protect against overfitting—more complex models will generally have higher maxima of the likelihood. In order to avoid problems with overfitting, frequentist procedures often maximize a *penalized* or *regularized* log likelihood (e.g. [3]). If the penalty or regularization term is interpreted as a log prior, then maximizing penalized likelihood appears identical to maximizing a posterior. However, there are subtle issues that make a Bayesian MAP procedure and maximum penalized likelihood different [4]. One difference is that the MAP estimate is not invariant to reparameterization, while the maximum of the penalized likelihood is invariant. The penalized likelihood is a function, not a density, and therefore does not increase or decrease depending on the Jacobian of the reparameterization.

2 Latent Variable Models

The framework described above can be applied to a wide range of models. No singe model is appropriate for all data sets. The art in machine learning is to develop models which are appropriate for the data set being analyzed, and which have certain desired properties. For example, for high dimensional data sets it might be necessary to use models that perform dimensionality reduction. Of course, ultimately, the machine should be able to decide on the appropriate model without any human intervention, but to achieve this in full generality requires significant advances in artificial intelligence.

In this section, we will consider probabilistic models that are defined in terms of some latent or hidden variables. These models can be used to do dimensionality reduction and clustering, the two cornerstones of unsupervised learning.

2.1 Factor Analysis

Let the data set $\mathcal{D}$ consist of D-dimensional real valued vectors, $\mathcal{D} = \{\mathbf{y}_1, \ldots, \mathbf{y}_N\}$. In factor analysis, the data is assumed to be generated from the following model

$$\mathbf{y} = \Lambda\mathbf{x} + \epsilon \quad (11)$$

where $\mathbf{x}$ is a K-dimensional zero-mean unit-variance multivariate Gaussian vector with elements corresponding to hidden (or latent) factors, Λ is a $D \times K$ matrix of parameters, known as the factor loading matrix, and ϵ is a D-dimensional zero-mean multivariate Gaussian noise vector with diagonal covariance matrix Ψ. Defining the parameters of the model to be $\theta = (\Psi, \Lambda)$, by integrating out the factors, one can readily derive that

$$p(\mathbf{y}|\theta) = \int p(\mathbf{x}|\theta)p(\mathbf{y}|\mathbf{x}, \theta)d\mathbf{x} = \mathcal{N}(0, \Lambda\Lambda^\top + \Psi) \tag{12}$$

where $\mathcal{N}(\mu, \Sigma)$ refers to a multivariate Gaussian density with mean μ and covariance matrix Σ. For more details refer to [5].

Factor analysis is an interesting model for several reasons. If the data is very high dimensional (D is large) then even a simple model like the full-covariance multivariate Gaussian will have too many parameters to reliably estimate or infer from the data. By choosing $K < D$, factor analysis makes it possible to model a Gaussian density for high dimensional data without requiring $\mathcal{O}(D^2)$ parameters. Moreover, given a new data point, one can compute the posterior over the hidden factors, $p(\mathbf{x}|\mathbf{y}, \theta)$; since $\mathbf{x}$ is lower dimensional than $\mathbf{y}$ this provides a low-dimensional representation of the data (for example, one could pick the mean of $p(\mathbf{x}|\mathbf{y}, \theta)$ as the representation for $\mathbf{y}$).

2.2   Principal Components Analysis (PCA)

Principal components analysis (PCA) is an important limiting case of factor analysis (FA). One can derive PCA by making two modifications to FA. First, the noise is assumed to be isotropic, in other words each element of ϵ has equal variance: $\Psi = \sigma^2 I$, where I is a $D \times D$ identity matrix. This model is called *probabilistic PCA* [6, 7]. Second, if we take the limit of $\sigma \to 0$ in probabilistic PCA, we obtain standard PCA (which also goes by the names Karhunen-Loève expansion, and singular value decomposition; SVD). Given a data set with covariance matrix Σ, for maximum likelihood factor analysis the goal is to find parameters Λ, and Ψ for which the model $\Lambda\Lambda^\top + \Psi$ has highest likelihood. In PCA, the goal is to find Λ so that the likelihood is highest for $\Lambda\Lambda^\top$. Note that this matrix is singular unless $K = D$, so the standard PCA model is not a sensible model. However, taking the limiting case, and further constraining the columns of Λ to be orthogonal, it can be derived that the principal components correspond to the K eigenvectors with largest eigenvalue of Σ. PCA is thus attractive because the solution can be found immediately after eigendecomposition of the covariance. Taking the limit $\sigma \to 0$ of $p(\mathbf{x}|\mathbf{y}, \Lambda, \sigma)$ we find that it is a delta-function at $\mathbf{x} = \Lambda^\top \mathbf{y}$, which is the projection of $\mathbf{y}$ onto the principal components.

2.3   Independent Components Analysis (ICA)

Independent components analysis (ICA) extends factor analysis to the case where the factors are non-Gaussian. This is an interesting extension because many real-world data sets have structure which can be modeled as linear combinations of sparse sources. This includes auditory data, images, biological signals such as EEG, etc. *Sparsity* simply corresponds to the assumption that the factors have distributions with higher kurtosis that the Gaussian. For example, $p(x) = \frac{\lambda}{2} \exp\{-\lambda|x|\}$ has a higher peak at zero and heavier tails than a Gaussian with corresponding mean and variance, so it would be considered sparse (strictly speaking, one would like a distribution which had non-zero probability mass at 0 to get true sparsity).

Models like PCA, FA and ICA can all be implemented using neural networks (multi-layer perceptrons) trained using various cost functions. It is not clear what advantage this implementation/interpretation has from a machine learning perspective, although it provides interesting ties to biological information processing.

Rather than ML estimation, one can also do Bayesian inference for the parameters of probabilistic PCA, FA, and ICA.

2.4 Mixture of Gaussians

The densities modeled by PCA, FA and ICA are all relatively simple in that they are unimodal and have fairly restricted parametric forms (Gaussian, in the case of PCA and FA). To model data with more complex structure such as clusters, it is very useful to consider mixture models. Although it is straightforward to consider mixtures of arbitrary densities, we will focus on Gaussians as a common special case. The density of each data point in a mixture model can be written:

$$p(\mathbf{y}|\theta) = \sum_{k=1}^{K} \pi_k \, p(\mathbf{y}|\theta_k) \tag{13}$$

where each of the K components of the mixture is, for example, a Gaussian with differing means and covariances $\theta_k = (\mu_k, \Sigma_k)$ and π_k is the mixing proportion for component k, such that $\sum_{k=1}^{K} \pi_k = 1$ and $\pi_k > 0$, $\forall k$.

A different way to think about mixture models is to consider them as latent variable models, where associated with each data point is a K-ary discrete latent (i.e. hidden) variable s which has the interpretation that $s = k$ if the data point was generated by component k. This can be written

$$p(\mathbf{y}|\theta) = \sum_{k=1}^{K} P(s = k|\pi)p(\mathbf{y}|s = k, \theta) \tag{14}$$

where $P(s = k|\pi) = \pi_k$ is the prior for the latent variable taking on value k, and $p(\mathbf{y}|s = k, \theta) = p(\mathbf{y}|\theta_k)$ is the density under component k, recovering Equation (13).

2.5 K-Means

The mixture of Gaussians model is closely related to an unsupervised clustering algorithm known as k-means as follows: Consider the special case where all the

Gaussians have common covariance matrix proportional to the identity matrix: $\Sigma_k = \sigma^2 I$, $\forall k$, and let $\pi_k = 1/K$, $\forall k$. We can estimate the maximum likelihood parameters of this model using the iterative algorithm which we are about to describe, known as EM. The resulting algorithm, as we take the limit $\sigma^2 \to 0$, becomes exactly the k-means algorithm. Clearly the model underlying k-means has only singular Gaussians and is therefore an unreasonable model of the data; however, k-means is usually justified from the point of view of clustering to minimize a distortion measure, rather than fitting a probabilistic models.

3   The EM Algorithm

The EM algorithm is an algorithm for estimating ML parameters of a model with latent variables. Consider a model with observed variables $\mathbf{y}$, hidden/latent variables $\mathbf{x}$, and parameters θ. We can lower bound the log likelihood for any data point as follows

$$L(\theta) = \log p(\mathbf{y}|\theta) = \log \int p(\mathbf{x}, \mathbf{y}|\theta)\, d\mathbf{x} \tag{15}$$

$$= \log \int q(\mathbf{x}) \frac{p(\mathbf{x}, \mathbf{y}|\theta)}{q(\mathbf{x})}\, d\mathbf{x} \tag{16}$$

$$\geq \int q(\mathbf{x}) \log \frac{p(\mathbf{x}, \mathbf{y}|\theta)}{q(\mathbf{x})}\, d\mathbf{x} \stackrel{\text{def}}{=} F(q, \theta) \tag{17}$$

where $q(\mathbf{x})$ is some arbitrary density over the hidden variables, and the lower bound holds due to the concavity of the log function (this inequality is known as Jensen's inequality). The lower bound F is a functional of both the density $q(\mathbf{x})$ and the model parameters θ. For a data set of N data points $\mathbf{y}^{(1)}, \ldots, \mathbf{y}^{(N)}$, this lower bound is formed for the log likelihood term corresponding to each data point, thus there is a separate density $q^{(n)}(\mathbf{x})$ for each point and $F(q, \theta) = \sum_n F^{(n)}(q^{(n)}, \theta)$.

The basic idea of the Expectation-Maximization (EM) algorithm is to iterate between optimizing this lower bound as a function of q and as a function of θ. We can prove that this will never decrease the log likelihood. After initializing the parameters somehow, the kth iteration of the algorithm consists of the following two steps:

E Step: *Optimize F with respect to the distribution q while holding the parameters fixed*

$$q_k(\mathbf{x}) = \arg\max_{q(\mathbf{x})} \int q(\mathbf{x}) \log \frac{p(\mathbf{x}, \mathbf{y}|\theta_{k-1})}{q(\mathbf{x})} \tag{18}$$

$$q_k(\mathbf{x}) = p(\mathbf{x}|\mathbf{y}, \theta_{k-1}) \tag{19}$$

M Step: *Optimize F with respect to the parameters θ while holding the distribution over hidden variables fixed*

$$\theta_k = \arg\max_{\theta} \int q_k(\mathbf{x}) \log \frac{p(\mathbf{x},\mathbf{y}|\theta)}{q_k(\mathbf{x})} \, d\mathbf{x} \tag{20}$$

$$\theta_k = \arg\max_{\theta} \int q_k(\mathbf{x}) \log p(\mathbf{x},\mathbf{y}|\theta) \, d\mathbf{x} \tag{21}$$

Let us be absolutely clear what happens for a data set of N data points: In the E step, for each data point, the distribution over the hidden variables is set to the posterior for that data point $q_k^{(n)}(\mathbf{x}) = p(\mathbf{x}|\mathbf{y}^{(n)}, \theta_{k-1})$, $\forall n$. In the M step the single set of parameters is re-estimated by maximizing the sum of the expected log likelihoods: $\theta_k = \arg\max_{\theta} \sum_n \int q_k^{(n)}(\mathbf{x}) \log p(\mathbf{x},\mathbf{y}^{(n)}|\theta) \, d\mathbf{x}$.

Two things are still unclear: how does (19) follow from (18), and how is this algorithm guaranteed to increase the likelihood? The optimization in (18) can be written as follows since $p(\mathbf{x},\mathbf{y}|\theta_{k-1}) = p(\mathbf{y}|\theta_{k-1})p(\mathbf{x}|\mathbf{y}, \theta_{k-1})$:

$$q_k(\mathbf{x}) = \arg\max_{q(\mathbf{x})} \left[\log p(\mathbf{y}|\theta_{k-1}) + \int q(\mathbf{x}) \log \frac{p(\mathbf{x}|\mathbf{y}, \theta_{k-1})}{q(\mathbf{x})} \, d\mathbf{x} \right] \tag{22}$$

Now, the first term is a constant w.r.t. $q(\mathbf{x})$ and the second term is the negative of the Kullback-Leibler divergence

$$\text{KL}(q(\mathbf{x})\|p(\mathbf{x}|\mathbf{y}, \theta_{k-1})) = \int q(\mathbf{x}) \log \frac{q(\mathbf{x})}{p(\mathbf{x}|\mathbf{y}, \theta_{k-1})} \, d\mathbf{x} \tag{23}$$

which we have seen in Equation (3) in its discrete form. This is minimized at $q(\mathbf{x}) = p(\mathbf{x}|\mathbf{y}, \theta_{k-1})$, where the KL divergence is zero. Intuitively, the interpretation of this is that in the E step of EM, the goal is to find the posterior distribution of the hidden variables given the observed variables and the current settings of the parameters. We also see that since the KL divergence is zero, at the end of the E step, $F(q_k, \theta_{k-1}) = L(\theta_{k-1})$.

In the M step, F is increased with respect to θ. Therefore, $F(q_k, \theta_k) \geq F(q_k, \theta_{k-1})$. Moreover, $L(\theta_k) = F(q_{k+1}, \theta_k) \geq F(q_k, \theta_k)$ after the next E step. We can put these steps together to establish that $L(\theta_k) \geq L(\theta_{k-1})$, establishing that the algorithm is guaranteed to increase the likelihood or keep it fixed (at convergence).

The EM algorithm can be applied to all the latent variable models described above, i.e. FA, probabilistic PCA, mixture models, and ICA. In the case of mixture models, the hidden variable is the discrete assignment s of data points to clusters; consequently the integrals turn into sums where appropriate. EM has wide applicability to latent variable models, although it is not always the fastest optimization method [8]. Moreover, we should note that the likelihood often has many local optima and EM will converge some local optimum which may not be the global one.

EM can also be used to estimate MAP parameters of a model, and as we will see in Section 11.4 there is a Bayesian generalization of EM as well.

4   Modeling Time Series and Other Structured Data

So far we have assumed that the data is *unstructured*, that is, the observations are assumed to be independent and identically distributed. This assumption is unreasonable for many data sets in which the observations arrive in a sequence and subsequent observations are correlated. Sequential data can occur in time series modeling (as in financial data or the weather) and also in situations where the sequential nature of the data is not necessarily tied to time (as in protein data which consist of sequences of amino acids).

As the most basic level, time series modeling consists of building a probabilistic model of the present observation given all past observations $p(\mathbf{y}_t | \mathbf{y}_{t-1}, \mathbf{y}_{t-2} \ldots)$. Because the history of observations grows arbitrarily large it is necessary to limit the complexity of such a model. There are essentially two ways of doing this.

The first approach is to limit the window of past observations. Thus one can simply model $p(\mathbf{y}_t | \mathbf{y}_{t-1})$ and assume that this relation holds for all t. This is known as a first-order Markov model. A second-order Markov model would be $p(\mathbf{y}_t | \mathbf{y}_{t-1}, \mathbf{y}_{t-2})$, and so on. Such Markov models have two limitations: First, the influence of past observations on present observations vanishes outside this window, which can be unrealistic. Second, it may be unnatural and unwieldy to model directly the relationship between raw observations at one time step and raw observations at a subsequent time step. For example, if the observations are noisy images, it would make more sense to de-noise them, extract some description of the objects, motions, illuminations, and then try to predict from that.

The second approach is to make use of latent or hidden variables. Instead of modeling directly the effect of $\mathbf{y}_{t-1}$ on $\mathbf{y}_t$, we assume that the observations were generated from some underlying hidden variable $\mathbf{x}_t$ which captures the dynamics of the system. For example, $\mathbf{y}$ might be noisy sonar readings of objects in a room, while $\mathbf{x}$ might be the actual locations and sizes of these objects. We usually call this hidden variable $\mathbf{x}$ the *state variable* since it is meant to capture all the aspects of the system relevant to predicting the future dynamical behavior of the system.

In order to understand more complex time series models, it is essential that one be familiar with state-space models (SSMs) and hidden Markov models (HMMs). These two classes of models have played a historically important role in control engineering, visual tracking, speech recognition, protein sequence modeling, and error decoding. They form the simplest building blocks from which other richer time-series models can be developed, in a manner completely analogous to the role that FA and mixture models play in building more complex models for i.i.d. data.

4.1   State-Space Models (SSMs)

In a state-space model, the sequence of observed data $\mathbf{y}_1, \mathbf{y}_2, \mathbf{y}_3, \ldots$ is assumed to have been generated from some sequence of hidden state variables $\mathbf{x}_1, \mathbf{x}_2, \mathbf{x}_3, \ldots$.

Letting $\mathbf{x}_{1:T}$ denote the sequence $\mathbf{x}_1, \ldots, \mathbf{x}_T$, the basic assumption in an SSM is that the joint probability of the hidden states and observations factors in the following way:

$$p(\mathbf{x}_{1:T}, \mathbf{y}_{1:T}|\theta) = \prod_{t=1}^{T} p(\mathbf{x}_t|\mathbf{x}_{t-1}, \theta)p(\mathbf{y}_t|\mathbf{x}_t, \theta) \qquad (24)$$

In order words, the observations are assumed to have been generated from the hidden states via $p(\mathbf{y}_t|\mathbf{x}_t, \theta)$, and the hidden states are assumed to have first-order Markov dynamics captured by $p(\mathbf{x}_t|\mathbf{x}_{t-1}, \theta)$. We can consider the first term $p(\mathbf{x}_1|\mathbf{x}_0, \theta)$ to be a prior on the initial state of the system $\mathbf{x}_1$.

The simplest kind of state-space model assumes that all variables are multivariate Gaussian distributed and all the relationships are linear. In such *linear-Gaussian state-space models*, we can write

$$\mathbf{y}_t = C\mathbf{x}_t + \mathbf{v}_t \qquad (25)$$
$$\mathbf{x}_t = A\mathbf{x}_{t-1} + \mathbf{w}_t \qquad (26)$$

where the matrices C and A define the linear relationships and $\mathbf{v}$ and $\mathbf{w}$ are zero-mean Gaussian noise vectors with covariance matrices R and Q respectively. If we assume that the prior on the initial state $p(\mathbf{x}_1)$ is also Gaussian, then all subsequent $\mathbf{x}$s and $\mathbf{y}$s are also Gaussian due the the fact that Gaussian densities are closed under linear transformations. This model can be generalized in many ways, for example by augmenting it to include a sequence of observed inputs $\mathbf{u}_1, \ldots, \mathbf{u}_T$ as well as the observed model outputs $\mathbf{y}_1, \ldots, \mathbf{y}_T$, but we will not discuss generalizations further.

By comparing equations (11) and (25) we see that linear-Gaussian SSMs can be thought of as a time-series generalization of factor analysis where the factors are assumed to have linear-Gaussian dynamics over time.

The parameters of this model are $\theta = (A, C, Q, R)$. To learn ML settings of these parameters one can make use of the EM algorithm [9]. The E step of the algorithm involves computing $q(\mathbf{x}_{1:T}) = p(\mathbf{x}_{1:T}|\mathbf{y}_{1:T}, \theta)$ which is the posterior over hidden state sequences. In fact, this whole posterior does not have to be computed or represented, all that is required are the marginals $q(\mathbf{x}_t)$ and pairwise marginals $q(\mathbf{x}_t, \mathbf{x}_{t+1})$. These can be computed via the *Kalman smoothing algorithm*, which is an efficient algorithm for inferring the distribution over the hidden states of a linear-Gaussian SSM. Since the model is linear, the M step of the algorithm requires solving a pair of weighted linear regression problems to re-estimate A and C, while Q and R are estimated from the residuals of those regressions. This is analogous to the M step of factor analysis, which also involves solving a linear regression problem.

4.2   Hidden Markov Models (HMMs)

Hidden Markov models are similar to state-space models in that the sequence of observations is assumed to have been generated from a sequence of underlying hidden states. The key difference is that in HMMs the state is assumed to be *discrete* rather than a continuous random vector. Let s_t denote the hidden state of an HMM at time t. We assume that s_t can take discrete values in $\{1, \ldots, K\}$. The model can again be written as in (24):

$$P(s_{1:T}, \mathbf{y}_{1:T}|\theta) = \prod_{t=1}^{T} P(s_t|s_{t-1}, \theta) P(\mathbf{y}_t|s_t, \theta) \tag{27}$$

where $P(s_1|s_0, \theta)$ is simply some initial distribution over the K settings of the first hidden state; we can call this discrete distribution $\boldsymbol{\pi}$, represented by a $K \times 1$ vector. The state-transition probabilities $P(s_t|s_{t-1}, \theta)$ are captured by a $K \times K$ transition matrix A, with elements $A_{ij} = P(s_t = i|s_{t-1} = j, \theta)$. The observations in an HMM can be either continuous or discrete. For continuous observations $\mathbf{y}_t$ one can for example choose a Gaussian density; thus $p(\mathbf{y}_t|s_t = i, \theta)$ would be a different Gaussian for each choice of $i \in \{1, \ldots, K\}$. This model is the dynamical generalization of a mixture of Gaussians. The marginal probability at each point in time is exactly a mixture of K Gaussians—the difference is that which component generates data point $\mathbf{y}_t$ and which component generated $\mathbf{y}_{t-1}$ are not independent random variables, but certain combinations are more and less probable depending on the entries in A. For $\mathbf{y}_t$ a discrete observation, let us assume that it can take on values $\{1, \ldots, L\}$. In that case the output probabilities $P(\mathbf{y}_t|s_t, \theta)$ can be captured by an $L \times K$ emission matrix, E.

The model parameters for a discrete-observation HMM are $\theta = (\boldsymbol{\pi}, A, E)$. Maximum likelihood learning of the model parameters can be approached using the EM algorithm, which in the case of HMMs is known as the *Baum-Welch algorithm*. The E step involves computing $Q(s_t)$ and $Q(s_t, s_{t+1})$ which are marginals of $Q(s_{1:T}) = P(s_{1:T}|\mathbf{y}_{1:T}, \theta)$. These marginals are computed as part of the *forward–backward algorithm* which as the name suggests sweeps forward and backward through the time series, and applies Bayes rule efficiently using the Markov conditional independence properties of the HMM, to compute the required marginals. The M step of HMM learning involves re-estimating $\boldsymbol{\pi}$, A, and E by adding up and normalizing expected counts for transitions and emissions that were computed in the E step.

4.3   Modeling Other Structured Data

We have considered the case of i.i.d. data and time series data. The observations in real world data sets can have many other possible structures as well. Let us mention a few examples, although it is not possible to strive for completeness.

In spatial data, the points are assumed to live in some metric, often Euclidean, space. Three examples of spatial data include epidemiological data which can be modeled as a function of the spatial location of the measurement; data from computer vision where the observations are measurements of features on a 2D input to the camera; and functional neuroimaging where the data can be physiological measurements related to neural activity located in 3D voxels defining coordinates in the brain. Generalizing HMMs, one can define Markov random field models where there are a set of hidden variables correlated to neighbors in some lattice, and related to the observed variables.

Hierarchical or tree-structured data contains known or unknown tree-like correlation structure between the data points or measured features. For example, the data points may be features of animals related through an evolutionary tree. A very different form of structured data is if each data point itself is tree-structured, for example if each point is a parse tree of a sentence in the English language.

Finally, one can take the structured dependencies between variables and consider the structure itself as an unknown part of the model. Such models are known as *probabilistic relational models* and are closely related to graphical models which we will discuss in Section 7.

5   Nonlinear, Factorial, and Hierarchical Models

The models we have described so far are attractive because they are relatively simple to understand and learn. However, their simplicity is also a limitation, since the intricacies of real-world data are unlikely to be well-captured by a simple statistical model. This motivates us to seek to describe and study learning in much more flexible models.

A simple combination of two of the ideas we have described for i.i.d. data is the *mixture of factor analyzers* [10, 11, 12]. This model performs simultaneous clustering and dimensionality reduction on the data, by assuming that the covariance in each Gaussian cluster can be modeled by an FA model. Thus, it becomes possible to apply a mixture model to very high dimensional data while allowing each cluster to span a different sub-space of the data.

As their name implies linear-Gaussian SSMs are limited by assumptions of linearity and Gaussian noise. In many realistic dynamical systems there are significant nonlinear effects, which make it necessary to consider learning in *nonlinear state-space models*. Such models can also be learned using the EM algorithm, but the E step must deal with inference in non-Gaussian and potentially very complicated densities (since non-linearities will turn Gaussians into non-Gaussians), and the M step is nonlinear regression, rather than linear regression [13]. There are many methods of dealing with inference in non-linear SSMs, including methods such as particle filtering [14, 15, 16, 17, 18, 19], linearization [20], the unscented filter [21, 22], the EP algorithm [23], and embedded HMMs [24].

Non-linear models are also important if we are to consider generalizing simple dimensionality reduction models such as PCA and FA. These models are limited in that they can only find a linear subspace of the data to capture the correlations between the observed variables. There are many interesting and important nonlinear dimensionality reduction models, including generative topographic mappings (GTM) [25] (a probabilistic alternative to Kohonen maps), multi-dimensional scaling (MDS) [26, 27], principal curves [28], Isomap [29], and locally linear embedding (LLE) [30].

Hidden Markov models also have their limitations. Even though they can model nonlinear dynamics by discretizing the hidden state space, an HMM with K hidden states can only capture $\log_2 K$ bits of information in its state variable about the past of the sequence. HMMs can be extended by allowing a *vector* of discrete state variables, in an architecture known as a *factorial HMM* [31]. Thus a vector of M variables, each of which can take K states, can capture K^M possible states in total, and $M \log_2 K$ bits of information about the past of the sequence. The problem is that such a model, if dealt with naively as an HMM would have exponentially many parameters and would take exponentially long to do inference in. Both the complexity in time and number of parameters can be alleviated by restricting the interactions between the hidden variables at one time step and at the next time step. A generalization of these ideas is the notion of a *dynamical Bayesian network (DBN)* [32].

A relatively old but still quite powerful class of models for binary data is the *Boltzmann machine* (BM) [33]. This is a simple model inspired from Ising models in statistical physics. A BM is a multivariate model for capturing correlations and higher order statistics in vectors of binary data. Consider data consisting of vectors of M binary variables (t he elements of the vector may, for example, be pixels in a black-and-white image). Clearly, each data point can be an instance of one of 2^M possible patterns. An arbitrary distribution over such patterns would require a table with $2^M - 1$ entries, again intractable in number of parameters, storage, and computation time. A BM allows one to define flexible distributions over the 2^M entries of this table by using $\mathcal{O}(M^2)$ parameters defining a symmetric matrix of weights connecting the variables. This can be augmented with hidden variables in order to enrich the model class, without adding exponentially many parameters. These hidden variables can be organized into layers of a hierarchy as in the Helmholtz machine [34]. Other hierarchical models include recent generalizations of ICA designed to capture higher order statistics in images [35].

6   Intractability

The problem with the models described in the previous section is that learning their parameters is in general computationally intractable. In a model with exponentially many settings for the hidden states, doing the E step of an EM algorithm would require computing appropriate marginals of a distribution over exponentially many possibilities.

Let us consider a simple example. Imagine we have a vector of N binary random variables $\mathbf{s} = (s_1, \ldots, s_N)$, where $s_i \in \{0, 1\}$ and a vector of N known integers $(r_1, \ldots, r_N)$ where $r_i \in \{1, 2, 3, \ldots, 10\}$. Let the variable $Y = \sum_{i=1}^{N} r_i s_i$. Assume that the binary variables are all independent and identically distributed with $P(s_i = 1) = 1/2, \forall i$. Let N be 100. Now imagine that we are told $Y = 430$. How do we compute $P(s_i = 1 | Y = 430)$? The problem is that even though the s_i were independent *before* we observed the value of Y, now that we know the value of Y, not all settings of $\mathbf{s}$ are possible anymore. To figure out for some s_i

the probability of $P(s_i = 1|Y = 430)$ requires that we enumerate all potentially exponentially many ways of achieving $Y = 430$ and counting how many of those had $s_i = 1$ vs $s_i = 0$.

This example illustrates the following ideas: Even if the prior is simple, the posterior can be very complicated. Whether two random variables are independent or not is a function of one's state of knowledge. Thus s_i and s_j may be independent if we are not told the value of Y but are certainly dependent given the value of Y. These type of phenomena are related to "explaining-away" which refers to the fact that if there are multiple potential causes for some effect, observing one, explains away the need for the others [36].

Intractability can thus occur if we have a model with discrete hidden variables which can take on exponentially many combinations. Intractability can also occur with continuous hidden variables if their density is not simply described, or if they interact with discrete hidden variables. Moreover, even for simple models, such as a mixture of Gaussians, intractability occurs when we consider the parameters to be unknown as well, and we attempt to do Bayesian inference on them. To deal with intractability it is essential to have good tools for representing multivariate distributions, such as graphical models.

7   Graphical Models

Graphical models are an important tool for representing the dependencies between random variables in a probabilistic model. They are important for two reasons. First, graphs are an intuitive way of visualizing dependencies. We are used to graphical depictions of dependency, for example in circuit diagrams and in phylogenetic trees. Second, by exploiting the structure of the graph it is possible to devise efficient message passing algorithms for computing marginal and conditional probabilities in a complicated model. We discuss message passing algorithms for inference in Section 8.

The main statistical property represented explicitly by the graph is *conditional independence* between variables. We say that X and Y are conditionally independent given Z, if $P(X, Y|Z) = P(X|Z)P(Y|Z)$ for all values of the variables X, Y, and Z where these quantities are defined (i.e. excepting settings z where $P(Z = z) = 0$). We use the notation $X \perp\!\!\!\perp Y|Z$ to denote the above conditional independence relation. Conditional independence generalists to sets of variables in the obvious way, and it is different from *marginal independence* which states that $P(X, Y) = P(X)P(Y)$, and is denoted $X \perp\!\!\!\perp Y$.

There are several different graphical formalisms for depicting conditional independence relationships. We focus on three of the main ones: undirected, factor, and directed graphs.

7.1   Undirected Graphs

In an *undirected graphical model* each random variable is represented by a node, and the edges of the graph indicate conditional independence relationships.

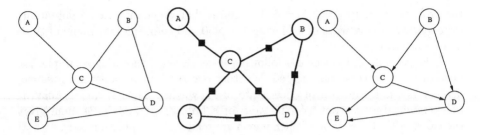

Fig. 1. Three kinds of probabilistic graphical model: undirected graphs, factor graphs and directed graphs

Specifically, let $\mathcal{X}, \mathcal{Y}$, and $\mathcal{Z}$ be sets of random variables. Then $\mathcal{X} \perp\!\!\!\perp \mathcal{Y} | \mathcal{Z}$ if every path on the graph from a node in $\mathcal{X}$ to a node in $\mathcal{Y}$ has to go through a node in $\mathcal{Z}$. Thus a variable X is conditionally independent of all other variables given the neighbors of X, and we say that the neighbors *separate* X from the rest of the graph. An example of an undirected graph is shown in Figure 1. In this graph $A \perp\!\!\!\perp B | C$ and $B \perp\!\!\!\perp E | \{C, D\}$, for example, and the neighbors of D are B, C, E.

A *clique* is a fully connected subgraph of a graph. A *maximal clique* is not contained in any other clique of the graph. It turns out that the set of conditional independence relations implied by the separation properties in the graph are satisfied by probability distributions which can be written as a normalized product of non-negative functions over the variables in the maximal cliques of the graph (this is known as the Hammersley-Clifford Theorem [37]). In the example in Figure 1, this implies that the probability distribution over (A, B, C, D, E) can be written as:

$$P(A, B, C, D, E) = c\, g_1(A, C) g_2(B, C, D) g_3(C, D, E) \qquad (28)$$

Here, c is the constant that ensures that the probability distribution sums to 1, and g_1, g_2 and g_3 are non-negative functions of their arguments. For example, if all the variables are binary the function g_2 is a table with a non-negative number for each of the $8 = 2 \times 2 \times 2$ possible settings of the variables B, C, D. These non-negative functions are supposed to represent how compatible these settings are with each other, with a 0 encoding logical incompatibility. For this reason, the g's are sometimes referred to as *compatibility functions*, other times as *potential functions*. Undirected graphical models are also sometimes referred to as *Markov networks*.

7.2   Factor Graphs

In a *factor graph* there are two kinds of nodes, *variable nodes* and *factor nodes*, usually denoted as open circles and filled dots (Figure 1). Like an undirected model, the factor graph represents a factorization of the joint probability distribution: each factor is a non-negative function of the variables connected to the corresponding factor node. Thus for the factor graph in Figure 1 we have:

$$P(A, B, C, D, E) = c g_1(A, C) g_2(B, C) g_3(B, D), g_4(C, D) g_5(C, E) g_6(D, E)$$
$$(29)$$

Factor nodes are also sometimes called function nodes. Again, as in an undirected graphical model, the variables in a set $\mathcal{X}$ are conditionally independent of the variables in a set $\mathcal{Y}$ given $\mathcal{Z}$ if all paths from $\mathcal{X}$ to $\mathcal{Y}$ go through variables in $\mathcal{Z}$. Note that the factor graph is Figure 1 has exactly the same conditional independence relations as the undirected graph, even though the factors in the former are contained in the factors in the latter. Factor graphs are particularly elegant and simple when it comes to implementing message passing algorithms for inference (Section 8).

7.3   Directed Graphs

In *directed graphical models*, also known as probabilistic directed acyclic graphs (DAGs), belief networks, and Bayesian networks, the nodes represent random variables and the directed edges represent statistical dependencies. If there exists an edge from A to B we say that A is a *parent* of B, and conversely B is a *child* of A. A directed graph corresponds to the factorization of the joint probability into a product of the conditional probabilities of each node given its parents. For the example in Figure 1 we write:

$$P(A, B, C, D, E) = P(A)P(B)P(C|A, B)P(D|B, C)P(E|C, D) \qquad (30)$$

In general we would write:

$$P(X_1, \ldots, X_N) = \prod_{i=1}^{N} P(X_i | X_{\mathrm{pa}_i}) \qquad (31)$$

where X_{pa_i} denotes the variables that are parents of X_i in the graph.

Assessing the conditional independence relations in a directed graph is slightly less trivial than in undirected and factor graphs. Rather than simply looking at separation between sets of variables, one has to consider the directions of the edges. The graphical test for two sets of variables being conditionally independent given a third is called *d-separation* [36]. D-separation takes into account the following fact about *v-structures* of the graph, which consist of two (or more) parents of a child, as in the $A \rightarrow C \leftarrow B$ subgraph in Figure 1. In such a v-structure $A \perp\!\!\!\perp B$, but it is not true that $A \perp\!\!\!\perp B | C$. That is, A and B are marginally independent, but conditionally *dependent* given C. This can be easily checked by writing out $P(A, B, C) = P(A)P(B)P(C|A, B)$. Summing out C leads to $P(A, B) = P(A)P(B)$. However, given the value of C, $P(A, B|C) = P(A)P(B)P(C|A, B)/P(C)$ which does not factor into separate functions of A and B. As a consequence of this property of v-structures, in a directed graph a variable X is independent of all other variables given the parents of X, the children of X, and the parents of the children of X. This is the minimal set that d-separates X from the rest of the graph and is known as the Markov boundary for X.

It is possible, though not always appropriate, to interpret a directed graphical model as a causal generative model of the data. The following procedure would generate data from the probability distribution defined by a directed graph: draw a random value from the marginal distribution of all variables which do not have any parents (e.g. $a \sim P(A)$, $b \sim P(B)$), then sample from the conditional distribution of the children of these variables (e.g. $c \sim P(C|A = a, B = a)$), and continue this procedure until all variables are assigned values. In the model, $P(C|A, B)$ can capture the causal relationship between the causes A and B and the effect C. Such causal interpretations are much less natural for undirected and factor graphs, since even generating a sample from such models cannot easily be done in a hierarchical manner starting from "parents" to "children" except in special cases. Moreover, the potential functions capture mutual compatibilities, rather than cause-effect relations.

A useful property of directed graphical models is that there is no global normalization constant c. This global constant can be computationally intractable to compute in undirected and factor graphs. In directed graphs, each term is a conditional probability and is therefore already normalized $\sum_x P(X_i = x|X_{\mathrm{pa}_i}) = 1$.

7.4   Expressive Power

Directed, undirected and factor graphs are complementary in their ability to express conditional independence relationships. Consider the directed graph consisting of a single v-structure $A \rightarrow C \leftarrow B$. This graph encodes $A \perp\!\!\!\perp B$ but not $A \perp\!\!\!\perp B|C$. There exists no undirected graph or factor graph over these three variables which captures exactly these independencies. For example, in $A - C - B$ it is not true that $A \perp\!\!\!\perp B$ but it is true that $A \perp\!\!\!\perp B|C$. Conversely, if we consider the undirected graph in Figure 2, we see that some independence relationships are better captured by undirected models (and factor graphs).

Fig. 2. No directed graph over 4 variables can represent the set of conditional independence relationships represented by this undirected graph

8   Exact Inference in Graphs

Probabilistic *inference* in a graph usually refers to the problem of computing the conditional probability of some variable X_i given the observed values of some other variables $X_{\mathrm{obs}} = x_{\mathrm{obs}}$ while marginalizing out all other variables. Starting from a joint distribution $P(X_1, \ldots, X_N)$, we can divide the set of all variables into three exhaustive and mutually exclusive sets $\{X_1, \ldots X_N\} = \{X_i\} \cup X_{\mathrm{obs}} \cup X_{\mathrm{other}}$. We wish to compute

$$P(X_i|X_{\text{obs}} = x_{\text{obs}}) = \frac{\sum_x P(X_i, X_{\text{other}} = x, X_{\text{obs}} = x_{\text{obs}})}{\sum_{x'} \sum_x P(X_i = x', X_{\text{other}} = x, X_{\text{obs}} = x_{\text{obs}})} \tag{32}$$

The problem is that the sum over x is exponential in the number of variables in X_{other}. For example. if there are M variables in X_{other} and each is binary, then there are 2^M possible values for x. If the variables are continuous, then the desired conditional probability is the ratio of two high-dimensional integrals, which could be intractable to compute. Probabilistic inference is essentially a problem of computing large sums and integrals.

There are several algorithms for computing these sums and integrals which exploit the structure of the graph to get the solution efficiently for certain graph structures (namely trees and related graphs). For general graphs the problem is fundamentally hard [38].

8.1   Elimination

The simplest algorithm conceptually is *variable elimination*. It is easiest to explain with an example. Consider computing $P(A = a|D = d)$ in the directed graph in Figure 1. This can be written

$$P(A = a|D = d) \propto \sum_c \sum_b \sum_e P(A = a, B = b, C = c, D = d, E = e)$$

$$= \sum_c \sum_b \sum_e P(A = a)P(B = b)P(C = c|A = a, B = b)$$

$$P(D = d|C = c, B = b)P(E = e|C = c, D = d)$$

$$= \sum_c \sum_b P(A = a)P(B = b)P(C = c|A = a, B = b)$$

$$P(D = d|C = c, B = b) \sum_e P(E = e|C = c, D = d)$$

$$= \sum_c \sum_b P(A = a)P(B = b)P(C = c|A = a, B = b)$$

$$P(D = d|C = c, B = b)$$

What we did was (1) exploit the factorization, (2) rearrange the sums, and (3) eliminate a variable, E. We could repeat this procedure and eliminate the variable C. When we do this we will need to compute a new function $\phi(A = a, B = b, D = d) \stackrel{\text{def}}{=} \sum_c P(C = c|A = a, B = b)P(D = d|C = c, B = b)$, resulting in:

$$P(A = a|D = d) \propto \sum_b P(A = a)P(B = b)\phi(A = a, B = b, D = d)$$

Finally, we eliminate B by computing $\phi'(A = a, D = d) \stackrel{\text{def}}{=} \sum_b P(B = b)\phi(A = a, B = b, D = d)$ to get our final answer which can be written

$$P(A = a|D = d) \propto P(A = a)\phi'(A = a, D = d) = \frac{P(A = a)\phi'(A = a, D = d)}{\sum_a P(A = a)\phi'(A = a, D = d)}$$

The functions we get when we eliminate variables can be thought of as messages sent by that variable to its neighbors. Eliminating transforms the graph by removing the eliminated node and drawing (undirected) edges between all the nodes in the Markov boundary of the eliminated node.

The same answer is obtained no matter what order we eliminate variables in; however, the computational complexity can depend dramatically on the ordering used.

8.2   Belief Propagation

The belief propagation (BP) algorithm is a message passing algorithm for computing conditional probabilities of any variable given the values of some set of other variables in a *singly-connected* directed acyclic graph [36]. The algorithm itself follows from the rules of probability and the conditional independence properties of the graph. Whereas variable elimination focuses on finding the conditional probability of a single variable X_i given $X_{\text{obs}} = x_{\text{obs}}$, belief propagation can compute at once all the conditionals $p(X_i|X_{\text{obs}} = x_{\text{obs}})$ for all i not observed.

We first need to define singly-connected directed graphs. A directed graph is singly connected if between every pair of nodes there is only one undirected path. An *undirected path* is a path along the edges of the graph ignoring the direction of the edges: in other words the path can traverse edges both upstream and downstream. If there is more than one undirected path between any pair of nodes then the graph is said to be *multiply connected*, or *loopy* (since it has loops).

Singly connected graphs have an important property which BP exploits. Let us call the set of observed variables the *evidence*, $e = X_{\text{obs}}$. Every node in the graph divides the evidence into upstream e_X^+ and downstream e_X^- parts. For example, in Figure 3 the variables $U_1 \ldots U_n$ their parents, ancestors, and children and descendents (not including X, its children and descendents) and anything else connected to X via an edge directed toward X are all considered to be *upstream* of X; anything connected to X via an edge away from X is considered *downstream* of X (e.g. Y_1, its children, the parents of its children, etc). Similarly, every edge $X \rightarrow Y$ in a singly connected graph divides the

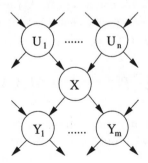

Fig. 3. Belief propagation in a directed graph

evidence into upstream and downstream parts. This separation of the evidence into upstream and downstream components does not generally occur in multiply-connected graphs.

Belief propagation uses three key ideas to compute the probability of some variable given the evidence $p(X|e)$, which we can call the "belief" about X.[4] First, the belief about X can be found by combining upstream and downstream evidence:

$$P(X|e) = \frac{P(X,e)}{P(e)} \propto P(X, e_X^+, e_X^-) \propto P(X|e_X^+)P(e_X^-|X) \qquad (33)$$

The last proportionality results from the fact that given X the downstream and upstream evidence are conditionally independent: $P(e_X^-|X, e_X^+) = P(e_X^-|X)$. Second, the effect of the upstream and downstream evidence on X can be computed via a local message passing algorithm between the nodes in the graph. Third, the message from X to Y has to be constructed carefully so that node X doesn't send back to Y any information that Y sent to X, otherwise the message passing algorithm would reverberate information between nodes amplifying and distorting the final beliefs.

Using these ideas and the basic rules of probability we can arrive at the following equations, where $\mathrm{ch}(X)$ and $\mathrm{pa}(X)$ are children and parents of X, respectively:

$$\lambda(X) \stackrel{\text{def}}{=} P(e_X^-|X) = \prod_{j \in \mathrm{ch}(X)} P(e_{XY_j}^-|X) \qquad (34)$$

$$\pi(X) \stackrel{\text{def}}{=} P(X|e_X^+) = \sum_{U_1 \ldots U_n} P(X|U_1, \ldots, U_n) \prod_{i \in \mathrm{pa}(X)} P(U_i|e_{U_i X}^+) \qquad (35)$$

Finally, the messages from parents to children (e.g. X to Y_j) and the messages from children to parents (e.g. X to U_i) can be computed as follows:

$$\pi_{Y_j}(X) \stackrel{\text{def}}{=} P(X|e_{XY_j}^+)$$
$$\propto \left[\prod_{k \neq j} P(e_{XY_k}^-|X) \right] \sum_{U_1, \ldots, U_n} P(X|U_1 \ldots U_n) \prod_i P(U_i|e_{U_i X}^+) \qquad (36)$$

$$\lambda_X(U_i) \stackrel{\text{def}}{=} P(e_{U_i X}^-|U_i)$$
$$= \sum_X P(e_X^-|X) \sum_{U_k: k \neq i} P(X|U_1 \ldots U_n) \prod_{k \neq i} P(U_k|e_{U_k X}^+) \qquad (37)$$

It is important to notice that in the computation of both the top-down message (36) and the bottom-up message (37) the recipient of the message is explicitly excluded. Pearl's [36] mnemonic of calling these messages λ and π messages is meant to reflect their role in computing "likelihood" and "prior" terms.

---

[4] There is considerably variety in the field regarding the naming of algorithms. Belief propagation is also known as the sum-product algorithm, a name which some people prefer since beliefs seem subjective.

BP includes as special cases two important algorithms: Kalman smoothing for linear-Gaussian state-space models, and the forward–backward algorithm for hidden Markov models. Although BP is only valid on singly connected graphs there is a large body of research on its application to multiply connected graphs— the use of BP on such graphs is called *loopy belief propagation* and has been analyzed by several researchers [39, 40]. Interest in loopy belief propagation arose out of its impressive performance in decoding error correcting codes [41, 42, 43, 44]. Although the beliefs are not guaranteed to be correct on loopy graphs, interesting connections can be made to approximate inference procedures inspired by statistical physics known as the Bethe and Kikuchi free energies [45].

8.3   Factor Graph Propagation

In belief propagation, there is an asymmetry between the messages a child sends its parents and the messages a parent sends its children. Propagation in singly-connected factor graphs is conceptually much simpler and easier to implement. In a factor graph, the joint probability distribution is written as a product of factors. Consider a vector of variables $\mathbf{x} = (x_1, \ldots, x_n)$

$$p(\mathbf{x}) = p(x_1, \ldots, x_n) = \frac{1}{Z} \prod_j f_j(\mathbf{x}_{S_j}) \qquad (38)$$

where Z is the normalisation constant, S_j denotes the subset of $\{1, \ldots, n\}$ which participate in factor f_j and $\mathbf{x}_{S_j} = \{x_i : i \in S_j\}$.

Let $\mathrm{n}(x)$ denote the set of factor nodes that are neighbours of x and let $\mathrm{n}(f)$ denote the set of variable nodes that are neighbours of f. We can compute probabilities in a factor graph by propagating messages from variable nodes to factor nodes and vice-versa. The message from variable x to function f is:

$$\mu_{x \to f}(x) = \prod_{h \in \mathrm{n}(x) \backslash \{f\}} \mu_{h \to x}(x) \qquad (39)$$

while the message from function f to variable x is:

$$\mu_{f \to x}(x) = \sum_{\mathbf{x} \backslash x} \left(f(\mathbf{x}) \prod_{y \in \mathrm{n}(f) \backslash \{x\}} \mu_{y \to f}(y) \right) \qquad (40)$$

Once a variable has received all messages from its neighbouring factor nodes we can compute the probability of that variable by multiplying all the messages and renormalising:

$$p(x) \propto \prod_{h \in \mathrm{n}(x)} \mu_{h \to x}(x) \qquad (41)$$

Again, these equations can be derived by using Bayes rule and the conditional independence relations in a singly-connected factor graph. For multiply-connected factor graphs (where there is more than one path between at least one pair of variable nodes) one can apply a loopy version of factor graph propagation. Since the algorithms for directed graphs and factor graphs are essentially based on the same ideas, we also call the loopy version of factor graph propagation "loopy belief propagation".

8.4   Junction Tree Algorithm

For multiply-connected graphs, the standard exact inference algorithms are based on the notion of a *junction tree* [46]. The basic idea of the junction tree algorithm is to group variables so as to convert the multiply-connected graph into a singly-connected undirected graph (tree) over sets of variables, and do inference in this tree.

We will not explain the algorithm in detail here, but rather give an overview of the steps involved. Starting from a directed graph, undirected edges are introduced between every pair of variables that share a child. This step is called "moralisation" in a tongue-in-cheek reference to the fact that it involves marrying the unmarried parents of every node. All the remaining edges are then changed from directed to undirected. We now have an undirected graph which does not imply any additional conditional or marginal independence relations which were not present in the original directed graph (although the undirected graph may easily have many fewer conditional or marginal independence relations than the directed graph). The next step of the algorithm is "triangulation" which introduces an edge cutting across every cycle of length 4. For example, the cycle $A - B - C - D - A$ which would look like Figure 2 would be triangulated either by adding an edge $A - C$ or an edge $B - D$. Once the graph has been triangulated, the maximal cliques of the graph are organised into a tree, where the nodes of the tree are cliques, by placing edges in the tree between some of the cliques with an overlap in variables (placing edges between all overlaps may not result in a tree). In general it may be possible to build several trees in this way, and triangulating the graph means than there exists a tree with the "running intersection property". This property ensures that none of the variable is represented in disjoint parts of the tree, as this would cause the algorithm to come up with multiple possibly inconsistent beliefs about the variable. Finally, once the tree with the running intersection property is built (the junction tree) it is possible to introduce the evidence into the tree and apply what is essentially a variant of belief propagation to this junction tree. This BP algorithm is operating on sets of variables contained in the cliques of the junction tree, rather than on individual variables in the original graph. As such, the complexity of the algorithm scales exponentially with the size of the largest clique in the junction tree. For example, if moralisation and triangulation results in a clique containing K binary variables, the junction tree algorithm would have to store and manipulate tables of size 2^K. Moreover, finding the optimal triangulation to get the most efficient junction tree for a particular graph is NP-complete [47, 48].

8.5   Cutest Conditioning

In certain graphs the simplest inference algorithm is *cutset conditioning* which is related to the idea of "reasoning by assumptions". The basic idea is very straightforward: find some small set of variables such that if they were given (i.e. you knew their values) it would make the remainder of the graph singly connected. For example, in the undirected graph in Figure 1, given C or D, the rest of the graph is singly connected. This set of variables is called the *cutset*. For each possible value of the variables in the cutset, run BP on the remainder of the graph to obtain the beliefs on the node of interest. These beliefs can be averaged with appropriate weights to obtain the true belief on the variable of interest. To make this more concrete, assume you want to find $P(X|e)$ and you discover a cutset consisting of a single variable C. Then

$$P(X|e) = \sum_c P(X|C = c, e)P(C = c\,|e) \qquad (42)$$

where the beliefs $P(X|C = c, e)$ and corresponding weights $P(C = c\,|e)$ are computed as part of BP, run once for each value of c.

9   Learning in Graphical Models

In Section 8 we described exact algorithms for inferring the value of variables in a graph with known parameters and structure. If the parameters and structure are unknown they can be learned from the data [49]. The learning problem can be divided into learning the graph parameters for a known structure, and learning the model structure (i.e. which edges should be present or absent).[5]

We focus here on directed graphs with discrete variables, although some of these issues become much more subtle for undirected and factor graphs [50]. The parameters of a directed graph with discrete variables parameterise the conditional probability tables $P(X_i|X_{\text{pa}_i})$. For each setting of X_{pa_i} this table contains a probability distribution over X_i. For example, if all variables are binary and X_i has K parents, then this *conditional probability table* has 2^{K+1} entries; however, since the probability over X_i has to sum to 1 for each setting of its parents there are only 2^K independent entries. The most general parameterisation would have a distinct parameter for each entry in this table, but this is often not a natural way to parameterise the dependency between variables. Alternatives (for binary data) are the noisy-or or sigmoid parameterisation of the dependencies [51]. Whatever the specific parameterisation, let $\boldsymbol{\theta}_i$ denote the parameters relating

---

[5] It should be noted that in Bayesian statistics there is no fundamental difference between parameters and variables, and therefore the learning and inference problems are really the same. All unknown quantities are treated as random variables, and learning is just inference about parameters and structure. It is however often useful to distinguish between parameters, which we assume to be fairly constant over the data, and variables, which we can assume to vary over each data point.

X_i to its parents, and let $\boldsymbol{\theta}$ denote all the parameters in the model. Let m denote the model structure, which corresponds to the set of edges in the graph. More generally the model structure can also contain the presence of additional hidden variables [52].

9.1   Learning Graph Parameters

We first consider the problem of learning graph parameters when the model structure is known and there are no missing or hidden variables. The presence of missing/hidden variables complicates the situation.

The Complete Data Case. Assume that the parameters controlling each *family* (a child and its parents) are distinct and that we observe N iid instances of all K variables in our graph. The data set is therefore $\mathcal{D} = \{X^{(1)} \dots X^{(N)}\}$ and the likelihood can be written

$$P(\mathcal{D}|\boldsymbol{\theta}) = \prod_{n=1}^{N} P(X^{(n)}|\boldsymbol{\theta}) = \prod_{n=1}^{N} \prod_{i=1}^{K} P(X_i^{(n)}|X_{\mathrm{pa}_i}^{(n)}, \boldsymbol{\theta}_i) \qquad (43)$$

Clearly, maximising the log likelihood with respect to the parameters results in K decoupled optimisation problems, one for each family, since the log likelihood can be written as a sum of K independent terms. Similarly, if the prior factors over the $\boldsymbol{\theta}_i$, then the Bayesian posterior is also factored: $P(\boldsymbol{\theta}|\mathcal{D}) = \prod_i P(\boldsymbol{\theta}_i|\mathcal{D})$.

The Incomplete Data Case. When there is missing/hidden data, the likelihood no longer factors over the variables. Divide the variables in $X^{(n)}$ into observed and missing components, $X_{\mathrm{obs}}^{(n)}$ and $X_{\mathrm{mis}}^{(n)}$. The observed data is now $\mathcal{D} = \{X_{\mathrm{obs}}^{(1)} \dots X_{\mathrm{obs}}^{(N)}\}$ and the likelihood is:

$$P(\mathcal{D}|\boldsymbol{\theta}) = \prod_{n=1}^{N} P(X_{\mathrm{obs}}^{(n)}|\boldsymbol{\theta}) \qquad (44)$$

$$= \prod_{n=1}^{N} \sum_{x_{\mathrm{mis}}^{(n)}} P(X_{\mathrm{mis}}^{(n)} = x_{\mathrm{mis}}^{(n)}, X_{\mathrm{obs}}^{(n)}|\boldsymbol{\theta}) \qquad (45)$$

$$= \prod_{n=1}^{N} \sum_{x_{\mathrm{mis}}^{(n)}} \prod_{i=1}^{K} P(X_i^{(n)}|X_{\mathrm{pa}_i}^{(n)}, \boldsymbol{\theta}_i) \qquad (46)$$

where in the last expression the missing variables are assumed to be set to the values $x_{\mathrm{mis}}^{(n)}$. Because of the missing data, the cost function can no longer be written as a sum of K independent terms and the parameters are all coupled. Similarly, even if the prior factors over the $\boldsymbol{\theta}_i$, the Bayesian posterior will couple all the $\boldsymbol{\theta}_i$.

One can still optimise the likelihood by making use of the EM algorithm (Section 3). The E step of EM infers the distribution over the hidden variables given

the current setting of the parameters. This can be done with BP for singly connected graphs or with the junction tree algorithm for multiply-connected graphs.
In the M step, the objective function being optimised conveniently factors in exactly the same way as in the complete data case (c.f. Equation (21)). Whereas
for the complete data case, the optimal ML parameters can often be computed
in closed form, in the incomplete data case an iterative algorithm such as EM is
usually required.

Bayesian parameter inference in the incomplete data case is also substantially
more complicated. The parameters and missing data are coupled in the posterior
distribution, as can be seen by multiplying (45) by the parameter prior and
normalising. Inference can be achieved via approximate inference methods such
as Markov chain Monte Carlo methods (Section 11.3, [53]) like Gibbs sampling,
and variational approximations (Section 11.4, [54]).

9.2   Learning Graph Structure

There are two basic components to learning the structure of a graph from data:
scoring and search. *Scoring* refers to computing a measure which can be used
to compare different structures m and m' given a data set $\mathcal{D}$. *Search* refers
to searching over the space of possible model structures, usually by proposing
changes to the current model, so as to find the model with the highest score. This
view of structure learning presupposes that the goal is to find a single structure
with the highest score, although of course in the Bayesian inference framework
it is desirable to infer the probability distribution over model structures given
the data.

Scoring Metrics. Assume that you have a prior $P(m)$ over model structures,
which is ideally based on some domain knowledge. The natural score to use is the
probability of the model given the data (although see [55]) or some monotonic
function of this:

$$s(m, \mathcal{D}) = P(m|\mathcal{D}) \propto P(\mathcal{D}|m)P(m). \tag{47}$$

This score requires computing the *marginal likelihood*

$$P(\mathcal{D}|m) = \int P(\mathcal{D}|\boldsymbol{\theta}, m)P(\boldsymbol{\theta}|m)d\boldsymbol{\theta}. \tag{48}$$

We discuss the intuitions behind the marginal likelihood as a natural score
for model comparison in Section 10.

For directed graphical models with fully-observed discrete variables and factored Dirichlet priors over the parameters of the conditional probability tables,
the integral in (48) is analytically tractable. For models with missing/hidden
data, alternative choices of priors and types of variables, the integral in (48) is
often intractable and approximation methods are required. Some of the standard
approximations that can be applied in this context and many other Bayesian inference problems are briefly reviewed in Section 11.

Search Algorithms. Given a way of scoring models, one can search over the space of all possible valid graphical models for the one with the highest score [56]. The space of all possible graphs is very large (exponential in the number of variables) and for directed graphs it can be expensive to check whether a particular change to the graph will result in a cycle being formed. Thus intelligent heuristics are needed to search the space efficiently [57]. An alternative to trying to find the most probable graph are methods that sample over the posterior distribution of graphs [58]. This has the advantage that it avoids the problem of overfitting which can occur for algorithms that select a single structure with highest score out of exponentially many.

10 Bayesian Model Comparison and Occam's Razor

So far in this chapter we have seen many different kinds of models. One of the most important problems in unsupervised learning is automatically determining which models are appropriate for a given data set. Model selection and comparison questions include all of the following:

- Are there clusters in the data and if so, how many? What are their shapes (e.g. Gaussian, t-distributed)?
- Does the data live on a low dimensional manifold? What dimensionality? Is this manifold flat or curved?
- Is the data discretised? If so, to what precision?
- Is the data a time series? If so, is it better modelled by an HMM, a state-space model? Linear or nonlinear? Gaussian or non-Gaussian noise? How many states should the HMM have? How many state variables should the SSM have?
- Can the data be modelled well by a directed graph? What is the structure of this graph? Does it have hidden variables? Are these continuous or discrete?

Clearly, this list could go on. A human may be able to answer these questions via careful use of visualisation, hypothesis testing, and guesswork. But ultimately, an intelligent unsupervised learning system should be able to answer all these questions automatically.

Fortunately, the framework of Bayesian inference can be used to provide a rational, coherent and automatic way of answering all of the above questions. This means that, *given a complete specification of the prior assumptions* there is an automatic procedure (based on Bayes rule) which provides a unique answer. Of course, as always, if the prior assumptions are very poor, the answers obtained could be useless. Therefore, it is essential to think carefully about the prior assumptions before turning the automatic Bayesian handle.

Let us go over this automatic procedure. Consider a model m_i coming from a set of possible models $\{m_1, m_2, m_3, \ldots\}$. For instance, the model m_i might correspond to a Gaussian mixture model with i components. The models need not be nested, nor does the space of models need to be discrete (although we'll focus on that case). Given data $\mathcal{D}$, the natural way to compare models is via their probability:

$$P(m_i|\mathcal{D}) = \frac{P(\mathcal{D}|m_i)P(m_i)}{P(\mathcal{D})} \qquad (49)$$

To compare models, the denominator, which sums over the potentially huge space of all possible models, $P(\mathcal{D}) = \sum_j P(\mathcal{D}|m_j)P(m_j)$ is not required. Prior preference for models can be included in $P(m_i)$. However, it is interesting to look closely at the *marginal likelihood* term (sometimes called the *evidence* for model m_i). Assume that model m_i has parameters $\boldsymbol{\theta}_i$ (e.g. the means and covariance matrices of the i Gaussians, along with the mixing proportions, c.f. Section 2.4). The marginal likelihood integrates over all possible parameter values

$$P(\mathcal{D}|m_i) = \int P(\mathcal{D}|\boldsymbol{\theta}_i, m_i)P(\boldsymbol{\theta}|m_i) \, d\boldsymbol{\theta}_i \qquad (50)$$

where $P(\boldsymbol{\theta}|m_i)$ is the prior over parameters, which is required for a complete specification of the model m_i.

The marginal likelihood has a very interesting interpretation. It is the probability of generating data set $\mathcal{D}$ from parameters that are *randomly sampled* from under the prior for m_i. This should be contrasted with the maximum likelihood for m_i which is the probability of the data under the single setting of the parameters $\hat{\boldsymbol{\theta}}_i$ that maximises $P(\mathcal{D}|\boldsymbol{\theta}_i, m_i)$. Clearly a more complicated model will have a higher maximum likelihood, which is the reason why maximising the likelihood results in *overfitting* — i.e. a preference for more complicated models than necessary. In contrast, the marginal likelihood can decrease as the model becomes more complicated. In a more complicated model sampling random parameter values can generate a wider range of possible data sets, but since the probability over data sets has to integrate to 1 (assuming a fixed number of data points) spreading the density to allow for more complicated data sets necessarily results in some simpler data sets having lower density under the model. This situation is diagrammed in Figure 4. The decrease in the marginal likelihood as additional parameters are added has been called the *automatic Occam's Razor* [59, 60, 61].

In theory all the questions posed at the beginning of this section could be addressed by defining appropriate priors and carefully computing marginal likelihoods of competing hypotheses. However, in practice the integral in (50) is usually very high dimensional and intractable. It is therefore necessary to approximate it.

11   Approximating Posteriors and Marginal Likelihoods

There are many ways of approximating the marginal likelihood of a model, and the corresponding parameter posterior. In this section, we review some of the most frequently used methods.

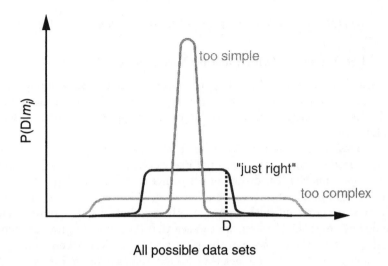

All possible data sets

Fig. 4. The marginal likelihood (evidence) as a function of an abstract one dimensional representation of "all possible" data sets of some size N. Because the evidence is a probability over data sets, it must normalise to one. Therefore very complex models which can account for many datasets only achieve modest evidence; simple models can reach high evidences, but only for a limited set of data. When a dataset $\mathcal{D}$ is observed, the evidence can be used to select between model complexities

11.1   Laplace Approximation

It can be shown that under some regularity conditions, for large amounts of data N relative to the number of parameters in the model, d, the parameter posterior is approximately Gaussian around the MAP estimate, $\hat{\theta}$:

$$p(\boldsymbol{\theta}|\mathcal{D},m) \approx (2\pi)^{-\frac{d}{2}}|A|^{\frac{1}{2}} \exp\left\{-\frac{1}{2}(\boldsymbol{\theta}-\hat{\boldsymbol{\theta}})^{\top}A\,(\boldsymbol{\theta}-\hat{\boldsymbol{\theta}})\right\} \qquad (51)$$

Here A is the $d \times d$ negative of the Hessian matrix which measures the curvature of the log posterior at the MAP estimate:

$$A_{ij} = -\left.\frac{d^2}{d\theta_i d\theta_j}\log p(\boldsymbol{\theta}|\mathcal{D},m)\right|_{\boldsymbol{\theta}=\hat{\boldsymbol{\theta}}} \qquad (52)$$

The matrix A is also referred to as the *observed information matrix*. Equation (51) is the *Laplace approximation* to the parameter posterior.

By Bayes rule, the marginal likelihood satisfies the following equality at any $\boldsymbol{\theta}$:

$$p(\mathcal{D}|m) = \frac{p(\boldsymbol{\theta},\mathcal{D}|m)}{p(\boldsymbol{\theta}|\mathcal{D},m)} \qquad (53)$$

The Laplace approximation to the marginal likelihood can be derived by evaluating the log of this expression at $\hat{\boldsymbol{\theta}}$, using the Gaussian approximation to the posterior from equation (51) in the denominator:

$$\log p(\mathcal{D}|m) \approx \log p(\hat{\boldsymbol{\theta}}|m) + \log p(\mathcal{D}|\hat{\boldsymbol{\theta}}, m) + \frac{d}{2} \log 2\pi - \frac{1}{2} \log |A| \qquad (54)$$

11.2   The Bayesian Information Criterion (BIC)

One of the disadvantages of the Laplace approximation is that it requires computing the determinant of the Hessian matrix. For models with many parameters, the Hessian matrix can be very large, and computing its determinant can be prohibitive.

The Bayesian Information Criterion (BIC) is a quick and easy way to compute an approximation to the marginal likelihood. BIC can be derived from the Laplace approximation by dropping all terms that do not depend on N, the number of data points. Starting from equation (54), we note that the first and third terms are constant with respect to the number of data points. Referring to the definition of the Hessian, we can see that its elements grow linearly with N. In the limit of large N we can therefore write $A = N\tilde{A}$, where $\tilde{A}$ is a matrix independent of N. We use the fact that for any scalar c and $d \times d$ matrix P, the determinant $|cP| = c^d|P|$, to get

$$\frac{1}{2} \log |A| \approx \frac{d}{2} \log N + \frac{1}{2} \log |\tilde{A}| \qquad (55)$$

The last term does not grow with N, so by dropping it and substituting into Eq. (54) we get the BIC approximation:

$$\log p(\mathcal{D}|m) \approx \log p(\mathcal{D}|\hat{\boldsymbol{\theta}}, m) - \frac{d}{2} \log N \qquad (56)$$

This expression is extremely easy to compute. Since the expression does not involve the prior it can be used either when $\hat{\boldsymbol{\theta}}$ is the MAP or the ML parameter estimate, the latter choice making the entire procedure independent of a prior. The likelihood is penalised by a term that depends linearly on the number of parameters in the model; this term is referred to as the *BIC penalty*. This is how BIC approximates the Bayesian Occam's Razor effect which penalises overcomplex models. The BIC criterion can also be derived from within the *Minimum Description Length* (MDL) framework.

The BIC penalty is clearly attractive since it does not require any costly integrals or matrix inversions. However this simplicity comes at a cost in accuracy which can sometimes be catastrophic. One of the dangers of BIC is that it relies on the number of parameters. The basic assumption underlying BIC, that the Hessian converges to N times a full-rank matrix, only holds for models in which all parameters are identifiable and well-determined. This is often not true.

11.3   Markov Chain Monte Carlo (MCMC)

Monte Carlo methods are a standard and often extremely effective way of computing complicated high dimensional integrals and sums. Many Bayesian inference problems can be seen as computing the integral (or sum) of some function $f(\boldsymbol{\theta})$ under some probability density $p(\boldsymbol{\theta})$:

$$\bar{f} \stackrel{\text{def}}{=} \int f(\boldsymbol{\theta}) p(\boldsymbol{\theta}) \, d\boldsymbol{\theta}. \tag{57}$$

For example, the marginal likelihood is the integral of the likelihood function under the prior. Simple Monte Carlo approximates (57) by sampling M independent draws $\boldsymbol{\theta}_i \sim p(\boldsymbol{\theta})$ and computing the sample average of f:

$$\bar{f} \approx \frac{1}{M} \sum_{i=1}^{M} f(\boldsymbol{\theta}_i) \tag{58}$$

There are many limitations of simple Monte Carlo, for example it is often not possible to draw directly from p. Generalisations of simple Monte Carlo such as rejection sampling and importance sampling attempt to overcome some of these limitations.

An important family of generalisations of Monte Carlo methods are Markov chain Monte Carlo (MCMC) methods. These are commonly used and powerful methods for approximating the posterior over parameters and the marginal likelihood. Unlike simple Monte Carlo methods, the samples are not drawn independently but rather *dependently* in the form of a Markov chain ... $\boldsymbol{\theta}_i \to \boldsymbol{\theta}_{i+1} \to \boldsymbol{\theta}_{t+2} \ldots$ where each sample depends on the value of the previous sample. MCMC estimates have the property that the asymptotic distribution of $\boldsymbol{\theta}_i$ is the desired distribution. That is, $\lim_{t \to \infty} p_t(\boldsymbol{\theta}_t) = p(\boldsymbol{\theta})$. Creating MCMC methods is somewhat of an art, and there are many MCMC methods available, some of which are reviewed in [53]. Some notable examples are Gibbs sampling, the Metropolis algorithm, and Hybrid Monte Carlo.

11.4   Variational Approximations

Variational methods can be used to derive a family of lower bounds on the marginal likelihood and to perform approximate Bayesian inference over the parameters of a probabilistic models [62, 63, 64]. Variational methods provide an alternative to the asymptotic and sampling-based approximations described above; they tend to be more accurate than the asymptotic approximations like BIC and faster than the MCMC approaches.

Let $\mathbf{y}$ denote the observed variables, $\mathbf{x}$ denote the latent variables, and $\boldsymbol{\theta}$ denote the parameters. The log marginal likelihood of data $\mathbf{y}$ can be lower bounded by introducing any distribution over both latent variables and parameters which has support where $p(\mathbf{x}, \boldsymbol{\theta} | \mathbf{y}, m)$ does, and then appealing to Jensen's inequality (due to the concavity of the logarithm function):

$$\ln p(\mathbf{y}|m) = \ln \int p(\mathbf{y}, \mathbf{x}, \boldsymbol{\theta}|m) \, d\mathbf{x} \, d\boldsymbol{\theta} = \ln \int q(\mathbf{x}, \boldsymbol{\theta}) \frac{p(\mathbf{y}, \mathbf{x}, \boldsymbol{\theta}|m)}{q(\mathbf{x}, \boldsymbol{\theta})} \, d\mathbf{x} \, d\boldsymbol{\theta} \tag{59}$$

$$\geq \int q(\mathbf{x}, \boldsymbol{\theta}) \ln \frac{p(\mathbf{y}, \mathbf{x}, \boldsymbol{\theta}|m)}{q(\mathbf{x}, \boldsymbol{\theta})} \, d\mathbf{x} \, d\boldsymbol{\theta}. \tag{60}$$

Maximising this lower bound with respect to the free distribution $q(\mathbf{x}, \boldsymbol{\theta})$ results in $q(\mathbf{x}, \boldsymbol{\theta}) = p(\mathbf{x}, \boldsymbol{\theta} | \mathbf{y}, m)$ which when substituted above turns the inequality into an equality (c.f. Section 3). This does not simplify the problem since evaluating the true posterior distribution $p(\mathbf{x}, \boldsymbol{\theta}|\mathbf{y}, m)$ requires knowing its normalising constant, the marginal likelihood. Instead we use a simpler, factorised approximation $q(\mathbf{x}, \boldsymbol{\theta}) = q_{\mathbf{x}}(\mathbf{x}) q_{\boldsymbol{\theta}}(\boldsymbol{\theta})$:

$$\ln p(\mathbf{y}|m) \geq \int q_{\mathbf{x}}(\mathbf{x}) q_{\boldsymbol{\theta}}(\boldsymbol{\theta}) \ln \frac{p(\mathbf{y}, \mathbf{x}, \boldsymbol{\theta}|m)}{q_{\mathbf{x}}(\mathbf{x}) q_{\boldsymbol{\theta}}(\boldsymbol{\theta})} \, d\mathbf{x} \, d\boldsymbol{\theta} \stackrel{\text{def}}{=} F_m(q_{\mathbf{x}}(\mathbf{x}), q_{\boldsymbol{\theta}}(\boldsymbol{\theta}), \mathbf{y}). \quad (61)$$

The quantity F_m is a functional of the free distributions, $q_{\mathbf{x}}(\mathbf{x})$ and $q_{\boldsymbol{\theta}}(\boldsymbol{\theta})$.

The variational Bayesian algorithm iteratively maximises F_m in equation (61) with respect to the free distributions, $q_{\mathbf{x}}(\mathbf{x})$ and $q_{\boldsymbol{\theta}}(\boldsymbol{\theta})$. We use elementary calculus of variations to take functional derivatives of the lower bound with respect to $q_{\mathbf{x}}(\mathbf{x})$ and $q_{\boldsymbol{\theta}}(\boldsymbol{\theta})$, each while holding the other fixed. This results in the following update equations where the superscript (t) denotes the iteration number:

$$q_{\mathbf{x}}^{(t+1)}(\mathbf{x}) \propto \exp \left[\int \ln p(\mathbf{x}, \mathbf{y}|\boldsymbol{\theta}, m) \, q_{\boldsymbol{\theta}}^{(t)}(\boldsymbol{\theta}) \, d\boldsymbol{\theta} \right] \quad (62)$$

$$q_{\boldsymbol{\theta}}^{(t+1)}(\boldsymbol{\theta}) \propto p(\boldsymbol{\theta}|m) \, \exp \left[\int \ln p(\mathbf{x}, \mathbf{y}|\boldsymbol{\theta}, m) \, q_{\mathbf{x}}^{(t+1)}(\mathbf{x}) \, d\mathbf{x} \right] \quad (63)$$

When there is more than one data point then there are different hidden variables $\mathbf{x}_i$ associated with each data point $\mathbf{y}_i$ and the step in (62) has to be carried out for each i, where the distributions are $q_{\mathbf{x}_i}^{(t)}(\mathbf{x}_i)$.

Clearly $q_{\boldsymbol{\theta}}(\boldsymbol{\theta})$ and $q_{\mathbf{x}_i}(\mathbf{x}_i)$ are coupled, so we iterate these equations until convergence. Recalling the EM algorithm (Section 3 and [65, 66]) we note the similarity between EM and the iterative algorithm in (62) and (63). This procedure is called the *Variational Bayesian EM Algorithm* and generalises the usual EM algorithm; see also [67] and [68].

Re-writing (61), it is easy to see that maximising F_m is equivalent to minimising the KL divergence between $q_{\mathbf{x}}(\mathbf{x}) \, q_{\boldsymbol{\theta}}(\boldsymbol{\theta})$ and the joint posterior $p(\mathbf{x}, \boldsymbol{\theta}|\mathbf{y}, m)$:

$$\ln p(\mathbf{y}|m) - F_m(q_{\mathbf{x}}(\mathbf{x}), q_{\boldsymbol{\theta}}(\boldsymbol{\theta}), \mathbf{y}) = \int q_{\mathbf{x}}(\mathbf{x}) \, q_{\boldsymbol{\theta}}(\boldsymbol{\theta}) \ln \frac{q_{\mathbf{x}}(\mathbf{x}) \, q_{\boldsymbol{\theta}}(\boldsymbol{\theta})}{p(\boldsymbol{\theta}, \mathbf{x}|\mathbf{y}, m)} \, d\mathbf{x} \, d\boldsymbol{\theta} = \mathrm{KL}(q\|p) \quad (64)$$

Note that while this factorisation of the posterior distribution over latent variables and parameters may seem drastic, one can think of it as replacing stochastic dependencies between $\mathbf{x}$ and $\boldsymbol{\theta}$ with deterministic dependencies between relevant moments of the two sets of variables. To compare between models m and m' one can evaluate F_m and $F_{m'}$. This approach can, for example, be used to score graphical model structures [54].

Summarising, the variational Bayesian EM algorithm simultaneously computes an approximation to the marginal likelihood and to the parameter posterior by maximising a lower bound.

11.5   Expectation Propagation (EP)

Expectation propagation (EP; [23, 69]) is another powerful method for approximate Bayesian inference. Consider a Bayesian inference problem in which you are given iid data $\mathcal{D} = \{\mathbf{x}^{(1)} \ldots, \mathbf{x}^{(N)}\}$ assumed to have come from a model $p(\mathbf{x}|\boldsymbol{\theta})$ parameterised by $\boldsymbol{\theta}$ with prior $p(\boldsymbol{\theta})$. The parameter posterior is:

$$p(\boldsymbol{\theta}|\mathcal{D}) = \frac{1}{p(\mathcal{D})} p(\boldsymbol{\theta}) \prod_{i=1}^{N} p(\mathbf{x}^{(i)}|\boldsymbol{\theta}). \tag{65}$$

To make the notation more general we can write the quantity we wish to approximate as a product of factors over $\boldsymbol{\theta}$,

$$\prod_{i=0}^{N} f_i(\boldsymbol{\theta}) = p(\boldsymbol{\theta}) \prod_{i=1}^{N} p(\mathbf{x}^{(i)}|\boldsymbol{\theta}) \tag{66}$$

where $f_0(\boldsymbol{\theta}) \stackrel{\text{def}}{=} p(\boldsymbol{\theta})$ and $f_i(\boldsymbol{\theta}) \stackrel{\text{def}}{=} p(\mathbf{x}^{(i)}|\boldsymbol{\theta})$ and we will ignore the normalising constants. We wish to approximate this by a product of *simpler* terms

$$q(\boldsymbol{\theta}) \stackrel{\text{def}}{=} \prod_{i=0}^{N} \tilde{f}_i(\boldsymbol{\theta}). \tag{67}$$

For example, consider a binary linear classification problem where $\boldsymbol{\theta}$ are the parameters of the classification hyperplane and $p(\boldsymbol{\theta})$ is a Gaussian prior ([69], Chapter 5). The true posterior is the product of this Gaussian and N likelihood terms, each of which defines a half-plane consistent with the class label observed. This posterior has a complicated shape, but we can approximate it using EP by assuming that each of the approximate likelihood terms $\tilde{f}_i$ is Gaussian in $\boldsymbol{\theta}$. Since the product of Gaussians is Gaussian, $q(\boldsymbol{\theta})$ will be a Gaussian approximation to the posterior. In general, one makes the approximate terms $\tilde{f}_i$ belong to some exponential family distribution so the overall approximation is in the same exponential family.

Having decided on the form of the approximation (67), let us consider how to tune this approximation so as to make it as accurate as possible. Ideally we would like to minimise the KL divergence between the true and the approximate distributions:

$$\min_{q(\boldsymbol{\theta})} \text{KL} \left(\prod_{i=0}^{N} f_i(\boldsymbol{\theta}) \middle\| \prod_{i=0}^{N} \tilde{f}_i(\boldsymbol{\theta}) \right). \tag{68}$$

For example, if $q(\boldsymbol{\theta})$ is a Gaussian density, minimising this KL divergence will result in finding the *exact* mean and covariance of the true posterior distribution over parameters. Unfortunately, this KL divergence involves averaging with respect to the true posterior distribution, which will generally be intractable. Note that the KL divergence in Equation (68) is different from the KL minimised by variational Bayesian methods (64); the former averages with respect to the true distribution and is therefore usually intractable, while the latter averages with respect to the approximate distribution and is often tractable. Moreover, for exponential family approximations the former KL has a unique global optimum, while the latter usually has multiple local optima.

Since we cannot minimise (68) we can instead consider minimising the KL divergence between each true term and the corresponding approximate term. That is, for each i:

$$\min_{\tilde{f}_i(\boldsymbol{\theta})} \mathrm{KL}\left(f_i(\boldsymbol{\theta}) \| \tilde{f}_i(\boldsymbol{\theta})\right). \tag{69}$$

This will usually be much easier to do, but each such approximate term will result in some error. Multiplying all the approximate terms together will probably result in an unacceptably inaccurate approximation. On the plus side, this approach is non-iterative in that once each term is approximated they are simply multiplied to get a final answer.

The Expectation Propagation (EP) algorithm is an iterative procedure which is as easy as the naive approach in (69) but which results in a much more accurate approximation. At each step of EP, one of the terms is optimised in the context of all the other approximate terms, i.e. for each i:

$$\min_{\tilde{f}_i(\boldsymbol{\theta})} \mathrm{KL}\left(f_i(\boldsymbol{\theta}) \prod_{j \neq i} \tilde{f}_j(\boldsymbol{\theta}) \,\middle\|\, \tilde{f}_i(\boldsymbol{\theta}) \prod_{j \neq i} \tilde{f}_j(\boldsymbol{\theta})\right). \tag{70}$$

Since the approximate terms depend on each other, this procedure is iterated. On the left hand side of the KL divergence the ith exact term is incorporated into $\prod_{j \neq i} \tilde{f}_j(\boldsymbol{\theta})$, which is assumed to be in the exponential family. The right hand side is an exponential-family approximation to this whole product. The minimisation is done by matching the appropriate moments (expectations) of $f_i(\boldsymbol{\theta}) \prod_{j \neq i} \tilde{f}_j(\boldsymbol{\theta})$. The name "Expectation Propagation" comes from the fact that each step corresponds to computing certain expectations, and the effect of these expectations is propagated to subsequent terms in the approximation. In fact, the messages in belief propagation can be derived as a particular form of EP where the approximating distribution is assumed to be a fully factored product of marginals over the variables in $\boldsymbol{\theta}$, i.e. $q(\boldsymbol{\theta}) = \prod_k q_k(\theta_k)$ [69].

In its simplest form, the EP algorithm can be summarised as in Figure 5. Although the algorithm as described here often converges, each step of the algorithm is not in fact decreasing any objective function so there is no guarantee of convergence. Convergent forms of EP can be derived by making use of the EP energy function [70] although these may not be as fast and simple to implement as the algorithm in Figure 5.

12   Conclusion

In this chapter, we have seen that unsupervised learning can be viewed from the perspective of statistical modelling. Statistics provides a coherent framework for learning from data and for reasoning under uncertainty. Many interesting statistical models used for unsupervised learning can be cast as latent variable models and graphical models. These types of models have played an important role in defining unsupervised learning systems for a variety of different kinds of data.

Input $f_0(\boldsymbol{\theta})\dots f_N(\boldsymbol{\theta})$
Initialise $\tilde{f}_0(\boldsymbol{\theta}) = f_0(\boldsymbol{\theta})$, $\tilde{f}_i(\boldsymbol{\theta}) = 1$ for $i > 0$, $q(\boldsymbol{\theta}) = \prod_i \tilde{f}_i(\boldsymbol{\theta})$
repeat
   for $i = 0\dots N$ **do**
     Deletion: $q_{\backslash i}(\boldsymbol{\theta}) \leftarrow \dfrac{q(\boldsymbol{\theta})}{\tilde{f}_i(\boldsymbol{\theta})} = \prod_{j\neq i} \tilde{f}_j(\boldsymbol{\theta})$
     Projection: $\tilde{f}_i^{\text{new}}(\boldsymbol{\theta}) \leftarrow \arg\min_{f(\boldsymbol{\theta})} \text{KL}(f_i(\boldsymbol{\theta})q_{\backslash i}(\boldsymbol{\theta})\|f(\boldsymbol{\theta})q_{\backslash i}(\boldsymbol{\theta}))$
     Inclusion: $q(\boldsymbol{\theta}) \leftarrow \tilde{f}_i^{\text{new}}(\boldsymbol{\theta})\,q_{\backslash i}(\boldsymbol{\theta})$
   end for
until convergence

Fig. 5. The EP algorithm. Some variations are possible: this assumes that f_0 is in the exponential family, and updates sequentially over i rather than randomly. The names for the steps (deletion, projection, inclusion) are not the same as in [69]

Graphical models have also played an important unifying framework for thinking about the role of conditional independence in inference in models with many variables. While for certain models exact inference is computationally tractable, for most of the models in this chapter we have seen that exact inference involves intractable sums and integrals. Thus, the study of unsupervised learning has lead us into focusing on ways of approximating high dimensional sums and integrals. We have reviewed many of the principal approximations, although of course in the limited space of this chapter one cannot hope to have a comprehensive review of approximation methods.

There are many interesting and relevant topics we did not get a chance to cover in this review of unsupervised learning. One of these is the interplay of unsupervised and supervised learning, in the form of semi-supervised learning. *Semi-supervised learning* refers to learning problems in which there is a small amount of labelled data and a large amount of unlabelled data. These problems are very natural, especially in domains where collecting data can be cheap (i.e. the internet) but labelling it can be expensive or time consuming. The key question in semi-supervised learning is how the data distribution from the unlabelled data should influence the supervised learning problem [71]. Many of the approaches to this problem attempt to infer a manifold, graph structure, or tree-structure from the unlabelled data and use spread in this structure to determine how labels will generalise to new unlabelled points [72, 73, 74, 75].

Another area of great interest which we did not have the space to cover are *nonparametric models*. The basic assumption of parametric statistical models is that the model is defined using a finite number of parameters. The number of parameters is assumed fixed regardless of the number of data points. Thus the parameters provide a finite summary of the data. In nonparametric models, the number of "parameters" in the model is allowed to grow with the size of the data set. With more data, the model becomes more complex, with no a-priori limit on the complexity of the model. For this reason nonparametric models are also sometimes called *infinite models*. An important example of this are *infinite mixture models*, more formally known as *Dirichlet Process mixtures* [76, 77]. These correspond to mixture models (Section 2.4) where the number of components is assumed to be infinite. Inference can be done in these models using MCMC methods [78, 79, 80], variational methods [81], or the EP algorithm [82]. Just as hidden Markov models can be seen as an extension of finite mixture models to model time series data, it is possible to extend infinite mixture models to hidden Markov models with infinitely many states [83]. Infinite models based on Dirichlet processes have also been generalised to be hierarchical in several different ways [84, 85]. Bayesian inference in nonparametric models is one of the most active areas of research in unsupervised learning, and there still remain many open problems.

As we have seen, the field of unsupervised learning can be understood formally within the framework of information theory and statistics. However, it is important not to lose sight of the tremendous influence ideas from neuroscience and psychology have had on the field. Many of the models we have reviewed here started life as models of brain function. These models were inspired by the brain's ability to extract statistical patterns from sensory data and to recognise complex visual scenes, sounds, and odours. Unsupervised learning theory and algorithms still have a long way to go to mimic some of the learning abilities of biological brains. As the boundaries of unsupervised learning get pushed forward, we will hopefully not only benefit from better learning machines and also improve our understanding of how the brain learns.

References

1. MacKay, D.J.C.: Information Theory, Inference, and Learning Algorithms. Cambridge University Press (2003)
2. Jaynes, E.T.: Probability Theory: The Logic of Science (Edited by G. Larry Bretthorst). Cambridge University Press (2003)
3. Girosi, F., Jones, M., Poggio, T.: Regularization theory and neural networks architectures. Neural Computation 7 (1995) 219–269
4. Green, P.J.: Penalized likelihood. In: Encyclopedia of Statistical Sciences, Update Volume 2. (1998)
5. Roweis, S.T., Ghahramani, Z.: A unifying review of linear Gaussian models. Neural Computation 11 (1999) 305–345
6. Roweis, S.T.: EM algorithms for PCA and SPCA. In Jordan, M.I., Kearns, M.J., Solla, S.A., eds.: Advances in Neural Information Processing Systems. Volume 10., The MIT Press (1998)
7. Tipping, M.E., Bishop, C.M.: Probabilistic principal component analysis. Journal of the Royal Statistical Society, Series B 61 (1999) 611–622
8. Salakhutdinov, R., Roweis, S.T., Ghahramani, Z.: Optimization with EM and Expectation-Conjugate-Gradient. In: International Conference on Machine Learning (ICML-2003). (2003) 672–679
9. Shumway, R.H., Stoffer, D.S.: An approach to time series smoothing and forecasting using the EM algorithm. J. Time Series Analysis 3 (1982) 253–264

10. Ghahramani, Z., Hinton, G.E.: The EM algorithm for mixtures of factor analyzers. University of Toronto, Technical Report CRG-TR-96-1 (1996)
11. Hinton, G.E., Dayan, P., Revow, M.: Modeling the manifolds of images of handwritten digits. IEEE Trans. Neural Networks **8** (1997) 65–74
12. Tipping, M.E., Bishop, C.M.: Mixtures of probabilistic principal component analyzers. Neural Computation **11** (1999) 443–482
13. Ghahramani, Z., Roweis, S.T.: Learning nonlinear dynamical systems using an EM algorithm. In: NIPS 11. (1999) 431–437
14. Handschin, J.E., Mayne, D.Q.: Monte Carlo techniques to estimate the conditional expectation in multi-stage non-linear filtering. International Journal of Control **9** (1969) 547–559
15. Gordon, N.J., Salmond, D.J., Smith, A.F.M.: A novel approach to nonlinear/non-Gaussian Bayesian state space estimation. IEE Proceedings F: Radar and Signal Processing **140** (1993) 107–113
16. Kanazawa, K., Koller, D., Russell, S.J.: Stochastic simulation algorithms for dynamic probabilistic networks. In Besnard, P., Hanks, S., eds.: Uncertainty in Artificial Intelligence. Proceedings of the Eleventh Conference. Morgan Kaufmann Publishers, San Francisco, CA (1995) 346–351
17. Kitagawa, G.: Monte Carlo filter and smoother for non-Gaussian nonlinear state space models. J. of Computational and Graphical Statistics **5** (1996) 1–25
18. Isard, M., Blake, A.: Condensation – conditional density propagation for visual tracking (1998)
19. Doucet, A., de Freitas, J.F.G., Gordon, N.: Sequential Monte Carlo Methods in Practice. Springer-Verlag, New York (2000)
20. Anderson, B.D.O., Moore, J.B.: Optimal Filtering. Prentice-Hall, Englewood Cliffs, NJ (1979)
21. Julier, S.J., Uhlmann, J.K.: A new extension of the Kalman filter to nonlinear systems. In: Int. Symp. Aerospace/Defense Sensing, Simulation and Controls. (1997)
22. Wan, E.A., van der Merwe, R., Nelson, A.T.: Dual estimation and the unscented transformation. In: NIPS 12. (2000) 666–672
23. Minka, T.P.: Expectation propagation for approximate Bayesian inference. In: Uncertainty in Artificial Intelligence: Proceedings of the Seventeenth Conference (UAI-2001), San Francisco, CA, Morgan Kaufmann Publishers (2001) 362–369
24. Neal, R.M., Beal, M.J., Roweis, S.T.: Inferring state sequences for non-linear systems with embedded hidden Markov models. In Thrun, S., Saul, L., Schölkopf, B., eds.: Advances in Neural Information Processing Systems 16, Cambridge, MA, MIT Press (2004)
25. Bishop, C.M., Svensen, M., Williams, C.K.I.: GTM: The generative topographic mapping. Neural Computation **10** (1998) 215–234
26. Shepard, R.N.: The analysis of proximities: multidimensional scaling with an unknown distance function i and ii. Psychometrika **27** (1962) 125–139 and 219–246
27. Kruskal, J.B.: Multidimensional scaling by optimizing goodness of fit to a nonmetric hypothesis. Psychometrika **29** (1964) 1–27 and 115–129
28. Hastie, T., Stuetzle, W.: Principle curves. Journal of the American Statistical Association **84** (1989) 502–516
29. Tenenbaum, J.B., de Silva, V., Langford, J.C.: A global geometric framework for nonlinear dimensionality reduction. Science **290** (2000) 2319–2323
30. Roweis, S.T., Saul, L.K.: Nonlinear dimensionality reduction by locally linear embedding. Science **290** (2000) 2323–2326

31. Ghahramani, Z., Jordan, M.I.: Factorial hidden Markov models. Machine Learning **29** (1997) 245–273
32. Murphy, K.P.: Dynamic Bayesian Networks: Representation, Inference and Learning. PhD thesis, UC Berkeley, Computer Science Division (2002)
33. Ackley, D.H., Hinton, G.E., Sejnowski, T.J.: A learning algorithm for Boltzmann machines. Cognitive Science **9** (1985) 147–169
34. Hinton, G.E., Dayan, P., Frey, B.J., Neal, R.M.: The wake-sleep algorithm for unsupervised neural networks. Science **268** (1995) 1158–1161
35. Karklin, Y., Lewicki, M.S.: Learning higher-order structures in natural images. Network: Computation in Neural Systems **14** (2003) 483–499
36. Pearl, J.: Probabilistic Reasoning in Intelligent Systems: Networks of Plausible Inference. Morgan Kaufmann, San Mateo, CA (1988)
37. Besag, J.: Spatial interaction and the statistical analysis of lattice systems. Journal of the Royal Statistical Society. Ser. B **6** (1974) 192–236
38. Cooper, G.F.: The computational complexity of probabilistic inference using Bayesian belief networks. Artificial Intelligence **42** (1990) 393–405
39. Weiss, Y.: Correctness of local probability propagation in graphical models with loops. Neural Computation **12** (2000) 1–41
40. Weiss, Y., Freeman, W.T.: On the optimality of solutions of the max-product belief-propagation algorithm in arbitrary graphs. IEEE Transactions on Information Theory, Special Issue on Codes on Graphs and Iterative Algorithms **47** (2001)
41. Gallager, R.G.: Low-Density Parity-Check Codes. MIT Press, Cambridge, MA (1963)
42. Berrou, C., Glavieux, A., Thitimajshima, P.: Near shannon limit error-correcting coding and decoding: Turbo-codes (1). In: Proc. ICC '93. (1993) 1064–1070
43. McEliece, R.J., MacKay, D.J.C., Cheng, J.F.: Turbo decoding as an instance of Pearl's 'Belief Propagation' algorithm. IEEE Journal on Selected Areas in Communications **16** (1998) 140–152
44. MacKay, D.J.C., Neal, R.M.: Good error-correcting codes based on very sparse matrices. IEEE Transactions on Information Theory **45** (1999) 399–431
45. Yedidia, J.S., Freeman, W.T., Weiss, Y.: Generalized belief propagation. In: NIPS 13, Cambridge, MA, MIT Press (2001)
46. Lauritzen, S.L., Spiegelhalter, D.J.: Local computations with probabilities on graphical structures and their application to expert systems. J. Royal Statistical Society B (1988) 157–224
47. Arnborg, S., Corneil, D.G., Proskurowski, A.: Complexity of finding embeddings in a k-tree. SIAM Journal of Algebraic and Discrete Methods **8** (1987) 277–284
48. Kjaerulff, U.: Triangulation of graphs—algorithms giving small total state space (1990)
49. Heckerman, D.: A tutorial on learning with Bayesian networks. Technical Report MSR-TR-95-06, Microsoft Research (1996)
50. Murray, I., Ghahramani, Z.: Bayesian learning in undirected graphical models: Approximate MCMC algorithms. In: Proceedings of UAI. (2004)
51. Neal, R.M.: Connectionist learning of belief networks. Artificial Intelligence **56** (1992) 71–113
52. Elidan, G., Lotner, N., Friedman, N., Koller, D.: Discovering hidden variables: A structure-based approach. In: Advances in Neural Information Processing Systems (NIPS). (2001)
53. Neal, R.M.: Probabilistic inference using Markov chain Monte Carlo methods. Technical report, Department of Computer Science, University of Toronto (1993)

54. Beal, M.J., Ghahramani, Z.: The variational Bayesian EM algorithm for incomplete data: With application to scoring graphical model structures. In Bernardo, J.M., Dawid, A.P., Berger, J.O., West, M., Heckerman, D., Bayarri, M.J., eds.: Bayesian Statistics 7, Oxford University Press (2003)
55. Heckerman, D., Chickering, D.M.: A comparison of scientific and engineering criteria for Bayesian model selection (1996)
56. Friedman, N.: The Bayesian structural EM algorithm. In: Proc. Fourteenth Conference on Uncertainty in Artificial Intelligence (UAI '98), San Francisco, CA, Morgan Kaufmann (1998)
57. Moore, A., Wong, W.K.: Optimal reinsertion: A new search operator for accelerated and more accurate Bayesian network structure learning. In Fawcett, T., Mishra, N., eds.: Proceedings of the 20th International Conference on Machine Learning (ICML '03), Menlo Park, California, AAAI Press (2003) 552–559
58. Friedman, N., Koller, D.: Being Bayesian about network structure: A Bayesian approach to structure discovery in Bayesian networks. Machine Learning **50** (2003) 95–126
59. Jefferys, W., Berger, J.: Ockham's razor and Bayesian analysis. American Scientist **80** (1992) 64–72
60. MacKay, D.J.C.: Probable networks and plausible predictions—a review of practical Bayesian methods for supervised neural networks. Network: Computation in Neural Systems **6** (1995) 469–505
61. Rasmussen, C.E., Ghahramani, Z.: Occam's razor. In: Advances in Neural Information Processing Systems 13, Cambridge, MA, MIT Press (2001)
62. Jordan, M.I., Ghahramani, Z., Jaakkola, T.S., Saul, L.K.: An introduction to variational methods in graphical models. Machine Learning **37** (1999) 183–233
63. Winn, J.: Variational Message Passing and its Applications. PhD thesis, Department of Physics, University of Cambridge (2003)
64. Wainwright, M.J., Jordan, M.I.: Graphical models, exponential families, and variational inference. Technical Report 649, UC Berkeley, Dept. of Statistics (2003)
65. Dempster, A., Laird, N., Rubin, D.: Maximum likelihood from incomplete data via the EM algorithm. J. Royal Statistical Society Series B **39** (1977) 1–38
66. Neal, R.M., Hinton, G.E.: A new view of the EM algorithm that justifies incremental, sparse, and other variants. In Jordan, M.I., ed.: Learning in Graphical Models. Kluwer Academic Press (1998)
67. Attias, H.: Inferring parameters and structure of latent variable models by variational Bayes. In: Proc. 15th Conf. on Uncertainty in Artificial Intelligence. (1999)
68. Ghahramani, Z., Beal, M.J.: Propagation algorithms for variational Bayesian learning. In: Advances in Neural Information Processing Systems 13, Cambridge, MA, MIT Press (2001)
69. Minka, T.P.: A family of algorithms for approximate Bayesian inference. PhD thesis, MIT (2001)
70. Minka, T.P.: The EP energy function and minimization schemes. Technical report (2001)
71. Seeger, M.: Learning with labeled and unlabeled data. Technical report, University of Edinburgh (2001)
72. Szummer, M., Jaakkola, T.S.: Partially labeled classification with Markov random walks. In: NIPS. (2001)
73. Zhu, X., Ghahramani, Z., Lafferty, J.: Semi-supervised learning using Gaussian fields and harmonic functions. In: The Twentieth International Conference on Machine Learning (ICML-2003). (2003)

74. Belkin, M., Niyogi, P.: Semi-supervised learning on Riemannian manifolds. Machine Learning **56** (2004) 209–239
75. Kemp, C., Griffiths, T.L., Stromsten, S., Tenenbaum, J.B.: Semi-supervised learning with trees. In: NIPS 16. (2004)
76. Antoniak, C.E.: Mixtures of Dirichlet processes with applications to Bayesian nonparametric problems. Annals of Statistics **2** (1974) 1152–1174
77. Ferguson, T.S.: Bayesian density estimation by mixtures of normal distributions. In: Recent Advances in Statistics, New York, Academic Press (1983) 287–302
78. Escobar, M.D., West, M.: Bayesian density estimation and inference using mixtures. Journal of the American Statistical Association **90** (1995) 577–588
79. Neal, R.M.: Markov chain sampling methods for Dirichlet process mixture models. Journal of Computational and Graphical Statistics **9** (2000) 249–265
80. Rasmussen, C.E.: The infinite Gaussian mixture model. In: Adv. Neur. Inf. Proc. Sys. 12. (2000) 554–560
81. Blei, D., Jordan, M.I.: Variational methods for the Dirichlet process. In: Proceedings of the 21st International Conference on Machine Learning. (2004)
82. Minka, T.P., Ghahramani, Z.: Expectation propagation for infinite mixtures. Technical report, Presented at NIPS'03 Workshop on Nonparametric Bayesian Methods and Infinite Models (2003)
83. Beal, M., Ghahramani, Z., Rasmussen, C.: The infinite hidden Markov model. In: Advances in Neural Information Processing Systems. Volume 14., MIT Press (2001)
84. Neal, R.M.: Density modeling and clustering using Dirichlet diffusion trees. In et al., J.M.B., ed.: Bayesian Statistics 7. (2003) 619–629
85. Teh, Y.W., Jordan, M.I., Beal, M.J., Blei, D.M.: Hierarchical Dirichlet processes. Technical Report 653, Department of Statistics, University of California at Berkeley (2004)

Monte Carlo Methods for Absolute Beginners

Christophe Andrieu

School of Mathematics, University of Bristol, University Walk, Bristol, BS8 1TW, UK
c.andrieu@bristol.ac.uk
http://www.stats.bris.ac.uk/~maxca

1 Motivation and Basic Principles of the Monte Carlo Method

The modern history of Monte Carlo techniques dates back from the 1940's and the Manhattan project. There are earlier descriptions of Monte Carlo experiments, Buffon's famous needle experiment is one them, but examples have been traced back to Babylonian and old testament times [13]. As we shall see these techniques are particularly useful in scenarios where it is of interest to perform calculations that involve - explicitly or implicitly - a probability distribution π on a space X (typically $X \subset \mathbb{R}^{n_x}$ for some integer n_x), for which closed-form calculations cannot be carried out due to the algebraic complexity of the problem. As we shall see the main principle of Monte Carlo techniques consists of replacing the algebraic representation of π, e.g. $1/\sqrt{2\pi} \exp(\frac{-1}{2}x^2)$ with a *sample* or *population* representation of π, e.g. a set of samples $X_1, X_2, \ldots, X_N \overset{iid}{\sim} \pi(x) = 1/\sqrt{2\pi} \exp(\frac{-1}{2}x^2)$. This proves in practice to be extremely powerful as difficult - if not impossible - *exact* algebraic calculations are typically replaced with simple calculations in the sample domain. One should however bear in mind that these are *random approximations* of the true quantity of interest. An important scenario where Monte Carlo methods can be of great help is when one is interested in evaluating expectations of functions, say f, of the type $\mathbb{E}_\pi(f(X))$ where π is the probability distributions that defines the expectation. The nature of the approach, where algebraic quantities are approximated by random quantities, requires one to quantify the random fluctuations around the true desired value. As we shall see, the power of Monte Carlo techniques lies in the fact that the *rate* at which the approximation converges towards the true value of interest is immune to the dimension n_x of the space X where π is defined. This is the second interest of Monte Carlo techniques.

These numerical techniques have been widely used in physics over the last 50 years, but their interest in the context of Bayesian statistics and more generally statistics was only fully realized in the late eighties early nineties. Although we will here mostly focus on their application in statistics, one should bear in mind that the material presented in this introduction to the topic has applications far beyond statistics.

The prerequisites for this introduction are a basic first year undergraduate background in probability and statistics. Keywords include random variable,

O. Bousquet et al. (Eds.): Machine Learning 2003, LNAI 3176, pp. 113–145, 2004.
© Springer-Verlag Berlin Heidelberg 2004

law of large numbers, estimators, central limit theorem and basic notions about Markov chains.

1.1   Motivating Example

In this section we motivate and illustrate the use of Monte Carlo methods with a toy example. We then point out the power of the approach on a "real" example.

Calculating π with the Help of Rain and the Law of Large Numbers

A Physical Experiment Consider the 2×2 square, say $\mathcal{S} \subset \mathbb{R}^2$, with inscribed disc $\mathcal{D}$ of radius 1 as in Figure 1.

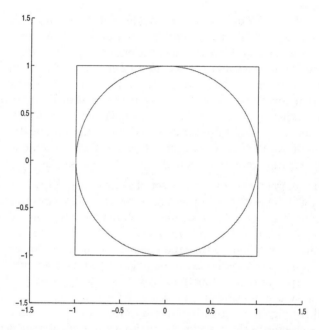

Fig. 1. A 2×2 square $\mathcal{S}$ with inscribed disk $\mathcal{D}$ of radius 1

Imagine that an "idealized" rain falls uniformly on the square $\mathcal{S}$, i.e. the probability for a drop to fall in a region $\mathcal{A}$ is proportional to the area of $\mathcal{A}$. More precisely, let D be the random variable defined on $X = \mathcal{S}$ representing the location of a drop and $\mathcal{A}$ a region of the square, then

$$\mathbb{P}(D \in \mathcal{A}) = \frac{\int_{\mathcal{A}} dxdy}{\int_{\mathcal{S}} dxdy}. \tag{1}$$

where x and y are the Cartesian coordinates. Now assume that we have observed N such *independent* drops, say $\{D_i, i = 1, \ldots, N\}$ as in Figure 2.

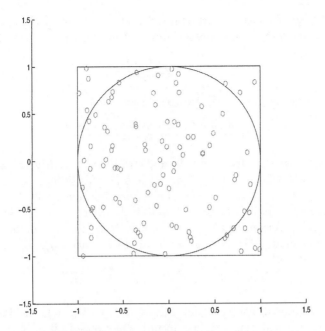

Fig. 2. A 2×2 square $\mathcal{S}$ with inscribed disk $\mathcal{D}$ of radius 1

Intuitively, without any knowledge of elementary statistics, a sensible technique to estimate the probability $\mathbb{P}(D \in \mathcal{A})$ of falling in a given region $\mathcal{A} \subset \mathcal{S}$ (and think for example of $\mathcal{A} = \mathcal{D}$) would consist of using the following formula

$$\mathbb{P}(D \in \mathcal{A}) \simeq \frac{\text{number of drops that fell in } \mathcal{A}}{N}.$$

This formula certainly makes sense, but we would like to be more rigorous and give a statistical justification to it.

$\mathbb{P}(D \in \mathcal{A})$ *as an Expectation.* Let us first introduce the indicator function of a set $\mathcal{A}$, defined as follows,

$$\mathbb{I}_{\mathcal{A}}(x, y) = \begin{cases} 1 \text{ if point } D = (x, y) \in \mathcal{A}, \\ 0 \text{ otherwise,} \end{cases}.$$

We define the random variable $V(D) := \mathbb{I}_{\mathcal{A}}(D) := \mathbb{I}_{\mathcal{A}}(X, Y)$, where X, Y are the random variables that represent the Cartesian coordinates of a uniformly distributed point on $\mathcal{S}$, denoted $D \sim \mathcal{U}_{\mathcal{S}}$. Using V, it is not hard to show that

$$\mathbb{P}(D \in \mathcal{A}) = \int_{\mathcal{S}} \mathbb{I}_{\mathcal{A}}(x, y) \frac{1}{4} dx dy = \mathbb{E}_{\mathcal{U}_{\mathcal{S}}}(V),$$

where for a probability distribution π we will denote $\mathbb{E}_{\pi}$ the expectation with respect to π.

The Law of Large Numbers. Now, similarly, let us introduce $\{V_i := V(D_i), i = 1, \ldots, N\}$ the random variables associated to the drops $\{D_i, i = 1, \ldots, N\}$ and consider the sum

$$S_N = \frac{\sum_{i=1}^N V_i}{N}. \tag{2}$$

We notice that an alternative expression for S_N is

$$S_N = \frac{\text{number of drops that fell in } \mathcal{A}}{N},$$

which corresponds precisely to the formula which we intuitively suggested to approximate $\mathbb{P}(D \in \mathcal{A})$. However Eq. (2) is statistically more explicit, in the sense that it tells us that our suggested approximation of $\mathbb{P}(D \in \mathcal{A})$ is the empirical average of independent and identically distributed random variables, $\{V_i, i = 1, \ldots, N\}$. Assuming that the rain lasts forever and therefore that $N \rightarrow +\infty$, then one can apply the *law of large numbers* (since $\mathbb{E}_{\mathcal{U}_s}(|V|) < +\infty$ here) and deduce that

$$\lim_{N \rightarrow +\infty} S_N = \mathbb{E}_{\mathcal{U}_s}(V), \text{ (almost surely)}.$$

As we have already proved that $\mathbb{P}(D \in \mathcal{A}) = \mathbb{E}_{\mathcal{U}_s}(V)$, the law of large numbers mathematically justifies our intuitive method of estimating $\mathbb{P}(D \in \mathcal{A})$, provided that N is large enough.

A Method of Approximating π. We note that as a special case we have defined a method of calculating π. Indeed,

$$\mathbb{P}(D \in \mathcal{D}) = \int_{\mathcal{D}} \frac{1}{4} dx dy = \frac{\pi}{4}.$$

S_N as defined in Eq. (2) with $\mathcal{A} = \mathcal{D}$ is an unbiased estimator of $\pi/4$, which is also ensured to converge towards $\pi/4$ for N very large. The quantity $S_N - \pi/4$ for a day of rain as a function of the number of drops for one rainfall is presented in Figure 3. However in practice one is interested in obtaining a result in finite time, i.e. for N finite. S_N is a random variable which can be rewritten as $S_N = \pi/4 + E_N$ where E_N is a random error term. It is naturally of interest to characterize the precision of our estimator, i.e. characterize the average magnitude of the fluctuations of the random error E_N, as illustrated in Figure 4. A simple measure of the average magnitude of E_N is its variance,

$$var(E_N) = var(S_N) = \frac{1}{N} var(V_1),$$

as the $\{V_i, i = 1, \ldots, N\}$ are independent. It is worth remembering that since S_N is unbiased,

$$\sqrt{var(S_N)} = \sqrt{\mathbb{E}\left[(S_N - \mathbb{P}(D \in \mathcal{D}))^2\right]},$$

which using the result above implies that the *mean square error* between S_N and $\mathbb{P}(D \in \mathcal{D})$ decreases as $1/\sqrt{N}$. This is illustrated in Figure 5 where the dotted

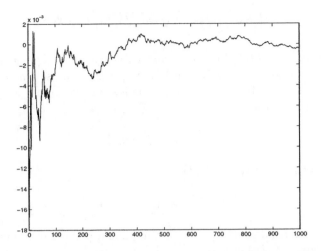

Fig. 3. Convergence of $S_N - \pi/4$ as a function of the number of samples, for one realization (or rainfall)

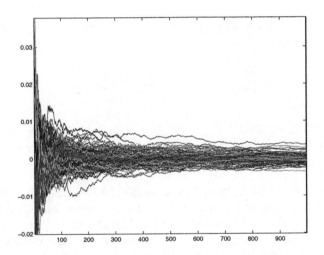

Fig. 4. Convergence of $S_N - \pi/4$ for 100 realizations of the rain

lines represent $\pm\sqrt{var(V)/N}$ and the dashed lines represent the empirical mean square error $S_N - \pi/4$ estimated from the 100 realizations in Figure 4. One can be slightly more precise and first invoke here an asymptotic result, the *central limit theorem* (which can be applied here as $var(V) < +\infty$). As $N \to +\infty$,

$$\sqrt{N}S_N \to_d \mathcal{N}(\pi/4, var(V)),$$

which implies that for N large enough the probability of the error being larger than $2\sqrt{var(V)/N}$ is

$$\mathbb{P}\left(|S_N - \pi/4| > 2\sqrt{var(V)/N}\right) \simeq 0.05,$$

with $2\sqrt{var(V)} = 0.8211$. In the present case (we are sampling here from a Bernoulli distribution) one can be much more precise and use a non-asymptotic result. Indeed, using a Bernstein type inequality, one can prove [22, p. 69] that for any integer $N \geq 1$ and $\varepsilon > 0$,

$$\mathbb{P}\left(|S_N - \pi/4| > \varepsilon\right) \leq 2\exp\left(-2N\varepsilon^2\right)$$

which tells us that for any $\alpha \in (0,1]$,

$$\mathbb{P}\left(|S_N - \pi/4| > \varepsilon\right) < \alpha$$

which on the one hand provides us with a minimum number of samples in order to achieve a given precision of α,

$$N = \left[\frac{\log(2/\alpha)}{2\varepsilon^2}\right],$$

where for a real x the quantity $[x]$ denotes the integer part of x, or alternatively tells us that for any $N \geq 1$,

$$\mathbb{P}\left(|S_N - \pi/4| > \sqrt{\frac{\log(40)}{2N}}\right) \leq 0.05$$

with $\sqrt{\log(40)/2} = 1.3541$.

Both results tell us that in some sense the approximation error is inversely proportional to $\sqrt{N}$.

A General and Powerful Method. Now consider the case where $X = \mathbb{R}^{n_x}$ for any integer n_x, and in particular large values of n_x. Replace now S and D above with a hypercube S^{n_x} and an inscribed hyperball D^{n_x} in X. If we could observe a hyper-rain, then it would not be difficult to see that the method described earlier to estimate the area of D could be used to estimate the volume of D^{n_x}. The only requirement is that one should be able to tell if a drop fell in D^{n_x} or not: in other words one should be able to calculate $\mathbb{I}_{D^{n_x}}(D)$ point-wise. Now a very important result is that the arguments that lead earlier to the formal validation of the Monte Carlo approach to estimate $\pi/4$ remain identical here (check it to convince yourself!). In particular the rate of convergence of the estimator in the mean square sense is again *independent of the dimension n_x*.

This would not be the case if we were using a deterministic method on a grid of regularly spaced points. Typically, the rate of convergence of such deterministic methods is of the form $1/N^{r/n_x}$ where r is related to the smoothness of the contours of region A, and is N the number of function (here $\mathbb{I}_A$) evaluations. Monte Carlo methods are thus extremely attractive when n_x is large.

A More General Context. In the previous subsection, we have seen that a simple experience involving the rain can help us to evaluate an *expectation* in an extremely simple way. In this subsection we generalist the ideas developed earlier in order to tackle the generic problem of estimating

$$\mathbb{E}_\pi(f(x)) \triangleq \int_X f(x)\pi(x)dx,$$

where $f : X \to \mathbb{R}^{n_f}$ and π is a probability distribution on $X \subset \mathbb{R}^{n_x}$. We will assume that $\mathbb{E}_\pi(|f(x)|) < +\infty$ but that it is difficult to obtain an analytical expression for $\mathbb{E}_\pi(f(x))$.

1.2   Generalization of the Rain Experiment

In the light of the square/circle example, assume that $N >> 1$ *i.i.d.* samples $X^{(i)} \sim \pi$ ($i = 1, \ldots, N$) are available to us (since it is unlikely that rain can generate samples from any distribution π, we will address the problem of sample generation in the next section). Now consider any set $\mathcal{A} \subset X$ and assume that we are interested in calculating $\pi(\mathcal{A}) = \mathbb{P}(X \in \mathcal{A})$ for $X \sim \pi$. We naturally choose the following estimator

$$\pi(\mathcal{A}) \simeq \frac{\text{number of samples in } \mathcal{A}}{\text{total number of samples}},$$

which by the law of large numbers is a consistent estimator of $\pi(\mathcal{A})$ since

$$\lim_{N \to +\infty} \frac{1}{N} \sum_{i=1}^N \mathbb{I}_\mathcal{A}(X_i) = \mathbb{E}_\pi(\mathbb{I}_\mathcal{A}(X)) = \pi(\mathcal{A}).$$

A way of generalizing this in order to evaluate $\mathbb{E}_\pi(f(x))$ consists of considering the estimator

$$S_N(f) = \frac{1}{N} \sum_{i=1}^N f(X_i),$$

which is unbiased. From the law of large numbers $S_N(f)$ will converge and

$$\lim_{N \to +\infty} \frac{1}{N} \sum_{i=1}^N f(X_i) = \mathbb{E}_\pi(f(X)) \; a.s.$$

Here again a good measure of the approximation is the variance of $S_N(f)$,

$$var_\pi[S_N(f)] = var_\pi \left[\frac{1}{N} \sum_{i=1}^N f(X^{(i)}) \right] = \frac{var_\pi[f(X)]}{N}.$$

Now the central limit theorem applies if $var_\pi[f(X)] < \infty$ and tells us that

$$S_N(f) \overset{N \to +\infty}{\to}_d \mathcal{N}\left(\sqrt{N}\mathbb{E}_\pi(f(X)), var_\pi[f(X)] \right),$$

and the conclusions drawn in the rain example are still valid here:

1. The rate of convergence is immune to the dimension of X.
2. It is easy to take complex integration domains into account.
3. It is easily implementable and general. The requirements are
   (a) to be able to evaluate $f(x)$ for any $x \in \mathsf{X}$,
   (b) to be able to produce samples distributed according to π.

1.3   From the Algebraic to the Sample Representation

In this subsection we make explicit the - approximate - sample representation of π. Let us first introduce the delta-Dirac function δ_{x_0} for $x_0 \in \mathsf{X}$, defined as follows

$$\int_\mathsf{X} f(x)\delta_{x_0}(x)dx = f(x_0),$$

for any $f : \mathsf{X} \to \mathbb{R}^{n_f}$. Note that this implies in particular that for $\mathcal{A} \subset \mathsf{X}$,

$$\int_\mathsf{X} \mathbb{I}_\mathcal{A}(x)\delta_{x_0}(x)dx = \int_\mathcal{A} \delta_{x_0}(x)dx = \mathbb{I}_\mathcal{A}(x_0).$$

Now, for $X_i \sim \pi$ for $i = 1, \ldots, N$, we can introduce the following mixture of delta-Dirac functions

$$\widehat{\pi}_N(x) := \frac{1}{N} \sum_{i=1}^N \delta_{X_i}(x),$$

which is the *empirical measure* of the sample, and consider for any $\mathcal{A} \subset \mathsf{X}$

$$\widehat{\pi}_N(\mathcal{A}) \triangleq \int_\mathcal{A} \widehat{\pi}_N(x)\,dx = \sum_{i=1}^N \int_\mathcal{A} \frac{1}{N}\delta_{X_i}(x) = \sum_{i=1}^N \frac{1}{N}\mathbb{I}_\mathcal{A}(x).$$

which is precisely $S_N(\mathbb{I}_\mathcal{A})$. What we have touched upon here is simply the sample representation of π, of which an illustration can be found in Figure 6 for a Gaussian distribution. **The concentration of points in a given region of the space represents** π. Note that this approach is in contrast with what is usually done in parametric statistics, i.e. start with samples and then introduce a distribution with an algebraic representation for the underlying population. Note that here each sample X_i has a weight of $1/N$, but that it is also possible to consider weighted sample representations of π: the approach is called *importance sampling* and will be covered later on.

Now consider the problem of estimating $\mathbb{E}_\pi(f)$. We simply replace π with its sample representation $\widehat{\pi}_N$ and obtain

$$\mathbb{E}_\pi(f) \simeq \int_\mathsf{X} f(x) \sum_{i=1}^N \frac{1}{N}\delta_{X_i}(x)\,dx = \sum_{i=1}^N \frac{1}{N} \int_\mathsf{X} f(x)\,\delta_{X_i}(x)\,dx = \frac{1}{N} \sum_{i=1}^N f(X_i),$$

which is precisely $S_N(f)$, the Monte Carlo estimator suggested earlier. The interest of this approximating representation of π will become clearer later, in particular in the context of importance sampling.

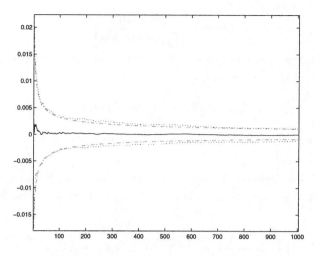

Fig. 5. Variance of $S_N - \pi/4$ across 100 realizations as a function of the number of samples and the theoretical variance

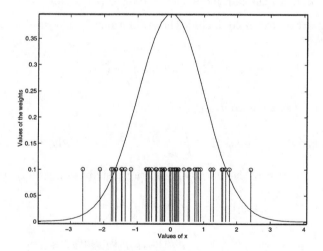

Fig. 6. Sample representation of a Gaussian distribution

1.4   Expectations in Statistics

The aim of this subsection is to illustrate why it is important to compute expectations in statistics, in particular in the Bayesian context.

Assume that we are given a Bayesian model, i.e. a likelihood $p(y|\theta)$ and a prior distribution $p(\theta)$. We observe some data y and wish to estimate θ. In a Bayesian framework, all the available information about θ is summarized by the posterior distribution, given by Bayes' rule,

$$p(\theta|y) = \frac{p(y|\theta)p(\theta)}{\int_\Theta p(y|\theta)p(\theta)d\theta}.$$

The expression looks simple, but the bottom of the fraction is an integral, and more precisely an expectation

$$\mathbb{E}_{p(\theta)}(p(y|\theta)) = \int_\Theta p(y|\theta)p(\theta)d\theta.$$

In many situations this integral typically does not admit a closed-form expression.

Example 1. We observe $y = (y_1, y_2, \ldots, y_T)$ which are *iid* such that $y_i \sim \mathcal{N}(\mu_j, \sigma_j^2)$ with probability p_j for $j = 1, 2$. Here $\theta = (\mu_1, \mu_2, \sigma_1^2, \sigma_2^2, p_1)$. The likelihood in this case is

$$p(y|\theta) = \prod_{i=1}^{T} \left[p_1 \frac{1}{\sqrt{2\pi\sigma_1^2}} e^{-\frac{(y_i-\mu_1)^2}{2\sigma_1^2}} + (1-p_1)\frac{1}{\sqrt{2\pi\sigma_2^2}} e^{-\frac{(y_i-\mu_2)^2}{2\sigma_2^2}} \right].$$

The normalizing constant of the posterior can be complicated, e.g. impose *a priori* constraints on the parameters $\sigma_1^2 < 10\sigma_2^2 + \sqrt{\mu_1\mu_2}$ and $\mu_2 < \pi$.

Other important examples include the evaluation of the posterior mean square estimate of θ,

$$\hat{\theta}_{MSE} := \mathbb{E}_{p(\theta|y)}(\theta) = \int_\Theta \theta p(\theta|y)d\theta,$$

the median, i.e. the solution $\hat{\theta}_{median}$ of

$$\mathbb{E}_{p(\theta|y)}(\mathbb{I}(\theta \leq \hat{\theta}_{median})) = \int_{-\infty}^{+\infty} \mathbb{I}(\theta \leq \hat{\theta}_{median})p(\theta|y)d\theta = 1/2.$$

but also the evaluation of the marginal posterior distribution $p(\theta_1|y)$ of $p(\theta_1, \theta_2|y)$,

$$p(\theta_1|y) = \int_\Theta p(\theta_1, \theta_2|y)d\theta_2$$

$$= \int_\Theta p(\theta_1|\theta_2, y)p(\theta_2|y)d\theta_2$$

$$= \mathbb{E}_{p(\theta_2|y)}(p(\theta_1|\theta_2, y)) \ldots$$

Similar problems are encountered when computing, marginal posterior means, posterior variances, posterior credibility regions.

1.5   A Simple Application

In 1786 Laplace was interested in determining if the probability θ of a male birth in Paris over a certain period of time was above 0.5 or not. The official figures gave $y_1 = 251,527$ males birth for $y_2 = 241,945$ female births. The observed proportion was therefore 0.509,. We choose a uniform distribution as prior distribution for θ the proportion of male births. The posterior distribution is

$$p(\theta|y) = \mathcal{B}e(\theta; 251528, 241946).$$

Imagine that we have no table and are interested in the posterior mean of this posterior distribution. Furthermore, imagine that we can sample (using a computer) a large number N of independent samples $(\theta_i, i = 1, \ldots, N)$ from this distribution. One could propose the following estimator

$$\frac{1}{N}\sum_{i=1}^{N}\theta_i$$

as from the law of large numbers,

$$\lim_{N\to+\infty}\frac{1}{N}\sum_{i=1}^{N}\theta_i = \mathbb{E}_{p(\theta|y)}(\theta).$$

We could also estimate the posterior variance as

$$\lim_{N\to+\infty}\frac{1}{N}\sum_{i=1}^{N}\theta_i^2 = \mathbb{E}_{p(\theta|y)}(\theta^2).$$

Now consider the following more challenging problems: we want to find estimates of the median of this posterior distribution, as well as a 95% credibility interval. We start with the median, and assume that we have ordered the samples, that is for any $i < j$, $\theta_i < \theta_j$ and for simplicity that N is an even number. Let $\bar{\theta}$ be the median of the posterior distribution. Then we know that

$$\mathbb{P}(\theta_i \geq \bar{\theta}) = \int_{-\infty}^{+\infty} \mathbb{I}(\bar{\theta} < \theta)p(\theta|y)d\theta = 1/2$$

$$\mathbb{P}(\theta_i \leq \bar{\theta}) = \int_{-\infty}^{+\infty} \mathbb{I}(\bar{\theta} < \theta)p(\theta|y)d\theta = 1/2$$

so that (assuming for simplicity that N is even and that we have ordered $(\theta_i, i = 1, \ldots, N)$), it is sensible to chose an estimate for $\bar{\theta}$ between $\theta_{N/2}$ and $\theta_{N/2+1}$. Now assume that we are looking for θ^- and θ^+ such that

$$\mathbb{P}(\theta^- \leq \theta \leq \theta^+) = \int_{-\infty}^{+\infty} I(\theta^- \leq \theta \leq \theta^+)p(\theta|y)d\theta = 0.95$$

or

$$\mathbb{P}(0 \leq \theta \leq \theta^-) = 0.025 \text{ and } \mathbb{P}(\theta^+ \leq \theta \leq 1) = 0.025$$

and assuming again for simplicity that $N = 1000$ and that the samples have been ordered. We find that a reasonable estimate of θ^- is between θ_{25} and θ_{26} and an estimate of θ^+ between θ_{975} and θ_{976}. Finally we might be interested in calculating

$$\mathbb{P}(\theta < 0.5) = \int_{0}^{0.5} p(\theta|y)d\theta = \int_{0}^{1} I(\theta \leq 0.5)p(\theta|y)d\theta$$

which suggests the following estimator of this probability

$$\mathbb{P}(\theta < 0.5) \simeq \frac{1}{N} \sum_{i=1}^{N} \mathbb{I}(\theta_i \leq 0.5).$$

(one can in fact find that $\mathbb{P}(\theta \leq 0.5 | y_1, y_2) = 1.146058490255674 \times 10^{-42}$).

1.6   Further Topic: Importance Sampling

In this subsection we explore the important method of importance sampling.[1] This method is of interest either in the case where samples from the desired distribution π are not available, but samples from a distribution q are, or as a way of possibly reducing the variance of an estimator.

Importance Sampling. Consider a probability distribution q such that $\pi(x) > 0 \Rightarrow q(x) > 0$. Then one can write

$$\mathbb{E}_\pi(f(x)) = \int_X f(x)\pi(x)dx = \int_X f(x)\underbrace{\frac{\pi(x)}{q(x)}}_{w(x)}q(x)dx = \mathbb{E}_q(w(x)f(x))$$

We are now integrating the function $w(x)f(x)$ with respect to the distribution q. Now provided that we can produce N *i.i.d.* samples $X_1, \ldots, X_N$ from q, then one can suggest the following estimator

$$\frac{1}{N} \sum_{i=1}^{N} \frac{\pi(X_i)}{q(X_i)} f(X_i) = \int_X f(x) \frac{1}{N} \sum_{i=1}^{N} \frac{\pi(X_i)}{q(X_i)} \delta_{X_i}(x) dx.$$

It is customary to call $w_i = \frac{\pi(X_i)}{q(X_i)}$ the *importance weight* and q the importance distribution. Now it is natural to introduce a delta-Dirac approximation of π is of the form

$$\widehat{\pi}_N(x) = \frac{1}{N} \sum_{i=1}^{N} w_i \delta_{X_i}(dx)$$

The interpretation of this weighted empirical measure is rather simple. Large w_i's indicate an underrepresentation of π by samples from q around X_i. Small w_i's indicate an overrepresentation of π by samples from q around X_i. This phenomenon is illustrated in Figure 1.6 where the importance weights required to represent a double exponential with samples from either a Gaussian or a t-Student are presented. Note that in the case where $q = \pi$ then $w_i = 1/N$ and we recover the representation presented earlier.

It is also worth noticing that if the normalizing constants of π and/or q are not known, then it is possible to define (with $\pi^*(x) \propto \pi(x)$ and $q^*(x) \propto q(x)$)

$$w_i = \frac{\pi^*(X_i)/q^*(X_i)}{\sum_{j=1}^{N} \pi^*(X_j)/q^*(X_j)}.$$

---

[1] This material can be skipped at first.

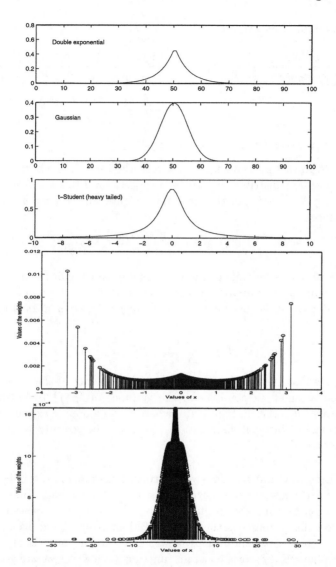

Fig. 7. Top: The three distributions. Middle: importance weights to represent a double exponential with samples from a Gaussian. Bottom: importance weights to represent a double exponential with samples from a t-Student

And consider the following estimator

$$I_N(f) = \sum_{i=1}^{N} w_i f(X_i) = \sum_{i=1}^{N} \frac{\pi^*(X_i)/q^*(X_i)}{\sum_{j=1}^{N} \pi^*(X_j)/q^*(X_j)} f(X_i).$$

This estimator is *biased*, but

$$\lim_{N \to \infty} \sum_{i=1}^{N} \frac{\pi^*(X_i)/q^*(X_i)}{\sum_{j=1}^{N} \pi^*(X_j)/q^*(X_j)} f(X_i) = \frac{\lim_{N \to \infty} \frac{1}{N} \sum_{i=1}^{N} \pi^*(X_i)/q^*(X_i)f(X_i)}{\lim_{N \to \infty} \frac{1}{N} \sum_{j=1}^{N} \pi^*(X_j)/q^*(X_j)}$$

$$= \frac{\int_X f(x) w(x) q(x) \, dx}{\int_X w(x) q(x) \, dx}$$

as the unknown normalizing constants cancel.

Example 2 (Naive). In a Bayesian framework the target distribution is $\pi(\theta) \triangleq p(\theta|y)$, the posterior distribution. One can suggest (and this is not necessarily a good choice) $q(\theta) \triangleq p(\theta)$. In this case the weights will be proportional to the likelihood since

$$w(\theta) = p(\theta|y)/p(\theta) \propto \frac{p(y|\theta)p(\theta)}{p(\theta)} \propto p(y|\theta).$$

Unfortunately this technique is not as general as it might seem. Let us consider the variance of the importance sampling estimator in the simple case where the normalizing constants are known and where $f = C$, i.e. is a constant. In this case

$$var_q(I_N(f)) = \frac{C}{N} \left[\mathbb{E}_q\left(w_1^2\right) - \mathbb{E}_q\left(w_1\right)^2 \right]$$

which suggests that even in the simplest case the variance of the weights should be finite and as small as possible for the variance of $I_N(f)$ to be small. The examples provided earlier in Figure 1.6, where π was a double exponential and q either a normal or t-Student distribution, illustrates the possibly large variations of the weights.

Zero Variance Estimator. Here we illustrate a possible interest of importance sampling, which is however specialized. We start with the trivial remark that the variance of a constant function is null, i.e. $var_\pi[f] = 0$ if f is a constant. We seek here to exploit this property in the context of Monte Carlo integration, although this might seem of little interest at first sight since no numerical method is needed to evaluate $\mathbb{E}_\pi(f)$ for a constant function f. However we are going to use this as a motivation to describe a method of reducing the variance of a Monte Carlo estimator for a fixed number of samples. Now assume that $\mathbb{E}_\pi(f)$ and that for simplicity $f \geq 0$. Using the convention $0/0 = 1$ we can rewrite $\mathbb{E}_\pi(f)$ as

$$\mathbb{E}_\pi(f) = \int_X f(x)\pi(x)dx = \int_X \frac{f(x)}{f(x)}\pi(x)f(x)dx$$

$$= \int_X 1 \times \int_X \pi(x'')f(x'')dx'' \frac{\pi(x)f(x)}{\int_X \pi(x')f(x')dx'}dx,$$

that is

$$\mathbb{E}_\pi(f) = \mathbb{E}_q(\mathbb{E}_\pi(f))$$

where

$$q(x) := \frac{\pi(x)f(x)}{\int_X \pi(x')f(x')dx'}$$

can be thought of as being a probability density. If we could sample from q then we could integrate the constant function $\int_X \pi(x'')f(x'')dx''$ and obtain a zero variance estimator. Naturally we have not solved the problem since the constant is precisely the integral that we are seeking to calculate!

The calculations above can be generalized to functions f that are not everywhere positive, with in this case,

$$q(x) = \frac{|f(x)|\,\pi(x)}{\int_X \pi(x')|f(x')|dx'}.$$

Despite our disappointing/absurd results, the strategy however suggests ways to improve the constant $var_\pi(f)$, by trying to sample from a distribution close to q. Note however that q depends on f, and that as a consequence such a method is therefore very specialized.

Conclusions. To summaries, the pros and cons of importance sampling are as follows:

- **Advantages.** Easy to implement, parallelizable, sequential version are possible (particle filter etc.). If q is a clever approximation of π, then we typically expect good results. It can be used a specialized way of reducing the variance of estimators.
- **Drawbacks.** If we do not have $var_\pi(w(x)) < +\infty$, then typically $\widehat{I}_N(f)$ can be a poor estimator since its variance is large. This poses the problem of the choice of $q(x)$? Where are the modes of $\pi(x)$? Importance sampling is typically limited to small dimensions for the parameter space, say $n_x = 10-50$ depending on the application.

Despite the possible drawbacks, importance sampling has proved to be extremely useful in the context of sequential importance sampling.

2   Classical "Exact" Simulation Methods

In this section we review some classical simulation techniques. We call those techniques "exact" as they allow one to generate samples in a *finite number of iterations* of a procedure. Note that the instant when a sample from the distribution of interest is produced is identifiable, that is we can stop the procedure and be sure that we have generated a sample from the distribution of interest. As we shall see in the next section this is not always the case. Unfortunately the simulation techniques presented in this chapter cannot typically be used in order to sample from complex distributions as they tend not to scale well with the dimension n_x and cases where little is known about π. However these techniques can be thought of as being building blocks of more complex algorithms that will be presented in the next chapter.

From now on we will assume that a computer can generate *independent uniformly distributed random variables,* or at least that it can generate a good approximation of such random variables (indeed computers should usually follow a deterministic behavior, and one must find ways around in order to produce something that looks random).

2.1   The cdf Inversion Method

We present here this method in the case where $X = \mathbb{R}$ for simplicity. The multivariate generalization is not difficult. First we consider a simple discrete example where $X \in X = \{1, 2, 3\}$ and such that

$$\mathbb{P}(X = 1) = \frac{1}{6}, \ \mathbb{P}(X = 2) = \frac{2}{6}, \ \mathbb{P}(X = 3) = \frac{1}{2}.$$

Define the cumulative probability distribution (cdf) of X as

$$F_X(x) = \mathbb{P}(X \le x) = \sum_{i=1}^{3} \mathbb{P}(X = i)\mathbb{I}(i \le x)$$

for $x \in [0, 3]$ and its inverse

$$F_X^{-1}(u) = \inf\{x \in X; F_X(x) \ge u\},$$

for $u \in [0, 1]$. The cdf corresponding to our example is represented in Figure 8. A method of sampling from this distribution consists of sampling $u \sim \mathcal{U}(0, 1)$ and find $x = F_X^{-1}(u)$. The probability of u falling in the vertical interval i is precisely equal to the probability $\mathbb{P}(X = i)$. The method indeed produces samples from the distribution of interest.

Now in the continuous case, and assuming that the distribution has a density the cdf takes the form

$$F_X(x) = \mathbb{P}(X \le x) = \int_{-\infty}^{+\infty} \pi(u) I(u \le x) du = \int_{-\infty}^{x} \pi(u) du.$$

A normal distribution and its cdf are presented in Figure 9. Intuitively the algorithm suggested in the discrete case should be valid here, since modes of π mean large variations of F_X and therefore a large probability for a uniform distribution to fall in these regions.

More rigorously, consider the algorithm

Sample $u \sim \mathcal{U}(0, 1)$ and set $Y = F_\pi^{-1}(u)$.

We prove that this algorithm produces samples from π. We calculate the cdf of X produced by the algorithm above. For any $y \in X$ we have

$$\mathbb{P}(Y \le y) = \mathbb{P}(Y = F_X^{-1}(u) \le y)$$
$$= \mathbb{P}(u \le F_X(y)) \text{ since } F_X \text{ is non decreasing}$$
$$= \int_0^1 I(u \le F_X(y)) \times 1 du = \int_0^{F_X(y)} du = F_X(y),$$

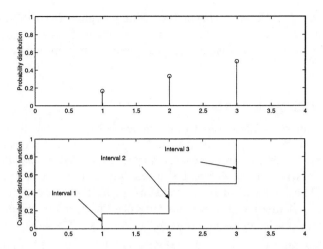

Fig. 8. The distribution and cdf of a discrete random variable

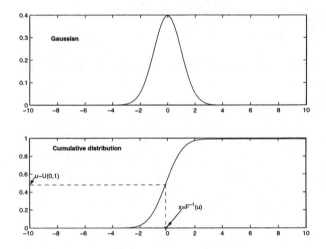

Fig. 9. The distribution and cdf of a normal distribution

which shows that the cdf of Y produced by the algorithm above is precisely the cdf of $X \sim \pi$.

Example 3. Consider the exponential distribution with parameter 1, i.e. $X \sim \pi(x) = \exp(-x) \mathbb{I}_{[0,+\infty)}(x)$. The cdf of X is $F_X(x) = 1 - \exp(-x)$. Now the inverse cdf is $F_X^{-1}(u) = -\log(1-u)$, and for $u \sim \mathcal{U}(0,1)$ then $-\log(1-u) \sim \pi$.

This example is interesting as it illustrates one of the fundamental idea of most simulation methods: sample from a distribution from which it is easy to sample (here the uniform distribution) and then transform this random variable (here through F_X^{-1}). However this method is only applicable to a limited number of cases as it requires a closed form expression of the inverse of the cdf, which is not explicit even for a distribution as simple and common as the normal distribution.

2.2   The Rejection Method

The rejection method allows one to sample according to a distribution π which is only known up to a proportionality constant, say $\pi^* \propto \pi$. It relies again on the assumption that samples can be generated from a so-called *proposal* distribution q defined on X, which might as well be known only up to a normalizing constant, say $q^* \propto q$. Then, instead of being transformed by a deterministic function as in the inverse cdf method, the samples produced from π are either rejected or accepted. More precisely, assume that for any $x \in$ X, $C = \sup_{x \in \mathsf{X}} \frac{\pi^*(x)}{q^*(x)} < +\infty$ (note that this imposes that for any $x \in$ X, $\pi^*(x) > 0 \Rightarrow q^*(x) > 0$) and consider $C' \geq C$. Then the accept/reject procedure proceeds as follows:

Accept/Reject procedure
1. Sample $Y \sim q$ and $u \sim \mathcal{U}(0,1)$.
2. If $u < \frac{\pi^*(Y)}{C'q^*(Y)}$ then return Y; otherwise return to step 1.

The intuition behind the method can be understood from Figure 10.

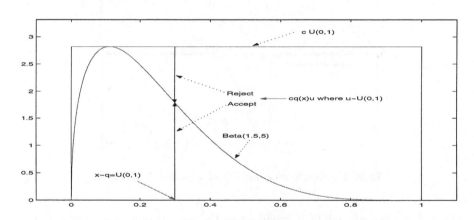

Fig. 10. The idea behind the rejection method

Now we prove that $\mathbb{P}(Y \leq x | Y \text{ accepted}) = \mathbb{P}(X \leq x)$. We will extensively use the trivial identity

$$q(x) = \frac{q^*(x)}{\int_\mathsf{X} q^*(y)dy}.$$

For any $x \in X$, consider the joint distribution

$$\mathbb{P}(Y \leq x \text{ and } Y \text{ accepted}) = \int_0^1 \int_{-\infty}^x I(u \leq \frac{\pi^*(y)}{C'q^*(y)})q(y) \times 1 dydu$$

$$= \int_{-\infty}^x \frac{\pi^*(y)}{C'q^*(y)}q(y)dy$$

$$= \frac{\int_{-\infty}^x \pi^*(y)dy}{C' \int_X q^*(y)dy},$$

and the probability of being accepted is the marginal of $\mathbb{P}(Y \leq x \text{ and } Y \text{ accepted})$, that is

$$\mathbb{P}(Y \text{ accepted}) = \int_X \frac{\pi^*(y)}{C'q^*(y)}q(y)dy = \frac{\int_X \pi^*(y)dy}{C' \int_X q^*(y)dy}. \tag{3}$$

Consequently

$$\mathbb{P}(Y \leq x | Y \text{ accepted}) = \frac{\int_{-\infty}^x \pi^*(y)dy}{\int_X \pi^*(y)dy} = \int_{-\infty}^x \pi(y)dy.$$

The expression for the probability of being accepted in Eq. (3) tells us that in order to design an efficient algorithm, C' should be chosen as small as possible, and that the optimal choice corresponds to C. However this constant might be very large, in particular for large n_x and C might not even be known. In the most favorable scenarios, at best an upper bound might be known.

Example 4. We want to sample from a $Be(x; \alpha, \beta) \propto x^{\alpha-1}(1-x)^{\beta-1}$ distribution. We can generate samples from $\mathcal{U}(0,1)$. One can find $\sup_{x \in [0,1]} \frac{x^{\alpha-1}(1-x)^{\beta-1}}{1}$ analytically for $\alpha, \beta > 1$! Note that we do not assume known the normalizing constant!

Example 5. Let us assume that one wants to simulate samples from $\pi(\theta) \triangleq p(\theta|y) \propto p(y|\theta)p(\theta)$. We assume that $p(y|\theta)$ is known analytically and $p(y|\theta) \leq C$ for any θ, where C is known. We also assume that we are able to simulate from $p(\theta)$. Thus one can choose $q(\theta) = p(\theta)$ and use the accept/reject procedure to sample from $p(\theta|y)$. Indeed

$$\frac{p(\theta|y)}{p(\theta)} = \frac{p(y|\theta)}{p(y)} \leq \frac{C}{p(y)} = M \tag{4}$$

is bounded and

$$\frac{\pi(\theta)}{Mq(\theta)} = \frac{p(\theta|y)}{\frac{C}{p(y)}p(\theta)} = \frac{p(y|\theta)}{C} \tag{5}$$

can be evaluated analytically. However, the acceptance rate $1/M$ is usually unknown as it involves $p(y)$ which is itself usually unknown.

We can summaries the pros and cons of the accept/reject procedure:

- **Advantages:**
    1. seems rather universal, and compared to the inverse cdf method requires less algebraic properties.
    2. in principle neither the normalization constant of π nor that of q are needed.
- **Drawbacks:**
    1. how to construct the proposal $q(x)$ to minimize C?
    2. typically C increases exponentially with n_x.

2.3   Deterministic Transformations

These methods rely on clever changes of variables, which transform one distribution to another. A typical setup is the following: consider $Y \sim q$ from which it is easy to sample, and consider $g : \mathsf{X} \to \mathsf{X}$ a differentiable and one-to-one transformation. Now define the transformed random variable

$$X = g(Y).$$

We know that the density, say π, of X can be expressed in terms of q and the Jacobian $\left|\frac{\partial g^{-1}(x)}{\partial x}\right|$ of the transformation g as follows

$$\pi(x) = q\left(g^{-1}(x)\right)\left|\frac{\partial g^{-1}(x)}{\partial x}\right|.$$

Naturally for a predefined π it is not always obvious to find proper g and q, but we present here a celebrated example. The Box-Muller transformation is a method of transforming two $i.i.d.$ uniformly distributed random variables Y_1 and Y_2 on $[0,1]$ into two $i.i.d.$ normally distributed random variables X_1 and X_2 with distribution $\mathcal{N}(0,1)$. The transformation is as follows

$$X_1 = \sqrt{-2\log(Y_1)}\cos(2\pi Y_2)$$
$$X_2 = \sqrt{-2\log(Y_1)}\sin(2\pi Y_2). \tag{6}$$

We compute the inverse transformation and find that

$$Y_1 = \exp\left(-(X_1^2 + X_2^2)/2\right)$$
$$Y_2 = \frac{1}{4} + \frac{1}{2\pi}\arctan\left(\frac{X_2}{X_1}\right)$$

Now one can check that the Jacobian of the transformation is

$$\frac{1}{\left(\sqrt{2\pi}\right)^2}\exp\left(-(x_1^2 + x_2^2)/2\right).$$

Consequently

$$\pi(x_1, x_2) = \frac{1}{\left(\sqrt{2\pi}\right)^2}\exp\left(-(x_1^2 + x_2^2)/2\right) \times 1,$$

which proves the result. This method is simple to implement on a computer, and is to a certain extent efficient in the sense that two uniformly distributed random variables Y_1 and Y_2 give two normally distributed random variables X_1 and X_2 through the deterministic transformation in Eq. (6). In this sense no computation is wasted in producing samples that are ultimately rejected. Note however that this transformation requires the evaluation of log and cos which can be costly in terms of computer time, and even more efficient alternatives have been proposed in the literature.

Although apparently limited, this type of transformation can be very useful in practice to sample from simple distributions that are then fed into more complex algorithms. Most of the efficient algorithms to sample from gamma's, beta's etc. are a mixture of such deterministic transformations and the accept/rejection method.

3   MCMC Methods

3.1   Motivation

So far we have seen methods of sampling from relatively low dimensional distributions, which in fact collapse for even modest dimensions. For example consider the following -over-used- Bayesian example, the nuclear pump data example (Gaver and O'Muircheartaigh, 1987). This example describes multiple failures in a nuclear plant with the data, say y, given in the following table:

Pump	1	2	3	4	5	6	7	8	9	10
Failures	5	1	5	14	3	19	1	1	4	22
Times	94.32	15.72	62.88	125.76	5.24	31.44	1.05	1.05	2.10	10.48

The modeling is based on the assumption that the failures of the i−th pump follow a Poisson process with parameter λ_i ($1 \le i \le 10$). For an observed time t_i, the number of failures p_i is thus a Poisson $\mathcal{P}(\lambda_i t_i)$ random variable. The unknowns here consist therefore of $\theta := (\lambda_1, \ldots, \lambda_{10}, \beta)$ and the aim here is to estimate quantities related to $p(\theta|y)$. For reasons invoked by the authors one chooses the following prior distributions,

$$\lambda_i \overset{iid}{\sim} \mathcal{G}a(\alpha, \beta) \text{ and } \beta \sim \mathcal{G}a(\gamma, \delta)$$

with $\alpha = 1.8$ and $\gamma = 0.01$ and $\delta = 1$. Note that this introduces a *hierarchical* parameterization of the problem, as the hyperparameter β is considered unknown here. A prior distribution is therefore ascribed to this hyperparameter, therefore robustifying the inference. The posterior distribution is proportional to

$$\prod_{i=1}^{10} \{(\lambda_i t_i)^{p_i} \exp(-\lambda_i t_i)\lambda_i^{\alpha-1}\exp(-\beta\lambda_i)\}\beta^{10\alpha}\beta^{\gamma-1}\exp(-\delta\beta)$$

$$\propto \prod_{i=1}^{10} \{\lambda_i^{p_i+\alpha-1}\exp(-(t_i+\beta)\lambda_i)\}\beta^{10\alpha+\gamma-1}\exp(-\delta\beta).$$

This multidimensional distribution is rather complex, and it is not obvious how the inverse cdf method, the rejection method or importance sampling could be used in this context. However one notices that the following conditionals have a familiar form,

$$\lambda_i|(\beta, t_i, p_i) \sim \mathcal{G}a(p_i + \alpha, t_i + \beta) \text{ for } 1 \le i \le 10$$

$$\beta|(\lambda_1, \ldots, \lambda_{10}) \sim \mathcal{G}a(\gamma + 10\alpha, \delta + \sum_{i=1}^{10} \lambda_i), \tag{7}$$

and instead of directly sampling the vector $\theta = (\lambda_1, \ldots, \lambda_{10}, \beta)$ at once, one could suggest sampling it progressively and iteratively, starting for example with the λ_i's for a given guess of β, followed by an update of β given the new samples $\lambda_1, \ldots, \lambda_{10}$. More precisely, given a sample, at iteration t, $\theta^t := (\lambda_1^t, \ldots, \lambda_{10}^t, \beta^t)$ one could proceed as follows at iteration $t + 1$,

1. $\lambda_i^{t+1}|(\beta^t, t_i, p_i) \sim \mathcal{G}a(p_i + \alpha, t_i + \beta^t)$ for $1 \le i \le 10$,
2. $\beta^{t+1}|(\lambda_1^{t+1}, \ldots, \lambda_{10}^{t+1}) \sim \mathcal{G}a(\gamma + 10\alpha, \delta + \sum_{i=1}^{10} \lambda_i^{t+1})$.

This suggestion is of great interest: indeed instead of directly sampling in a space with 11 dimensions one samples in spaces of dimension 1, which can be achieved using either of the methods reviewed in previous sections. However the structure of the algorithm calls for many questions: by sampling from these conditional distributions are we sampling from the desired joint distribution? If yes, how many times should the iteration above be repeated? In fact the validity of the approach described here stems from the fact that the sequence $\{\theta^t\}$ defined above is a Markov chain and, as we shall see, some Markov chains have very nice properties.

3.2   Intuitive Approach to MCMC

Basic Concepts. Assume that we wish to sample from a distribution π. The idea of MCMC consists of running an ergodic Markov chain. In order to illustrate this intuitively, consider Figure 11. The target distribution corresponds to the continuous line. It is a normal distribution. We consider here 1000 Markov chains run in parallel, and independent. We assume that the initial distribution of these Markov chains is a uniform distribution on $[0, 20]$. We then apply a (specially designed) Markov transition probability to all of the 1000 samples, in an independent manner. Observe how the histograms of these samples evolve with the iterations. Obviously the normal distribution seems to "attract" the distribution of the samples and even to be a fixed point of the algorithm. This is is what we wanted to achieve, i.e. it seems that we have produced 1000 independent samples from the normal distribution. The numbers $1, 2, 3, 4$ and 5 correspond to the location of samples $1, 2, 3, 4$ and 5 along the iterations. In fact one can show that in many situations of interest it is not necessary to run N Markov chains in parallel in order to obtain 1000 samples, but that one can consider a unique Markov chain, and build the histogram from this single Markov chain by forming

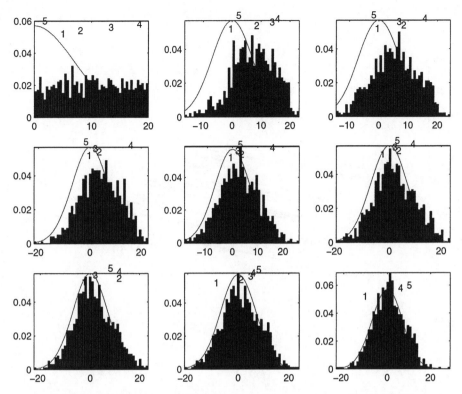

Fig. 11. From top left to bottom right: histograms of 1000 independent Markov chains with a normal distribution as target distribution

histograms from one trajectory. This idea is illustrated in Figure 12. The target distribution is here a mixture of normal distributions. Notice that the estimate of the target distribution, through the series of histograms, improves with the number of iterations. Assume that we have stored $\{X_i, 1 \le i \le N\}$ for N large and wish to estimate $\int_X f(x)\pi(x)dx$. In the light of the numerical experiments above, one can suggest the estimator

$$\frac{1}{N} \sum_{i=1}^{N} f(X_i),$$

which is exactly the estimator that we would use if $\{X_i, 1 \le i \le N\}$ were independent. In fact, it can be proved, under relatively mild conditions, that such an estimator is consistent *despite the fact that the samples are NOT independent!* Under additional conditions, a central limit theorem also holds for this estimator, and the rate of convergence is again $1/\sqrt{N}$. Note however that the constant involved in the CLT will be different from the constant in the independent case, as it will take into account the fact that the samples are not independent.

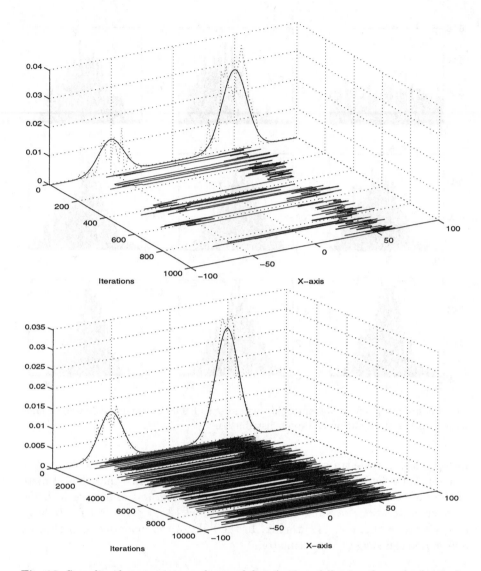

Fig. 12. Sampling from a mixture of normal distributions following the path of a single Markov chain. Full line: the target distribution - Dashed line: histogram of the path. Top: 1000 iterations only. Bottom: 10000 iterations

Unfortunately not all Markov chains, with transition probability say P, will have the following three important properties observed above:

1. The desired distribution π is a "fixed point" of the algorithm or, in more appropriate terms, an *invariant distribution* of the Markov chain, i.e.

$$\int_X \pi(x)P(x,y) = \pi(y).$$

2. The successive distributions of the Markov chains are "attracted" by π, or converge towards π.
3. The estimator

$$\frac{1}{N} \sum_{i=1}^{N} f(X_i)$$

is consistent, and converges towards $\mathbb{E}_\pi(f(X))$.

The first point is easily solved: the Metropolis-Hastings algorithm provides us with a *generic* mechanism of building Markov chains that admit a given distribution π as invariant distribution, whose density is known *only up to a normalizing constant*. Note that this later property is very convenient in a Bayesian framework! The reason for which the Metropolis-Hastings algorithm admits any desired distribution π as invariant distributions stems from the fact that it is *reversible* with respect to π, i.e. for any $x, y \in \mathsf{X}$,

$$\pi(x)P(x,y) = \pi(y)P(y,x)$$

and therefore automatically admits π as invariant distribution (indeed integrate the equality above with respect to x over X). In order to answer the second and third points one needs to introduce two notions: *irreducibility* and *aperiodicity*. The notion of reducibility (i.e. non-irreducibility) is illustrated in Figure 13: the Markov chain cannot reach a region of the space X where the distribution π has positive mass. Therefore irreducibility means that two arbitrarily chosen points in X with positive densities, can always communicate in a finite number of iterations. It is quit remarkable that under this simple condition, provided that π is an invariant distribution of the Markov chain and $\mathbb{E}_\pi(|f(x)|) < +\infty$, then $N^{-1} \sum_{i=1}^{N} f(x_i)$ is consistent (see [24]). In order to ensure that the series of distributions of the Markov chain converges it is furthermore necessary to ensure aperiodicity. To illustrate this, consider the following toy example. $\mathsf{X} = \{1, 2\}$ and $P(1, 2) = 1$ and $P(2, 1) = 1$. One easily checks that

$$\pi^{\mathsf{T}} P = \pi^{\mathsf{T}} \begin{pmatrix} 0 & 1 \\ 1 & 0 \end{pmatrix} = \pi^{\mathsf{T}},$$

admits the solution $\pi = (1/2, 1/2)^{\mathsf{T}}$, i.e. π is an invariant distribution of the Markov chain. Clearly this chain has a periodic behavior, with period 2, so that if at iteration $i = 0$ the chain always starts in 1, i.e. $\mu = (1, 0)^{\mathsf{T}}$, then the distributions of the Markov chain are

$$\mu^{\mathsf{T}} P^{2k} = \mu^{\mathsf{T}}$$
$$\mu^{\mathsf{T}} P^{2k+1} = (0, 1)^{\mathsf{T}} \ k \geq 0,$$

that is the distributions do not converge. On the other hand the proportions of time spent in state 1 and 2 converge to $1/2, 1/2$ and we expect $N^{-1} \sum_{i=1}^{N} f(X_i)$ to be consistent.

138   C. Andrieu

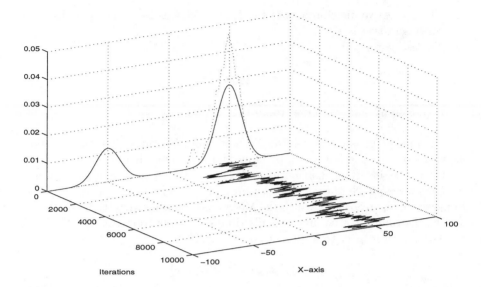

Fig. 13. In this case the Markov chain cannot explore the complete distribution: this is an illustration of reducibility (or in fact here quasi-reducibility)

The Gibbs Sampler. In the light of the appendix on Markov chains, one can ask if the following algorithm is likely to produce samples from the required posterior distribution,

$$\lambda_i | (\beta, t_i, p_i) \sim \mathcal{G}a(p_i + \alpha, t_i + \beta) \text{ for } 1 \le i \le 10$$

$$\beta | (\lambda_1, \ldots, \lambda_{10}) \sim \mathcal{G}a(\gamma + 10\alpha, \delta + \sum_{i=1}^{10} \lambda_i).$$

There are many ways of sampling from these unidimensional distribution (including rejection sampling, but there are even much more efficient ways). The idea of the Gibbs sampler consists of replacing a difficult global update of θ, with successive updates of the components of θ (or in fact in general groups of components of θ). Given the simple and familiar expressions of the conditional distributions above, one can suggest the following algorithm

1. $\lambda_i^{t+1} | (\beta^t, t_i, p_i) \sim \mathcal{G}a(p_i + \alpha, t_i + \beta^t)$ for $1 \le i \le 10$,
2. $\beta^{t+1} | (\lambda_1^{t+1}, \ldots, \lambda_{10}^{t+1}) \sim \mathcal{G}a(\gamma + 10\alpha, \delta + \sum_{i=1}^{10} \lambda_i^{t+1})$.

Maybe surprisingly, this algorithm produces samples from the posterior distribution $p(\theta|y)$, provided that the required distribution is invariant and the Markov chain irreducibility and aperiodicity are satisfied. We start with a result, in a simple case for simplicity. The generalization is trivial.

Proposition 1. *Let $p(a, b)$ be a probability density. Consider the Gibbs sampler which updates (a, b) using the conditional distributions $p(a|b)$ and $p(b|a)$. The*

Markov chain generated by this algorithm admits $p(a, b)$ as invariant distribution.

Proof. From the definition of invariance, we want to prove that for any a', b',

$$\int_X p(a, b)p(a'|b)p(b'|a')dadb \stackrel{?}{=} p(a', b').$$

We start from the left hand side, and apply basic probability rules

$$\int_X p(a, b)p(a'|b)p(b'|a')dadb = \int_X p(b)p(a'|b)p(b'|a')db$$

$$= \int_X p(a', b)p(b'|a')db$$

$$= \int_X p(b|a')p(a')p(b'|a')db$$

$$= p(a', b') \times 1.$$

Now, in order to ensure the convergence of estimators of the type $N^{-1} \sum_{i=1}^{N} f(X_i)$, it is sufficient to ensure irreducibility. This is not automatically verified for a Gibbs sampler, as illustrated in Figure 14 with a simple example. However in the nuclear pumps failure data, irreducibility is automatic: all the conditional distributions are strictly positive on the domain of definition of the parameters $((0, +\infty)$ for each of them). One can therefore reach any set A from any starting point x with positive probability in one iteration of the Gibbs sampler.

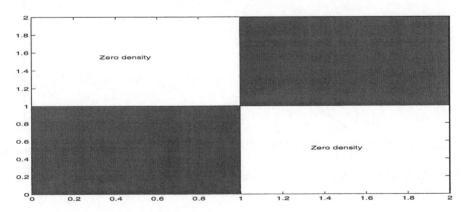

Fig. 14. A distribution that can lead to a reducible Gibbs sampler

It is relatively easy to prove aperiodicity as well, but we will not stress on this here, as we are in practice mostly interested in estimators of the type $N^{-1} \sum_{i=1}^{N} f(X_i)$.

Although natural, generally easy to implement, the Gibbs sampler does not come without problems. First it is clear that it requires one to be able to identify conditional distributions in the model, from which it is routine to sample. This is in fact rarely the case with realistic models. It is however generally the case when distributions from an exponential family are involved in the modeling. Another problem of the Gibbs sampler, is that its speed of convergence is directly influenced by the correlation properties of the target distribution π. Indeed, consider the toy two-dimensional example in Figure 15. This is a bidimensional normal distribution with strong correlation between x and y. A Gibbs sampler along the x and y axis will require many iterations to go from one point to another point that is far apart, and is somehow strongly constrained by the properties (both in terms of shape and algebraic properties) of π.

In contrast the Metropolis-Hastings algorithm which is presented in the next subsection possesses an extra degree of freedom, its proposal distribution which will determine how π is explored. This is illustrated in Figure 16, where for a good choice of the proposal distribution, the distribution π is better explored than in Figure 15, for the same number of iterations.

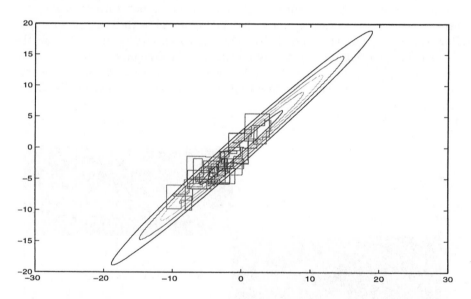

Fig. 15. A distribution for which the Gibbs sampler along the x and y axis might be very slow

The Metropolis-Hastings Algorithm. Let π be the density of a probability distribution on X and let $\{\theta \in X : q(\theta, \cdot)\}$ be a family of probability densities from which it is possible to sample. The Metropolis-Hastings algorithm proceeds as follows.

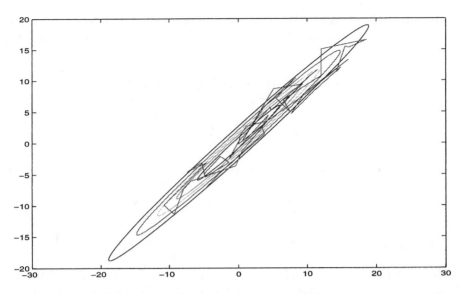

Fig. 16. A distribution for which the Gibbs sampler might be very slow, but here explored with an appropriate Metropolis-Hastings algorithm

---

Metropolis-Hastings Algorithm

1. Initialization, $i = 0$. Set randomly or deterministically θ_0.
2. Iteration i, $i \geq 1$.
   - Propose a candidate $\theta \sim q(\theta_{i-1}, \cdot)$.
   - Evaluate the acceptance probability

$$\alpha(\theta_{i-1}, \theta) = \min \left\{ 1, \frac{\pi(\theta)/q(\theta_{i-1}, \theta)}{\pi(\theta_{i-1})/q(\theta, \theta_{i-1})} \right\} \tag{8}$$

   - Then $\theta_i = \theta$ with probability $\alpha(\theta_{i-1}, \theta)$ otherwise $\theta_i = \theta_{i-1}$.

Example 6. Let us assume that we want to simulate a set of samples from $p(\theta|y)$. Using Bayes' theorem we have $p(\theta|y) \propto p(y|\theta)p(\theta)$. A MH procedure consists of simulating some candidates θ' according to $q(\theta, \theta')$, evaluating some quantities $\alpha(\theta, \theta') = \min \left\{ 1, \frac{p(y|\theta')p(\theta')q(\theta', \theta)}{p(y|\theta)p(\theta)q(\theta, \theta')} \right\}$, and accepting these candidates with probability $\alpha(\theta, \theta')$.

As pointed out earlier, q is to a certain extent an extra degree of freedom compared to the Gibbs sampler and an infinite number of possible choices for q is possible. We here briefly review two classical choices.

Random Walk: A simple choice consists of proposing as candidate a perturbation of the current state, i.e. $\theta' = \theta + z$ where z is a random increment of density $\varphi(z)$.

– This algorithm corresponds to the particular case $q(\theta, \theta') = \varphi(\theta' - \theta)$. We obtain the following acceptance probability:

$$\alpha(\theta, \theta') = \min\left\{1, \frac{\pi(\theta')\,\varphi(\theta - \theta')}{\pi(\theta)\,\varphi(\theta' - \theta)}\right\} \tag{9}$$

– If $q(\theta, \theta') = \varphi(\theta - \theta') = \varphi(\theta' - \theta)$ then we obtain

$$\alpha(\theta, \theta') = \min\left\{1, \frac{\pi(\theta')}{\pi(\theta)}\right\} \tag{10}$$

This algorithm is called the Metropolis algorithm [15].

Independent Metropolis-Hastings: In this case, we select the candidate independently of the current state according to a distribution $\varphi(\theta')$. Thus $q(\theta, \theta') = \varphi(\theta')$ and we obtain the following acceptance probability:

$$\alpha(\theta, \theta') = \min\left\{1, \frac{\pi(\theta')\,\varphi(\theta)}{\pi(\theta)\,\varphi(\theta')}\right\} \tag{11}$$

In the case where $\pi(\theta)/\varphi(\theta)$ is bounded, i.e. we could also apply the accept/reject procedure, this procedure shows (fortunately) better asymptotic performance in terms of variance of ergodic averages.

Example 7. In a Bayesian framework, if we want to sample from $p(\theta|y) \propto p(y|\theta)p(\theta)$ then one can take $p(\theta)$ as candidate distribution. Then the acceptance reduces to

$$\alpha(\theta, \theta') = \min\left\{\frac{p(y|\theta')}{p(y|\theta)}, 1\right\} \tag{12}$$

There are many possible variations on this theme, see [24] and [2].

Metropolis-Hastings One-at-a-Time. It should not be surprising if the problems encountered with classical sampling techniques are also problems with the plain MH algorithm. In particular, when θ is high-dimensional, it typically becomes very difficult to select a good proposal distribution: either the acceptance probability is very low or very large and the chain does not explore π very rapidly, or the chain explores only one mode of the distribution. To solve this problem one can use the strategy adopted by the Gibbs sampler. Define a partition of $\theta := (\theta_1, \ldots, \theta_p)$. Then each component θ_k can be updated according to a MH update with proposal distribution, say q_k which admits the conditional distribution $\pi(\theta_k|\theta_{-k})$ (where $\theta_{-k} := (\theta_1, \ldots, \theta_{k-1}, \theta_{k+1}, \ldots, \theta_p)$) as invariant distribution.

MH One-at-a-Time

1. Initialization, $i = 0$. Set randomly or deterministically $\theta^{(0)} = \theta_0$.
2. Iteration i, $i \geq 1$.

– For $k = 1$ to p

– Sample $\theta_k^{(i)}$ according to a MH step with proposal distribution

$$q_k((\theta_{-k}^{(i)}, \theta_k^{(i-1)}), \theta_k) \tag{13}$$

and invariant distribution $\pi(\theta_k|\theta_{-k}^{(i)})$.
End For.

This algorithm includes the Gibbs sampler as a special case. Indeed, this latter corresponds to the particular case where the proposal distributions of the MH steps are equal to the full conditional distributions, $i.e.$ $q_k((\theta_{-k}^{(i)}, \theta_k^{(i-1)}), \theta_k) = \pi(\theta_k|\theta_{-k}^{(i)})$, so that the acceptance probabilities are equal to 1 and no candidate is rejected.

Theoretical Aspects of the MH Algorithm. In this subsection we establish that the MH transition probability admits π as invariant distribution, and then briefly discuss the irreducibility and aperiodicity issues. The transition probability of the Metropolis-Hastings algorithm is for $x, A \in \mathsf{X}, \mathcal{B}(\mathsf{X})$

$$P(x, A) = \int_A \alpha(x, y)q(x, y)dy + \mathbb{I}_A(x) \int_{\mathsf{X}} (1 - \alpha(x, y))q(x, y)dy$$
$$= \int_A \alpha(x, y)q(x, y)dy + \mathbb{I}_A(x)[1 - \int_{\mathsf{X}} \alpha(x, y)q(x, y)dy].$$

We now prove that P is reversible with respect to π. First notice that

$$\alpha(x, y)\pi(x)q(x, y) = \min\{1, \frac{\pi(y)q(y, x)}{\pi(x)q(x, y)}\}\pi(x)q(x, y)$$
$$= \min\{\pi(x)q(x, y), \pi(y)q(y, x)\}$$
$$= \pi(y)q(y, x) \min\{\frac{\pi(x)q(x, y)}{\pi(y)q(y, x)}, 1\}$$
$$= \pi(y)q(y, x)\alpha(y, x).$$

Consequently for any $A, B \in \mathcal{B}(\mathsf{X})$,

$$
\begin{aligned}
\int_B \pi(x)P(x,A)dx &= \int_B \int_A \pi(x)\alpha(x,y)q(x,y)dxdy \\
&\quad + \int_B I_A(x)\pi(x)[1 - \int_{\mathsf{X}} \alpha(x,y)q(x,y)dy]dx \\
&= \int_A \int_B \pi(y)q(y,x)\alpha(y,x)dxdy \\
&\quad + \int_{\mathsf{X}} \mathbb{I}_{A \cap B}(x)\pi(x)[1 - \int_{\mathsf{X}} \alpha(x,y)q(x,y)dy]dx \\
&= \int_A \int_B \pi(y)q(y,x)\alpha(y,x)dxdy \\
&\quad + \int_A \mathbb{I}_B(x)\pi(x)[1 - \int_{\mathsf{X}} \alpha(x,y)q(x,y)dy]dx \\
&= \int_A \pi(y)P(y,B)dy.
\end{aligned}
$$

A simple condition which ensures the irreducibility and the aperiodicity of the MH algorithm is that $q(x,y)$ is continuous and strictly positive on the support of π for any x [20].

References

1. D. Gammerman, *Markov Chain Monte Carlo*, Chapman and Hall, London, 1997.
2. Monte Carlo Statistical Methods, Springer-Verlag, 2000.
3. **The MCMC preprint service provides papers in the MCMC field:** http://www.statslab.cam.ac.uk/~mcmc/
4. J.M. Bernardo and A.F.M. Smith, *Bayesian Theory*, John Wiley & Sons, 1995.
5. S. Brooks, "Markov Chain Monte Carlo Method and its Application", *The Statistician*, vol. 47, 69-100, 1998.
6. S. Chib and E. Greenberg, "Markov Chain Monte Carlo Simulation Methods in Econometrics", *Econometric Theory*, 12, 409-431, 1996.
7. L. Devroye, *Non-Uniform Random Variate Generation*, Springer, New-York, 1986.
8. A.E. Gelfand and A.F.M. Smith, "Sampling-based Approaches to Calculating Marginal Densities", *J. Am. Statis. Assoc.*, vol. 85, no. 410, 398-409, 1990.
9. A. Gelman, G.O. Roberts and W.R. Gilks, "Efficient Metropolis Jumping Rules", in *Bayesian Statistics V*, Clarendon Press, Oxford, 599-608, 1996.
10. A. Gelman and D.B. Rubin, "Markov Chain Monte Carlo Methods in Biostatistics", *Stat. Meth. Med. Res.*, 339-355, 1996.
11. J. Geweke, "Bayesian Inference in Econometrics Models using Monte Carlo Integration", *Econometrica*, vol. 57, 1317-1339, 1989.
12. W.R. Gilks, S. Richardson and D.J. Spiegelhalter (editors), *Markov Chain Monte Carlo in Practice*, Chapman&Hall, 1996.
13. J.H. Halton, "A retrospective and prospective survey of the Monte Carlo method," SIAM Review, vol. 12, no. 1, January 1970.

14. W.K. Hastings, "Monte Carlo Sampling Methods using Markov Chains and their Applications", *Biometrika* 57, 97-109, 1970.
15. N. Metropolis, N. Rosenblutt, A.W. Rosenblutt, M.N. Teller, A.H. Teller, "Equations of State Calculations by Fast Computing Machines", *Journal of Chemical Physics,* 21, 1087-1092, 1953.
16. S.P. Meyn and R.L. Tweedie, *Markov Chains and Stochastic Stability*, Springer-Verlag, 1993.
17. B.D. Ripley, *Stochastic Simulation*, Wiley, New York, 1987.
18. C.P. Robert, *The Bayesian Choice*, Springer-Verlag, 1996.
19. C.P. Robert and G. Casella, *Monte Carlo Statistical Methods*, Springer-Verlag, 1999.
20. A.F.M. Smith and A.E. Gelfand, "Bayesian Statistics without Tears: a Sampling-Resampling Perspective", *American Statistician*, vol. 46, no. 2, 84-88, 1992.
21. A.F.M. Smith and G.O. Roberts, "Bayesian Computation via the Gibbs sampler and Related Markov Chain Monte Carlo Methods", *J. Roy. Stat. Soc. B*, vol. 55, 3-23, 1993.
22. A.N. Shiryaev, Probability, 2nd edition, Springer.
23. M.A. Tanner, *Tools for statistical inference : methods for the exploration of posterior distributions and likelihood functions*, Springer-Verlag, New York, 1993.
24. L. Tierney, "Markov Chains for Exploring Posterior Distributions", *The Annals of Statistics*, vol. 22, 1701-1762, 1994.

Stochastic Learning

Léon Bottou

NEC Labs of America, 4 Independence Way, Princeton NJ08540, USA
leonb@bottou.org
http://leon.bottou.org

Abstract. This contribution presents an overview of the theoretical and practical aspects of the broad family of learning algorithms based on Stochastic Gradient Descent, including Perceptrons, Adalines, K-Means, LVQ, Multi-Layer Networks, and Graph Transformer Networks.

1 Introduction

This contribution reviews some material presented during the "Stochastic Learning" lecture given at the 2003 Machine Learning Summer School in Tübingen. It defines a broad family of learning algorithms that can be formalized as stochastic gradient descent algorithms and describes their common properties. This includes numerous well known algorithms such as Perceptrons, Adalines, K-Means, LVQ, and Multi-Layer Networks.

Stochastic learning algorithms are also effective for training large systems with rich structure, such as Graph Transformer Networks [8, 24]. Such large scale systems have been designed and industrially deployed with considerable success.

- Section 2 presents the basic framework and illustrates it with a number of well known learning algorithms.
- Section 3 presents the basic mathematical tools for establishing the convergence of stochastic learning algorithms.
- Section 4 discusses the learning speed of stochastic learning algorithms applied to large datasets. This discussion covers both statistical efficiency and computational requirements.

These concepts were previously discussed in [9, 10, 14, 12]. Readers interested by the practice of stochastic gradient algorithms should also read [25] and investigate applied contributions such as [39, 37, 46, 6, 24, 26].

2 Foundations

Almost all of the early work on *Learning Systems* focused on online algorithms [18, 34, 44, 2, 19]. In these early days, the algorithmic simplicity of online algorithms was a requirement. This is still the case when it comes to handling large, real-life training sets [23, 30, 25, 26].

O. Bousquet et al. (Eds.): Machine Learning 2003, LNAI 3176, pp. 146–168, 2004.
© Springer-Verlag Berlin Heidelberg 2004

The early *Recursive Adaptive Algorithms* were introduced during the same years [33] and very often by the same people [45]. First developed in the engineering world, recursive adaptation algorithms have turned into a mathematical discipline, namely *Stochastic Approximations* [22, 27, 7].

2.1   Expected Risk Function

In [40, 41], the goal of a learning system consists of finding the minimum of a function $C(w)$ named the *expected risk function*[1]. This function is decomposed as follows:

$$C(w) \stackrel{\triangle}{=} \mathbf{E}_z \, Q(z,w) \stackrel{\triangle}{=} \int Q(z,w) \, dP(z) \tag{1}$$

The minimization variable w is meant to represent the part of the learning system which must be adapted as a response to observing events z occurring in the real world. The *loss function* $Q(z, w)$ measures the performance of the learning system with parameter w under the circumstances described by event z. Common mathematical practice suggests to represent both w and z by elements of adequately chosen spaces $\mathcal{W}$ and $\mathcal{Z}$.

2.2   Gradient Based Learning

The expected risk function (1) cannot be minimized directly because the grand truth distribution is unknown. It is however possible to compute an approximation of $C(w)$ by simply using a finite *training set* of independent observations $z_1, \ldots, z_L$.

$$C(w) \approx \hat{C}_L(w) \stackrel{\triangle}{=} \frac{1}{L} \sum_{n=1}^{L} Q(z_n, w) \tag{2}$$

General theorems [42] show that minimizing the *empirical risk* $\hat{C}_L(w)$ can provide a good estimate of the minimum of the expected risk $C(w)$ when the training set is large enough. This line of work has provided a way to understand the *generalization* phenomenon, i.e. the ability of a system to learn from a finite training set and yet provide results that are valid in general.

Batch Gradient Descent. Minimizing the empirical risk $\hat{C}_L(w)$ can be achieved using a *batch gradient descent* algorithm. Successive estimates w_t of the optimal parameter are computed using the following formula

$$w_{t+1} \;=\; w_t - \gamma_t \nabla_w \hat{C}_L(w_t) \;=\; w_t - \gamma_t \frac{1}{L} \sum_{i=1}^{L} \nabla_w \, Q(z_n, w_t) \tag{3}$$

where the learning rate γ_t is a positive number.

---

[1] The origin of this statistical framework is unclear. It has been popularized by Vapnik's work [42] but was already discussed in Tsypkin's work [40] or even [16]. Vapnik told me that "someone wrote this on the blackboard during a seminar"; he does not remember who did.

The properties of this optimization algorithm are well known: When the learning rate γ_t are small enough[2], the algorithm converges towards a local minimum of the empirical risk $\hat{C}_L(w)$. Each iteration of the batch gradient descent algorithm however involves a burdening computation of the average of the gradients of the loss function $\nabla_w Q(z_n, w)$ over the entire training set. Significant computer resources must be allocated in order to store a large enough training set and compute this average.

Online Gradient Descent. The elementary *online gradient descent* algorithm is obtained by dropping the averaging operation in the batch gradient descent algorithm (3). Instead of averaging the gradient of the loss over the complete training set, each iteration of the online gradient descent consists of choosing an example z_t at random, and updating the parameter w_t according to the following formula.

$$w_{t+1} = w_t - \gamma_t \nabla_w Q(z_t, w_t) \qquad (4)$$

Averaging this update over all possible choices of the training example z_t would restore the batch gradient descent algorithm. The online gradient descent simplification relies on the hope that the random noise introduced by this procedure will not perturbate the average behavior of the algorithm. Significant empirical evidence substantiate this hope.

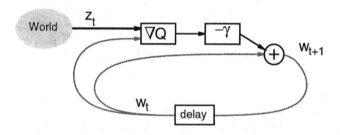

Fig. 1. Online Gradient Descent. The parameters of the learning system are updated using information extracted from real world observations

Many variants of (4) have been defined. Parts of this contribution discuss two significant variants: Section 2.4 replaces the gradient $\nabla_w Q(z, w)$ by a general term $U(z, w)$ satisfying $\mathbf{E}_z U(z, w) = \nabla_w C(w)$. Section 4 replaces the learning rates γ_t by positive symmetric matrices (equation (27).)

Online gradient descent can also be described without reference to a training set. Instead of drawing examples from a training set, we can directly use the events z_t observed in the real world, as shown in Figure 1. This formulation is particularly adequate for describing *adaptive algorithms* that simultaneously

---

[2] Convergence occurs for constant learning rates, smaller than a critical learning rate related to the maximal curvature of the cost function. See [25] for instance.

process an observation and learn to perform better. Such adaptive algorithms are very useful for tracking a phenomenon that evolves in time.

Formulating online gradient descent without reference to a training set also presents a theoretical interest. Each iteration of the algorithm uses an example z_t drawn from the grand truth distribution instead of a finite training set. The average update therefore is a gradient descent algorithm which directly optimizes the expected risk. This shortcuts the usual discussion about differences between optimizing the empirical risk and the expected risk [42, 43]. Proving the convergence of an online algorithm towards the minimum of the expected risk provides an alternative to the Vapnik proofs of the consistency of learning algorithms. Non-asymptotic bounds for online algorithms are rare.

2.3   Examples: Online Least Mean Squares

Widrow's Adaline. The *Adaline* [44] is one of the few learning systems designed at the very beginning of the computer age. Online gradient descent was then a very attractive proposition requiring little hardware. The adaline could fit in a refrigerator sized cabinet containing a forest of potentiometers and electrical motors.

The Adaline (Figure 2) learning algorithm adapts the parameters of a single *threshold unit*. Input patterns x are recognized as class $y = +1$ or $y = -1$ according to the sign of $w'x + \beta$. It is practical to consider an *augmented input* pattern x containing an extra constant coefficient equal to 1. The bias β then is represented as an extra coefficient in the parameter vector w. With this convention, the output of the threshold unit can be written as

$$\hat{y}_w(x) \overset{\triangle}{=} \text{sign}(w'x) = \text{sign}\sum_i w_i x_i \tag{5}$$

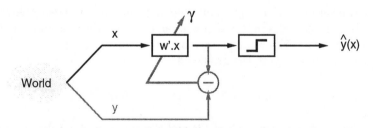

Fig. 2. Widrow's Adaline. The adaline computes a binary indicator by thresholding a linear combination of its input. Learning is achieved using the *delta rule*

During training, the Adaline is provided with pairs $z = (x, y)$ representing input patterns and desired output for the Adaline. The parameter w is adjusted after using the *delta rule* (the "prime" denotes transposed vectors):

$$w_{t+1} = w_t - \gamma_t(y_t - w'_t x_t)' x_t \tag{6}$$

This delta rule is nothing more than an iteration of the online gradient descent algorithm (4) with the following loss function:

$$Q_{\text{adaline}}(z, w) \triangleq (y - w'x)^2 \tag{7}$$

This loss function does not take the discontinuity of the threshold unit (5) into account. This linear approximation is a real breakthrough over the apparently more natural loss function $(y - \hat{y}_w(x))^2$. This discontinuous loss function is difficult to minimize because its gradient is zero almost everywhere. Furthermore, all solutions achieving the same misclassification rate would have the same cost $C(w)$, regardless of the margins separating the examples from the decision boundary implemented by the threshold unit.

Multi-layer Networks. *Multi-Layer Networks* were initially designed to overcome the computational limitation of the threshold units [29]. Arbitrary binary mappings can be implemented by stacking several layers of threshold units, each layer using the outputs of the previous layers as inputs. The Adaline linear approximation could not be used in this framework, because ignoring the discontinuities would make the entire system linear regardless of the number of layers. The key of a learning algorithm for multi-layer networks [35] consisted of noticing that the discontinuity of the threshold unit could be represented by a smooth non-linear approximation.

$$\text{sign}(w'x) \approx \tanh(w'x) \tag{8}$$

Using such *sigmoid units* does not reduce the computational capabilities of a multi-layer network, because the approximation of a step function by a sigmoid can be made arbitrarily good by scaling the coefficients of the parameter vector w.

A multi-layer network of sigmoidal units implements a differentiable function $f(x, w)$ of the input pattern x and the parameters w. Given an input pattern x and the desired network output y, the *back-propagation* algorithm, [35] provides an efficient way to compute the gradients of the mean square loss function.

$$Q_{\text{mse}}(z, w) = \frac{1}{2}(y - f(x, w))^2 \tag{9}$$

Both the batch gradient descent (3) and the online gradient descent (4) have been used with considerable success. On large, redundant data sets, the online version converges much faster then the batch version, sometimes by orders of magnitude [30]. An intuitive explanation can be found in the following extreme example. Consider a training set composed of two copies of the same subset. The batch algorithm (3) averages the gradient of the loss function over the whole training set, causing redundant computations. On the other hand, running online gradient descent (4) on all examples of the training set would amount to performing two complete learning iterations over the duplicated subset.

2.4   Examples: Non Differentiable Loss Functions

Many interesting examples involve a loss function $Q(z, w)$ which is not differentiable on a subset of points with probability zero. Intuition suggests that this is a minor problems because the iterations of the online gradient descent have zero probability to reach one of these points. Even if we reach one of these points, we can just draw another example z.

This can be formalized as replacing the gradient $\nabla_w Q(z, w)$ in equation (4) by an update term $U(z, w)$ defined as follows:

$$U(z, w) = \begin{cases} \nabla_w Q(z, w) & \text{when differentiable} \\ 0 & \text{otherwise} \end{cases} \qquad (10)$$

The convergence study (Section 3) shows that this works if the expectation of the update term $U(z, w)$ is equal to gradient of the cost $C(w)$:

$$\mathbf{E}_z U(z, w) \stackrel{?}{=} \nabla_w C(w)$$

$$\int \nabla_w Q(z, w) \, dP(z) \stackrel{?}{=} \nabla_w \int Q(z, w) \, dP(z) \qquad (11)$$

The Lebesgue integration theory provides a sufficient condition for swapping the integration ($\int$) and differentiation (∇_w) operators as in (11). For each parameter value w reached by the online algorithm, it is sufficient to find an integrable function $\Phi(z, w)$ and a neighborhood $\vartheta(w)$ of w such that:

$$\forall z, \ \forall v \in \vartheta(w), \ \ |Q(z, v) - Q(z, w)| \ \leq \ |w - v| \, \Phi(z, w) \qquad (12)$$

This condition (12) tests that the maximal slope of the loss function $Q(z, w)$ is conveniently bounded. This is obviously true when the loss function $Q(z, w)$ is differentiable and has an integrable gradient. This is obviously false when the loss function is not continuous. Given our previous assumption concerning the zero probability of the non differentiable points, condition (12) is a sufficient condition for safely ignoring a few non differentiable points.

Rosenblatt's Perceptron. During the early days of the computer age, the *Perceptron* [34] generated considerable interest as a possible architecture for general purpose computers. This interest faded after the disclosure of its computational limitations [29]. Figure 3 represents the perceptron architecture. An *associative area* produces a feature vector x by applying predefined transformations to the *retina* input. The feature vector is then processed by a *threshold unit* (cd. Adaline).

The perceptron learning algorithm adapts the parameters w of the threshold unit. Whenever a misclassification occurs, the parameters are updated according to the *perceptron rule*.

$$w_{t+1} = w_t + 2\gamma_t y_t \, x_t \qquad (13)$$

This learning rule can be derived as an online gradient descent applied to the following loss function:

$$Q_{\text{perceptron}}(z, w) = (\text{sign}(w'x) - y) \, w'x \qquad (14)$$

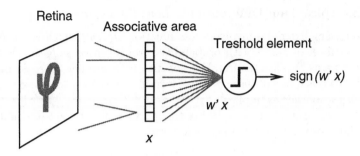

Fig. 3. Rosenblatt's Perceptron is composed of a fixed preprocessing and of a trainable threshold unit

Although this loss function is non differentiable when $w'x$ is null, is meets condition (12) as soon as the expectation $\mathbf{E}(x)$ is defined. We can therefore ignore the non differentiability and apply the online gradient descent algorithm:

$$w_{t+1} = w_t - \gamma_t (\text{sign}(w'_t x_t) - y_t)\, x_t \tag{15}$$

Since the desired class is either $+1$ or -1, the weights are not modified when the pattern x is correctly classified. Therefore this parameter update (15) is equivalent to the perceptron rule (13).

The perceptron loss function (14) is zero when the pattern x is correctly recognized as a member of class $y = \pm 1$. Otherwise its value is positive and proportional to the dot product $w'x$. The corresponding cost function reaches its minimal value zero when all examples are properly recognized or when the weight vector w is null.

Such *hinge loss functions* [17, 36] have recently drawn much interest because of their links with the Support Vector Machines and the AdaBoost algorithm.

K-Means. The *K-Means* algorithm [28] is a popular clustering method which dispatches K centroids $w(k)$ in order to find clusters in a set of points $x_1, \ldots, x_L$. This algorithm can be derived by performing the online gradient descent with the following loss function.

$$Q_{\text{kmeans}}(x, w) \overset{\triangle}{=} \min_{k=1}^{K} (x - w(k))^2 \tag{16}$$

This loss function measures the quantification error, that is to say the error on the position of point x when we replace it by the closest centroid. The corresponding cost function measures the average quantification error.

This loss function is not differentiable on points located on the Voronoï boundaries of the set of centroids, but meets condition (12) as soon as the expectations $\mathbf{E}(x)$ and $\mathbf{E}(x^2)$ are defined. On the remaining points, the derivative of the loss is the derivative of the distance to the nearest centroid w^-. We can therefore ignore the non-differentiable points and apply the online gradient descent algorithm.

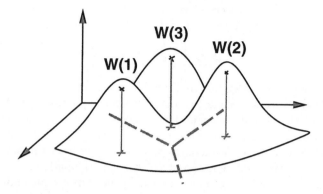

Fig. 4. K-Means dispatches a predefined number of cluster centroids in a way that minimizes the quantification error

$$w_{t+1}^- = w_t^- + \gamma_t(x_t - w_t^-) \qquad (17)$$

This formula describes an elementary iteration of the K-Means algorithm. A very efficient choice of learning rates γ_t will be suggested in Section 4.6.

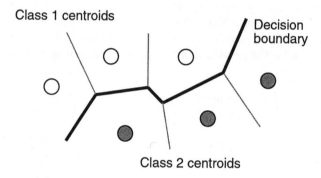

Fig. 5. Kohonen's LVQ2 pattern recognition scheme outputs the class associated with the closest reference point to the input pattern

Learning Vector Quantization 2. Kohonen's *Learning Vector Quantization 2* (LVQ2) rule [20] is a powerful pattern recognition algorithm. Like K-Means, it uses a fixed set of reference points $w(k)$. A class $y(k)$ is associated with each reference point. As shown in Figure 5, an unknown pattern x is then recognized as a member of the class associated with the nearest reference point.

Given a training pattern x, let us denote w^- the nearest reference point and denote w^+ the nearest reference point among those associated with the correct class y. Adaptation only occurs when the closest reference point w^- is associated with an incorrect class while the closest correct reference point w^+ is not too far away:

$$\text{if } \begin{cases} x \text{ is misclassified } (w^- \neq w^+) \\ \text{and } (x - w^+)^2 < (1 + \delta)(x - w^-)^2 \end{cases} \tag{18}$$

$$\text{then } \begin{cases} w_{t+1}^- = w_t^- - \varepsilon_t(x - w_t^-) \\ w_{t+1}^+ = w_t^+ + \varepsilon_t(x - w_t^+) \end{cases}$$

Reference points are only updated when the pattern x is misclassified. Furthermore, the distance to the closest correct reference point w^+ must not exceed the distance to the closest (incorrect) reference point w^- by more than a percentage defined by parameter δ. When both conditions are met, the algorithm pushes the closest (incorrect) reference point w^- away from the pattern x, and pulls the closest correct reference point w^+ towards the pattern x.

This intuitive algorithm can be derived by performing an online gradient descent with the following loss function:

$$Q_{\text{lvq2}}(z, w) \triangleq \begin{cases} 0 & \text{if } x \text{ is well classified } (w^+ = w^-) \\ 1 & \text{if } (x - w^+)^2 \geq (1 + \delta)(x - w^-)^2 \\ \frac{(x-w^+)^2 - (x-w^-)^2}{\delta(x-w^-)^2} & \text{otherwise} \end{cases} \tag{19}$$

This function is a continuous approximation to a binary variable indicating whether pattern x is misclassified. The corresponding cost function therefore is a continuous approximation of the system misclassification rate [9]. This analysis helps understanding how the LVQ2 algorithm works.

Although the above loss function is not differentiable for some values of w, it meets condition (12) as soon as the expectations $\mathbf{E}(x)$ and $\mathbf{E}(x^2)$ are defined. We can therefore ignore the non-differentiable points and apply the online gradient descent algorithm:

$$\text{if } \begin{cases} x \text{ is misclassified } (w^- \neq w^+) \\ \text{and } (x - w^+)^2 < (1 + \delta)(x - w^-)^2 \end{cases} \tag{20}$$

$$\text{then } \begin{cases} w_{t+1}^- = w_t^- - \gamma_t k_1(x - w_t^-) \\ w_{t+1}^+ = w_t^+ + \gamma_t k_2(x - w_t^+) \end{cases}$$

$$\text{with } k_2 = \frac{1}{\delta(x - w^-)^2} \text{ and } k_1 = k_2 \frac{(x - w^+)^2}{(x - w^-)^2} \tag{21}$$

This online gradient descent algorithm (20) is similar to the usual LVQ2 learning algorithm (18). The difference between the two scalar coefficients k_1 and k_2 can be viewed as a minor variation on the learning rates.

3   Convergence

Given a suitable choice of the learning rates γ_t, the batch gradient descent algorithm (3) is known to converge to a local minimum of the cost function. This local minimum is a function of the initial parameters w_0. The parameter trajectory follows the meanders of the local attraction basin and eventually reaches the corresponding minimum.

The random noise introduced by stochastic gradient descent (4) disrupts this deterministic picture. The parameter trajectory can jump from basin to basin. One usually distinguish a *search phase* that explores the parameter space and a *final phase* that takes place in the vicinity of a minimum.

- The final phase takes place in the vicinity of a single local minimum w^* where the cost function is essentially convex. This is discussed in Section 3.1.
- Our understanding of the search phase is still very spotty. Section 3.2 presents sufficient conditions to guarantee that the convergence process will eventually reach the final phase.

3.1   Final Convergence Phase

The following discussion rely on the *general convexity assumption*[3]. Everywhere in the parameter space, the opposite of the gradient must point toward a unique minimum w^*.

$$\forall \varepsilon > 0, \quad \inf_{(w-w^*)^2 > \varepsilon} (w - w^*) \, \nabla_w C(w) > 0 \qquad (22)$$

Such a strong assumption is only valid for a few simple learning algorithms such as the Adaline, Section 2.3). Nevertheless these results are useful for understanding the final convergence phase. The assumption usually holds within the final convergence region because the cost function is locally convex.

The parameter updates $\gamma_t \nabla_w Q(z, w)$ must become smaller and smaller when the parameter vector w approaches the optimum w^*. This implies that either the gradients or the learning rates must vanish in the vicinity of the optimum. More specifically one can write:

$$\mathbf{E}_z \left[\nabla_w Q(z, w)^2 \right] = \mathbf{E}_z \left[(\nabla_w Q(z, w) - \nabla_w C(w))^2 \right] + \| \nabla_w C(w) \|^2$$

The first term is the variance of the stochastic gradient. It is reasonable to assume that it does not grow faster than the norm of the real gradient itself. In the vicinity of w^* we can write:

$$\| \nabla_w C(w) \|^2 = \| \nabla_w C(w) - \nabla_w C(w^*) \|^2 \le \frac{1}{2} \| \nabla \nabla_w C(w^*) \|^2 \, \| w - w^* \|^2$$

It is therefore reasonable to assume that $\| \nabla_w C(w) \|^2$ behaves quadratically within the final convergence region. Both assumptions are conveniently expressed as follows:

$$\mathbf{E}_z \left[\nabla_w Q(z, w)^2 \right] < A + B \, (w - w^*)^2 \quad \text{with } A \ge 0, \, B \ge 0 \qquad (23)$$

The constant A must be greater than the residual variance $\mathbf{E}_z \left[\nabla_w Q(z, w^*)^2 \right]$ of the gradients at the optimum. This residual variance can be zero for certain

---

[3] The optimization literature often defines such extended notions of convexity. Small details are important. For instance, in (22), one cannot simply replace the infimum by $\forall w \ne w^*$. Consider function $C(w) = 1 - \exp(-\|w\|^2)$ as a counter-example.

rare noiseless problems where w^* simultaneously optimizes the loss for every examples. It is strictly positive in most practical cases. The average norm of the gradients then does not vanish when the parameter vector w approaches the optimum. Therefore one must use *decreasing learning rates*, e.g.:

$$\sum \gamma_t^2 < \infty \qquad (24)$$

The presence of constant A in (23) marks a critical difference between stochastic and ordinary gradient descent. There is no such constant in the case of the ordinary gradient descent. A simple analysis then yields an expression for the maximal constant learning rate [25]. In the stochastic gradient case, this analysis suggests that the parameter vector eventually hovers around the minimum w^* at a distance roughly proportional to γ_t. Quickly decreasing the learning rate is therefore tempting. Suppose however that the learning rates decrease so fast that $\sum \gamma_t = R < \infty$. This would effectively maintain the parameters within a certain radius of their initial value. It is therefore necessary to enforce the following condition:

$$\sum \gamma_t = \infty \qquad (25)$$

Convex Convergence Theorem. *The general convexity (22) and the three conditions (23), (24) and (25) are sufficient conditions for the almost sure convergence of the stochastic gradient descent (4) to the optimum w^*.*

The following discussion provides a sketch of the proof. This proof is simply an extension of the convergence proofs for the continuous gradient descent and the discrete gradient descent.

The continuous gradient descent proof studies the convergence of the function $w(t)$ defined by the following differential equation:

$$\frac{\mathrm{d}w}{\mathrm{d}t} = -\nabla_w C(w)$$

This proof follows three steps:

A) *Definition of a Lyapunov function* — A Lyapunov function is a function whose convergence to zero implies the convergence of $w(t)$ to w^* when t grows to the infinity. For the continuous gradient we simply use $h(t) = (w - w^*)^2$.
B) *Convergence of the Lyapunov function* — Using (22), it is easy to see that $\mathrm{d}h/\mathrm{d}t = 2(w - w^*)\nabla_w C(w) \le 0$. Function $h(t)$ converges because it is both positive and decreasing.
C) *The limit of the Lyapunov function must be zero.* We know that $\mathrm{d}h/\mathrm{d}t \to 0$ because $h(t)$ converges. Assumption (22) then implies that $(w - w^*)^2 \to 0$.

The convergence proofs for both the discrete (3) and stochastic (4) gradient descents follow the same three steps. Each step requires increasingly sophisticated mathematical tools summarized in the following table.

	Continuous	Discrete	Stochastic
Step A Define Lyapunov criterion.	Function $h(t) = (w(t) - w^*)^2$	Sequence $h_t = (w_t - w^*)^2$	Random Process $h_t = (w_t - w^*)^2$
Step B Lyapunov criterion converges.	Decreasing positive function	Positive sequence with bounded positive increments	Positive quasi-martingales
Step C Lyapunov criterion converges to zero.	General Convexity		

Full details can be found in [9, 10].

3.2   Search Phase

This section discusses the convergence of the stochastic gradient algorithm (4) without the general convexity assumption (22). Since the cost function $C(w)$ can have several local minima, this discussion encompasses the search phase. Although our understanding of the search phase is still very incomplete, empirical and theoretical evidence indicate that stochastic gradient algorithms enjoy significant advantages over batch algorithms. Stochastic gradient descent benefit from the redundancies of the training set. Consider the extreme case where a training set of size 1000 is inadvertently composed of 10 identical copies of a set with 100 samples. Averaging the gradient over all 1000 patterns gives the exact same result as computing the gradient based on just the first 100. Batch gradient descent is wasteful because it re-computes the same quantity 10 times before one parameter update. On the other hand, stochastic gradient will see a full epoch as 10 iterations through a 100-long training set.

In the case of the continuous and discrete gradient descent, it is usually sufficient to partition the parameter space into several attraction basins, discuss the conditions under which the algorithm confines the parameters w_t in a single attraction basin, define a suitable Lyapunov criterion [21], and proceed as in the convex case. This approach does not work well with stochastic gradient because the parameter trajectory can always jump from basin to basin.

Let us instead assume that the cost function becomes large when one wanders far from the origin. The global landscape then looks like a single large attraction basin. The local minima structure only shows when one gives a closer look to in the vicinity of the apparent minimum.

This situation can be expressed by the following assumptions:

i.) $\inf C(w) > -\infty$

ii.) $\exists D > 0,\ \inf_{w^2 > D} w\, \nabla_w C(w) > 0$

iii.) $\mathbf{E}_z (\nabla_w Q(z, w))^2 \leq A + Bw^2$

iv.) $\exists E > D,\ \forall z,\ \sup_{w^2 < E} ||\nabla_w Q(z, w)|| \leq Constant$

Assumption (i) indicates that the cost is bounded from below. Assumption (ii) indicates that the gradient far away from the origin always drives us back towards the origin. Assumptions (iii) and (iv) limit the variance of the stochastic gradient and the asymptotic growth of the real gradients[4].

Global Confinement Theorem: *The four assumptions (i) to (iv) above, and the two learning rate assumptions (24) and (25) guarantee that the parameter w_t defined by the stochastic gradient update (4) will almost surely remain confined within distance $\sqrt{E}$ of the origin.*

This global confinement result [10] is obtained using the same proof technique as in the convex case. The Lyapunov criterion is simply defined as $h_t = \max(E, w_t^2)$.

Global confinement shows that w_t evolves in a compact domain where nothing dramatic can happen. In fact, it even implies that the stochastic gradient descent will soon or later reach the final convergence phase. This is formalized by the following result:

Gradient Convergence Theorem. *The four assumptions (i) to (iv) above, and the two learning rate assumptions (24) and (25) guarantee that the gradients $\nabla_w C(w_t)$ converges almost surely to zero.*

The proof of this final convergence result [10] again is very similar to the convergence proofs for the convex case with suitable choices for the Lyapunov criterion. The details of the proof extensively rely on the global confinement result.

4   Convergence Speed and Learning Speed

The main purpose of this section is to illustrate a critical difference between optimization algorithms and learning algorithm. It will then appear that stochastic gradient descent is simultaneously a very poor optimization algorithm and a very effective learning algorithm.

4.1   Convergence Speed for Batch Gradient Descent

Simple batch gradient descent enjoy *linear*[5] convergence speed (see for instance Section 5 of [25]). The convergence speed of batch gradient descent drastically improves when one replaces the scalar learning rates γ_t by a definite positive symmetric matrix Φ_t that approximates the inverse of the Hessian of the cost function.

$$\Phi_t \approx H^{-1}(w_t), \qquad H(w) = \nabla\nabla_w C(w) \tag{26}$$

This leads to very effective optimization algorithms such as Newton's algorithm, Levemberg-Marquardt, Conjugate Gradient and BFGS (see [15] for a

---

[4] See also the discussion for convex assumption (23).

[5] Linear convergence speed: $(\log 1/(w_t - w^*)^2)$ grows linearly with t.

review). These algorithms achieve *superlinear* or even *quadratic*[6] convergence speeds.

4.2   Convergence Speed for Stochastic Algorithms

Whereas online algorithms may converge to the general area of the optimum at least as fast as batch algorithms [25], the optimization proceeds rather slowly during the final convergence phase [14]. The noisy gradient estimate causes the parameter vector to fluctuate around the optimum in a bowl whose size depends on the decreasing learning rates and is therefore constrained by (25). It can be shown that this size decreases like $1/t$ at best[7].

Stochastic gradient descent nevertheless benefits from using similar second order methods. The gradient vector is rescaled using a positive symmetric matrix Φ_t that approximates the inverse hessian (26) in a manner analogous to Newton's algorithm[8]. The same convergence results apply as long as the eigenvalues of the scaling matrix Φ_t are bounded.

$$w_{t+1} = w_t - \frac{1}{t} \Phi_t \nabla_w Q(z_t, w_t) \tag{27}$$

For simplicity, this section only addresses the case $\gamma_t = 1/t$ which satisfies both conditions (24) and (25). It is however important to understand that the second order stochastic algorithm (27) still experiences the stochastic noise resulting from the random selection of the examples z_t. Its convergence speed still depends on the choice of decreasing learning rates γ_t and is therefore constrained by condition (25). This is a sharp contrast with the case of batch algorithms where the same scaling matrix yields superlinear convergence.

Stochastic gradient descent is a hopeless optimization algorithm. It is tempting to conclude that it is also a very poor learning algorithm. Yet experience suggests otherwise [4].

4.3   Optimization Versus Learning

This apparent contradiction is resolved when one considers that the above discussion compares the speed of two different convergences:

– Batch algorithms converge towards a minimum of the *empirical risk* $\hat{C}_L(w)$, which is defined as an average on L training examples (2).
– Stochastic algorithms converge towards a minimum of the *expected risk* $C(w)$, which is defined as an expectation with respect to the probability distribution from which we draw the examples (1).

---

[6] Quadratic convergence speed: $(\log \log 1/(w_t - w^*)^2)$ grows linearly with t.

[7] Convergence speed of stochastic gradient: $(1/(w_t - w^*)^2)$ grows linearly with t.

[8] Such second order stochastic approximations are standard practice in the Stochastic Approximation literature [22, 27, 7].

In a learning problem, we are interested in knowing the speed of convergence towards the minimum of the expected risk $C(w)$ because it reflects the generalization error. Replacing the expected risk $C(w)$ by the empirical risk $\hat{C}_L(w)$ is by itself an approximation. As shown in the next section, this approximation spoils the potential benefits of running an optimization algorithm with ambitious convergence speed.

4.4   Optimizing the Empirical Risk Is a Stochastic Process

We consider in this section an infinite sequence of independent training examples $(z_1, \ldots, z_t, \ldots)$. Let w_t^* be the minimum of the empirical risk $\hat{C}_t(w)$ defined on a training set composed of the first t examples $(z_1, \ldots, z_t)$. We assume that all the w_t^* are located in the vicinity of the minimum w^* of the expected risk $C(w)$.

Manipulating a Taylor expansion of the gradient of $\hat{C}_{t+1}(w)$ in the vicinity of w_t^* provides the following recursive relation:

$$w_{t+1}^* = w_t^* - \frac{1}{t+1} \Psi_t \nabla_w Q(z_t, w_t^*) + \mathcal{O}\left(\frac{1}{t^2}\right) \tag{28}$$

with

$$\Psi_t \triangleq \left(\frac{1}{t+1} \sum_{i=1}^{t+1} \nabla \nabla_w Q(z_i, w_t^*)\right)^{-1} \xrightarrow[t \to \infty]{} H^{-1}(w_t^*)$$

The similarity between (28) and (27) suggests that both the batch sequence (w_t^*) and online sequence (w_t) converge at the same speed for adequate choices of the scaling matrix Φ_t. Theoretical analysis indeed shows that [31, 13]:

$$\mathbf{E}\left[(w_t^* - w^*)^2\right] = \frac{K}{t} + o\left(\frac{1}{t}\right) \tag{29}$$

$$\Phi_t \xrightarrow[t \to \infty]{} H^{-1}(w^*) \implies \mathbf{E}\left[(w_t - w^*)^2\right] = \frac{K}{t} + o\left(\frac{1}{t}\right) \tag{30}$$

where

$$K = \text{trace}\left(H^{-1}(w^*) \cdot \mathbf{E}_z\left[(\nabla_w Q(z, w^*))(\nabla_w Q(z, w^*))'\right] \cdot H^{-1}(w^*)\right)$$

Not only does this result establish that both sequences have $\mathcal{O}(1/t)$ convergence, but also it provides the value of the common constant K. This constant is neither affected by the second order terms of (28) nor by the convergence speed of the scaling matrix Φ_t towards the inverse Hessian [13].

Following [40], we say that a second order stochastic algorithm is *optimal* when Φ_t converges to $H^{-1}(w^*)$. Figure 6 summarizes the behavior of such optimal algorithms. After t iterations on fresh examples, the point w_t reached by an optimal stochastic learning algorithm is asymptotically as good as the solution w_t^* of a batch algorithm trained on the same t examples.

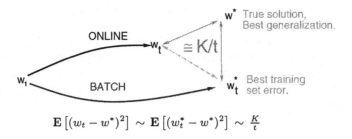

$$\mathbf{E}\left[(w_t - w^*)^2\right] \sim \mathbf{E}\left[(w_t^* - w^*)^2\right] \sim \frac{K}{t}$$

Fig. 6. After t iterations on fresh examples, the point w_t reached by an optimal stochastic learning algorithm is asymptotically as good as the solution w_t^* of a batch algorithm trained on the same t examples

4.5   Comparing Computational Complexities

The discussion so far has established that a properly designed online learning algorithm performs as well as any batch learning algorithm for a same number of examples. We now establish that, given the same computing resources, a stochastic learning algorithm can asymptotically process more examples than a batch learning algorithm.

Each iteration of a batch learning algorithm running on N training examples requires a time $K_1 N + K_2$. Constants K_1 and K_2 respectively represent the time required to process each example, and the time required to update the parameters. Result (29) provides the following asymptotic equivalence:

$$\mathbf{E}\left[(w_N^* - w^*)^2\right] \sim \frac{1}{N}$$

The batch algorithm must perform enough iterations to approach the empirical optimum w_N^* with at least the same accuracy ($\sim 1/N$). A very efficient algorithm with quadratic convergence achieves this after a number of iterations asymptotically proportional to $(\log\log N)$.

Running a stochastic learning algorithm requires a constant time K_3 per processed example. Let us call T the number of examples processed by the stochastic learning algorithm using the same computing resources as the batch algorithm. We then have:

$$K_3 T \sim (K_1 N + K_2)\log\log N \quad \Longrightarrow \quad T \sim N \log\log N$$

The parameter w_T of the stochastic algorithm also converges according to (30). Comparing the accuracies of both algorithms shows that the stochastic algorithm asymptotically provides a better solution by a factor $\sim (\log\log N)$.

$$\mathbf{E}\left[(w_T - w^*)^2\right] \sim \frac{1}{N \log\log N} \ll \frac{1}{N} \sim \mathbf{E}\left[(w_N^* - w^*)^2\right] \qquad (31)$$

This $(\log\log N)$ factor corresponds to the number of iterations required by the batch algorithm. This number increases slowly with the desired accuracy of the solution. In practice, this factor is much less significant than the actual value of the constants K_1, K_2 and K_3. Experience shows however that stochastic algorithms are considerably easier to implement. Each iteration of the batch algorithm involves a large summation over all the available examples. Memory must be allocated to hold these examples. On the other hand, each iteration of the stochastic algorithm only involves one random example which can then be discarded.

4.6   Examples

Optimal Learning Rate for K-Means. Second derivative information can be used to determine very efficient learning rates for the K-Means algorithm (Section 2.4). A simple analysis of the loss function (16) shows that the Hessian of the cost function is a diagonal matrix [11] whose coefficients $\lambda_{(k)}$ are equal to the probabilities that an example x is associated with the corresponding centroid $w_{(k)}$.

These probabilities can be estimated by simply counting how many examples $n_{(k)}$ have been associated with each centroid $w_{(k)}$. Each iteration of the corresponding stochastic algorithm consists in drawing a random example x_t, finding the closest centroid $w_{(k)}$, and updating both the count and the centroid with the following equations:

$$\begin{bmatrix} n_{t+1}(k) = n_t(k) + 1 \\ w_{t+1}(k) = w_t(k) + \frac{1}{n_{t+1}(k)}(x_t - w_t(k)) \end{bmatrix} \tag{32}$$

Algorithm (32) very quickly locates the relative position of clusters in the data. Terminal convergence however is slowed down by the noise implied by the random choice of the examples. Experimental evidence [11] suggest that the best optimization speed is achieved by first using the stochastic algorithm (32) and then switching to a batch super-linear version of K-means.

Kalman Algorithms. The Kalman filter theory has introduced an efficient way to compute an approximation of the inverse of the Hessian of certain cost functions. This idea is easily demonstrated in the case of linear algorithms such as the Adaline (Section 2.3). Consider stochastic gradient descent applied to the minimization of the following mean square cost function:

$$C(w) = \int Q(z, w)\, dP(z) \quad \text{with} \quad Q(z, w) \stackrel{\triangle}{=} (y - w'x)^2 \tag{33}$$

Each iteration of this algorithm consists of drawing a new pair $z_t = (x_t, y_t)$ from the distribution $dP(z)$ and applying a parameter update formula similar to (27):

$$w_{t+1} = w_t - H_t^{-1}\nabla_w Q(z_t, w_t) = w_t - H_t^{-1}(y_t - w'_t x_t)' x_t \tag{34}$$

where H_t denotes the Hessian of an empirical estimate $C_t(w)$ of the cost function $C(w)$ based on the examples $z_1, \ldots, z_t$ observed so far.

$$C_t(w) \;\stackrel{\triangle}{=}\; \frac{1}{2}\sum_{i=1}^{t} Q(z_i, w) \;=\; \frac{1}{2}\sum_{i=1}^{t}(y_i - w'x_i)^2 \tag{35}$$

$$H_t \;\stackrel{\triangle}{=}\; \nabla_w^2 C_t(w) \;=\; \sum_{i=1}^{t} x_i x_i' \tag{36}$$

Directly computing the matrix H_t^{-1} at each iteration would be very expensive. We can take advantage however of the recursion $H_t = H_{t-1} + x_t x_t'$ using the well known matrix equality:

$$(A + BB')^{-1} = A^{-1} - (A^{-1}B)\,(I + B'A^{-1}B)^{-1}\,(A^{-1}B)' \tag{37}$$

Algorithm (34) then can be rewritten recursively using the Kalman matrix $K_t = H_{t-1}^{-1}$. The resulting algorithm (38) converges much faster than the delta rule (6) and yet remains quite easy to implement:

$$\left[\begin{aligned} K_{t+1} &= K_t - \frac{(K_t x_t)(K_t x_t)'}{1 + x_t' K_t x_t} \\ w_{t+1} &= w_t - K_{t+1}\,(y_t - w_t' x_t)' x_t \end{aligned} \right. \tag{38}$$

Gauss Newton Algorithms. Non linear least mean square algorithms, such as the multi-layer networks (Section 2.3) can also benefit from non-scalar learning rates. The idea consists of using an approximation of the Hessian matrix. The second derivatives of the loss function (9) can be written as:

$$\frac{1}{2}\nabla_w^2 \,(y - f(x,w))^2 = \nabla_w f(x,w)\,\nabla_w' f(x,w) - (y - f(x,w))\nabla_w^2 f(x,w)$$

$$\approx \nabla_w f(x,w)\,\nabla_w' f(x,w) \tag{39}$$

Approximation (39), known as the *Gauss Newton Approximation*, neglects the impact of the non linear function f on the curvature of the cost function. With this approximation, the Hessian of the empirical stochastic cost takes a very simple form.

$$H_t(w) \;\approx\; \sum_{i=1}^{t} \nabla_w f(x_i, w)\,\nabla_w' f(x_i, w) \tag{40}$$

Although the real Hessian can be negative, this approximated Hessian is always positive, a useful property for convergence. Its expression (40) is reminiscent of the linear case (36). Its inverse can be computed using similar recursive equations.

Natural Gradient. Information geometry [1] provides an elegant description of the geometry of the cost function. It is best introduced by casting the learning problem as a density estimation problem. A multilayer perceptron $f(x,w)$, for instance, can be regarded as a parametric regression model $y = f(x,w) + \varepsilon$

where ε represents an additive Gaussian noise. The network function $f(x, w)$ then becomes part of the Gaussian location model:

$$p(z|w) = C_\sigma \exp\left(-\frac{(y - f(x, w))^2}{2\sigma^2}\right) \tag{41}$$

The optimal parameters are found by minimizing the Kullback-Leibler divergence between $p(z|w)$ and the ground truth $P(z)$. This is equivalent to the familiar optimization of the mean square loss (9):

$$\mathbf{E}_z \log \frac{P(z)}{p(z|w)} = \frac{1}{\sigma^2}\mathbf{E}_z Q_{mse}(z, w) + \text{Constant} \tag{42}$$

The essential idea consists of endowing the space of the parameters w with a distance that reflects the proximity of the distributions $p(z|w)$ instead of the proximity of the parameters w. Multilayer networks, for instance, can implement the same function with very different weights vectors. The new distance distorts the geometry of the parameter space in order to represent the closeness of these weight vectors.

The infinitesimal distance between distributions $p(z|w)$ and $p(z|w + dw)$ can be written as follows:

$$D(w\|w + dw) \approx dw'\mathcal{G}(w)dw \tag{43}$$

where $\mathcal{G}(w)$ is the Fisher Information matrix:

$$\mathcal{G}(w) \stackrel{\triangle}{=} \int \left(\nabla_w \log p(z|w)\nabla_w \log p(z|w)'\right) p(z|w)dz$$

The determinant $|\mathcal{G}(w)|$ of the Fisher information matrix usually is a smooth function of the parameter w. The parameter space is therefore composed of Riemannian domains where $|\mathcal{G}(w)| \neq 0$ separated by critical sub-spaces where $|\mathcal{G}(w)| = 0$.

The *Natural Gradient* algorithm [3] provides a principled way to search a Riemannian domain. The gradient $\nabla_w C(w)$ defines the steepest descent direction in the Euclidean space. The steepest descent direction in a Riemannian domain differs from the Euclidexan one. It is defined as the vector dw which maximizes $C(w) - C(w + dw)$ in the δ-neighborhood:

$$D(w\|w + dw) \approx dw'\mathcal{G}(w)dw \leq \delta. \tag{44}$$

A simple derivation then shows that multiplying the gradient by the inverse of the Fisher Information matrix yields the steepest Riemannian direction. The Natural Gradient algorithm applies the same correction to the stochastic gradient descent algorithm (4):

$$w_{t+1} = w_t - \gamma_t \mathcal{G}^{-1}(w_t)\nabla_w Q(z, w_t), \tag{45}$$

The similarity between the update rules (27) and (45) is obvious. This link becomes clearer when the Fisher Information matrix is written in Hessian form,

$$\mathcal{G}(w) \triangleq \int - \left(\nabla_w^2 \log p(z|w) \right) p(z|w)dz$$

where ∇_w^2 denotes a second derivative. When the parameter approaches the optimum, distribution $p(z|w)$ becomes closer to the ground truth $dP(z)$, and the Fisher Information matrix $\mathcal{G}(w)$ aligns with the Hessian matrix $\nabla_w^2 \mathbf{E}_z Q(z, w)$. The natural gradient asymptotically behaves like a second order algorithm.

Remark. The above algorithms are all derived from (27) and suffer from the same limitation. The number of coefficients in matrix Φ_t scales like the square of the number of parameters. Manipulating such large matrices often requires excessive computer time and memory.

Result (30) holds when $\Phi_t \longrightarrow H^{-1}(w^*)$. This implies that Φ_t must be a full rank approximation of H^{-1}. Suppose instead that Φ_t converges to a more economical approximation of H^{-1} involving a limited number of coefficients. With a proper choice of learning rates γ_t, such an approximate second order stochastic gradient algorithm keeps the $\mathcal{O}(1/t)$ behavior (30) with a worse constant $K_A > K$. Such a stochastic algorithm will eventually outperform batch algorithms because $(\log \log N)$ will eventually become larger than the ratio K_A/K. In practice this can take a very long time...

Approximate second order stochastic algorithms are still desirable because it might be simply impossible to simply store a full rank matrix Φ_t, and because manipulating the approximation of the Hessian might bring computational gains that compare well with ratio K_A/K. The simplest approximation [5] involves a diagonal approximation of Φ_t. More sophisticated schemes [32, 38] attempt to approximate the average value of $\Phi_t \nabla_w Q(z, w_t)$ using simpler calculations for each example.

5   Conclusion

A broad family of learning algorithms can be formalized as stochastic gradient descent algorithms. It includes numerous well known algorithms such as Perceptrons, Adalines, K-Means, LVQ, and Multi-Layer Networks as well as more ambitious learning systems such as Graph Transformer Networks.

All these algorithms share common convergence properties. In particular, stochastic gradient descent simultaneously is a very poor optimization algorithm and a very effective learning algorithm.

References

1. S.-I. Amari. *Differential-geometrical methods in statistics.* Springer Verlag, Berlin, New York, 1990.
2. S.I. Amari. A theory of adaptive pattern classifiers. *IEEE Transactions on Electronic Computers*, EC-16:299–307, 1967.
3. Sun-Ichi Amari. Natural learning in structured parameter spaces – natural riemannian gradient. In *Neural Information Processing Systems*, volume 9, pages 127–133, Cambridge, MA., 1996. MIT Press.

4. Roberto Battiti. First- and second-order methods for learning: Between steepest descent and newton's method. *Neural Computation*, 4:141–166, 1992.
5. S. Becker and Y. Le Cun. Improving the convergence of back-propagation learning with second-order methods. In D. Touretzky, G. Hinton, and T Sejnowski, editors, *Proceedings of the 1988 Connectionist Models Summer School*, pages 29–37, San Mateo, 1989. Morgan Kaufman.
6. Y. Bengio, Y. LeCun, C. Nohl, and C. Burges. Lerec: A nn/hmm hybrid for on-line handwriting recognition. *Neural Computation*, 7(6), November 1995.
7. A. Benveniste, M. Metivier, and P. Priouret. *Adaptive Algorithms and Stochastic Approximations*. Springer Verlag, Berlin, New York, 1990.
8. L. Bottou, Y. Le Cun, and Y. Bengio. Global training of document processing systems using graph transformer networks. In *Proc. of Computer Vision and Pattern Recognition*, pages 489–493, Puerto-Rico, 1997. IEEE.
9. Léon Bottou. *Une Approche théorique de l'Apprentissage Connexionniste: Applications à la Reconnaissance de la Parole*. PhD thesis, Université de Paris XI, Orsay, France, 1991.
10. Léon Bottou. Online algorithms and stochastic approximations. In David Saad, editor, *Online Learning and Neural Networks*. Cambridge University Press, Cambridge, UK, 1998.
11. Léon Bottou and Yoshua Bengio. Convergence properties of the kmeans algorithm. In *Advances in Neural Information Processing Systems*, volume 7, Denver, 1995. MIT Press.
12. Léon Bottou and Yann LeCun. Large scale online learning. In *Advances in Neural Information Processing Systems*, volume 16. MIT Press, 2004.
13. Léon Bottou and Yann LeCun. On-line learning for very large datasets. *Applied Stochastic Models in Business and Industry*, 2004. To appear, Special issue.
14. Léon Bottou and Noboru Murata. Stochastic approximations and efficient learning. In M. A. Arbib, editor, *The Handbook of Brain Theory and Neural Networks, Second edition,*. The MIT Press, Cambridge, MA, 2002.
15. J. E., Jr. Dennis and R. B. Schnabel. *Numerical Methods For Unconstrained Optimization and Nonlinear Equations*. Prentice-Hall, Inc., Englewood Cliffs, New Jersey, 1983.
16. R.O. Duda and P.E. Hart. *Pattern Classification And Scene Analysis*. Wiley and Son, 1973.
17. C. Gentile and M. K. Warmuth. Linear hinge loss and average margin. In *Neural Information Processing Systems*, volume 11, pages 255–231, Cambridge, MA., 1999. MIT Press.
18. D. O. Hebb. *The Organization of Behavior*. Wiley, New York, 1949.
19. T. Kohonen. Self-organized formation of topologically correct feature maps. *Biological Cybernetics*, 43:59–69, 1982.
20. T. Kohonen, G. Barna, and R. Chrisley. Statistical pattern recognition with neural network: Benchmarking studies. In *Proceedings of the IEEE Second International Conference on Neural Networks*, volume 1, pages 61–68, San Diego, 1988.
21. A. A. Krasovskii. *Dynamic of continuous self-Organizing Systems*. Fizmatgiz, Moscow, 1963. (in russian).
22. H. J. Kushner and D. S. Clark. *Stochastic Approximation for Constrained and Unconstrained Systems*. Applied Math. Sci. 26. Springer Verlag, Berlin, New York, 1978.
23. Y. Le Cun, B. Boser, J. S. Denker, D. Henderson, R. E. Howard, W. Hubbard, and L. D. Jackel. Backpropagation applied to handwritten zip code recognition. *Neural Computation*, 1(4):541–551, Winter 1989.

24. Yann Le Cun, Léon Bottou, Yoshua Bengio, and Patrick Haffner. Gradient based learning applied to document recognition. *Proceedings of IEEE*, 86(11):2278–2324, 1998.
25. Yann Le Cun, Léon Bottou, Genevieve B. Orr, and Klaus-Robert Müller. Efficient backprop. In *Neural Networks, Tricks of the Trade*, Lecture Notes in Computer Science 1524. Springer Verlag, 1998.
26. Yann LeCun, Léon Bottou, and Jie HuangFu. Learning methods for generic object recognition with invariance to pose and lighting. In *Proc. of Computer Vision and Pattern Recognition*, Washington, D.C., 2004. IEEE.
27. L. Ljung and T. Söderström. *Theory and Practice of recursive identification*. MIT Press, Cambridge, MA, 1983.
28. J. MacQueen. Some methods for classification and analysis of multivariate observations. In L. M. LeCam and J. Neyman, editors, *Proceedings of the Fifth Berkeley Symposium on Mathematics, Statistics, and Probabilities*, volume 1, pages 281–297, Berkeley and Los Angeles, (Calif), 1967. University of California Press.
29. M. Minsky and S. Papert. *Perceptrons*. MIT Press, Cambridge, MA, 1969.
30. U. Müller, A. Gunzinger, and W. Guggenbühl. Fast neural net simulation with a DSP processor array. *IEEE Trans. on Neural Networks*, 6(1):203–213, 1995.
31. Noboru Murata and Sun-ichi Amari. Statistical analysis of learning dynamics. *Signal Processing*, 74(1):3–28, 1999.
32. Genevieve B. Orr and Todd K. Leen. Momentum and optimal stochastic search. In M. C. Mozer, P. Smolensky, D. S. Touretzky, J. L. Elman, and A. S. Weigend, editors, *Proceedings of the 1993 Connectionist Models Summer School*, pages 351–357. Lawrence Erlbaum Associates, 1994.
33. H. Robbins and S. Monro. A stochastic approximation model. *Ann. Math. Stat.*, 22:400–407, 1951.
34. F. Rosenblatt. The perceptron: A perceiving and recognizing automaton. Technical Report 85-460-1, Project PARA, Cornell Aeronautical Lab, 1957.
35. D. E. Rumelhart, G. E. Hinton, and R. J. Williams. Learning internal representations by error propagation. In *Parallel distributed processing: Explorations in the microstructure of cognition*, volume I, pages 318–362. Bradford Books, Cambridge, MA, 1986.
36. Ji Zhu Saharon Rosset and Trevor Hastie. Margin maximizing loss functions. In *Advances in Neural Information Processing Systems*, volume 16. MIT Press, 2004.
37. M. Schenkel, H. Weissman, I. Guyon, C. Nohl, and D. Henderson. Recognition-based segmentation of on-line hand-printed words. In S. J. Hanson, J. D. Cowan, and C. L. Giles, editors, *Advances in Neural Information Processing Systems 5*, pages 723–730, Denver, CO, 1993.
38. N. Schraudolph and T. Graepel. Conjugate directions for stochastic gradient descent. In *Proceedings of the International Conference on Artificial Neural Networks (ICANN 2002).*, Berlin, 2002. Springer Verlag.
39. T. J. Sejnowski and C. R. Rosenberg. Parallel networks that learn to pronounce english text. *Complex Systems*, 1:145–168, 1987.
40. Ya Tsypkin. *Adaptation and Learning in automatic systems*. Academic Press, New York, 1971.
41. Ya Tsypkin. *Foundations of the theory of learning systems*. Academic Press, New York, 1973.
42. V. N. Vapnik. *Estimation of dependences based on empirical data*. Springer Series in Statistics. Springer Verlag, Berlin, New York, 1982.
43. V. N. Vapnik. *The Nature of Statistical Learning Theory*. Springer Verlag, Berlin, New York, 1995.

44. B. Widrow and M. E. Hoff. Adaptive switching circuits. In *IRE WESCON Conv. Record, Part 4.*, pages 96–104, 1960.
45. B. Widrow and S. D. Stearns. *Adaptive Signal Processing*. Prentice-Hall, 1985.
46. R. Wolf and J. Platt. Postal address block location using a convolutional locator network. In J. D. Cowan, G. Tesauro, and J. Alspector, editors, *Advances in Neural Information Processing Systems 6*, pages 745–752, 1994.

Introduction to Statistical Learning Theory

Olivier Bousquet[1], Stéphane Boucheron[2], and Gábor Lugosi[3]

[1] Max-Planck Institute for Biological Cybernetics
Spemannstr. 38, D-72076 Tübingen, Germany
olivier.bousquet@m4x.org
http://www.kyb.mpg.de/~bousquet
[2] Université de Paris-Sud, Laboratoire d'Informatique
Bâtiment 490, F-91405 Orsay Cedex, France
stephane.boucheron@lri.fr
http://www.lri.fr/~bouchero
[3] Department of Economics, Pompeu Fabra University
Ramon Trias Fargas 25-27, 08005 Barcelona, Spain
lugosi@upf.es
http://www.econ.upf.es/~lugosi

Abstract. The goal of statistical learning theory is to study, in a statistical framework, the properties of learning algorithms. In particular, most results take the form of so-called error bounds. This tutorial introduces the techniques that are used to obtain such results.

1 Introduction

The main goal of statistical learning theory is to provide a framework for studying the problem of inference, that is of gaining knowledge, making predictions, making decisions or constructing models from a set of data. This is studied in a statistical framework, that is there are assumptions of statistical nature about the underlying phenomena (in the way the data is generated).

As a motivation for the need of such a theory, let us just quote V. Vapnik:

(Vapnik, [1]) Nothing is more practical than a good theory.

Indeed, a theory of inference should be able to give a formal definition of words like learning, generalization, overfitting, and also to characterize the performance of learning algorithms so that, ultimately, it may help design better learning algorithms.

There are thus two goals: make things more precise and derive new or improved algorithms.

1.1 Learning and Inference

What is under study here is the process of inductive inference which can roughly be summarized as the following steps:

O. Bousquet et al. (Eds.): Machine Learning 2003, LNAI 3176, pp. 169–207, 2004.
© Springer-Verlag Berlin Heidelberg 2004

1. Observe a phenomenon
2. Construct a model of that phenomenon
3. Make predictions using this model

Of course, this definition is very general and could be taken more or less as the goal of Natural Sciences. The goal of Machine Learning is to actually *automate* this process and the goal of Learning Theory is to *formalize* it.

In this tutorial we consider a special case of the above process which is the supervised learning framework for pattern recognition. In this framework, the data consists of instance-label pairs, where the label is either $+1$ or -1. Given a set of such pairs, a learning algorithm constructs a function mapping instances to labels. This function should be such that it makes few mistakes when predicting the label of unseen instances.

Of course, given some training data, it is always possible to build a function that fits exactly the data. But, in the presence of noise, this may not be the best thing to do as it would lead to a poor performance on unseen instances (this is usually referred to as overfitting). The general idea behind the design of learning algorithms is thus to look for *regularities* (in a sense to be defined later) in the observed phenomenon (i.e. training data). These can then be *generalized* from the observed past to the future. Typically, one would look, in a collection of possible models, for one which fits well the data, but at the same time is as simple as possible (see Figure 1). This immediately raises the question of how to measure and quantify simplicity of a model (i.e. a $\{-1, +1\}$-valued function).

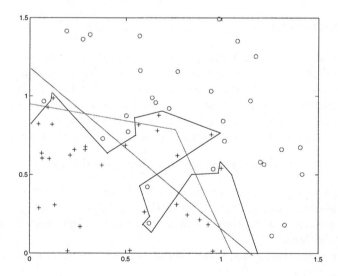

Fig. 1. Trade-off between fit and complexity

It turns out that there are many ways to do so, but no best one. For example in Physics, people tend to prefer models which have a small number of constants and that correspond to simple mathematical formulas. Often, the length of description of a model in a coding language can be an indication of its complexity. In classical statistics, the number of free parameters of a model is usually a measure of its complexity. Surprisingly as it may seem, there is no universal way of measuring simplicity (or its counterpart complexity) and the choice of a specific measure inherently depends on the problem at hand. It is actually in this choice that the designer of the learning algorithm introduces knowledge about the specific phenomenon under study.

This lack of universally best choice can actually be formalized in what is called the *No Free Lunch* theorem, which in essence says that, if there is no assumption on how the past (i.e. training data) is related to the future (i.e. test data), prediction is impossible. Even more, if there is no a priori restriction on the possible phenomena that are expected, it is impossible to generalize and there is thus no better algorithm (any algorithm would be beaten by another one on some phenomenon).

Hence the need to make assumptions, like the fact that the phenomenon we observe can be explained by a simple model. However, as we said, simplicity is not an absolute notion, and this leads to the statement that data cannot replace knowledge, or in pseudo-mathematical terms:

Generalization = Data + Knowledge

1.2   Assumptions

We now make more precise the assumptions that are made by the Statistical Learning Theory framework. Indeed, as we said before we need to assume that the future (i.e. test) observations are related to the past (i.e. training) ones, so that the phenomenon is somewhat stationary.

At the core of the theory is a probabilistic model of the phenomenon (or data generation process). Within this model, the relationship between past and future observations is that they both are sampled independently from the same distribution (i.i.d.). The independence assumption means that each new observation yields maximum information. The identical distribution means that the observations give information about the underlying phenomenon (here a probability distribution).

An immediate consequence of this very general setting is that one can construct algorithms (e.g. k-nearest neighbors with appropriate k) that are *consistent*, which means that, as one gets more and more data, the predictions of the algorithm are closer and closer to the optimal ones. So this seems to indicate that we can have some sort of universal algorithm. Unfortunately, any (consistent) algorithm can have an arbitrarily bad behavior when given a finite training set. These notions are formalized in Appendix B.

Again, this discussion indicates that generalization can only come when one adds specific knowledge to the data. Each learning algorithm encodes specific knowledge (or a specific assumption about how the optimal classifier looks like), and works best when this assumption is satisfied by the problem to which it is applied.

Bibliographical Remarks. Several textbooks, surveys, and research monographs have been written on pattern classification and statistical learning theory. A partial list includes Anthony and Bartlett [2], Breiman, Friedman, Olshen, and Stone [3], Devroye, Györfi, and Lugosi [4], Duda and Hart [5], Fukunaga [6], Kearns and Vazirani [7], Kulkarni, Lugosi, and Venkatesh [8], Lugosi [9], McLachlan [10], Mendelson [11], Natarajan [12], Vapnik [13, 14, 1], and Vapnik and Chervonenkis [15].

2   Formalization

We consider an input space $\mathcal{X}$ and output space $\mathcal{Y}$. Since we restrict ourselves to binary classification, we choose $\mathcal{Y} = \{-1, 1\}$. Formally, we assume that the pairs $(X, Y) \in \mathcal{X} \times \mathcal{Y}$ are random variables distributed according to an *unknown* distribution P. We observe a sequence of n i.i.d. pairs (X_i, Y_i) sampled according to P and the goal is to construct a function $g : \mathcal{X} \to \mathcal{Y}$ which *predicts* Y from X.

We need a criterion to choose this function g. This criterion is a low probability of error $P(g(X) \neq Y)$. We thus define the *risk* of g as

$$R(g) = P(g(X) \neq Y) = \mathbb{E}\left[\mathbb{1}_{g(X) \neq Y}\right] .$$

Notice that P can be decomposed as $P_X \times P(Y|X)$. We introduce the *regression function* $\eta(x) = \mathbb{E}[Y|X = x] = 2\mathbb{P}[Y = 1|X = x]-1$ and the *target function* (or Bayes classifier) $t(x) = \operatorname{sgn} \eta(x)$. This function achieves the minimum risk over all possible measurable functions:

$$R(t) = \inf_g R(g) .$$

We will denote the value $R(t)$ by R^*, called the Bayes risk. In the deterministic case, one has $Y = t(X)$ almost surely ($\mathbb{P}[Y = 1|X] \in \{0, 1\}$) and $R^* = 0$. In the general case we can define the *noise level* as $s(x) = \min(\mathbb{P}[Y = 1|X = x], 1 - \mathbb{P}[Y = 1|X = x]) = (1 - \eta(x))/2$ ($s(X) = 0$ almost surely in the deterministic case) and this gives $R^* = \mathbb{E}s(X)$.

Our goal is thus to identify this function t, but since P is unknown we cannot directly measure the risk and we also cannot know directly the value of t at the data points. We can only measure the agreement of a candidate function with the data. This is called the *empirical risk*:

$$R_n(g) = \frac{1}{n} \sum_{i=1}^{n} \mathbb{1}_{g(X_i) \neq Y_i} .$$

It is common to use this quantity as a criterion to select an estimate of t.

2.1   Algorithms

Now that the goal is clearly specified, we review the common strategies to (approximately) achieve it. We denote by g_n the function returned by the algorithm.

Because one cannot compute $R(g)$ but only approximate it by $R_n(g)$, it would be unreasonable to look for the function minimizing $R_n(g)$ among all possible functions. Indeed, when the input space is infinite, one can always construct a function g_n which perfectly predicts the labels of the training data (i.e. $g_n(X_i) = Y_i$, and $R_n(g_n) = 0$), but behaves on the other points as the opposite of the target function t, i.e. $g_n(X) = -Y$ so that $R(g_n) = 1$[1]. So one would have minimum empirical risk but maximum risk.

It is thus necessary to prevent this overfitting situation. There are essentially two ways to do this (which can be combined). The first one is to restrict the class of functions in which the minimization is performed, and the second is to modify the criterion to be minimized (e.g. adding a penalty for 'complicated' functions).

Empirical Risk Minimization. This algorithm is one of the most straight-forward, yet it is usually efficient. The idea is to choose a *model* $\mathcal{G}$ of possible functions and to minimize the empirical risk in that model:

$$g_n = \arg\min_{g \in \mathcal{G}} R_n(g).$$

Of course, this will work best when the target function belongs to $\mathcal{G}$. However, it is rare to be able to make such an assumption, so one may want to enlarge the model as much as possible, while preventing overfitting.

Structural Risk Minimization. The idea here is to choose an infinite sequence $\{\mathcal{G}_d : d = 1, 2, \ldots\}$ of models of increasing size and to minimize the empirical risk in each model with an added penalty for the size of the model:

$$g_n = \arg\min_{g \in \mathcal{G}_d, d \in \mathbb{N}} R_n(g) + \mathrm{pen}(d, n).$$

The penalty $\mathrm{pen}(d, n)$ gives preference to models where estimation error is small and measures the size or *capacity* of the model.

Regularization. Another, usually easier to implement approach consists in choosing a large model $\mathcal{G}$ (possibly dense in the continuous functions for example) and to define on $\mathcal{G}$ a *regularizer*, typically a norm $\|g\|$. Then one has to minimize the regularized empirical risk:

$$g_n = \arg\min_{g \in \mathcal{G}} R_n(g) + \lambda \|g\|^2.$$

Compared to SRM, there is here a free parameter λ, called the *regularization parameter* which allows to choose the right trade-off between fit and complexity.

---

[1] Strictly speaking this is only possible if the probability distribution satisfies some mild conditions (e.g. has no atoms). Otherwise, it may not be possible to achieve $R(g_n) = 1$ but even in this case, provided the support of P contains infinitely many points, a similar phenomenon occurs.

Tuning λ is usually a hard problem and most often, one uses extra validation data for this task.

Most existing (and successful) methods can be thought of as regularization methods.

Normalized Regularization. There are other possible approaches when the regularizer can, in some sense, be 'normalized', i.e. when it corresponds to some probability distribution over $\mathcal{G}$.

Given a probability distribution π defined on $\mathcal{G}$ (usually called a prior), one can use as a regularizer $-\log \pi(g)^2$. Reciprocally, from a regularizer of the form $\|g\|^2$, if there exists a measure μ on $\mathcal{G}$ such that $\int e^{-\lambda\|g\|^2} d\mu(g) < \infty$ for some $\lambda > 0$, then one can construct a prior corresponding to this regularizer. For example, if $\mathcal{G}$ is the set of hyperplanes in $\mathbb{R}^d$ going through the origin, $\mathcal{G}$ can be identified with $\mathbb{R}^d$ and, taking μ as the Lebesgue measure, it is possible to go from the Euclidean norm regularizer to a spherical Gaussian measure on $\mathbb{R}^d$ as a prior[3].

This type of normalized regularizer, or prior, can be used to construct another probability distribution ρ on $\mathcal{G}$ (usually called posterior), as

$$\rho(g) = \frac{e^{-\gamma R_n(g)}}{Z(\gamma)} \pi(g) \,,$$

where $\gamma \geq 0$ is a free parameter and $Z(\gamma)$ is a normalization factor.

There are several ways in which this ρ can be used. If we take the function maximizing it, we recover regularization as

$$\arg \max_{g \in \mathcal{G}} \rho(g) = \arg \min_{g \in \mathcal{G}} \gamma R_n(g) - \log \pi(g) \,,$$

where the regularizer is $-\gamma^{-1} \log \pi(g)^4$.

Also, ρ can be used to *randomize* the predictions. In that case, before computing the predicted label for an input x, one samples a function g according to ρ and outputs $g(x)$. This procedure is usually called Gibbs classification.

Another way in which the distribution ρ constructed above can be used is by taking the expected prediction of the functions in $\mathcal{G}$:

$$g_n(x) = \text{sgn}(\mathbb{E}_\rho(g(x))) \,.$$

This is typically called Bayesian averaging.

---

[2] This is fine when $\mathcal{G}$ is countable. In the continuous case, one has to consider the density associated to π. We omit these details.

[3] Generalization to infinite dimensional Hilbert spaces can also be done but it requires more care. One can for example establish a correspondence between the norm of a reproducing kernel Hilbert space and a Gaussian process prior whose covariance function is the kernel of this space.

[4] Note that minimizing $\gamma R_n(g) - \log \pi(g)$ is equivalent to minimizing $R_n(g) - \gamma^{-1} \log \pi(g)$.

At this point we have to insist again on the fact that the choice of the class $\mathcal{G}$ and of the associated regularizer or prior, has to come from *a priori* knowledge about the task at hand, and there is no universally best choice.

2.2   Bounds

We have presented the framework of the theory and the type of algorithms that it studies, we now introduce the kind of results that it aims at. The overall goal is to characterize the risk that some algorithm may have in a given situation. More precisely, a learning algorithm takes as input the data $(X_1, Y_1), \ldots, (X_n, Y_n)$ and produces a function g_n which depends on this data. We want to estimate the risk of g_n. However, $R(g_n)$ is a random variable (since it depends on the data) and it cannot be computed from the data (since it also depends on the unknown P). Estimates of $R(g_n)$ thus usually take the form of probabilistic bounds.

Notice that when the algorithm chooses its output from a model $\mathcal{G}$, it is possible, by introducing the best function g^* in $\mathcal{G}$, with $R(g^*) = \inf_{g \in \mathcal{G}} R(g)$, to write

$$R(g_n) - R^* = [R(g^*) - R^*] + [R(g_n) - R(g^*)].$$

The first term on the right hand side is usually called the approximation error, and measures how well can functions in $\mathcal{G}$ approach the target (it would be zero if $t \in \mathcal{G}$). The second term, called estimation error is a random quantity (it depends on the data) and measures how close is g_n to the best possible choice in $\mathcal{G}$.

Estimating the approximation error is usually hard since it requires knowledge about the target. Classically, in Statistical Learning Theory it is preferable to avoid making specific assumptions about the target (such as its belonging to some model), but the assumptions are rather on the value of R^*, or on the noise function s.

It is also known that for any (consistent) algorithm, the rate of convergence to zero of the approximation error[5] can be arbitrarily slow if one does not make assumptions about the regularity of the target, while the rate of convergence of the estimation error can be computed without any such assumption. We will thus focus on the estimation error.

Another possible decomposition of the risk is the following:

$$R(g_n) = R_n(g_n) + [R(g_n) - R_n(g_n)].$$

In this case, one estimates the risk by its empirical counterpart, and some quantity which approximates (or upper bounds) $R(g_n) - R_n(g_n)$.

To summarize, we write the three type of results we may be interested in.

- *Error bound*: $R(g_n) \leq R_n(g_n) + B(n, \mathcal{G})$. This corresponds to the estimation of the risk from an empirical quantity.

---

[5] For this converge to mean anything, one has to consider algorithms which choose functions from a class which grows with the sample size. This is the case for example of Structural Risk Minimization or Regularization based algorithms.

- *Error bound relative to the best in the class*: $R(g_n) \leq R(g^*) + B(n, \mathcal{G})$. This tells how "optimal" is the algorithm given the model it uses.
- *Error bound relative to the Bayes risk*: $R(g_n) \leq R^* + B(n, \mathcal{G})$. This gives theoretical guarantees on the convergence to the Bayes risk.

3   Basic Bounds

In this section we show how to obtain simple error bounds (also called generalization bounds). The elementary material from probability theory that is needed here and in the later sections is summarized in Appendix A.

3.1   Relationship to Empirical Processes

Recall that we want to estimate the risk $R(g_n) = \mathbb{E}\left[\mathbb{1}_{g_n(X) \neq Y}\right]$ of the function g_n returned by the algorithm after seeing the data $(X_1, Y_1), \ldots, (X_n, Y_n)$. This quantity cannot be observed (P is unknown) and is a random variable (since it depends on the data). Hence one way to make a statement about this quantity is to say how it relates to an estimate such as the empirical risk $R_n(g_n)$. This relationship can take the form of upper and lower bounds for

$$\mathbb{P}\left[R(g_n) - R_n(g_n) > \varepsilon\right] .$$

For convenience, let $Z_i = (X_i, Y_i)$ and $Z = (X, Y)$. Given $\mathcal{G}$ define the *loss class*

$$\mathcal{F} = \{f : (x, y) \mapsto \mathbb{1}_{g(x) \neq y} : g \in \mathcal{G}\} . \tag{1}$$

Notice that $\mathcal{G}$ contains functions with range in $\{-1, 1\}$ while $\mathcal{F}$ contains non-negative functions with range in $\{0, 1\}$. In the remainder of the tutorial, we will go back and forth between $\mathcal{F}$ and $\mathcal{G}$ (as there is a bijection between them), sometimes stating the results in terms of functions in $\mathcal{F}$ and sometimes in terms of functions in $\mathcal{G}$. It will be clear from the context which classes $\mathcal{G}$ and $\mathcal{F}$ we refer to, and $\mathcal{F}$ will always be derived from the last mentioned class $\mathcal{G}$ in the way of (1).

We use the shorthand notation $Pf = \mathbb{E}\left[f(X, Y)\right]$ and $P_n f = \frac{1}{n}\sum_{i=1}^{n} f(X_i, Y_i)$. P_n is usually called the *empirical measure* associated to the training sample. With this notation, the quantity of interest (difference between true and empirical risks) can be written as

$$Pf_n - P_n f_n . \tag{2}$$

An empirical process is a collection of random variables indexed by a class of functions, and such that each random variable is distributed as a sum of i.i.d. random variables (values taken by the function at the data):

$$\{Pf - P_n f\}_{f \in \mathcal{F}} .$$

One of the most studied quantity associated to empirical processes is their supremum:

$$\sup_{f \in \mathcal{F}} Pf - P_n f .$$

It is clear that if we know an upper bound on this quantity, it will be an upper bound on (2). This shows that the theory of empirical processes is a great source of tools and techniques for Statistical Learning Theory.

3.2   Hoeffding's Inequality

Let us rewrite again the quantity we are interested in as follows

$$R(g) - R_n(g) = \mathbb{E}\left[f(Z)\right] - \frac{1}{n}\sum_{i=1}^{n} f(Z_i).$$

It is easy to recognize here the difference between the expectation and the empirical average of the random variable $f(Z)$. By the law of large numbers, we immediately obtain that

$$\mathbb{P}\left[\lim_{n\to\infty} \frac{1}{n}\sum_{i=1}^{n} f(Z_i) - \mathbb{E}\left[f(Z)\right] = 0\right] = 1.$$

This indicates that with enough samples, the empirical risk of a function is a good approximation to its true risk.

It turns out that there exists a quantitative version of the law of large numbers when the variables are bounded.

Theorem 1 (Hoeffding). *Let* $Z_1, \ldots, Z_n$ *be* n *i.i.d. random variables with* $f(Z) \in [a,b]$. *Then for all* $\varepsilon > 0$, *we have*

$$\mathbb{P}\left[\left|\frac{1}{n}\sum_{i=1}^{n} f(Z_i) - \mathbb{E}\left[f(Z)\right]\right| > \varepsilon\right] \leq 2\exp\left(-\frac{2n\varepsilon^2}{(b-a)^2}\right).$$

Let us rewrite the above formula to better understand its consequences. Denote the right hand side by δ. Then

$$\mathbb{P}\left[|P_n f - Pf| > (b-a)\sqrt{\frac{\log \frac{2}{\delta}}{2n}}\right] \leq \delta,$$

or (by inversion, see Appendix A) with probability at least $1 - \delta$,

$$|P_n f - Pf| \leq (b-a)\sqrt{\frac{\log \frac{2}{\delta}}{2n}}.$$

Applying this to $f(Z) = \mathbb{1}_{g(X) \neq Y}$ we get that for any g, and any $\delta > 0$, with probability at least $1 - \delta$

$$R(g) \leq R_n(g) + \sqrt{\frac{\log \frac{2}{\delta}}{2n}}. \tag{3}$$

Notice that one has to consider a fixed function g and the probability is with respect to the sampling of the data. If the function depends on the data this does not apply!

3.3   Limitations

Although the above result seems very nice (since it applies to any class of bounded functions), it is actually severely limited. Indeed, what it essentially says is that for each (fixed) function $f \in \mathcal{F}$, there is a set S of samples for which $Pf - P_n f \leq \sqrt{\frac{\log \frac{2}{\delta}}{2n}}$ (and this set of samples has measure $\mathbb{P}[S] \geq 1 - \delta$). However, these sets S may be different for different functions. In other words, for the observed sample, only some of the functions in $\mathcal{F}$ will satisfy this inequality.

Another way to explain the limitation of Hoeffding's inequality is the following. If we take for $\mathcal{G}$ the class of all $\{-1, 1\}$-valued (measurable) functions, then for any fixed sample, there exists a function $f \in \mathcal{F}$ such that

$$Pf - P_n f = 1 \, .$$

To see this, take the function which is $f(X_i) = Y_i$ on the data and $f(X) = -Y$ everywhere else. This does not contradict Hoeffding's inequality but shows that it does not yield what we need.

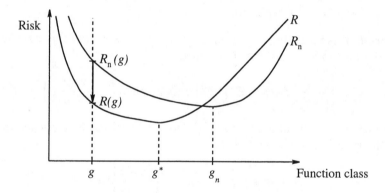

Fig. 2. Convergence of the empirical risk to the true risk over the class of functions

Figure 2 illustrates the above argumentation. The horizontal axis corresponds to the functions in the class. The two curves represent the true risk and the empirical risk (for some training sample) of these functions. The true risk is fixed, while for each different sample, the empirical risk will be a different curve. If we observe a fixed function g and take several different samples, the point on the empirical curve will fluctuate around the true risk with fluctuations controlled by Hoeffding's inequality. However, for a fixed sample, if the class $\mathcal{G}$ is big enough, one can find somewhere along the axis, a function for which the difference between the two curves will be very large.

3.4   Uniform Deviations

Before seeing the data, we do not know which function the algorithm will choose. The idea is to consider *uniform* deviations

$$R(f_n) - R_n(f_n) \leq \sup_{f \in \mathcal{F}} (R(f) - R_n(f)) \tag{4}$$

In other words, if we can upper bound the supremum on the right, we are done. For this, we need a bound which holds simultaneously for all functions in a class.

Let us explain how one can construct such uniform bounds. Consider two functions f_1, f_2 and define

$$C_i = \{(x_1, y_1), \ldots, (x_n, y_n) : Pf_i - P_n f_i > \varepsilon\}.$$

This set contains all the 'bad' samples, i.e. those for which the bound fails. From Hoeffding's inequality, for each i

$$\mathbb{P}[C_i] \leq \delta.$$

We want to measure how many samples are 'bad' for $i = 1$ or $i = 2$. For this we use (see Appendix A)

$$\mathbb{P}[C_1 \cup C_2] \leq \mathbb{P}[C_1] + \mathbb{P}[C_2] \leq 2\delta.$$

More generally, if we have N functions in our class, we can write

$$\mathbb{P}[C_1 \cup \ldots \cup C_N] \leq \sum_{i=1}^{N} \mathbb{P}[C_i]$$

As a result we obtain

$$\mathbb{P}[\exists f \in \{f_1, \ldots, f_N\} : Pf - P_n f > \varepsilon]$$
$$\leq \sum_{i=1}^{N} \mathbb{P}[Pf_i - P_n f_i > \varepsilon]$$
$$\leq N \exp\left(-2n\varepsilon^2\right)$$

Hence, for $\mathcal{G} = \{g_1, \ldots, g_N\}$, for all $\delta > 0$ with probability at least $1 - \delta$,

$$\forall g \in \mathcal{G}, \ R(g) \leq R_n(g) + \sqrt{\frac{\log N + \log \frac{1}{\delta}}{2n}}$$

This is an error bound. Indeed, if we know that our algorithm picks functions from $\mathcal{G}$, we can apply this result to g_n itself.

Notice that the main difference with Hoeffding's inequality is the extra $\log N$ term on the right hand side. This is the term which accounts for the fact that we want N bounds to hold simultaneously. Another interpretation of this term is as the number of bits one would require to specify one function in $\mathcal{G}$. It turns out that this kind of coding interpretation of generalization bounds is often possible and can be used to obtain error estimates [16].

3.5   Estimation Error

Using the same idea as before, and with no additional effort, we can also get a bound on the estimation error. We start from the inequality

$$R(g^*) \leq R_n(g^*) + \sup_{g \in \mathcal{G}}(R(g) - R_n(g)),$$

which we combine with (4) and with the fact that since g_n minimizes the empirical risk in $\mathcal{G}$,

$$R_n(g^*) - R_n(g_n) \geq 0$$

Thus we obtain

$$\begin{aligned}
R(g_n) &= R(g_n) - R(g^*) + R(g^*) \\
&\leq R_n(g^*) - R_n(g_n) + R(g_n) - R(g^*) + R(g^*) \\
&\leq 2 \sup_{g \in \mathcal{G}} |R(g) - R_n(g)| + R(g^*)
\end{aligned}$$

We obtain that with probability at least $1 - \delta$

$$R(g_n) \leq R(g^*) + 2\sqrt{\frac{\log N + \log \frac{2}{\delta}}{2n}}.$$

We notice that in the right hand side, both terms depend on the size of the class $\mathcal{G}$. If this size increases, the first term will decrease, while the second will increase.

3.6   Summary and Perspective

At this point, we can summarize what we have exposed so far.

- Inference requires to put assumptions on the process generating the data (data sampled i.i.d. from an unknown P), generalization requires knowledge (e.g. restriction, structure, or prior).
- The error bounds are valid with respect to the repeated sampling of training sets.
- For a fixed function g, for most of the samples

$$R(g) - R_n(g) \approx 1/\sqrt{n}$$

- For most of the samples if $|\mathcal{G}| = N$

$$\sup_{g \in \mathcal{G}} R(g) - R_n(g) \approx \sqrt{\log N / n}$$

The extra variability comes from the fact that the chosen g_n changes with the data.

So the result we have obtained so far is that with high probability, for a finite class of size N,

$$\sup_{g \in \mathcal{G}}(R(g) - R_n(g)) \leq \sqrt{\frac{\log N + \log \frac{1}{\delta}}{2n}}.$$

There are several things that can be improved:

- Hoeffding's inequality only uses the boundedness of the functions, not their variance.
- The union bound is as bad as if all the functions in the class were independent (i.e. if $f_1(Z)$ and $f_2(Z)$ were independent).
- The supremum over $\mathcal{G}$ of $R(g) - R_n(g)$ is not necessarily what the algorithm would choose, so that upper bounding $R(g_n) - R_n(g_n)$ by the supremum might be loose.

4   Infinite Case: Vapnik-Chervonenkis Theory

In this section we show how to extend the previous results to the case where the class $\mathcal{G}$ is infinite. This requires, in the non-countable case, the introduction of tools from Vapnik-Chervonenkis Theory.

4.1   Refined Union Bound and Countable Case

We first start with a simple refinement of the union bound that allows to extend the previous results to the (countably) infinite case.

Recall that by Hoeffding's inequality, for each $f \in \mathcal{F}$, for each $\delta > 0$ (possibly depending on f, which we write $\delta(f)$),

$$\mathbb{P}\left[Pf - P_n f > \sqrt{\frac{\log \frac{1}{\delta(f)}}{2n}}\right] \leq \delta(f).$$

Hence, if we have a countable set $\mathcal{F}$, the union bound immediately yields

$$\mathbb{P}\left[\exists f \in \mathcal{F} : Pf - P_n f > \sqrt{\frac{\log \frac{1}{\delta(f)}}{2n}}\right] \leq \sum_{f \in \mathcal{F}} \delta(f).$$

Choosing $\delta(f) = \delta p(f)$ with $\sum_{f \in \mathcal{F}} p(f) = 1$, this makes the right-hand side equal to δ and we get the following result. With probability at least $1 - \delta$,

$$\forall f \in \mathcal{F}, \, Pf \leq P_n f + \sqrt{\frac{\log \frac{1}{p(f)} + \log \frac{1}{\delta}}{2n}}.$$

We notice that if $\mathcal{F}$ is finite (with size N), taking a uniform p gives the $\log N$ as before.

Using this approach, it is possible to put knowledge about the algorithm into $p(f)$, but p should be chosen before seeing the data, so it is not possible to 'cheat' by setting all the weight to the function returned by the algorithm after seeing the data (which would give the smallest possible bound). But, in general, if p is well-chosen, the bound will have a small value. Hence, the bound can be improved if one knows ahead of time the functions that the algorithm is likely to pick (i.e. knowledge improves the bound).

4.2   General Case

When the set $\mathcal{G}$ is uncountable, the previous approach does not directly work. The general idea is to look at the function class 'projected' on the sample. More precisely, given a sample $z_1, \ldots, z_n$, we consider

$$\mathcal{F}_{z_1,\ldots,z_n} = \{(f(z_1), \ldots, f(z_n)) : f \in \mathcal{F}\}$$

The size of this set is the number of possible ways in which the data $(z_1, \ldots, z_n)$ can be classified. Since the functions f can only take two values, this set will always be finite, no matter how big $\mathcal{F}$ is.

Definition 1 (Growth Function). *The growth function is the maximum number of ways into which n points can be classified by the function class:*

$$S_{\mathcal{F}}(n) = \sup_{(z_1,\ldots,z_n)} |\mathcal{F}_{z_1,\ldots,z_n}|.$$

We have defined the growth function in terms of the loss class $\mathcal{F}$ but we can do the same with the initial class $\mathcal{G}$ and notice that $S_{\mathcal{F}}(n) = S_{\mathcal{G}}(n)$.

It turns out that this growth function can be used as a measure of the 'size' of a class of function as demonstrated by the following result.

Theorem 2 (Vapnik-Chervonenkis). *For any $\delta > 0$, with probability at least $1 - \delta$,*

$$\forall g \in \mathcal{G}, \ R(g) \leq R_n(g) + 2\sqrt{2\frac{\log S_{\mathcal{G}}(2n) + \log \frac{2}{\delta}}{n}}.$$

Notice that, in the finite case where $|\mathcal{G}| = N$, we have $S_{\mathcal{G}}(n) \leq N$ so that this bound is always better than the one we had before (except for the constants).

But the problem becomes now one of computing $S_{\mathcal{G}}(n)$.

4.3   VC Dimension

Since $g \in \{-1, 1\}$, it is clear that $S_{\mathcal{G}}(n) \leq 2^n$. If $S_{\mathcal{G}}(n) = 2^n$, there is a set of size n such that the class of functions can generate any classification on these points (we say that $\mathcal{G}$ *shatters* the set).

Definition 2 (VC Dimension). *The VC dimension of a class $\mathcal{G}$ is the largest n such that*

$$S_{\mathcal{G}}(n) = 2^n.$$

In other words, the VC dimension of a class $\mathcal{G}$ is the size of the largest set that it can shatter.

In order to illustrate this definition, we give some examples. The first one is the set of half-planes in $\mathbb{R}^d$ (see Figure 3). In this case, as depicted for the case $d = 2$, one can shatter a set of $d + 1$ points but no set of $d + 2$ points, which means that the VC dimension is $d + 1$.

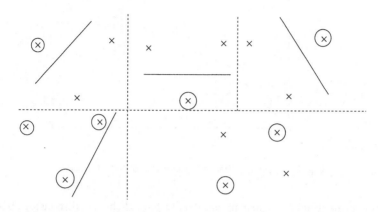

Fig. 3. Computing the VC dimension of hyperplanes in dimension 2: a set of 3 points can be shattered, but no set of four points

It is interesting to notice that the number of parameters needed to define half-spaces in $\mathbb{R}^d$ is d, so that a natural question is whether the VC dimension is related to the number of parameters of the function class. The next example, depicted in Figure 4, is a family of functions with one parameter only:

$$\{\mathrm{sgn}(\sin(tx)) : t \in \mathbb{R}\}$$

which actually has infinite VC dimension (this is an exercise left to the reader).

It remains to show how the notion of VC dimension can bring a solution to the problem of computing the growth function. Indeed, at first glance, if we

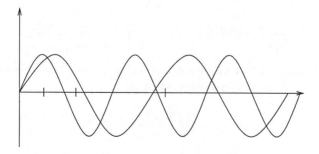

Fig. 4. VC dimension of sinusoids

know that a class has VC dimension h, it entails that for all $n \leq h$, $S_{\mathcal{G}}(n) = 2^n$ and $S_{\mathcal{G}}(n) < 2^n$ otherwise. This seems of little use, but actually, an intriguing phenomenon occurs for $n \geq h$ as depicted in Figure 5. The growth function

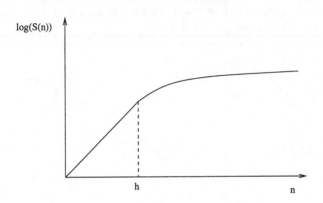

Fig. 5. Typical behavior of the log growth function

which is exponential (its logarithm is linear) up until the VC dimension, becomes polynomial afterwards.

This behavior is captured in the following lemma.

Lemma 1 (Vapnik and Chervonenkis, Sauer, Shelah). *Let $\mathcal{G}$ be a class of functions with finite VC-dimension h. Then for all $n \in \mathbb{N}$,*

$$S_{\mathcal{G}}(n) \leq \sum_{i=0}^{h} \binom{n}{i},$$

and for all $n \geq h$,

$$S_{\mathcal{G}}(n) \leq \left(\frac{en}{h}\right)^h.$$

Using this lemma along with Theorem 2 we immediately obtain that if $\mathcal{G}$ has VC dimension h, with probability at least $1 - \delta$,

$$\forall g \in \mathcal{G}, \ R(g) \leq R_n(g) + 2\sqrt{2\frac{h\log\frac{2en}{h} + \log\frac{2}{\delta}}{n}}.$$

What is important to recall from this result, is that the difference between the true and empirical risk is at most of order

$$\sqrt{\frac{h\log n}{n}}.$$

An interpretation of VC dimension and growth functions is that they measure the *effective* size of the class, that is the size of the projection of the class onto finite samples. In addition, this measure does not just 'count' the number of functions in the class but depends on the geometry of the class (rather its projections). Finally, the finiteness of the VC dimension ensures that the empirical risk will converge uniformly over the class to the true risk.

4.4   Symmetrization

We now indicate how to prove Theorem 2. The key ingredient to the proof is the so-called *symmetrization* lemma. The idea is to replace the true risk by an estimate computed on an independent set of data. This is of course a mathematical technique and does not mean one needs to have more data to be able to apply the result. The extra data set is usually called 'virtual' or 'ghost sample'.

We will denote by $Z'_1, \ldots, Z'_n$ an independent (ghost) sample and by P'_n the corresponding empirical measure.

Lemma 2 (Symmetrization). *For any $t > 0$, such that $nt^2 \geq 2$,*

$$\mathbb{P}\left[\sup_{f \in \mathcal{F}}(P - P_n)f \geq t\right] \leq 2\mathbb{P}\left[\sup_{f \in \mathcal{F}}(P'_n - P_n)f \geq t/2\right].$$

Proof. Let f_n be the function achieving the supremum (note that it depends on $Z_1, \ldots, Z_n$). One has (with $\wedge$ denoting the conjunction of two events),

$$\mathbb{1}_{(P-P_n)f_n > t}\mathbb{1}_{(P-P'_n)f_n < t/2} = \mathbb{1}_{(P-P_n)f_n > t \wedge (P'_n - P)f_n \geq -t/2}$$
$$\leq \mathbb{1}_{(P'_n - P_n)f_n > t/2}.$$

Taking expectations with respect to the second sample gives

$$\mathbb{1}_{(P-P_n)f_n > t}\mathbb{P}'\left[(P - P'_n)f_n < t/2\right] \leq \mathbb{P}'\left[(P'_n - P_n)f_n > t/2\right].$$

By Chebyshev's inequality (see Appendix A),

$$\mathbb{P}'\left[(P - P'_n)f_n \geq t/2\right] \leq \frac{4\mathrm{Var}f_n}{nt^2} \leq \frac{1}{nt^2}.$$

Indeed, a random variable with range in $[0, 1]$ has variance less than $1/4$. Hence

$$\mathbb{1}_{(P-P_n)f_n > t}(1 - \frac{1}{nt^2}) \leq \mathbb{P}'\left[(P'_n - P_n)f_n > t/2\right].$$

Taking expectation with respect to first sample gives the result.   □

This lemma allows to replace the expectation Pf by an empirical average over the ghost sample. As a result, the right hand side only depends on the *projection* of the class $\mathcal{F}$ on the double sample:

$$\mathcal{F}_{Z_1, \ldots, Z_n, Z'_1, \ldots, Z'_n},$$

which contains finitely many different vectors. One can thus use the simple union bound that was presented before in the finite case. The other ingredient that is needed to obtain Theorem 2 is again Hoeffding's inequality in the following form:

$$\mathbb{P}\left[P_n f - P_n' f > t\right] \le e^{-nt^2/2}.$$

We now just have to put the pieces together:

$$
\begin{aligned}
&\mathbb{P}\left[\sup_{f\in\mathcal{F}}(P - P_n)f \ge t\right] \\
&\le 2\mathbb{P}\left[\sup_{f\in\mathcal{F}}(P_n' - P_n)f \ge t/2\right] \\
&= 2\mathbb{P}\left[\sup_{f\in\mathcal{F}_{Z_1,\dots,Z_n,Z_1',\dots,Z_n'}}(P_n' - P_n)f \ge t/2\right] \\
&\le 2S_{\mathcal{F}}(2n)\mathbb{P}\left[(P_n' - P_n)f \ge t/2\right] \\
&\le 4S_{\mathcal{F}}(2n)e^{-nt^2/8}.
\end{aligned}
$$

Using inversion finishes the proof of Theorem 2.

4.5   VC Entropy

One important aspect of the VC dimension is that it is *distribution independent*. Hence, it allows to get bounds that do not depend on the problem at hand: the same bound holds for any distribution. Although this may be seen as an advantage, it can also be a drawback since, as a result, the bound may be loose for most distributions.

We now show how to modify the proof above to get a distribution-dependent result. We use the following notation $N(\mathcal{F}, z_1^n) := |\mathcal{F}_{z_1,\dots,z_n}|$.

Definition 3 (VC Entropy). *The (annealed) VC entropy is defined as*

$$H_{\mathcal{F}}(n) = \log \mathbb{E}\left[N(\mathcal{F}, Z_1^n)\right].$$

Theorem 3. *For any $\delta > 0$, with probability at least $1 - \delta$,*

$$\forall g \in \mathcal{G}, \ R(g) \le R_n(g) + 2\sqrt{2\frac{H_{\mathcal{G}}(2n) + \log\frac{2}{\delta}}{n}}.$$

Proof.   We again begin with the symmetrization lemma so that we have to upper bound the quantity

$$I = \mathbb{P}\left[\sup_{f\in\mathcal{F}_{Z_1^n,Z_1^{n'}}}(P_n' - P_n)f \ge t/2\right].$$

Let $\sigma_1,\dots,\sigma_n$ be n independent random variables such that $P(\sigma_i = 1) = P(\sigma_i = -1) = 1/2$ (they are called Rademacher variables). We notice that the quantities $(P_n' - P_n)f$ and $\frac{1}{n}\sum_{i=1}^n \sigma_i(f(Z_i') - f(Z_i))$ have the same distribution since changing one σ_i corresponds to exchanging Z_i and Z_i'. Hence we have

$$I \leq \mathbb{E}\left[\mathbb{P}_\sigma\left[\sup_{f\in\mathcal{F}_{Z_1^n,Z_1^{n\prime}}} \frac{1}{n}\sum_{i=1}^n \sigma_i(f(Z_i') - f(Z_i)) \geq t/2\right]\right],$$

and the union bound leads to

$$I \leq \mathbb{E}\left[N\left(\mathcal{F}, Z_1^n, Z_1^{n\prime}\right) \max_f \mathbb{P}\left[\frac{1}{n}\sum_{i=1}^n \sigma_i(f(Z_i') - f(Z_i)) \geq t/2\right]\right].$$

Since $\sigma_i(f(Z_i') - f(Z_i)) \in [-1,1]$, Hoeffding's inequality finally gives

$$I \leq \mathbb{E}\left[N\left(\mathcal{F}, Z, Z'\right)\right] e^{-nt^2/8}.$$

The rest of the proof is as before. □

5   Capacity Measures

We have seen so far three measures of *capacity* or size of classes of function: the VC dimension and growth function both distribution independent, and the VC entropy which depends on the distribution. Apart from the VC dimension, they are usually hard or impossible to compute. There are however other measures which not only may give sharper estimates, but also have properties that make their computation possible from the data only.

5.1   Covering Numbers

We start by endowing the function class $\mathcal{F}$ with the following (random) metric

$$d_n(f, f') = \frac{1}{n}|\{f(Z_i) \neq f'(Z_i) : i = 1,\ldots,n\}|.$$

This is the normalized Hamming distance of the 'projections' on the sample. Given such a metric, we say that a set $f_1,\ldots,f_N$ *covers* $\mathcal{F}$ at radius ε if

$$\mathcal{F} \subset \cup_{i=1}^N B(f_i, \varepsilon).$$

We then define the covering numbers of $\mathcal{F}$ as follows.

Definition 4 (Covering Number). *The covering number of $\mathcal{F}$ at radius ε, with respect to d_n, denoted by $N(\mathcal{F}, \varepsilon, n)$ is the minimum size of a cover of radius ε.*

Notice that it does not matter if we apply this definition to the original class $\mathcal{G}$ or the loss class $\mathcal{F}$, since $N(\mathcal{F}, \varepsilon, n) = N(\mathcal{G}, \varepsilon, n)$.

The covering numbers characterize the size of a function class as measured by the metric d_n. The rate of growth of the logarithm of $N(\mathcal{G}, \varepsilon, n)$ usually called the metric entropy, is related to the classical concept of vector dimension. Indeed, if $\mathcal{G}$ is a compact set in a d-dimensional Euclidean space, $N(\mathcal{G}, \varepsilon, n) \approx \varepsilon^{-d}$.

When the covering numbers are finite, it is possible to approximate the class $\mathcal{G}$ by a finite set of functions (which cover $\mathcal{G}$). Which again allows to use the finite union bound, provided we can relate the behavior of all functions in $\mathcal{G}$ to that of functions in the cover. A typical result, which we provide without proof, is the following.

Theorem 4. *For any* $t > 0$,

$$\mathbb{P}\left[\exists g \in \mathcal{G} : R(g) > R_n(g) + t\right] \leq 8\mathbb{E}\left[N(\mathcal{G}, t, n)\right] e^{-nt^2/128}.$$

Covering numbers can also be defined for classes of real-valued functions.

We now relate the covering numbers to the VC dimension. Notice that, because the functions in $\mathcal{G}$ can only take two values, for all $\varepsilon > 0$, $N(\mathcal{G}, \varepsilon, n) \leq |\mathcal{G}_{Z_1^n}| = N(\mathcal{G}, Z_1^n)$. Hence the VC entropy corresponds to log covering numbers at minimal scale, which implies $N(\mathcal{G}, \varepsilon, n) \leq h \log \frac{en}{h}$, but one can have a considerably better result.

Lemma 3 (Haussler). *Let* $\mathcal{G}$ *be a class of VC dimension* h. *Then, for all* $\varepsilon > 0$, *all* n, *and any sample*,

$$N(\mathcal{G}, \varepsilon, n) \leq Ch(4e)^h \varepsilon^{-h}.$$

The interest of this result is that the upper bound does not depend on the sample size n.

The covering number bound is a generalization of the VC entropy bound where the scale is adapted to the error. It turns out that this result can be improved by considering all scales (see Section 5.2).

5.2   Rademacher Averages

Recall that we used in the proof of Theorem 3 Rademacher random variables, i.e. independent $\{-1, 1\}$-valued random variables with probability $1/2$ of taking either value.

For convenience we introduce the following notation (signed empirical measure) $R_n f = \frac{1}{n} \sum_{i=1}^n \sigma_i f(Z_i)$. We will denote by $\mathbb{E}_\sigma$ the expectation taken with respect to the Rademacher variables (i.e. conditionally to the data) while $\mathbb{E}$ will denote the expectation with respect to all the random variables (i.e. the data, the ghost sample and the Rademacher variables).

Definition 5 (Rademacher Averages). *For a class* $\mathcal{F}$ *of functions, the Rademacher average is defined as*

$$\mathcal{R}(\mathcal{F}) = \mathbb{E} \sup_{f \in \mathcal{F}} R_n f,$$

and the conditional Rademacher average is defined as

$$\mathcal{R}_n(\mathcal{F}) = \mathbb{E}_\sigma \sup_{f \in \mathcal{F}} R_n f.$$

We now state the fundamental result involving Rademacher averages.

Theorem 5. *For all $\delta > 0$, with probability at least $1 - \delta$,*

$$\forall f \in \mathcal{F}, Pf \leq P_n f + 2\mathcal{R}(\mathcal{F}) + \sqrt{\frac{\log \frac{1}{\delta}}{2n}},$$

and also, with probability at least $1 - \delta$,

$$\forall f \in \mathcal{F}, Pf \leq P_n f + 2\mathcal{R}_n(\mathcal{F}) + \sqrt{\frac{2\log \frac{2}{\delta}}{n}}.$$

It is remarkable that one can obtain a bound (second part of the theorem) which depends solely on the data.

The proof of the above result requires a powerful tool called a concentration inequality for empirical processes.

Actually, Hoeffding's inequality is a (simple) concentration inequality, in the sense that when n increases, the empirical average is concentrated around the expectation. It is possible to generalize this result to functions that depend on i.i.d. random variables as shown in the theorem below.

Theorem 6 (McDiarmid [17]). *Assume for all $i = 1, \ldots, n$,*

$$\sup_{z_1,\ldots,z_n,z_i'} |F(z_1, \ldots, z_i, \ldots, z_n) - F(z_1, \ldots, z_i', \ldots, z_n)| \leq c,$$

then for all $\varepsilon > 0$,

$$\mathbb{P}\left[|F - \mathbb{E}[F]| > \varepsilon\right] \leq 2\exp\left(-\frac{2\varepsilon^2}{nc^2}\right).$$

The meaning of this result is thus that, as soon as one has a function of n independent random variables, which is such that its variation is bounded when one variable is modified, the function will satisfy a Hoeffding-like inequality.

Proof of Theorem 5. To prove Theorem 5, we will have to follow the following three steps:

1. Use *concentration* to relate $\sup_{f \in \mathcal{F}} Pf - P_n f$ to its expectation,
2. use *symmetrization* to relate the expectation to the Rademacher average,
3. use *concentration* again to relate the Rademacher average to the conditional one.

We first show that McDiarmid's inequality can be applied to $\sup_{f \in \mathcal{F}} Pf - P_n f$. We denote temporarily by P_n^i the empirical measure obtained by modifying one element (e.g. Z_i is replaced by Z_i') of the sample. It is easy to check that the following holds

$$|\sup_{f \in \mathcal{F}}(Pf - P_n f) - \sup_{f \in \mathcal{F}}(Pf - P_n^i f)| \leq \sup_{f \in \mathcal{F}} |P_n^i f - P_n f|.$$

Since $f \in \{0, 1\}$ we obtain

$$|P_n^i f - P_n f| = \frac{1}{n} |f(Z_i') - f(Z_i)| \leq \frac{1}{n},$$

and thus McDiarmid's inequality can be applied with $c = 1/n$. This concludes the first step of the proof.

We next prove the (first part of the) following symmetrization lemma.

Lemma 4. *For any class $\mathcal{F}$,*

$$\mathbb{E} \sup_{f \in \mathcal{F}} Pf - P_n f \leq 2\mathbb{E} \sup_{f \in \mathcal{F}} R_n f,$$

and

$$\mathbb{E} \sup_{f \in \mathcal{F}} |Pf - P_n f| \geq \frac{1}{2} \mathbb{E} \sup_{f \in \mathcal{F}} R_n f - \frac{1}{2\sqrt{n}}.$$

Proof.   We only prove the first part. We introduce a ghost sample and its corresponding measure P_n'. We successively use the fact that $\mathbb{E} P_n' f = Pf$ and the supremum is a convex function (hence we can apply Jensen's inequality, see Appendix A):

$$\mathbb{E} \sup_{f \in \mathcal{F}} Pf - P_n f$$

$$= \mathbb{E} \sup_{f \in \mathcal{F}} \mathbb{E} [P_n' f] - P_n f$$

$$\leq \mathbb{E} \sup_{f \in \mathcal{F}} P_n' f - P_n f$$

$$= \mathbb{E}_\sigma \mathbb{E} \left[\sup_{f \in \mathcal{F}} \frac{1}{n} \sum_{i=1}^n \sigma_i (f(Z_i') - f(Z_i)) \right]$$

$$\leq \mathbb{E}_\sigma \mathbb{E} \left[\sup_{f \in \mathcal{F}} \frac{1}{n} \sum_{i=1}^n \sigma_i f(Z_i') \right] + \mathbb{E}_\sigma \mathbb{E} \left[\sup_{f \in \mathcal{F}} \frac{1}{n} \sum_{i=1}^n -\sigma_i f(Z_i)) \right]$$

$$= 2\mathbb{E} \sup_{f \in \mathcal{F}} R_n f.$$

where the third step uses the fact that $f(Z_i) - f(Z_i')$ and $\sigma_i(f(Z_i) - f(Z_i'))$ have the same distribution and the last step uses the fact that the $\sigma_i f(Z_i)$ and $-\sigma_i f(Z_i')$ have the same distribution.   □

The above already establishes the first part of Theorem 5. For the second part, we need to use concentration again. For this we apply McDiarmid's inequality to the following functional

$$F(Z_1, \ldots, Z_n) = \mathcal{R}_n(\mathcal{F}).$$

It is easy to check that F satisfies McDiarmid's assumptions with $c = \frac{1}{n}$. As a result, $\mathbb{E} F = \mathcal{R}(\mathcal{F})$ can be sharply estimated by $F = \mathcal{R}_n(\mathcal{F})$.

Loss Class and Initial Class. In order to make use of Theorem 5 we have to relate the Rademacher average of the loss class to those of the initial class. This can be done with the following derivation where one uses the fact that σ_i and $\sigma_i Y_i$ have the same distribution.

$$
\begin{aligned}
\mathcal{R}(\mathcal{F}) &= \mathbb{E}\left[\sup_{g \in \mathcal{G}} \frac{1}{n} \sum_{i=1}^{n} \sigma_i \mathbb{1}_{g(X_i) \neq Y_i}\right] \\
&= \mathbb{E}\left[\sup_{g \in \mathcal{G}} \frac{1}{n} \sum_{i=1}^{n} \sigma_i \frac{1}{2}(1 - Y_i g(X_i))\right] \\
&= \frac{1}{2}\mathbb{E}\left[\sup_{g \in \mathcal{G}} \frac{1}{n} \sum_{i=1}^{n} \sigma_i Y_i g(X_i)\right] = \frac{1}{2}\mathcal{R}(\mathcal{G}).
\end{aligned}
$$

Notice that the same is valid for conditional Rademacher averages, so that we obtain that with probability at least $1 - \delta$,

$$
\forall g \in \mathcal{G}, R(g) \leq R_n(g) + \mathcal{R}_n(\mathcal{G}) + \sqrt{\frac{2\log\frac{2}{\delta}}{n}}.
$$

Computing the Rademacher Averages. We now assess the difficulty of actually computing the Rademacher averages. We write the following.

$$
\begin{aligned}
\frac{1}{2}\mathbb{E}&\left[\sup_{g \in \mathcal{G}} \frac{1}{n} \sum_{i=1}^{n} \sigma_i g(X_i)\right] \\
&= \frac{1}{2} + \mathbb{E}\left[\sup_{g \in \mathcal{G}} \frac{1}{n} \sum_{i=1}^{n} -\frac{1 - \sigma_i g(X_i)}{2}\right] \\
&= \frac{1}{2} - \mathbb{E}\left[\inf_{g \in \mathcal{G}} \frac{1}{n} \sum_{i=1}^{n} \frac{1 - \sigma_i g(X_i)}{2}\right] \\
&= \frac{1}{2} - \mathbb{E}\left[\inf_{g \in \mathcal{G}} R_n(g, \sigma)\right].
\end{aligned}
$$

This indicates that, given a sample and a choice of the random variables $\sigma_1, \ldots, \sigma_n$, computing $\mathcal{R}_n(\mathcal{G})$ is not harder than computing the empirical risk minimizer in $\mathcal{G}$. Indeed, the procedure would be to generate the σ_i randomly and minimize the empirical error in $\mathcal{G}$ with respect to the labels σ_i.

An advantage of rewriting $\mathcal{R}_n(\mathcal{G})$ as above is that it gives an intuition of what it actually measures: it measures how much the class $\mathcal{G}$ can fit random noise. If the class $\mathcal{G}$ is very large, there will always be a function which can perfectly fit the σ_i and then $\mathcal{R}_n(\mathcal{G}) = 1/2$, so that there is no hope of uniform convergence to zero of the difference between true and empirical risks.

For a finite set with $|\mathcal{G}| = N$, one can show that

$$
\mathcal{R}_n(\mathcal{G}) \leq 2\sqrt{\log N/n},
$$

where we again see the logarithmic factor $\log N$. A consequence of this is that, by considering the projection on the sample of a class $\mathcal{G}$ with VC dimension h, and using Lemma 1, we have

$$\mathcal{R}(\mathcal{G}) \leq 2\sqrt{\frac{h \log \frac{en}{h}}{n}}.$$

This result along with Theorem 5 allows to recover the Vapnik Chervonenkis bound with a concentration-based proof.

Although the benefit of using concentration may not be entirely clear at that point, let us just mention that one can actually improve the dependence on n of the above bound. This is based on the so-called *chaining* technique. The idea is to use covering numbers at all scales in order to capture the geometry of the class in a better way than the VC entropy does.

One has the following result, called Dudley's entropy bound

$$\mathcal{R}_n(\mathcal{F}) \leq \frac{C}{\sqrt{n}} \int_0^\infty \sqrt{\log N(\mathcal{F}, t, n)}\, dt.$$

As a consequence, along with Haussler's upper bound, we can get the following result

$$\mathcal{R}_n(\mathcal{F}) \leq C\sqrt{\frac{h}{n}}.$$

We can thus, with this approach, remove the unnecessary $\log n$ factor of the VC bound.

6   Advanced Topics

In this section, we point out several ways in which the results presented so far can be improved. The main source of improvement actually comes, as mentioned earlier, from the fact that Hoeffding and McDiarmid inequalities do not make use of the variance of the functions.

6.1   Binomial Tails

We recall that the functions we consider are binary valued. So, if we consider a fixed function f, the distribution of $P_n f$ is actually a binomial law of parameters Pf and n (since we are summing n i.i.d. random variables $f(Z_i)$ which can either be 0 or 1 and are equal to 1 with probability $\mathbb{E}f(Z_i) = Pf$). Denoting $p = Pf$, we can have an exact expression for the deviations of $P_n f$ from Pf:

$$\mathbb{P}\left[Pf - P_n f \geq t\right] = \sum_{k=0}^{\lfloor n(p-t) \rfloor} \binom{n}{k} p^k (1-p)^{n-k}.$$

Since this expression is not easy to manipulate, we have used an upper bound provided by Hoeffding's inequality. However, there exist other (sharper) upper bounds. The following quantities are an upper bound on $\mathbb{P}\left[Pf - P_n f \geq t\right]$,

$$\left(\frac{1-p}{1-p-t}\right)^{n(1-p-t)} \left(\frac{p}{p+t}\right)^{n(p+t)} \quad \text{(exponential)}$$

$$e^{-\frac{np}{1-p}\left((1-t/p)\log(1-t/p)+t/p\right)} \quad \text{(Bennett)}$$

$$e^{-\frac{nt^2}{2p(1-p)+2t/3}} \quad \text{(Bernstein)}$$

$$e^{-2nt^2} \quad \text{(Hoeffding)}$$

Examining the above bounds (and using inversion), we can say that roughly speaking, the small deviations of $Pf - P_n f$ have a Gaussian behavior of the form $\exp(-nt^2/2p(1-p))$ (i.e. Gaussian with variance $p(1-p)$) while the large deviations have a Poisson behavior of the form $\exp(-3nt/2)$.

So the tails are heavier than Gaussian, and Hoeffding's inequality consists in upper bounding the tails with a Gaussian with maximum variance, hence the term $\exp(-2nt^2)$.

Each function $f \in \mathcal{F}$ has a different variance $Pf(1 - Pf) \leq Pf$. Moreover, for each $f \in \mathcal{F}$, by Bernstein's inequality, with probability at least $1 - \delta$,

$$Pf \leq P_n f + \sqrt{\frac{2Pf \log \frac{1}{\delta}}{n}} + \frac{2\log \frac{1}{\delta}}{3n} \, .$$

The Gaussian part (second term in the right hand side) dominates (for Pf not too small, or n large enough), and it depends on Pf. We thus want to combine Bernstein's inequality with the union bound and the symmetrization.

6.2   Normalization

The idea is to consider the ratio

$$\frac{Pf - P_n f}{\sqrt{Pf}} \, .$$

Here ($f \in \{0, 1\}$), $\mathsf{Var} f \leq Pf^2 = Pf$

The reason for considering this ration is that after normalization, fluctuations are more 'uniform' in the class $\mathcal{F}$. Hence the supremum in

$$\sup_{f \in \mathcal{F}} \frac{Pf - P_n f}{\sqrt{Pf}}$$

not necessarily attained at functions with large variance as it was the case previously.

Moreover, we know that our goal is to find functions with small error Pf (hence small variance). The normalized supremum takes this into account.

We now state a result similar to Theorem 2 for the normalized supremum.

Theorem 7 (Vapnik-Chervonenkis, [18]). *For $\delta > 0$ with probability at least $1 - \delta$,*

$$\forall f \in \mathcal{F}, \frac{Pf - P_nf}{\sqrt{Pf}} \le 2\sqrt{\frac{\log S_{\mathcal{F}}(2n) + \log \frac{4}{\delta}}{n}},$$

and also with probability at least $1 - \delta$,

$$\forall f \in \mathcal{F}, \frac{P_nf - Pf}{\sqrt{P_nf}} \le 2\sqrt{\frac{\log S_{\mathcal{F}}(2n) + \log \frac{4}{\delta}}{n}}.$$

Proof. We only give a sketch of the proof. The first step is a variation of the symmetrization lemma

$$\mathbb{P}\left[\sup_{f \in \mathcal{F}} \frac{Pf - P_nf}{\sqrt{Pf}} \ge t\right] \le 2\mathbb{P}\left[\sup_{f \in \mathcal{F}} \frac{P_n'f - P_nf}{\sqrt{(P_nf + P_n'f)/2}} \ge t\right].$$

The second step consists in randomization (with Rademacher variables)

$$\cdots = 2\mathbb{E}\left[\mathbb{P}_\sigma\left[\sup_{f \in \mathcal{F}} \frac{\frac{1}{n}\sum_{i=1}^n \sigma_i(f(Z_i') - f(Z_i))}{\sqrt{(P_nf + P_n'f)/2}} \ge t\right]\right].$$

Finally, one uses a tail bound of Bernstein type. □

Let us explore the consequences of this result.
From the fact that for non-negative numbers A, B, C,

$$A \le B + C\sqrt{A} \Rightarrow A \le B + C^2 + \sqrt{BC},$$

we easily get for example

$$\forall f \in \mathcal{F}, Pf \le P_nf + 2\sqrt{P_nf \frac{\log S_{\mathcal{F}}(2n) + \log \frac{4}{\delta}}{n}}$$
$$+ 4\frac{\log S_{\mathcal{F}}(2n) + \log \frac{4}{\delta}}{n}.$$

In the ideal situation where there is no noise (i.e. $Y = t(X)$ almost surely), and $t \in \mathcal{G}$, denoting by g_n the empirical risk minimizer, we have $R^* = 0$ and also $R_n(g_n) = 0$. In particular, when $\mathcal{G}$ is a class of VC dimension h, we obtain

$$R(g_n) = O\left(\frac{h \log n}{n}\right).$$

So, in a way, Theorem 7 allows to interpolate between the best case where the rate of convergence is $O(h \log n/n)$ and the worst case where the rate is $O(\sqrt{h \log n/n})$ (it does not allow to remove the $\log n$ factor in this case).

It is also possible to derive from Theorem 7 relative error bounds for the minimizer of the empirical error. With probability at least $1 - \delta$,

$$R(g_n) \leq R(g^*) + 2\sqrt{R(g^*)\frac{\log S_{\mathcal{G}}(2n) + \log \frac{4}{\delta}}{n}}$$
$$+4\frac{\log S_{\mathcal{G}}(2n) + \log \frac{4}{\delta}}{n}.$$

We notice here that when $R(g^*) = 0$ (i.e. $t \in \mathcal{G}$ and $R^* = 0$), the rate is again of order $1/n$ while, as soon as $R(g^*) > 0$, the rate is of order $1/\sqrt{n}$. Therefore, it is not possible to obtain a rate with a power of n in between $-1/2$ and -1.

The main reason is that the factor of the square root term $R(g^*)$ is not the right quantity to use here since it does not vary with n. We will see later that one can have instead $R(g_n) - R(g^*)$ as a factor, which is usually converging to zero with n increasing. Unfortunately, Theorem 7 cannot be applied to functions of the type $f - f^*$ (which would be needed to have the mentioned factor), so we will need a refined approach.

6.3   Noise Conditions

The refinement we seek to obtain requires certain specific assumptions about the noise function $s(x)$. The ideal case being when $s(x) = 0$ everywhere (which corresponds to $R^* = 0$ and $Y = t(X)$). We now introduce quantities that measure how well-behaved the noise function is.

The situation is favorable when the regression function $\eta(x)$ is not too close to 0, or at least not too often close to $1/2$. Indeed, $\eta(x) = 0$ means that the noise is maximum at x ($s(x) = 1/2$) and that the label is completely undetermined (any prediction would yield an error with probability $1/2$).

Definitions. There are two types of conditions.

Definition 6 (Massart's Noise Condition). *For some $c > 0$, assume*

$$|\eta(X)| > \frac{1}{c} \; almost \; surely.$$

This condition implies that there is no region where the decision is completely random, or the noise is bounded away from $1/2$.

Definition 7 (Tsybakov's Noise Condition). *Let $\alpha \in [0, 1]$, assume that one the following equivalent conditions is satisfied*

(i) $\exists c > 0, \; \forall g \in \{-1, 1\}^{\mathcal{X}}$,
$$\mathbb{P}\left[g(X)\eta(X) \leq 0\right] \leq c(R(g) - R^*)^\alpha$$

(ii) $\exists c > 0, \; \forall A \subset \mathcal{X}, \; \int_A dP(x) \leq c(\int_A |\eta(x)|dP(x))^\alpha$

(iii) $\exists B > 0, \; \forall t \geq 0, \; \mathbb{P}\left[|\eta(X)| \leq t\right] \leq Bt^{\frac{\alpha}{1-\alpha}}$

Condition (iii) is probably the easiest to interpret: it means that $\eta(x)$ is close to the critical value 0 with low probability.

We indicate how to prove that conditions $(i), (ii)$ and (iii) are indeed equivalent:

$(i) \Leftrightarrow (ii)$ It is easy to check that $R(g) - R^* = \mathbb{E}\left[|\eta(X)|\mathbb{1}_{g\eta \leq 0}\right]$. For each function g, there exists a set A such that $\mathbb{1}_A = \mathbb{1}_{g\eta \leq 0}$

$(ii) \Rightarrow (iii)$ Let $A = \{x : |\eta(x)| \leq t\}$

$$\mathbb{P}\left[|\eta| \leq t\right] = \int_A dP(x) \leq c(\int_A |\eta(x)|dP(x))^\alpha$$

$$\leq ct^\alpha(\int_A dP(x))^\alpha$$

$$\Rightarrow \mathbb{P}\left[|\eta| \leq t\right] \leq c^{\frac{1}{1-\alpha}} t^{\frac{\alpha}{1-\alpha}}$$

$(iii) \Rightarrow (i)$ We write

$$R(g) - R^* = \mathbb{E}\left[|\eta(X)|\, g\eta \leq 0\right]$$

$$\geq t\mathbb{E}\left[\mathbb{1}_{g\eta \leq 0}\mathbb{1}_{|\eta|t}\right]$$

$$= t\mathbb{P}\left[|\eta| t\right] - t\mathbb{E}\left[\mathbb{1}_{g\eta > 0}\mathbb{1}_{|\eta|t}\right]$$

$$\geq t(1 - Bt^{\frac{\alpha}{1-\alpha}}) - t\mathbb{P}\left[g\eta > 0\right] = t(\mathbb{P}\left[g\eta \leq 0\right] - Bt^{\frac{\alpha}{1-\alpha}}).$$

Taking $t = \left(\frac{(1-\alpha)\mathbb{P}[g\eta \leq 0]}{B}\right)^{(1-\alpha)/\alpha}$ finally gives

$$\mathbb{P}\left[g\eta \leq 0\right] \leq \frac{B^{1-\alpha}}{(1-\alpha)^{(1-\alpha)}\alpha^\alpha}(R(g) - R^*)^\alpha.$$

We notice that the parameter α has to be in $[0,1]$. Indeed, one has the opposite inequality

$$R(g) - R^* = \mathbb{E}\left[|\eta(X)|\mathbb{1}_{g\eta \leq 0}\right] \leq \mathbb{E}\left[\mathbb{1}_{g\eta \leq 0}\right] = \mathbb{P}\left[g(X)\eta(X) \leq 0\right],$$

which is incompatible with condition (i) if $\alpha > 1$.

We also notice that when $\alpha = 0$, Tsybakov's condition is void, and when $\alpha = 1$, it is equivalent to Massart's condition.

Consequences. The conditions we impose on the noise yield a crucial relationship between the variance and the expectation of functions in the so-called relative loss class defined as

$$\tilde{\mathcal{F}} = \{(x,y) \mapsto f(x,y) - \mathbb{1}_{t(x) \neq y} : f \in \mathcal{F}\}.$$

This relationship will allow to exploit Bernstein type inequalities applied to this latter class.

Under Massart's condition, one has (written in terms of the initial class) for $g \in \mathcal{G}$,

$$\mathbb{E}\left[(\mathbb{1}_{g(X) \neq Y} - \mathbb{1}_{t(X) \neq Y})^2\right] \leq c(R(g) - R^*),$$

or, equivalently, for $f \in \tilde{\mathcal{F}}$, $\mathrm{Var} f \leq P f^2 \leq c P f$. Under Tsybakov's condition this becomes for $g \in \mathcal{G}$,

$$\mathbb{E}\left[(\mathbb{1}_{g(X) \neq Y} - \mathbb{1}_{t(X) \neq Y})^2\right] \leq c(R(g) - R^*)^\alpha,$$

and for $f \in \tilde{\mathcal{F}}$, $\mathrm{Var} f \leq P f^2 \leq c(P f)^\alpha$.

In the finite case, with $|\mathcal{G}| = N$, one can easily apply Bernstein's inequality to $\tilde{\mathcal{F}}$ and the finite union bound to get that with probability at least $1 - \delta$, for all $g \in \mathcal{G}$,

$$R(g) - R^* \leq R_n(g) - R_n(t) + \sqrt{\frac{8c(R(g) - R^*)^\alpha \log \frac{N}{\delta}}{n}} + \frac{4 \log \frac{N}{\delta}}{3n}.$$

As a consequence, when $t \in \mathcal{G}$, and g_n is the minimizer of the empirical error (hence $R_n(g) \leq R_n(t)$), one has

$$R(g_n) - R^* \leq C \left(\frac{\log \frac{N}{\delta}}{n}\right)^{\frac{1}{2-\alpha}},$$

which always better than $n^{-1/2}$ for $\alpha > 0$ and is valid even if $R^* > 0$.

6.4   Local Rademacher Averages

In this section we generalize the above result by introducing a localized version of the Rademacher averages. Going from the finite to the general case is more involved than what has been seen before. We first give the appropriate definitions, then state the result and give a proof sketch.

Definitions. Local Rademacher averages refer to Rademacher averages of subsets of the function class determined by a condition on the variance of the function.

Definition 8 (Local Rademacher Average). *The local Rademacher average at radius $r \geq 0$ for the class $\mathcal{F}$ is defined as*

$$\mathcal{R}(\mathcal{F}, r) = \mathbb{E} \sup_{f \in \mathcal{F}: P f^2 \leq r} R_n f.$$

The reason for this definition is that, as we have seen before, the crucial ingredient to obtain better rates of convergence is to use the variance of the functions. Localizing the Rademacher average allows to focus on the part of the function class where the fast rate phenomenon occurs, that are functions with small variance.

Next we introduce the concept of a sub-root function, a real-valued function with certain monotony properties.

Definition 9 (Sub-root Function). *A function* $\psi : \mathbb{R} \rightarrow \mathbb{R}$ *is sub-root if*

(i) ψ *is non-decreasing,*
(ii) ψ *is non negative,*
(iii) $\psi(r)/\sqrt{r}$ *is non-increasing.*

An immediate consequence of this definition is the following result.

Lemma 5. *A sub-root function*

(i) *is continuous,*
(ii) *has a unique (non-zero)* fixed point r^* *satisfying* $\psi(r^*) = r^*$.

Figure 6 shows a typical sub-root function and its fixed point.

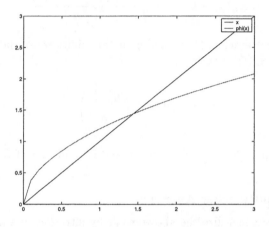

Fig. 6. An example of a sub-root function and its fixed point

Before seeing the rationale for introducing the sub-root concept, we need yet another definition, that of a 'star-hull' (somewhat similar to a convex hull).

Definition 10 (Star-Hull). *Let $\mathcal{F}$ be a set of functions. Its star-hull is defined as*

$$\star \mathcal{F} = \{\alpha f : f \in \mathcal{F}, \, \alpha \in [0,1]\}.$$

Now, we state a lemma that indicates that by taking the star-hull of a class of functions, we are guaranteed that the local Rademacher average behaves like a sub-root function, and thus has a unique fixed point. This fixed point will turn out to be the key quantity in the relative error bounds.

Lemma 6. *For any class of functions $\mathcal{F}$,*

$$\mathcal{R}_n(\star \mathcal{F}, r) \text{ is sub-root.}$$

One legitimate question is whether taking the star-hull does not enlarge the class too much. One way to see what the effect is on the size of the class is to compare the metric entropy (log covering numbers) of $\mathcal{F}$ and of $\star \mathcal{F}$. It is possible to see that the entropy increases only by a logarithmic factor, which is essentially negligible.

Result. We now state the main result involving local Rademacher averages and their fixed point.

Theorem 8. *Let $\mathcal{F}$ be a class of bounded functions (e.g. $f \in [-1, 1]$) and r^* be the fixed point of $\mathcal{R}(\star\mathcal{F}, r)$. There exists a constant $C > 0$ such that with probability at least $1 - \delta$,*

$$\forall f \in \mathcal{F}, \ Pf - P_n f \leq C \left(\sqrt{r^* \mathsf{Var} f} + \frac{\log \frac{1}{\delta} + \log \log n}{n} \right).$$

If in addition the functions in $\mathcal{F}$ satisfy $\mathsf{Var} f \leq c(Pf)^\beta$, then one obtains that with probability at least $1 - \delta$,

$$\forall f \in \mathcal{F}, \ Pf \leq C \left(P_n f + (r^*)^{\frac{1}{2-\beta}} + \frac{\log \frac{1}{\delta} + \log \log n}{n} \right).$$

Proof. We only give the main steps of the proof.

1. The starting point is Talagrand's inequality for empirical processes, a generalization of McDiarmid's inequality of Bernstein type (i.e. which includes the variance). This inequality tells that with high probability,

$$\sup_{f \in \mathcal{F}} Pf - P_n f \leq \mathbb{E} \left[\sup_{f \in \mathcal{F}} Pf - P_n f \right] + c \sqrt{\sup_{f \in \mathcal{F}} \mathsf{Var} f / n} + c'/n,$$

for some constants c, c'.

2. The second step consists in 'peeling' the class, that is splitting the class into subclasses according to the variance of the functions

$$\mathcal{F}_k = \{f : \mathsf{Var} f \in [x^k, x^{k+1})\},$$

3. We can then apply Talagrand's inequality to each of the sub-classes separately to get with high probability

$$\sup_{f \in \mathcal{F}_k} Pf - P_n f \leq \mathbb{E} \left[\sup_{f \in \mathcal{F}_k} Pf - P_n f \right] + c\sqrt{x \mathsf{Var} f / n} + c'/n,$$

4. Then the symmetrization lemma allows to introduce local Rademacher averages. We get that with high probability

$$\forall f \in \mathcal{F}, \ Pf - P_n f \leq 2\mathcal{R}(\mathcal{F}, x \mathsf{Var} f) + c\sqrt{x \mathsf{Var} f / n} + c'/n.$$

5. We then have to 'solve' this inequality. Things are simple if $\mathcal{R}$ behaves like a square root function since we can upper bound the local Rademacher average by the value of its fixed point. With high probability,

$$Pf - P_n f \leq 2\sqrt{r^* \mathsf{Var} f} + c\sqrt{x \mathsf{Var} f / n} + c'/n.$$

6. Finally, we use the relationship between variance and expectation

$$\mathrm{Var} f \leq c(Pf)^\alpha ,$$

and solve the inequality in Pf to get the result.

□

We will not got into the details of how to apply the above result, but we give some remarks about its use.

An important example is the case where the class $\mathcal{F}$ is of finite VC dimension h. In that case, one has

$$\mathcal{R}(\mathcal{F}, r) \leq C\sqrt{\frac{rh\log n}{n}} ,$$

so that $r^* \leq C\frac{h\log n}{n}$. As a consequence, we obtain, under Tsybakov condition, a rate of convergence of Pf_n to Pf^* is $O(1/n^{1/(2-\alpha)})$. It is important to note that in this case, the rate of convergence of $P_n f$ to Pf in $O(1/\sqrt{n})$. So we obtain a fast rate by looking at the relative error. These fast rates can be obtained provided $t \in \mathcal{G}$ (but it is not needed that $R^* = 0$). This requirement can be removed if one uses structural risk minimization or regularization.

Another related result is that, as in the global case, one can obtain a bound with data-dependent (i.e. conditional) local Rademacher averages

$$\mathcal{R}_n(\mathcal{F}, r) = \mathbb{E}_\sigma \sup_{f \in \mathcal{F}: Pf^2 \leq r} R_n f .$$

The result is the same as before (with different constants) under the same conditions as in Theorem 8. With probability at least $1 - \delta$,

$$Pf \leq C\left(P_n f + (r_n^*)^{\frac{1}{2-\alpha}} + \frac{\log\frac{1}{\delta} + \log\log n}{n} \right)$$

where r_n^* is the fixed point of a sub-root upper bound of $\mathcal{R}_n(\mathcal{F}, r)$.

Hence, we can get improved rates when the noise is well-behaved and these rates interpolate between $n^{-1/2}$ and n^{-1}. However, it is not in general possible to estimate the parameters (c and α) entering in the noise conditions, but we will not discuss this issue further here. Another point is that although the capacity measure that we use seems 'local', it does depend on all the functions in the class, but each of them is implicitly appropriately rescaled. Indeed, in $\mathcal{R}(\star\mathcal{F}, r)$, each function $f \in \mathcal{F}$ with $Pf^2 \geq r$ is considered at scale r/Pf^2.

Bibliographical Remarks. Hoeffding's inequality appears in [19]. For a proof of the contraction principle we refer to Ledoux and Talagrand [20].

Vapnik-Chervonenkis-Sauer-Shelah's lemma was proved independently by Sauer [21], Shelah [22], and Vapnik and Chervonenkis [18]. For related combinatorial results we refer to Alesker [23], Alon, Ben-David, Cesa-Bianchi, and

Haussler [24], Cesa-Bianchi and Haussler [25], Frankl [26], Haussler [27], Szarek and Talagrand [28].

Uniform deviations of averages from their expectations is one of the central problems of empirical process theory. Here we merely refer to some of the comprehensive coverages, such as Dudley [29], Giné [30], Vapnik [1], van der Vaart and Wellner [31]. The use of empirical processes in classification was pioneered by Vapnik and Chervonenkis [18, 15] and re-discovered 20 years later by Blumer, Ehrenfeucht, Haussler, and Warmuth [32], Ehrenfeucht, Haussler, Kearns, and Valiant [33]. For surveys see Anthony and Bartlett [2], Devroye, Györfi, and Lugosi [4], Kearns and Vazirani [7], Natarajan [12], Vapnik [14, 1].

The question of how $\sup_{f \in \mathcal{F}}(P(f) - P_n(f))$ behaves has been known as the Glivenko-Cantelli problem and much has been said about it. A few key references include Alon, Ben-David, Cesa-Bianchi, and Haussler [24], Dudley [34, 35, 36], Talagrand [37, 38], Vapnik and Chervonenkis [18, 39].

The VC dimension has been widely studied and many of its properties are known. We refer to Anthony and Bartlett [2], Assouad [40], Cover [41], Dudley [42, 29], Goldberg and Jerrum [43], Karpinski and A. Macintyre [44], Khovanskii [45], Koiran and Sontag [46], Macintyre and Sontag [47], Steele [48], and Wenocur and Dudley [49].

The bounded differences inequality was formulated explicitly first by McDiarmid [17] who proved it by martingale methods (see the surveys [17], [50]), but closely related concentration results have been obtained in various ways including information-theoretic methods (see Alhswede, Gács, and Körner [51], Marton [52], [53],[54], Dembo [55], Massart [56] and Rio [57]), Talagrand's induction method [58],[59],[60] (see also Luczak and McDiarmid [61], McDiarmid [62], Panchenko [63, 64, 65]) and the so-called "entropy method", based on logarithmic Sobolev inequalities, developed by Ledoux [66],[67], see also Bobkov and Ledoux [68], Massart [69], Rio [57], Boucheron, Lugosi, and Massart [70], [71], Boucheron, Bousquet, Lugosi, and Massart [72], and Bousquet [73].

Symmetrization lemmas can be found in Giné and Zinn [74] and Vapnik and Chervonenkis [18, 15].

The use of Rademacher averages in classification was first promoted by Koltchinskii [75] and Bartlett, Boucheron, and Lugosi [76], see also Koltchinskii and Panchenko [77, 78], Bartlett and Mendelson [79], Bartlett, Bousquet, and Mendelson [80], Bousquet, Koltchinskii, and Panchenko [81], Kégl, Linder, and Lugosi [82].

A   Probability Tools

This section recalls some basic facts from probability theory that are used throughout this tutorial (sometimes without explicitly mentioning it).

We denote by A and B some events (i.e. elements of a σ-algebra), and by X some real-valued random variable.

A.1   Basic Facts

– Union:
$$\mathbb{P}[A \text{ or } B] \le \mathbb{P}[A] + \mathbb{P}[B] .$$

– Inclusion: If $A \Rightarrow B$, then $\mathbb{P}[A] \le \mathbb{P}[B]$.
– Inversion: If $\mathbb{P}[X > t] \le F(t)$ then with probability at least $1 - \delta$,
$$X \le F^{-1}(\delta) .$$

– Expectation: If $X \ge 0$,
$$\mathbb{E}[X] = \int_0^\infty \mathbb{P}[X \ge t]\, dt .$$

A.2   Basic Inequalities

All the inequalities below are valid as soon as the right-hand side exists.

– Jensen: for f convex,
$$f(\mathbb{E}[X]) \le \mathbb{E}[f(X)] .$$

– Markov: If $X \ge 0$ then for all $t > 0$,
$$\mathbb{P}[X \ge t] \le \frac{\mathbb{E}[X]}{t} .$$

– Chebyshev: for $t > 0$,
$$\mathbb{P}[|X - \mathbb{E}[X]| \ge t] \le \frac{\operatorname{Var} X}{t^2} .$$

– Chernoff: for all $t \in \mathbb{R}$,
$$\mathbb{P}[X \ge t] \le \inf_{\lambda \ge 0} \mathbb{E}\left[e^{\lambda(X - t)}\right] .$$

B   No Free Lunch

We can now give a formal definition of consistency and state the core results about the impossibility of universally good algorithms.

Definition 11 (Consistency). *An algorithm is consistent if for any probability measure P,*
$$\lim_{n \to \infty} R(g_n) = R^* \text{ almost surely.}$$

It is important to understand the reasons that make possible the existence of consistent algorithms. In the case where the input space $\mathcal{X}$ is countable, things are somehow easy since even if there is no relationship at all between inputs and outputs, by repeatedly sampling data independently from P, one will get to see an increasing number of different inputs which will eventually converge to all the inputs. So, in the countable case, an algorithm which would simply learn 'by heart' (i.e. makes a majority vote when the instance has been seen before, and produces an arbitrary prediction otherwise) would be consistent.

In the case where $\mathcal{X}$ is not countable (e.g. $\mathcal{X} = \mathbb{R}$), things are more subtle. Indeed, in that case, there is a seemingly innocent assumption that becomes crucial: to be able to define a probability measure P on $\mathcal{X}$, one needs a σ-algebra on that space, which is typically the Borel σ-algebra. So the hidden assumption is that P is a Borel measure. This means that the topology of $\mathbb{R}$ plays a role here, and thus, the target function t will be Borel measurable. In a sense this guarantees that it is possible to approximate t from its value (or approximate value) at a finite number of points. The algorithms that will achieve consistency are thus those who use the topology in the sense of 'generalizing' the observed values to neighborhoods (e.g. local classifiers). In a way, the measurability of t is one of the crudest notions of smoothness of functions.

We now cite two important results. The first one tells that for a fixed sample size, one can construct arbitrarily bad problems for a given algorithm.

Theorem 9 (No Free Lunch, see e.g. [4]). *For any algorithm, any n and any $\varepsilon > 0$, there exists a distribution P such that $R^* = 0$ and*

$$\mathbb{P}\left[R(g_n) \geq \frac{1}{2} - \varepsilon\right] = 1.$$

The second result is more subtle and indicates that given an algorithm, one can construct a problem for which this algorithm will converge as slowly as one wishes.

Theorem 10 (No Free Lunch at All, see e.g. [4]). *For any algorithm, and any sequence (a_n) that converges to 0, there exists a probability distribution P such that $R^* = 0$ and*

$$R(g_n) \geq a_n.$$

In the above theorem, the 'bad' probability measure is constructed on a countable set (where the outputs are not related at all to the inputs so that no generalization is possible), and is such that the rate at which one gets to see new inputs is as slow as the convergence of a_n.

Finally we mention other notions of consistency.

Definition 12 (VC Consistency of ERM). *The ERM algorithm is consistent if for any probability measure P,*

$$R(g_n) \to R(g^*) \text{ in probability,}$$

and

$$R_n(g_n) \to R(g^*) \text{ in probability.}$$

Definition 13 (VC Non-trivial Consistency of ERM). *The ERM algorithm is non-trivially consistent for the set $\mathcal{G}$ and the probability distribution P if for any $c \in \mathbb{R}$,*

$$\inf_{f \in \mathcal{F}: Pf > c} P_n(f) \to \inf_{f \in \mathcal{F}: Pf > c} P(f) \text{ in probability.}$$

References

1. Vapnik, V.: Statistical Learning Theory. John Wiley, New York (1998)
2. Anthony, M., Bartlett, P.L.: Neural Network Learning: Theoretical Foundations. Cambridge University Press, Cambridge (1999)
3. Breiman, L., Friedman, J., Olshen, R., Stone, C.: Classification and Regression Trees. Wadsworth International, Belmont, CA (1984)
4. Devroye, L., Györfi, L., Lugosi, G.: A Probabilistic Theory of Pattern Recognition. Springer-Verlag, New York (1996)
5. Duda, R., Hart, P.: Pattern Classification and Scene Analysis. John Wiley, New York (1973)
6. Fukunaga, K.: Introduction to Statistical Pattern Recognition. Academic Press, New York (1972)
7. Kearns, M., Vazirani, U.: An Introduction to Computational Learning Theory. MIT Press, Cambridge, Massachusetts (1994)
8. Kulkarni, S., Lugosi, G., Venkatesh, S.: Learning pattern classification—a survey. IEEE Transactions on Information Theory 44 (1998) 2178–2206 Information Theory: 1948–1998. Commemorative special issue.
9. Lugosi, G.: Pattern classification and learning theory. In Györfi, L., ed.: Principles of Nonparametric Learning, Springer, Viena (2002) 5–62
10. McLachlan, G.: Discriminant Analysis and Statistical Pattern Recognition. John Wiley, New York (1992)
11. Mendelson, S.: A few notes on statistical learning theory. In Mendelson, S., Smola, A., eds.: Advanced Lectures in Machine Learning. LNCS 2600, Springer (2003) 1–40
12. Natarajan, B.: Machine Learning: A Theoretical Approach. Morgan Kaufmann, San Mateo, CA (1991)
13. Vapnik, V.: Estimation of Dependencies Based on Empirical Data. Springer-Verlag, New York (1982)
14. Vapnik, V.: The Nature of Statistical Learning Theory. Springer-Verlag, New York (1995)
15. Vapnik, V., Chervonenkis, A.: Theory of Pattern Recognition. Nauka, Moscow (1974) (in Russian); German translation: *Theorie der Zeichenerkennung*, Akademie Verlag, Berlin, 1979.
16. von Luxburg, U., Bousquet, O., Schölkopf, B.: A compression approach to support vector model selection. The Journal of Machine Learning Research 5 (2004) 293–323
17. McDiarmid, C.: On the method of bounded differences. In: Surveys in Combinatorics 1989, Cambridge University Press, Cambridge (1989) 148–188
18. Vapnik, V., Chervonenkis, A.: On the uniform convergence of relative frequencies of events to their probabilities. Theory of Probability and its Applications 16 (1971) 264–280

19. Hoeffding, W.: Probability inequalities for sums of bounded random variables. Journal of the American Statistical Association **58** (1963) 13–30
20. Ledoux, M., Talagrand, M.: Probability in Banach Space. Springer-Verlag, New York (1991)
21. Sauer, N.: On the density of families of sets. Journal of Combinatorial Theory Series A **13** (1972) 145–147
22. Shelah, S.: A combinatorial problem: Stability and order for models and theories in infinity languages. Pacific Journal of Mathematics **41** (1972) 247–261
23. Alesker, S.: A remark on the Szarek-Talagrand theorem. Combinatorics, Probability, and Computing **6** (1997) 139–144
24. Alon, N., Ben-David, S., Cesa-Bianchi, N., Haussler, D.: Scale-sensitive dimensions, uniform convergence, and learnability. Journal of the ACM **44** (1997) 615–631
25. Cesa-Bianchi, N., Haussler, D.: A graph-theoretic generalization of the Sauer-Shelah lemma. Discrete Applied Mathematics **86** (1998) 27–35
26. Frankl, P.: On the trace of finite sets. Journal of Combinatorial Theory, Series A **34** (1983) 41–45
27. Haussler, D.: Sphere packing numbers for subsets of the boolean n-cube with bounded Vapnik-Chervonenkis dimension. Journal of Combinatorial Theory, Series A **69** (1995) 217–232
28. Szarek, S., Talagrand, M.: On the convexified Sauer-Shelah theorem. Journal of Combinatorial Theory, Series B **69** (1997) 183–192
29. Dudley, R.: Uniform Central Limit Theorems. Cambridge University Press, Cambridge (1999)
30. Giné, E.: Empirical processes and applications: an overview. Bernoulli **2** (1996) 1–28
31. van der Waart, A., Wellner, J.: Weak convergence and empirical processes. Springer-Verlag, New York (1996)
32. Blumer, A., Ehrenfeucht, A., Haussler, D., Warmuth, M.: Learnability and the Vapnik-Chervonenkis dimension. Journal of the ACM **36** (1989) 929–965
33. Ehrenfeucht, A., Haussler, D., Kearns, M., Valiant, L.: A general lower bound on the number of examples needed for learning. Information and Computation **82** (1989) 247–261
34. Dudley, R.: Central limit theorems for empirical measures. Annals of Probability **6** (1978) 899–929
35. Dudley, R.: Empirical processes. In: Ecole de Probabilité de St. Flour 1982, Lecture Notes in Mathematics #1097, Springer-Verlag, New York (1984)
36. Dudley, R.: Universal Donsker classes and metric entropy. Annals of Probability **15** (1987) 1306–1326
37. Talagrand, M.: The Glivenko-Cantelli problem. Annals of Probability **15** (1987) 837–870
38. Talagrand, M.: Sharper bounds for Gaussian and empirical processes. Annals of Probability **22** (1994) 28–76
39. Vapnik, V., Chervonenkis, A.: Necessary and sufficient conditions for the uniform convergence of means to their expectations. Theory of Probability and its Applications **26** (1981) 821–832
40. Assouad, P.: Densité et dimension. Annales de l'Institut Fourier **33** (1983) 233–282
41. Cover, T.: Geometrical and statistical properties of systems of linear inequalities with applications in pattern recognition. IEEE Transactions on Electronic Computers **14** (1965) 326–334
42. Dudley, R.: Balls in R^k do not cut all subsets of $k + 2$ points. Advances in Mathematics **31** (**3**) (1979) 306–308

43. Goldberg, P., Jerrum, M.: Bounding the Vapnik-Chervonenkis dimension of concept classes parametrized by real numbers. Machine Learning 18 (1995) 131–148
44. Karpinski, M., Macintyre, A.: Polynomial bounds for VC dimension of sigmoidal and general Pfaffian neural networks. Journal of Computer and System Science 54 (1997)
45. Khovanskii, A.G.: Fewnomials. Translations of Mathematical Monographs, vol. 88, American Mathematical Society (1991)
46. Koiran, P., Sontag, E.: Neural networks with quadratic VC dimension. Journal of Computer and System Science 54 (1997)
47. Macintyre, A., Sontag, E.: Finiteness results for sigmoidal "neural" networks. In: Proceedings of the 25th Annual ACM Symposium on the Theory of Computing, Association of Computing Machinery, New York (1993) 325–334
48. Steele, J.: Existence of submatrices with all possible columns. Journal of Combinatorial Theory, Series A 28 (1978) 84–88
49. Wenocur, R., Dudley, R.: Some special Vapnik-Chervonenkis classes. Discrete Mathematics 33 (1981) 313–318
50. McDiarmid, C.: Concentration. In Habib, M., McDiarmid, C., Ramirez-Alfonsin, J., Reed, B., eds.: Probabilistic Methods for Algorithmic Discrete Mathematics, Springer, New York (1998) 195–248
51. Ahlswede, R., Gács, P., Körner, J.: Bounds on conditional probabilities with applications in multi-user communication. Zeitschrift für Wahrscheinlichkeitstheorie und verwandte Gebiete 34 (1976) 157–177 (correction in 39:353–354,1977).
52. Marton, K.: A simple proof of the blowing-up lemma. IEEE Transactions on Information Theory 32 (1986) 445–446
53. Marton, K.: Bounding $\bar{d}$-distance by informational divergence: a way to prove measure concentration. Annals of Probability 24 (1996) 857–866
54. Marton, K.: A measure concentration inequality for contracting Markov chains. Geometric and Functional Analysis 6 (1996) 556–571 Erratum: 7:609–613, 1997.
55. Dembo, A.: Information inequalities and concentration of measure. Annals of Probability 25 (1997) 927–939
56. Massart, P.: Optimal constants for Hoeffding type inequalities. Technical report, Mathematiques, Université de Paris-Sud, Report 98.86 (1998)
57. Rio, E.: Inégalités de concentration pour les processus empiriques de classes de parties. Probability Theory and Related Fields 119 (2001) 163–175
58. Talagrand, M.: A new look at independence. Annals of Probability 24 (1996) 1–34 (Special Invited Paper).
59. Talagrand, M.: Concentration of measure and isoperimetric inequalities in product spaces. Publications Mathématiques de l'I.H.E.S. 81 (1995) 73–205
60. Talagrand, M.: New concentration inequalities in product spaces. Inventiones Mathematicae 126 (1996) 505–563
61. Luczak, M.J., McDiarmid, C.: Concentration for locally acting permutations. Discrete Mathematics (2003) to appear
62. McDiarmid, C.: Concentration for independent permutations. Combinatorics, Probability, and Computing 2 (2002) 163–178
63. Panchenko, D.: A note on Talagrand's concentration inequality. Electronic Communications in Probability 6 (2001)
64. Panchenko, D.: Some extensions of an inequality of Vapnik and Chervonenkis. Electronic Communications in Probability 7 (2002)
65. Panchenko, D.: Symmetrization approach to concentration inequalities for empirical processes. Annals of Probability to appear (2003)

66. Ledoux, M.: On Talagrand's deviation inequalities for product measures. ESAIM: Probability and Statistics **1** (1997) 63–87 http://www.emath.fr/ps/.
67. Ledoux, M.: Isoperimetry and Gaussian analysis. In Bernard, P., ed.: Lectures on Probability Theory and Statistics, Ecole d'Eté de Probabilités de St-Flour XXIV-1994 (1996) 165–294
68. Bobkov, S., Ledoux, M.: Poincaré's inequalities and Talagrands's concentration phenomenon for the exponential distribution. Probability Theory and Related Fields **107** (1997) 383–400
69. Massart, P.: About the constants in Talagrand's concentration inequalities for empirical processes. Annals of Probability **28** (2000) 863–884
70. Boucheron, S., Lugosi, G., Massart, P.: A sharp concentration inequality with applications. Random Structures and Algorithms **16** (2000) 277–292
71. Boucheron, S., Lugosi, G., Massart, P.: Concentration inequalities using the entropy method. The Annals of Probability **31** (2003) 1583–1614
72. Boucheron, S., Bousquet, O., Lugosi, G., Massart, P.: Moment inequalities for functions of independent random variables. The Annals of Probability (2004) to appear.
73. Bousquet, O.: A Bennett concentration inequality and its application to suprema of empirical processes. C. R. Acad. Sci. Paris **334** (2002) 495–500
74. Giné, E., Zinn, J.: Some limit theorems for empirical processes. Annals of Probability **12** (1984) 929–989
75. Koltchinskii, V.: Rademacher penalties and structural risk minimization. IEEE Transactions on Information Theory **47** (2001) 1902–1914
76. Bartlett, P., Boucheron, S., Lugosi, G.: Model selection and error estimation. Machine Learning **48** (2001) 85–113
77. Koltchinskii, V., Panchenko, D.: Empirical margin distributions and bounding the generalization error of combined classifiers. Annals of Statistics **30** (2002)
78. Koltchinskii, V., Panchenko, D.: Rademacher processes and bounding the risk of function learning. In Giné, E., Mason, D., Wellner, J., eds.: High Dimensional Probability II. (2000) 443–459
79. Bartlett, P., Mendelson, S.: Rademacher and Gaussian complexities: risk bounds and structural results. Journal of Machine Learning Research **3** (2002) 463–482
80. Bartlett, P., Bousquet, O., Mendelson, S.: Localized Rademacher complexities. In: Proceedings of the 15th annual conference on Computational Learning Theory. (2002) 44–48
81. Bousquet, O., Koltchinskii, V., Panchenko, D.: Some local measures of complexity of convex hulls and generalization bounds. In: Proceedings of the 15th Annual Conference on Computational Learning Theory, Springer (2002) 59–73
82. Antos, A., Kégl, B., Linder, T., Lugosi, G.: Data-dependent margin-based generalization bounds for classification. Journal of Machine Learning Research **3** (2002) 73–98

Concentration Inequalities

Stéphane Boucheron[1], Gábor Lugosi[2], and Olivier Bousquet[3]

[1] Université de Paris-Sud, Laboratoire d'Informatique
Bâtiment 490, F-91405 Orsay Cedex, France
stephane.boucheron@lri.fr
http://www.lri.fr/~bouchero
[2] Department of Economics, Pompeu Fabra University
Ramon Trias Fargas 25-27, 08005 Barcelona, Spain
lugosi@upf.es
http://www.econ.upf.es/~lugosi
[3] Max-Planck Institute for Biological Cybernetics
Spemannstr. 38, D-72076 Tübingen, Germany
olivier.bousquet@m4x.org
http://www.kyb.mpg.de/~bousquet

Abstract. Concentration inequalities deal with deviations of functions of independent random variables from their expectation. In the last decade new tools have been introduced making it possible to establish simple and powerful inequalities. These inequalities are at the heart of the mathematical analysis of various problems in machine learning and made it possible to derive new efficient algorithms. This text attempts to summarize some of the basic tools.

1 Introduction

The laws of large numbers of classical probability theory state that sums of independent random variables are, under very mild conditions, close to their expectation with a large probability. Such sums are the most basic examples of random variables concentrated around their mean. More recent results reveal that such a behavior is shared by a large class of general functions of independent random variables. The purpose of these notes is to give an introduction to some of these general concentration inequalities.

The inequalities discussed in these notes bound tail probabilities of general functions of independent random variables. Several methods have been known to prove such inequalities, including martingale methods (see Milman and Schechtman [1] and the surveys of McDiarmid [2, 3]), information-theoretic methods (see Alhswede, Gács, and Körner [4], Marton [5, 6, 7], Dembo [8], Massart [9] and Rio [10]), Talagrand's induction method [11, 12, 13] (see also Luczak and McDiarmid [14], McDiarmid [15] and Panchenko [16, 17, 18]), the decoupling method surveyed by de la Peña and Giné [19], and the so-called "entropy method", based on logarithmic Sobolev inequalities, developed by Ledoux [20, 21], see also Bobkov

O. Bousquet et al. (Eds.): Machine Learning 2003, LNAI 3176, pp. 208–240, 2004.

and Ledoux [22], Massart [23], Rio [10], Klein [24], Boucheron, Lugosi, and Massart [25, 26], Bousquet [27, 28], and Boucheron, Bousquet, Lugosi, and Massart [29]. Also, various problem-specific methods have been worked out in random graph theory, see Janson, Luczak, and Ruciński [30] for a survey.

First of all we recall some of the essential basic tools needed in the rest of these notes. For any nonnegative random variable X,

$$\mathbb{E}X = \int_0^\infty \mathbb{P}\{X \geq t\}dt .$$

This implies *Markov's inequality*: for any nonnegative random variable X, and $t > 0$,

$$\mathbb{P}\{X \geq t\} \leq \frac{\mathbb{E}X}{t}.$$

If follows from Markov's inequality that if ϕ is a strictly monotonically increasing nonnegative-valued function then for any random variable X and real number t,

$$\mathbb{P}\{X \geq t\} = \mathbb{P}\{\phi(X) \geq \phi(t)\} \leq \frac{\mathbb{E}\phi(X)}{\phi(t)}.$$

An application of this with $\phi(x) = x^2$ is *Chebyshev's inequality*: if X is an arbitrary random variable and $t > 0$, then

$$\mathbb{P}\{|X - \mathbb{E}X| \geq t\} = \mathbb{P}\left\{|X - \mathbb{E}X|^2 \geq t^2\right\} \leq \frac{\mathbb{E}\left[|X - \mathbb{E}X|^2\right]}{t^2} = \frac{\mathsf{Var}\{X\}}{t^2}.$$

More generally taking $\phi(x) = x^q$ ($x \geq 0$), for any $q > 0$ we have

$$\mathbb{P}\{|X - \mathbb{E}X| \geq t\} \leq \frac{\mathbb{E}\left[|X - \mathbb{E}X|^q\right]}{t^q}.$$

In specific examples one may choose the value of q to optimize the obtained upper bound. Such moment bounds often provide with very sharp estimates of the tail probabilities. A related idea is at the basis of *Chernoff's bounding method*. Taking $\phi(x) = e^{sx}$ where s is an arbitrary positive number, for any random variable X, and any $t > 0$, we have

$$\mathbb{P}\{X \geq t\} = \mathbb{P}\{e^{sX} \geq e^{st}\} \leq \frac{\mathbb{E}e^{sX}}{e^{st}}.$$

In Chernoff's method, we find an $s > 0$ that minimizes the upper bound or makes the upper bound small.

Next we recall some simple inequalities for sums of independent random variables. Here we are primarily concerned with upper bounds for the probabilities of deviations from the mean, that is, to obtain inequalities for $\mathbb{P}\{S_n - \mathbb{E}S_n \geq t\}$, with $S_n = \sum_{i=1}^n X_i$, where $X_1, \ldots, X_n$ are independent real-valued random variables.

Chebyshev's inequality and independence immediately imply

$$\mathbb{P}\{|S_n - \mathbb{E}S_n| \geq t\} \leq \frac{\mathsf{Var}\{S_n\}}{t^2} = \frac{\sum_{i=1}^n \mathsf{Var}\{X_i\}}{t^2}.$$

In other words, writing $\sigma^2 = \frac{1}{n}\sum_{i=1}^{n} \mathsf{Var}\{X_i\}$,

$$\mathbb{P}\left\{\left|\frac{1}{n}\sum_{i=1}^{n}X_i - \mathbb{E}X_i\right| \geq \epsilon\right\} \leq \frac{\sigma^2}{n\epsilon^2}.$$

Chernoff's bounding method is especially convenient for bounding tail probabilities of sums of independent random variables. The reason is that since the expected value of a product of independent random variables equals the product of the expected values, Chernoff's bound becomes

$$\mathbb{P}\{S_n - \mathbb{E}S_n \geq t\} \leq e^{-st}\mathbb{E}\left[\exp\left(s\sum_{i=1}^{n}(X_i - \mathbb{E}X_i)\right)\right]$$

$$= e^{-st}\prod_{i=1}^{n}\mathbb{E}\left[e^{s(X_i - \mathbb{E}X_i)}\right] \quad \text{(by independence).} \tag{1}$$

Now the problem of finding tight bounds comes down to finding a good upper bound for the moment generating function of the random variables $X_i - \mathbb{E}X_i$. There are many ways of doing this. For bounded random variables perhaps the most elegant version is due to Hoeffding [31] which we state without proof.

Lemma 1. HOEFFDING'S INEQUALITY. *Let X be a random variable with $\mathbb{E}X = 0$, $a \leq X \leq b$. Then for $s > 0$,*

$$\mathbb{E}\left[e^{sX}\right] \leq e^{s^2(b-a)^2/8}.$$

This lemma, combined with (1) immediately implies Hoeffding's tail inequality [31]:

Theorem 1. *Let $X_1, \ldots, X_n$ be independent bounded random variables such that X_i falls in the interval $[a_i, b_i]$ with probability one. Then for any $t > 0$ we have*

$$\mathbb{P}\{S_n - \mathbb{E}S_n \geq t\} \leq e^{-2t^2/\sum_{i=1}^{n}(b_i-a_i)^2}$$

and

$$\mathbb{P}\{S_n - \mathbb{E}S_n \leq -t\} \leq e^{-2t^2/\sum_{i=1}^{n}(b_i-a_i)^2}.$$

The theorem above is generally known as *Hoeffding's inequality*. For binomial random variables it was proved by Chernoff [32] and Okamoto [33].

A disadvantage of Hoeffding's inequality is that it ignores information about the variance of the X_i's. The inequalities discussed next provide an improvement in this respect.

Assume now without loss of generality that $\mathbb{E}X_i = 0$ for all $i = 1, \ldots, n$. Our starting point is again (1), that is, we need bounds for $\mathbb{E}\left[e^{sX_i}\right]$. Introduce the notation $\sigma_i^2 = \mathbb{E}[X_i^2]$, and

$$F_i = \mathbb{E}[\psi(sX_i)] = \sum_{r=2}^{\infty}\frac{s^{r-2}\mathbb{E}[X_i^r]}{r!\sigma_i^2}.$$

Also, let $\psi(x) = \exp(x) - x - 1$, and observe that $\psi(x) \leq x^2/2$ for $x \leq 0$ and $\psi(sx) \leq x^2\psi(s)$ for $s \geq 0$ and $x \in [0,1]$. Since $e^{sx} = 1 + sx + \psi(sx)$, we may write

$$
\begin{aligned}
\mathbb{E}\left[e^{sX_i}\right] &= 1 + s\mathbb{E}[X_i] + \mathbb{E}[\psi(sX_i)] \\
&= 1 + \mathbb{E}[\psi(sX_i)] \quad (\text{since } \mathbb{E}[X_i] = 0.) \\
&\leq 1 + \mathbb{E}[\psi(s(X_i)_+) + \psi(-s(X_i)_-)] \\
&\quad (\text{where } x_+ = \max(0, x) \text{ and } x_- = \max(0, -x)) \\
&\leq 1 + \mathbb{E}[\psi(s(X_i)_+) + \frac{s^2}{2}(X_i)^2_-] \quad (\text{using } \psi(x) \leq x^2/2 \text{ for } x \leq 0.) \ .
\end{aligned}
$$

Now assume that the X_i's are bounded such that $X_i \leq 1$. Thus, we have obtained

$$
\mathbb{E}\left[e^{sX_i}\right] \leq 1 + \mathbb{E}[\psi(s)(X_i)^2_+ + \frac{s^2}{2}(X_i)^2_-] \leq 1 + \psi(s)\mathbb{E}[X_i^2] \leq \exp\left(\psi(s)\mathbb{E}[X_i^2]\right)
$$

Returning to (1) and using the notation $\sigma^2 = (1/n)\sum \sigma_i^2$, we get

$$
\mathbb{P}\left\{\sum_{i=1}^n X_i > t\right\} \leq e^{n\sigma^2\psi(s) - st}.
$$

Now we are free to choose s. The upper bound is minimized for

$$
s = \log\left(1 + \frac{t}{n\sigma^2}\right).
$$

Resubstituting this value, we obtain *Bennett's inequality* [34]:

Theorem 2. BENNETT'S INEQUALITY. *Let $X_1, \ldots, X_n$ be independent real-valued random variables with zero mean, and assume that $X_i \leq 1$ with probability one. Let*

$$
\sigma^2 = \frac{1}{n}\sum_{i=1}^n \mathsf{Var}\{X_i\}.
$$

Then for any $t > 0$,

$$
\mathbb{P}\left\{\sum_{i=1}^n X_i > t\right\} \leq \exp\left(-n\sigma^2 h\left(\frac{t}{n\sigma^2}\right)\right).
$$

where $h(u) = (1 + u)\log(1 + u) - u$ for $u \geq 0$.

The message of this inequality is perhaps best seen if we do some further bounding. Applying the elementary inequality $h(u) \geq u^2/(2 + 2u/3)$, $u \geq 0$ (which may be seen by comparing the derivatives of both sides) we obtain a classical inequality of Bernstein [35]:

Theorem 3. BERNSTEIN'S INEQUALITY. *Under the conditions of the previous theorem, for any $\epsilon > 0$,*

$$\mathbb{P}\left\{\frac{1}{n}\sum_{i=1}^{n}X_i > \epsilon\right\} \leq \exp\left(-\frac{n\epsilon^2}{2(\sigma^2 + \epsilon/3)}\right).$$

Bernstein's inequality points out an interesting phenomenon: if $\sigma^2 < \epsilon$, then the upper bound behaves like $e^{-n\epsilon}$ instead of the $e^{-n\epsilon^2}$ guaranteed by Hoeffding's inequality. This might be intuitively explained by recalling that a Binomial$(n, \lambda/n)$ distribution can be approximated, for large n, by a Poisson(λ) distribution, whose tail decreases as $e^{-\lambda}$.

2   The Efron-Stein Inequality

The main purpose of these notes is to show how many of the tail inequalities for sums of independent random variables can be extended to general functions of independent random variables. The simplest, yet surprisingly powerful inequality of this kind is known as the *Efron-Stein inequality*. It bounds the variance of a general function. To obtain tail inequalities, one may simply use Chebyshev's inequality.

Let $\mathcal{X}$ be some set, and let $g : \mathcal{X}^n \to \mathbb{R}$ be a measurable function of n variables. We derive inequalities for the difference between the random variable $Z = g(X_1, \ldots, X_n)$ and its expected value $\mathbb{E}Z$ when $X_1, \ldots, X_n$ are arbitrary independent (not necessarily identically distributed!) random variables taking values in $\mathcal{X}$.

The main inequalities of this section follow from the next simple result. To simplify notation, we write $\mathbb{E}_i$ for the expected value with respect to the variable X_i, that is, $\mathbb{E}_i Z = \mathbb{E}[Z|X_1, \ldots, X_{i-1}, X_{i+1}, \ldots, X_n]$.

Theorem 4.

$$\mathsf{Var}(Z) \leq \sum_{i=1}^{n} \mathbb{E}\left[(Z - \mathbb{E}_i Z)^2\right].$$

Proof. The proof is based on elementary properties of conditional expectation. Recall that if X and Y are arbitrary bounded random variables, then $\mathbb{E}[XY] = \mathbb{E}[\mathbb{E}[XY|Y]] = \mathbb{E}[Y\mathbb{E}[X|Y]]$.

Introduce the notation $V = Z - \mathbb{E}Z$, and define

$$V_i = \mathbb{E}[Z|X_1, \ldots, X_i] - \mathbb{E}[Z|X_1, \ldots, X_{i-1}], \qquad i = 1, \ldots, n.$$

Clearly, $V = \sum_{i=1}^{n} V_i$. (Thus, V is written as a sum of martingale differences.) Then

$$\mathsf{Var}(Z) = \mathbb{E}\left[\left(\sum_{i=1}^{n} V_i\right)^2\right]$$

$$= \mathbb{E}\sum_{i=1}^{n} V_i^2 + 2\mathbb{E}\sum_{i>j} V_i V_j$$

$$= \mathbb{E}\sum_{i=1}^{n} V_i^2 \ ,$$

since, for any $i > j$,

$$\mathbb{E}V_i V_j = \mathbb{E}\mathbb{E}\left[V_i V_j | X_1, \ldots, X_j\right] = \mathbb{E}\left[V_j \mathbb{E}\left[V_i | X_1, \ldots, X_j\right]\right] = 0 \ .$$

To bound $\mathbb{E}V_i^2$, note that, by Jensen's inequality,

$$V_i^2 = \left(\mathbb{E}[Z|X_1, \ldots, X_i] - \mathbb{E}[Z|X_1, \ldots, X_{i-1}]\right)^2$$

$$= \left(\mathbb{E}\left[\mathbb{E}[Z|X_1, \ldots, X_n] - \mathbb{E}[Z|X_1, \ldots, X_{i-1}, X_{i+1}, \ldots, X_n]\Big| X_1, \ldots, X_i\right]\right)^2$$

$$\leq \mathbb{E}\left[\left(\mathbb{E}[Z|X_1, \ldots, X_n] - \mathbb{E}[Z|X_1, \ldots, X_{i-1}, X_{i+1}, \ldots, X_n]\right)^2 \Big| X_1, \ldots, X_i\right]$$

$$= \mathbb{E}\left[\left(Z - \mathbb{E}_i Z\right)^2 \Big| X_1, \ldots, X_i\right] \ .$$

Taking expected values on both sides, we obtain the statement.   □

Now the Efron-Stein inequality follows easily. To state the theorem, let X_1', $\ldots, X_n'$ form an independent copy of $X_1, \ldots, X_n$ and write

$$Z_i' = g(X_1, \ldots, X_i', \ldots, X_n) \ .$$

Theorem 5. EFRON-STEIN INEQUALITY (EFRON AND STEIN [36], STEELE [37]).

$$\mathsf{Var}(Z) \leq \frac{1}{2}\sum_{i=1}^{n} \mathbb{E}\left[(Z - Z_i')^2\right]$$

Proof. The statement follows by Theorem 4 simply by using (conditionally) the elementary fact that if X and Y are independent and identically distributed random variables, then $\mathsf{Var}(X) = (1/2)\mathbb{E}[(X - Y)^2]$, and therefore

$$\mathbb{E}_i\left[\left(Z - \mathbb{E}_i Z\right)^2\right] = \frac{1}{2}\mathbb{E}_i\left[(Z - Z_i')^2\right] \ .$$ □

Remark. Observe that in the case when $Z = \sum_{i=1}^{n} X_i$ is a sum of independent random variables (of finite variance) then the inequality in Theorem 5 becomes an equality. Thus, the bound in the Efron-Stein inequality is, in a sense, not improvable. This example also shows that, among all functions of independent random variables, sums, in some sense, are the least concentrated. Below we will see other evidences for this extremal property of sums.

Another useful corollary of Theorem 4 is obtained by recalling that, for any random variable X, $\mathsf{Var}(X) \leq \mathbb{E}[(X - a)^2]$ for any constant $a \in \mathbb{R}$. Using this fact conditionally, we have, for every $i = 1, \ldots, n$,

$$\mathbb{E}_i\left[(Z - \mathbb{E}_i Z)^2\right] \leq \mathbb{E}_i\left[(Z - Z_i)^2\right]$$

where $Z_i = g_i(X_1, \ldots, X_{i-1}, X_{i+1}, \ldots, X_n)$ for arbitrary measurable functions $g_i : \mathcal{X}^{n-1} \to \mathbb{R}$ of $n - 1$ variables. Taking expected values and using Theorem 4 we have the following.

Theorem 6.

$$\mathsf{Var}(Z) \leq \sum_{i=1}^n \mathbb{E}\left[(Z - Z_i)^2\right] .$$

In the next two sections we specialize the Efron-Stein inequality and its variant Theorem 6 to functions which satisfy some simple easy-to-verify properties.

2.1   Functions with Bounded Differences

We say that a function $g : \mathcal{X}^n \to \mathbb{R}$ has the *bounded differences property* if for some nonnegative constants $c_1, \ldots, c_n$,

$$\sup_{\substack{x_1, \ldots, x_n, \\ x_i' \in \mathcal{X}}} |g(x_1, \ldots, x_n) - g(x_1, \ldots, x_{i-1}, x_i', x_{i+1}, \ldots, x_n)| \leq c_i , \quad 1 \leq i \leq n .$$

In other words, if we change the i-th variable of g while keeping all the others fixed, the value of the function cannot change by more than c_i. Then the Efron-Stein inequality implies the following:

Corollary 1. *If g has the bounded differences property with constants $c_1, \ldots, c_n$, then*

$$\mathsf{Var}(Z) \leq \frac{1}{2} \sum_{i=1}^n c_i^2 .$$

Next we list some interesting applications of this corollary. In all cases the bound for the variance is obtained effortlessly, while a direct estimation of the variance may be quite involved.

Example. UNIFORM DEVIATIONS. One of the central quantities of statistical learning theory and empirical process theory is the following: let $X_1, \ldots, X_n$ be i.i.d. random variables taking their values in some set $\mathcal{X}$, and let $\mathcal{A}$ be a collection of subsets of $\mathcal{X}$. Let μ denote the distribution of X_1, that is, $\mu(A) = \mathbb{P}\{X_1 \in A\}$, and let μ_n denote the empirical distribution:

$$\mu_n(A) = \frac{1}{n} \sum_{i=1}^n \mathbb{1}_{\{X_n \in A\}} .$$

The quantity of interest is

$$Z = \sup_{A \in \mathcal{A}} |\mu_n(A) - \mu(A)|.$$

If $\lim_{n \to \infty} \mathbb{E}Z = 0$ for every distribution of the X_i's, then $\mathcal{A}$ is called a *uniform Glivenko-Cantelli class*, and Vapnik and Chervonenkis [38] gave a beautiful combinatorial characterization of such classes. But regardless of what $\mathcal{A}$ is, by changing one X_i, Z can change by at most $1/n$, so regardless of the behavior of $\mathbb{E}Z$, we always have

$$\mathsf{Var}(Z) \leq \frac{1}{2n} .$$

For more information on the behavior of Z and its role in learning theory see, for example, Devroye, Györfi, and Lugosi [39], Vapnik [40], van der Vaart and Wellner [41], Dudley [42].

Next we show how a closer look at the the Efron-Stein inequality implies a significantly better bound for the variance of Z. We do this in a slightly more general framework of empirical processes. Let $\mathcal{F}$ be a class of real-valued functions and define $Z = g(X_1, \ldots, X_n) = \sup_{f \in \mathcal{F}} \sum_{j=1}^{n} f(X_j)$. Assume that the functions $f \in \mathcal{F}$ are such that $\mathbb{E}[f(X_i)] = 0$ and take values in $[-1, 1]$. Let Z_i be defined as

$$Z_i = \sup_{f \in \mathcal{F}} \sum_{j \neq i} f(X_j) .$$

Let $\hat{f}$ be the function achieving the supremum[1] in the definition of Z, that is $Z = \sum_{i=1}^{n} \hat{f}(X_i)$ and similarly $\hat{f}_i$ be such that $Z_i = \sum_{j \neq i} \hat{f}_i(X_j)$. We have

$$\hat{f}_i(X_i) \leq Z - Z_i \leq \hat{f}(X_i),$$

and thus $\sum_{i=1}^{n} Z - Z_i \leq Z$. As $\hat{f}_i$ and X_i are independent, $\mathbb{E}_i[\hat{f}_i(X_i)] = 0$. On the other hand,

$$(Z - Z_i)^2 - \hat{f}_i^2(X_i) = (Z - Z_i + \hat{f}_i(X_i))(Z - Z_i - \hat{f}_i(X_i))$$
$$\leq 2(Z - Z_i + \hat{f}_i(X_i)) .$$

Summing over all i and taking expectations,

$$\mathbb{E}\left[\sum_{i=1}^{n}(Z - Z_i)^2\right] \leq \mathbb{E}\left[\sum_{i=1}^{n} \hat{f}_i^2(X_i) + 2(Z - Z_i) + 2\hat{f}_i(X_i)\right]$$
$$\leq n \sup_{f \in \mathcal{F}} \mathbb{E}[f^2(X_1)] + 2\mathbb{E}[Z]$$

where at the last step we used the facts that $\mathbb{E}[\hat{f}_i(X_i)^2] \leq \sup_{f \in \mathcal{F}} \mathbb{E}[f^2(X_1)]$, $\sum_{i=1}^{n}(Z - Z_i) \leq Z$, and $\mathbb{E}\hat{f}_i(X_i) = 0$. Thus, by the Efron-Stein inequality

$$\mathsf{Var}(Z) \leq n \sup_{f \in \mathcal{F}} \mathbb{E}[f^2(X_1)] + 2\mathbb{E}[Z]$$

---

[1] If the supremum is not attained the proof can be modified to yield the same result. We omit the details here.

From just the bounded differences property we derived $\mathsf{Var}(Z) \leq 2n$. The new bound may be a significant improvement whenever the maximum of $\mathbb{E}f(X_i)^2$ over $f \in \mathcal{F}$ is small. (Note that if the class $\mathcal{F}$ is not too large, $\mathbb{E}Z$ is typically of the order of $\sqrt{n}$.) The exponential tail inequality due to Talagrand [12] extends this variance inequality, and is one of the most important recent results of the theory of empirical processes, see also Ledoux [20], Massart [23], Rio [10], Klein [24], and Bousquet [27, 28].

Example. MINIMUM OF THE EMPIRICAL LOSS. Concentration inequalities have been used as a key tool in recent developments of model selection methods in statistical learning theory. For the background we refer to the the recent work of Koltchinskii and Panchenko [43], Massart [44], Bartlett, Boucheron, and Lugosi [45], Lugosi and Wegkamp [46], Bousquet [47].

Let $\mathcal{F}$ denote a class of $\{0, 1\}$-valued functions on some space $\mathcal{X}$. For simplicity of the exposition we assume that $\mathcal{F}$ is finite. The results remain true for general classes as long as the measurability issues are taken care of. Given an i.i.d. sample $D_n = (\langle X_i, Y_i \rangle)_{i \leq n}$ of n pairs of random variables $\langle X_i, Y_i \rangle$ taking values in $\mathcal{X} \times \{0, 1\}$, for each $f \in \mathcal{F}$ we define the empirical loss

$$L_n(f) = \frac{1}{n} \sum_{i=1}^{n} \ell(f(X_i), Y_i)$$

where the loss function ℓ is defined on $\{0, 1\}^2$ by

$$\ell(y, y') = \mathbb{1}_{y \neq y'} \ .$$

In nonparametric classification and learning theory it is common to select an element of $\mathcal{F}$ by minimizing the empirical loss. The quantity of interest in this section is the minimal empirical loss

$$\widehat{L} = \inf_{f \in \mathcal{F}} L_n(f).$$

Corollary 1 immediately implies that $\mathsf{Var}(\widehat{L}) \leq 1/(2n)$. However, a more careful application of the Efron-Stein inequality reveals that $\widehat{L}$ may be much more concentrated than predicted by this simple inequality. Getting tight results for the fluctuations of $\widehat{L}$ provides better insight into the calibration of penalties in certain model selection methods.

Let $Z = n\widehat{L}$ and let Z_i' be defined as in Theorem 5, that is,

$$Z_i' = \min_{f \in \mathcal{F}} \left[\sum_{j \neq i} \ell(f(X_j), Y_j) + \ell(f(X_i'), Y_i') \right]$$

where $\langle X_i', Y_i' \rangle$ is independent of D_n and has the same distribution as $\langle X_i, Y_i \rangle$. Now the convenient form of the Efron-Stein inequality is the following:

$$\mathsf{Var}(Z) \leq \frac{1}{2} \sum_{i=1}^{n} \mathbb{E}\left[(Z - Z_i')^2 \right] = \sum_{i=1}^{n} \mathbb{E}\left[(Z - Z_i')^2 \mathbb{1}_{Z_i' > Z} \right]$$

Let f^* denote a (possibly non-unique) minimizer of the empirical risk so that $Z = \sum_{j=1}^{n} \ell(f^*(X_j), Y_j)$. The key observation is that

$$(Z - Z_i')^2 \mathbb{1}_{Z_i' > Z} \leq (\ell(f^*(X_i'), Y_i') - \ell(f^*(X_i), Y_i))^2 \mathbb{1}_{Z_i' > Z}$$
$$= \ell(f^*(X_i'), Y_i') \mathbb{1}_{\ell(f^*(X_i), Y_i) = 0} .$$

Thus,

$$\sum_{i=1}^{n} \mathbb{E}\left[(Z - Z_i')^2 \mathbb{1}_{Z_i' > Z}\right] \leq \mathbb{E} \sum_{i: \ell(f^*(X_i), Y_i) = 0} \mathbb{E}_{X_i', Y_i'}[\ell(f^*(X_i'), Y_i')] \leq n \mathbb{E} L(f^*)$$

where $\mathbb{E}_{X_i', Y_i'}$ denotes expectation with respect to the variables X_i', Y_i' and for each $f \in \mathcal{F}$, $L(f) = \mathbb{E}\ell(f(X), Y)$ is the true (expected) loss of f. Therefore, the Efron-Stein inequality implies that

$$\mathsf{Var}(\widehat{L}) \leq \frac{\mathbb{E} L(f^*)}{n} .$$

This is a significant improvement over the bound $1/(2n)$ whenever $\mathbb{E} L(f^*)$ is much smaller than $1/2$. This is very often the case. For example, we have

$$L(f^*) = \widehat{L} - (L_n(f^*) - L(f^*)) \leq \frac{Z}{n} + \sup_{f \in \mathcal{F}}(L(f) - L_n(f))$$

so that we obtain

$$\mathsf{Var}(\widehat{L}) \leq \frac{\mathbb{E}\widehat{L}}{n} + \frac{\mathbb{E} \sup_{f \in \mathcal{F}}(L(f) - L_n(f))}{n} .$$

In most cases of interest, $\mathbb{E} \sup_{f \in \mathcal{F}}(L(f) - L_n(f))$ may be bounded by a constant (depending on $\mathcal{F}$) times $n^{-1/2}$ (see, e.g., Lugosi [48]) and then the second term on the right-hand side is of the order of $n^{-3/2}$. For exponential concentration inequalities for $\widehat{L}$ we refer to Boucheron, Lugosi, and Massart [26].

Example. KERNEL DENSITY ESTIMATION. Let $X_1, \ldots, X_n$ be i.i.d. samples drawn according to some (unknown) density f on the real line. The density is estimated by the kernel estimate

$$f_n(x) = \frac{1}{nh} \sum_{i=1}^{n} K\left(\frac{x - X_i}{h}\right),$$

where $h > 0$ is a smoothing parameter, and K is a nonnegative function with $\int K = 1$. The performance of the estimate is measured by the L_1 error

$$Z = g(X_1, \ldots, X_n) = \int |f(x) - f_n(x)| dx.$$

It is easy to see that

$$|g(x_1, \ldots, x_n) - g(x_1, \ldots, x_i', \ldots, x_n)| \leq \frac{1}{nh} \int \left| K\left(\frac{x - x_i}{h}\right) - K\left(\frac{x - x_i'}{h}\right) \right| dx$$
$$\leq \frac{2}{n},$$

so without further work we get

$$\mathrm{Var}(Z) \leq \frac{2}{n} .$$

It is known that for every f, $\sqrt{n}\mathbb{E}g \to \infty$ (see Devroye and Györfi [49]) which implies, by Chebyshev's inequality, that for every $\epsilon > 0$

$$\mathbb{P}\left\{\left|\frac{Z}{\mathbb{E}Z} - 1\right| \geq \epsilon\right\} = \mathbb{P}\{|Z - \mathbb{E}Z| \geq \epsilon\mathbb{E}Z\} \leq \frac{\mathrm{Var}(Z)}{\epsilon^2(\mathbb{E}Z)^2} \to 0$$

as $n \to \infty$. That is, $Z/\mathbb{E}Z \to 0$ in probability, or in other words, Z is *relatively stable*. This means that the random L_1-error behaves like its expected value. This result is due to Devroye [50], [51]. For more on the behavior of the L_1 error of the kernel density estimate we refer to Devroye and Györfi [49], Devroye and Lugosi [52].

2.2   Self-Bounding Functions

Another simple property which is satisfied for many important examples is the so-called *self-bounding* property. We say that a nonnegative function $g : \mathcal{X}^n \to \mathbb{R}$ has the self-bounding property if there exist functions $g_i : \mathcal{X}^{n-1} \to \mathbb{R}$ such that for all $x_1, \ldots, x_n \in \mathcal{X}$ and all $i = 1, \ldots, n$,

$$0 \leq g(x_1, \ldots, x_n) - g_i(x_1, \ldots, x_{i-1}, x_{i+1}, \ldots, x_n) \leq 1$$

and also

$$\sum_{i=1}^{n} \left(g(x_1, \ldots, x_n) - g_i(x_1, \ldots, x_{i-1}, x_{i+1}, \ldots, x_n)\right) \leq g(x_1, \ldots, x_n) .$$

Concentration properties for such functions have been studied by Boucheron, Lugosi, and Massart [25], Rio [10], and Bousquet [27, 28]. For self-bounding functions we clearly have

$$\sum_{i=1}^{n} \left(g(x_1, \ldots, x_n) - g_i(x_1, \ldots, x_{i-1}, x_{i+1}, \ldots, x_n)\right)^2 \leq g(x_1, \ldots, x_n) .$$

and therefore Theorem 6 implies

Corollary 2. *If g has the self-bounding property, then*

$$\mathrm{Var}(Z) \leq \mathbb{E}Z .$$

Next we mention some applications of this simple corollary. It turns out that in many cases the obtained bound is a significant improvement over what we would obtain by using simply Corollary 1.

Remark. RELATIVE STABILITY. Bounding the variance of Z by its expected value implies, in many cases, the relative stability of Z. A sequence of non-negative random variables (Z_n) is said to be relatively stable if $Z_n/\mathbb{E}Z_n \to 1$ in probability. This property guarantees that the random fluctuations of Z_n around its expectation are of negligible size when compared to the expectation, and therefore most information about the size of Z_n is given by $\mathbb{E}Z_n$. If Z_n has the self-bounding property, then, by Chebyshev's inequality, for all $\epsilon > 0$,

$$\mathbb{P}\left\{\left|\frac{Z_n}{\mathbb{E}Z_n} - 1\right| > \epsilon\right\} \le \frac{\mathsf{Var}(Z_n)}{\epsilon^2(\mathbb{E}Z_n)^2} \le \frac{1}{\epsilon^2 \mathbb{E}Z_n} .$$

Thus, for relative stability, it suffices to have $\mathbb{E}Z_n \to \infty$.

Example. RADEMACHER AVERAGES. A less trivial example for self-bounding functions is the one of Rademacher averages. Let $\mathcal{F}$ be a class of functions with values in $[-1, 1]$. If $\sigma_1, \ldots, \sigma_n$ denote independent symmetric $\{-1, 1\}$-valued random variables, independent of the X_i's (the so-called Rademacher random variables), then we define the *conditional Rademacher average* as

$$Z = \mathbb{E}\left[\sup_{f \in \mathcal{F}} \sum_{j=1}^{n} \sigma_j f(X_j) | X_1^n \right] ,$$

where the notation X_1^n is a shorthand for $X_1, \ldots, X_n$. Thus, the expected value is taken with respect to the Rademacher variables and Z is a function of the X_i's. Quantities like Z have been known to measure effectively the complexity of model classes in statistical learning theory, see, for example, Koltchinskii [53], Bartlett, Boucheron, and Lugosi [45], Bartlett and Mendelson [54], Bartlett, Bousquet, and Mendelson [55]. It is immediate that Z has the bounded differences property and Corollary 1 implies $\mathsf{Var}(Z) \le n/2$. However, this bound may be improved by observing that Z also has the self-bounding property, and therefore $\mathsf{Var}(Z) \le \mathbb{E}Z$. Indeed, defining

$$Z_i = \mathbb{E}\left[\sup_{f \in \mathcal{F}} \sum_{\substack{j=1 \\ j \neq i}}^{n} \sigma_j f(X_j) | X_1^n \right]$$

it is easy to see that $0 \le Z - Z_i \le 1$ and $\sum_{i=1}^{n}(Z - Z_i) \le Z$ (the details are left as an exercise). The improvement provided by Lemma 2 is essential since it is well-known in empirical process theory and statistical learning theory that in many cases when $\mathcal{F}$ is a relatively small class of functions, $\mathbb{E}Z$ may be bounded by something like $Cn^{1/2}$ where the constant C depends on the class $\mathcal{F}$, see, e.g., Vapnik [40], van der Vaart and Wellner [41], Dudley [42].

Configuration Functions. An important class of functions satisfying the self-bounding property consists of the so-called *configuration functions* defined by Talagrand [11, section 7]. Our definition, taken from [25] is a slight modification of Talagrand's.

Assume that we have a property P defined over the union of finite products of a set $\mathcal{X}$, that is, a sequence of sets $P_1 \in \mathcal{X}, P_2 \in \mathcal{X} \times \mathcal{X}, \ldots, P_n \in \mathcal{X}^n$. We say that $(x_1, \ldots x_m) \in \mathcal{X}^m$ satisfies the property P if $(x_1, \ldots x_m) \in P_m$. We assume that P is *hereditary* in the sense that if $(x_1, \ldots x_m)$ satisfies P then so does any subsequence $(x_{i_1}, \ldots x_{i_k})$ of $(x_1, \ldots x_m)$. The function g_n that maps any tuple $(x_1, \ldots x_n)$ to the size of the largest subsequence satisfying P is the *configuration function* associated with property P.

Corollary 2 implies the following result:

Corollary 3. *Let g_n be a configuration function, and let $Z = g_n(X_1, \ldots, X_n)$, where $X_1, \ldots, X_n$ are independent random variables. Then for any $t \geq 0$,*

$$\mathsf{Var}(Z) \leq \mathbb{E}Z .$$

Proof. By Corollary 2 it suffices to show that any configuration function is self bounding. Let $Z_i = g_{n-1}(X_1, \ldots, X_{i-1}, X_{i+1}, \ldots, X_n)$. The condition $0 \leq Z - Z_i \leq 1$ is trivially satisfied. On the other hand, assume that $Z = k$ and let $\{X_{i_1}, \ldots, X_{i_k}\} \subset \{X_1, \ldots, X_n\}$ be a subsequence of cardinality k such that $f_k(X_{i_1}, \ldots, X_{i_k}) = k$. (Note that by the definition of a configuration function such a subsequence exists.) Clearly, if the index i is such that $i \notin \{i_1, \ldots, i_k\}$ then $Z = Z_i$, and therefore

$$\sum_{i=1}^{n}(Z - Z_i) \leq Z$$

is also satisfied, which concludes the proof. $\square$

To illustrate the fact that configuration functions appear rather naturally in various applications, we describe a prototypical example:

Example. VC DIMENSION. One of the central quantities in statistical learning theory is the *Vapnik-Chervonenkis dimension*, see Vapnik and Chervonenkis [38, 56], Blumer, Ehrenfeucht, Haussler, and Warmuth [57], Devroye, Györfi, and Lugosi [39], Anthony and Bartlett [58], Vapnik [40], etc.

Let $\mathcal{A}$ be an arbitrary collection of subsets of $\mathcal{X}$, and let $x_1^n = (x_1, \ldots, x_n)$ be a vector of n points of $\mathcal{X}$. Define the *trace* of $\mathcal{A}$ on x_1^n by

$$\mathrm{tr}(x_1^n) = \{A \cap \{x_1, \ldots, x_n\} : A \in \mathcal{A}\} .$$

The *shatter coefficient*, (or *Vapnik-Chervonenkis growth function*) of $\mathcal{A}$ in x_1^n is $T(x_1^n) = |\mathrm{tr}(x_1^n)|$, the size of the trace. $T(x_1^n)$ is the number of different subsets of the n-point set $\{x_1, \ldots, x_n\}$ generated by intersecting it with elements of $\mathcal{A}$. A subset $\{x_{i_1}, \ldots, x_{i_k}\}$ of $\{x_1, \ldots, x_n\}$ is said to be *shattered* if

$2^k = T(x_{i_1}, \ldots, x_{i_k})$. The VC *dimension* $D(x_1^n)$ of $\mathcal{A}$ (with respect to x_1^n) is the cardinality k of the largest shattered subset of x_1^n. From the definition it is obvious that $g_n(x_1^n) = D(x_1^n)$ is a configuration function (associated to the property of "shatteredness", and therefore if $X_1, \ldots, X_n$ are independent random variables, then

$$\mathsf{Var}(D(X_1^n)) \leq \mathbb{E}D(X_1^n) .$$

3   The Entropy Method

In the previous section we saw that the Efron-Stein inequality serves as a powerful tool for bounding the variance of general functions of independent random variables. Then, via Chebyshev's inequality, one may easily bound the tail probabilities of such functions. However, just as in the case of sums of independent random variables, tail bounds based on inequalities for the variance are often not satisfactory, and essential improvements are possible. The purpose of this section is to present a methodology which allows one to obtain exponential tail inequalities in many cases. The pursuit of such inequalities has been an important topics in probability theory in the last few decades. Originally, martingale methods dominated the research (see, e.g., McDiarmid [2, 3], Rhee and Talagrand [59], Shamir and Spencer [60]) but independently information-theoretic methods were also used with success (see Alhswede, Gács, and Körner [4], Marton [5, 6, 7], Dembo [8], Massart [9], Rio [10], and Samson [61]). Talagrand's induction method [11, 12, 13] caused an important breakthrough both in the theory and applications of exponential concentration inequalities. In this section we focus on so-called "entropy method", based on logarithmic Sobolev inequalities developed by Ledoux [20, 21], see also Bobkov and Ledoux [22], Massart [23], Rio [10], Boucheron, Lugosi, and Massart [25], [26], and Bousquet [27, 28]. This method makes it possible to derive exponential analogues of the Efron-Stein inequality perhaps the simplest way.

The method is based on an appropriate modification of the "tensorization" inequality Theorem 4. In order to prove this modification, we need to recall some of the basic notions of information theory. To keep the material at an elementary level, we prove the modified tensorization inequality for discrete random variables only. The extension to arbitrary distributions is straightforward.

3.1   Basic Information Theory

In this section we summarize some basic properties of the entropy of a discrete-valued random variable. For a good introductory book on information theory we refer to Cover and Thomas [62].

Let X be a random variable taking values in the countable set $\mathcal{X}$ with distribution $\mathbb{P}\{X = x\} = p(x)$, $x \in \mathcal{X}$. The *entropy* of X is defined by

$$H(X) = \mathbb{E}[-\log p(X)] = -\sum_{x \in \mathcal{X}} p(x) \log p(x)$$

(where log denotes natural logarithm and $0 \log 0 = 0$). If X, Y is a pair of discrete random variables taking values in $\mathcal{X} \times \mathcal{Y}$ then the *joint entropy* $H(X, Y)$ of X and Y is defined as the entropy of the pair (X, Y). The *conditional entropy* $H(X|Y)$ is defined as

$$H(X|Y) = H(X, Y) - H(Y) .$$

Observe that if we write $p(x, y) = \mathbb{P}\{X = x, Y = y\}$ and $p(x|y) = \mathbb{P}\{X = x|Y = y\}$ then

$$H(X|Y) = - \sum_{x \in \mathcal{X}, y \in \mathcal{Y}} p(x, y) \log p(x|y)$$

from which we see that $H(X|Y) \geq 0$. It is also easy to see that the defining identity of the conditional entropy remains true conditionally, that is, for any three (discrete) random variables X, Y, Z,

$$H(X, Y|Z) = H(Y|Z) + H(X|Y, Z) .$$

(Just add $H(Z)$ to both sides and use the definition of the conditional entropy.) A repeated application of this yields the *chain rule for entropy*: for arbitrary discrete random variables $X_1, \ldots, X_n$,

$$H(X_1, \ldots, X_n) = H(X_1) + H(X_2|X_1) + H(X_3|X_1, X_2) + \cdots + H(X_n|X_1, \ldots, X_{n-1}).$$

Let P and Q be two probability distributions over a countable set $\mathcal{X}$ with probability mass functions p and q. Then the *Kullback-Leibler divergence* or *relative entropy* of P and Q is

$$D(P\|Q) = \sum_{x \in \mathcal{X}} p(x) \log \frac{p(x)}{q(x)} .$$

Since $\log x \leq x - 1$,

$$D(P\|Q) = - \sum_{x \in \mathcal{X}} p(x) \log \frac{q(x)}{p(x)} \geq - \sum_{x \in \mathcal{X}} p(x) \left(\frac{q(x)}{p(x)} - 1 \right) = 0 ,$$

so that the relative entropy is always nonnegative, and equals zero if and only if $P = Q$. This simple fact has some interesting consequences. For example, if $\mathcal{X}$ is a finite set with N elements and X is a random variable with distribution P and we take Q to be the uniform distribution over $\mathcal{X}$ then $D(P\|Q) = \log N - H(X)$ and therefore the entropy of X never exceeds the logarithm of the cardinality of its range.

Consider a pair of random variables X, Y with joint distribution $P_{X,Y}$ and marginal distributions P_X and P_Y. Noting that $D(P_{X,Y}\|P_X \times P_Y) = H(X) - H(X|Y)$, the nonnegativity of the relative entropy implies that $H(X) \geq H(X|Y)$, that is, conditioning reduces entropy. It is similarly easy to see that this fact remains true for conditional entropies as well, that is,

$$H(X|Y) \geq H(X|Y, Z) .$$

Now we may prove the following inequality of Han [63]

Theorem 7. HAN'S INEQUALITY. *Let $X_1, \ldots, X_n$ be discrete random variables. Then*

$$H(X_1, \ldots, X_n) \leq \frac{1}{n-1} \sum_{i=1}^{n} H(X_1, \ldots, X_{i-1}, X_{i+1}, \ldots, X_n)$$

Proof. For any $i = 1, \ldots, n$, by the definition of the conditional entropy and the fact that conditioning reduces entropy,

$$H(X_1, \ldots, X_n)$$
$$= H(X_1, \ldots, X_{i-1}, X_{i+1}, \ldots, X_n) + H(X_i | X_1, \ldots, X_{i-1}, X_{i+1}, \ldots, X_n)$$
$$\leq H(X_1, \ldots, X_{i-1}, X_{i+1}, \ldots, X_n) + H(X_i | X_1, \ldots, X_{i-1}) \qquad i = 1, \ldots, n \, .$$

Summing these n inequalities and using the chain rule for entropy, we get

$$nH(X_1, \ldots, X_n) \leq \sum_{i=1}^{n} H(X_1, \ldots, X_{i-1}, X_{i+1}, \ldots, X_n) + H(X_1, \ldots, X_n)$$

which is what we wanted to prove.   □

We finish this section by an inequality which may be regarded as a version of Han's inequality for relative entropies. As it was pointed out by Massart [44], this inequality may be used to prove the key tensorization inequality of the next section.

To this end, let $\mathcal{X}$ be a countable set, and let P and Q be probability distributions on $\mathcal{X}^n$ such that $P = P_1 \times \cdots \times P_n$ is a product measure. We denote the elements of $\mathcal{X}^n$ by $x_1^n = (x_1, \ldots, x_n)$ and write $x^{(i)} = (x_1, \ldots, x_{i-1}, x_{i+1}, \ldots, x_n)$ for the $(n-1)$-vector obtained by leaving out the i-th component of x_1^n. Denote by $Q^{(i)}$ and $P^{(i)}$ the marginal distributions of x_1^n according to Q and P, that is,

$$Q^{(i)}(x) = \sum_{x \in \mathcal{X}} Q(x_1, \ldots, x_{i-1}, x, x_{i+1}, \ldots, x_n)$$

and

$$P^{(i)}(x) = \sum_{x \in \mathcal{X}} P(x_1, \ldots, x_{i-1}, x, x_{i+1}, \ldots, x_n)$$
$$= \sum_{x \in \mathcal{X}} P_1(x_1) \cdots P_{i-1}(x_{i-1}) P_i(x) P_{i+1}(x_{i+1}) \cdots P_n(x_n) \, .$$

Then we have the following.

Theorem 8. HAN'S INEQUALITY FOR RELATIVE ENTROPIES.

$$D(Q \| P) \geq \frac{1}{n-1} \sum_{i=1}^{n} D(Q^{(i)} \| P^{(i)})$$

or equivalently,

$$D(Q \| P) \leq \sum_{i=1}^{n} \left(D(Q \| P) - D(Q^{(i)} \| P^{(i)}) \right) \, .$$

Proof. The statement is a straightforward consequence of Han's inequality. Indeed, Han's inequality states that

$$\sum_{x_1^n \in \mathcal{X}^n} Q(x_1^n) \log Q(x_1^n) \geq \frac{1}{n-1} \sum_{i=1}^{n} \sum_{x^{(i)} \in \mathcal{X}^{n-1}} Q^{(i)}(x^{(i)}) \log Q^{(i)}(x^{(i)}) \ .$$

Since

$$D(Q\|P) = \sum_{x_1^n \in \mathcal{X}^n} Q(x_1^n) \log Q(x_1^n) - \sum_{x_1^n \in \mathcal{X}^n} Q(x_1^n) \log P(x_1^n)$$

and

$$D(Q^{(i)}\|P^{(i)}) = \sum_{x^{(i)} \in \mathcal{X}^{n-1}} \left(Q^{(i)}(x^{(i)}) \log Q^{(i)}(x^{(i)}) - Q^{(i)}(x^{(i)}) \log P^{(i)}(x^{(i)}) \right) \ ,$$

it suffices to show that

$$\sum_{x_1^n \in \mathcal{X}^n} Q(x_1^n) \log P(x_1^n) = \frac{1}{n-1} \sum_{i=1}^{n} \sum_{x^{(i)} \in \mathcal{X}^{n-1}} Q^{(i)}(x^{(i)}) \log P^{(i)}(x^{(i)}) \ .$$

This may be seen easily by noting that by the product property of P, we have $P(x_1^n) = P^{(i)}(x^{(i)}) P_i(x_i)$ for all i, and also $P(x_1^n) = \prod_{i=1}^{n} P_i(x_i)$, and therefore

$$\sum_{x_1^n \in \mathcal{X}^n} Q(x_1^n) \log P(x_1^n) = \frac{1}{n} \sum_{i=1}^{n} \sum_{x_1^n \in \mathcal{X}^n} Q(x_1^n) \left(\log P^{(i)}(x^{(i)}) + \log P_i(x_i) \right)$$

$$= \frac{1}{n} \sum_{i=1}^{n} \sum_{x_1^n \in \mathcal{X}^n} Q(x_1^n) \log P^{(i)}(x^{(i)}) + \frac{1}{n} Q(x_1^n) \log P(x_i^n) \ .$$

Rearranging, we obtain

$$\sum_{x_1^n \in \mathcal{X}^n} Q(x_1^n) \log P(x_1^n) = \frac{1}{n-1} \sum_{i=1}^{n} \sum_{x_1^n \in \mathcal{X}^n} Q(x_1^n) \log P^{(i)}(x^{(i)})$$

$$= \frac{1}{n-1} \sum_{i=1}^{n} \sum_{x^{(i)} \in \mathcal{X}^{n-1}} Q^{(i)}(x^{(i)}) \log P^{(i)}(x^{(i)})$$

where we used the defining property of $Q^{(i)}$.   □

3.2   Tensorization of the Entropy

We are now prepared to prove the main exponential concentration inequalities of these notes. Just as in Section 2, we let $X_1, \ldots, X_n$ be independent random variables, and investigate concentration properties of $Z = g(X_1, \ldots, X_n)$. The basis of Ledoux's entropy method is a powerful extension of Theorem 4. Note that Theorem 4 may be rewritten as

$$\mathsf{Var}(Z) \leq \sum_{i=1}^{n} \mathbb{E}\left[\mathbb{E}_i(Z^2) - (\mathbb{E}_i(Z))^2\right]$$

or, putting $\phi(x) = x^2$,

$$\mathbb{E}\phi(Z) - \phi(\mathbb{E}Z) \leq \sum_{i=1}^{n} \mathbb{E}\left[\mathbb{E}_i\phi(Z) - \phi(\mathbb{E}_i(Z))\right] \ .$$

As it turns out, this inequality remains true for a large class of convex functions ϕ, see Beckner [64], Latała and Oleszkiewicz [65], Ledoux [20], Boucheron, Bousquet, Lugosi, and Massart [29], and Chafaï [66]. The case of interest in our case is when $\phi(x) = x \log x$. In this case, as seen in the proof below, the left-hand side of the inequality may be written as the relative entropy between the distribution induced by Z on $\mathcal{X}^n$ and the distribution of X_1^n. Hence the name "tensorization inequality of the entropy", (see, e.g., Ledoux [20]).

Theorem 9. *Let $\phi(x) = x \log x$ for $x > 0$. Let $X_1 \ldots, X_n$ be independent random variables taking values in $\mathcal{X}$ and let f be a positive-valued function on $\mathcal{X}^n$. Letting $Y = f(X_1, \ldots, X_n)$, we have*

$$\mathbb{E}\phi(Y) - \phi(\mathbb{E}Y) \leq \sum_{i=1}^{n} \mathbb{E}\left[\mathbb{E}_i\phi(Y) - \phi(\mathbb{E}_i(Y))\right] \ .$$

Proof. We only prove the statement for discrete random variables $X_1 \ldots, X_n$. The extension to the general case is technical but straightforward. The theorem is a direct consequence of Han's inequality for relative entropies. First note that if the inequality is true for a random variable Y then it is also true for cY where c is a positive constant. Hence we may assume that $\mathbb{E}Y = 1$. Now define the probability measure Q on $\mathcal{X}^n$ by

$$Q(x_1^n) = f(x_1^n)P(x_1^n)$$

where P denotes the distribution of $X_1^n = X_1, \ldots, X_n$. Then clearly,

$$\mathbb{E}\phi(Y) - \phi(\mathbb{E}Y) = \mathbb{E}[Y \log Y] = D(Q\|P)$$

which, by Theorem 8, does not exceed $\sum_{i=1}^{n}\left(D(Q\|P) - D(Q^{(i)}\|P^{(i)})\right)$. However, straightforward calculation shows that

$$\sum_{i=1}^{n}\left(D(Q\|P) - D(Q^{(i)}\|P^{(i)})\right) = \sum_{i=1}^{n}\mathbb{E}\left[\mathbb{E}_i\phi(Y) - \phi(\mathbb{E}_i(Y))\right]$$

and the statement follows. $\square$

The main idea in Ledoux's entropy method for proving concentration inequalities is to apply Theorem 9 to the positive random variable $Y = e^{sZ}$. Then, denoting the moment generating function of Z by $F(s) = \mathbb{E}[e^{sZ}]$, the left-hand side of the inequality in Theorem 9 becomes

$$s\mathbb{E}\left[Ze^{sZ}\right] - \mathbb{E}\left[e^{sZ}\right]\log\mathbb{E}\left[e^{sZ}\right] = sF'(s) - F(s)\log F(s) .$$

Our strategy, then is to derive upper bounds for the derivative of $F(s)$ and derive tail bounds via Chernoff's bounding. To do this in a convenient way, we need some further bounds for the right-hand side of the inequality in Theorem 9. This is the purpose of the next section.

3.3   Logarithmic Sobolev Inequalities

Recall from Section 2 that we denote $Z_i = g_i(X_1, \ldots, X_{i-1}, X_{i+1}, \ldots, X_n)$ where g_i is some function over $\mathcal{X}^{n-1}$. Below we further develop the right-hand side of Theorem 9 to obtain important inequalities which serve as the basis in deriving exponential concentration inequalities. These inequalities are closely related to the so-called *logarithmic Sobolev inequalities* of analysis, see Ledoux [20, 67, 68], Massart [23].

First we need the following technical lemma:

Lemma 2. *Let Y denote a positive random variable. Then for any $u > 0$,*

$$\mathbb{E}[Y\log Y] - (\mathbb{E}Y)\log(\mathbb{E}Y) \le \mathbb{E}[Y\log Y - Y\log u - (Y - u)] .$$

Proof.   As for any $x > 0$, $\log x \le x - 1$, we have

$$\log\frac{u}{\mathbb{E}Y} \le \frac{u}{\mathbb{E}Y} - 1 ,$$

hence

$$\mathbb{E}Y\log\frac{u}{\mathbb{E}Y} \le u - \mathbb{E}Y$$

which is equivalent to the statement.   □

Theorem 10.   A LOGARITHMIC SOBOLEV INEQUALITY. *Denote $\psi(x) = e^x - x - 1$. Then*

$$s\mathbb{E}\left[Ze^{sZ}\right] - \mathbb{E}\left[e^{sZ}\right]\log\mathbb{E}\left[e^{sZ}\right] \le \sum_{i=1}^{n}\mathbb{E}\left[e^{sZ}\psi\left(-s(Z - Z_i)\right)\right] .$$

Proof.   We bound each term on the right-hand side of Theorem 9. Note that Lemma 2 implies that if Y_i is a positive function of $X_1, \ldots, X_{i-1}, X_{i+1}, \ldots, X_n$, then

$$\mathbb{E}_i(Y\log Y) - \mathbb{E}_i(Y)\log\mathbb{E}_i(Y) \le \mathbb{E}_i\left[Y(\log Y - \log Y_i) - (Y - Y_i)\right]$$

Applying the above inequality to the variables $Y = e^{sZ}$ and $Y_i = e^{sZ_i}$, one gets

$$\mathbb{E}_i(Y\log Y) - \mathbb{E}_i(Y)\log\mathbb{E}_i(Y) \le \mathbb{E}_i\left[e^{sZ}\psi(-s(Z - Z^{(i)}))\right]$$

and the proof is completed by Theorem 9.   □

The following symmetrized version, due to Massart [23], will also be useful. Recall that $Z_i' = g(X_1, \ldots, X_i', \ldots, X_n)$ where the X_i' are independent copies of the X_i.

Theorem 11. SYMMETRIZED LOGARITHMIC SOBOLEV INEQUALITY. *If ψ is defined as in Theorem 10 then*

$$s\mathbb{E}\left[Ze^{sZ}\right] - \mathbb{E}\left[e^{sZ}\right]\log\mathbb{E}\left[e^{sZ}\right] \le \sum_{i=1}^{n}\mathbb{E}\left[e^{sZ}\psi\left(-s(Z - Z_i')\right)\right].$$

Moreover, denote $\tau(x) = x(e^x - 1)$. Then for all $s \in \mathbb{R}$,

$$s\mathbb{E}\left[Ze^{sZ}\right] - \mathbb{E}\left[e^{sZ}\right]\log\mathbb{E}\left[e^{sZ}\right] \le \sum_{i=1}^{n}\mathbb{E}\left[e^{sZ}\tau(-s(Z - Z_i'))\mathbb{1}_{Z > Z_i'}\right],$$

$$s\mathbb{E}\left[Ze^{sZ}\right] - \mathbb{E}\left[e^{sZ}\right]\log\mathbb{E}\left[e^{sZ}\right] \le \sum_{i=1}^{n}\mathbb{E}\left[e^{sZ}\tau(s(Z_i' - Z))\mathbb{1}_{Z < Z_i'}\right].$$

Proof. The first inequality is proved exactly as Theorem 10, just by noting that, just like Z_i, Z_i' is also independent of X_i. To prove the second and third inequalities, write

$$e^{sZ}\psi\left(-s(Z - Z_i')\right) = e^{sZ}\psi\left(-s(Z - Z_i')\right)\mathbb{1}_{Z > Z_i'} + e^{sZ}\psi\left(s(Z_i' - Z)\right)\mathbb{1}_{Z < Z_i'}.$$

By symmetry, the conditional expectation of the second term may be written as

$$\mathbb{E}_i\left[e^{sZ}\psi\left(s(Z_i' - Z)\right)\mathbb{1}_{Z < Z_i'}\right] = \mathbb{E}_i\left[e^{sZ_i'}\psi\left(s(Z - Z_i')\right)\mathbb{1}_{Z > Z_i'}\right]$$
$$= \mathbb{E}_i\left[e^{sZ}e^{-s(Z - Z_i')}\psi\left(s(Z - Z_i')\right)\mathbb{1}_{Z > Z_i'}\right].$$

Summarizing, we have

$$\mathbb{E}\left[e^{sZ}\psi\left(-s(Z - Z_i')\right)\right]$$
$$= \mathbb{E}_i\left[\left(\psi\left(-s(Z - Z_i')\right) + e^{-s(Z - Z_i')}\psi\left(s(Z - Z_i')\right)\right)e^{sZ}\mathbb{1}_{Z > Z_i'}\right].$$

The second inequality of the theorem follows simply by noting that $\psi(x) + e^x\psi(-x) = x(e^x - 1) = \tau(x)$. The last inequality follows similarly. $\square$

3.4   First Example: Bounded Differences and More

The purpose of this section is to illustrate how the logarithmic Sobolev inequalities shown in the previous section may be used to obtain powerful exponential concentration inequalities. The first result is rather easy to obtain, yet it turns out to be very useful. Also, its proof is prototypical, in the sense that it shows, in a transparent way, the main ideas.

Theorem 12. *Assume that there exists a positive constant C such that, almost surely,*

$$\sum_{i=1}^{n}(Z - Z_i')^2 \leq C .$$

Then for all $t > 0$,

$$\mathbb{P}\left[|Z - \mathbb{E}Z| > t\right] \leq 2e^{-t^2/4C} .$$

Proof. Observe that for $x > 0$, $\tau(-x) \leq x^2$, and therefore, for any $s > 0$, Theorem 11 implies

$$s\mathbb{E}\left[Ze^{sZ}\right] - \mathbb{E}\left[e^{sZ}\right]\log\mathbb{E}\left[e^{sZ}\right] \leq \mathbb{E}\left[e^{sZ}\sum_{i=1}^{n}s^2(Z - Z_i')^2\mathbb{1}_{Z>Z_i'}\right]$$

$$\leq s^2\mathbb{E}\left[e^{sZ}\sum_{i=1}^{n}(Z - Z_i')^2\right]$$

$$\leq s^2 C\mathbb{E}\left[e^{sZ}\right] ,$$

where at the last step we used the assumption of the theorem. Now denoting the moment generating function of Z by $F(s) = \mathbb{E}\left[e^{sZ}\right]$, the above inequality may be re-written as

$$sF'(s) - F(s)\log F(s) \leq Cs^2 F(s) .$$

After dividing both sides by $s^2 F(s)$, we observe that the left-hand side is just the derivative of $H(s) = s^{-1}\log F(s)$, that is, we obtain the inequality

$$H'(s) \leq C .$$

By l'Hospital's rule we note that $\lim_{s\to 0} H(s) = F'(0)/F(0) = \mathbb{E}Z$, so by integrating the above inequality, we get $H(s) \leq \mathbb{E}Z + sC$, or in other words,

$$F(s) \leq e^{s\mathbb{E}Z+s^2 C} .$$

Now by Markov's inequality,

$$\mathbb{P}\left[Z > \mathbb{E}Z + t\right] \leq F(s)e^{-s\mathbb{E}Z-st} \leq e^{s^2 C-st} .$$

Choosing $s = t/2C$, the upper bound becomes $e^{-t^2/4C}$. Replace Z by $-Z$ to obtain the same upper bound for $\mathbb{P}\left[Z < \mathbb{E}Z - t\right]$.   □

Remark. It is easy to see that the condition of Theorem 12 may be relaxed in the following way: if

$$\mathbb{E}\left[\sum_{i=1}^{n}(Z - Z_i')^2\mathbb{1}_{Z>Z_i'}\bigg|\mathbf{X}\right] \leq c$$

then for all $t > 0$,

$$\mathbb{P}\left[Z > \mathbb{E}Z + t\right] \leq e^{-t^2/4c}$$

and if

$$\mathbb{E}\left[\sum_{i=1}^{n}(Z - Z_i')^2 \mathbb{1}_{Z_i' > Z} \Big| \mathbf{X}\right] \le c\,,$$

then

$$\mathbb{P}\left[Z < \mathbb{E}Z - t\right] \le e^{-t^2/4c}\,.$$

An immediate corollary of Theorem 12 is a subgaussian tail inequality for functions of bounded differences.

Corollary 4. BOUNDED DIFFERENCES INEQUALITY. *Assume the function g satisfies the bounded differences assumption with constants $c_1, \ldots, c_n$, then*

$$\mathbb{P}\left[|Z - \mathbb{E}Z| > t\right] \le 2e^{-t^2/4C}$$

where $C = \sum_{i=1}^{n} c_i^2$.

We remark here that the constant appearing in this corollary may be improved. Indeed, using the martingale method, McDiarmid [2] showed that under the conditions of Corollary 4,

$$\mathbb{P}\left[|Z - \mathbb{E}Z| > t\right] \le 2e^{-2t^2/C}$$

(see the exercises). Thus, we have been able to extend Corollary 1 to an exponential concentration inequality. Note that by combining the variance bound of Corollary 1 with Chebyshev's inequality, we only obtained

$$\mathbb{P}\left[|Z - \mathbb{E}Z| > t\right] \le \frac{C}{2t^2}$$

and therefore the improvement is essential. Thus the applications of Corollary 1 in all the examples shown in Section 2.1 are now improved in an essential way without further work.

However, Theorem 12 is much stronger than Corollary 4. To understand why, just observe that the conditions of Theorem 12 do not require that g has bounded differences. All that's required is that

$$\sup_{\substack{x_1, \ldots, x_n, \\ x_1', \ldots, x_n' \in \mathcal{X}}} \sum_{i=1}^{n} |g(x_1, \ldots, x_n) - g(x_1, \ldots, x_{i-1}, x_i', x_{i+1}, \ldots, x_n)|^2 \le \sum_{i=1}^{n} c_i^2\,,$$

an obviously much milder requirement.

3.5   Exponential Inequalities for Self-Bounding Functions

In this section we prove exponential concentration inequalities for self-bounding functions discussed in Section 2.2. Recall that a variant of the Efron-Stein inequality (Theorem 2) implies that for self-bounding functions $\mathsf{Var}(Z) \le \mathbb{E}(Z)$.

Based on the logarithmic Sobolev inequality of Theorem 10 we may now obtain exponential concentration bounds. The theorem appears in Boucheron, Lugosi, and Massart [25] and builds on techniques developed by Massart [23].

Recall the definition of following two functions that we have already seen in Bennett's inequality and in the logarithmic Sobolev inequalities above:

$$h(u) = (1+u)\log(1+u) - u \quad (u \geq -1),$$
$$\text{and} \quad \psi(v) = \sup_{u \geq -1} [uv - h(u)] = e^v - v - 1 .$$

Theorem 13. *Assume that g satisfies the self-bounding property. Then for every $s \in \mathbb{R}$,*

$$\log \mathbb{E}\left[e^{s(Z-\mathbb{E}Z)}\right] \leq \mathbb{E}Z\psi(s) .$$

Moreover, for every $t > 0$,

$$\mathbb{P}[Z \geq \mathbb{E}Z + t] \leq \exp\left[-\mathbb{E}Zh\left(\frac{t}{\mathbb{E}Z}\right)\right]$$

and for every $0 < t \leq \mathbb{E}Z$,

$$\mathbb{P}[Z \leq \mathbb{E}Z - t] \leq \exp\left[-\mathbb{E}Zh\left(-\frac{t}{\mathbb{E}Z}\right)\right]$$

By recalling that $h(u) \geq u^2/(2 + 2u/3)$ for $u \geq 0$ (we have already used this in the proof of Bernstein's inequality) and observing that $h(u) \geq u^2/2$ for $u \leq 0$, we obtain the following immediate corollaries: for every $t > 0$,

$$\mathbb{P}[Z \geq \mathbb{E}Z + t] \leq \exp\left[-\frac{t^2}{2\mathbb{E}Z + 2t/3}\right]$$

and for every $0 < t \leq \mathbb{E}Z$,

$$\mathbb{P}[Z \leq \mathbb{E}Z - t] \leq \exp\left[-\frac{t^2}{2\mathbb{E}Z}\right] .$$

Proof. We apply Lemma 10. Since the function ψ is convex with $\psi(0) = 0$, for any s and any $u \in [0,1]$, $\psi(-su) \leq u\psi(-s)$. Thus, since $Z - Z_i \in [0,1]$, we have that for every s, $\psi(-s(Z - Z_i)) \leq (Z - Z_i)\psi(-s)$ and therefore, Lemma 10 and the condition $\sum_{i=1}^{n}(Z - Z_i) \leq Z$ imply that

$$s\mathbb{E}\left[Ze^{sZ}\right] - \mathbb{E}\left[e^{sZ}\right]\log\mathbb{E}\left[e^{sZ}\right] \leq \mathbb{E}\left[\psi(-s)e^{sZ}\sum_{i=1}^{n}(Z - Z_i)\right]$$
$$\leq \psi(-s)\mathbb{E}\left[Ze^{sZ}\right].$$

Introduce $\widetilde{Z} = Z - \mathbb{E}[Z]$ and define, for any s, $\tilde{F}(s) = \mathbb{E}\left[e^{s\widetilde{Z}}\right]$. Then the inequality above becomes

$$[s - \psi(-s)]\frac{\tilde{F}'(s)}{\tilde{F}(s)} - \log\tilde{F}(s) \leq \mathbb{E}Z\psi(-s) ,$$

which, writing $G(s) = \log F(s)$, implies

$$\left(1 - e^{-s}\right) G'(s) - G(s) \leq \mathbb{E}Z\psi(-s) \ .$$

Now observe that the function $G_0 = \mathbb{E}Z\psi$ is a solution of the ordinary differential equation $(1 - e^{-s}) G'(s) - G(s) = \mathbb{E}Z\psi(-s)$. We want to show that $G \leq G_0$. In fact, if $G_1 = G - G_0$, then

$$\left(1 - e^{-s}\right) G_1'(s) - G_1(s) \leq 0. \tag{2}$$

Hence, defining $\tilde{G}(s) = G_1(s)/(e^s - 1)$, we have

$$\left(1 - e^{-s}\right)(e^s - 1) \tilde{G}'(s) \leq 0.$$

Hence $\tilde{G}'$ is non-positive and therefore $\tilde{G}$ is non-increasing. Now, since $\tilde{Z}$ is centered $G_1'(0) = 0$. Using the fact that $s(e^s - 1)^{-1}$ tends to 1 as s goes to 0, we conclude that $\tilde{G}(s)$ tends to 0 as s goes to 0. This shows that $\tilde{G}$ is non-positive on $(0, \infty)$ and non-negative over $(-\infty, 0)$, hence G_1 is everywhere non-positive, therefore $G \leq G_0$ and we have proved the first inequality of the theorem. The proof of inequalities for the tail probabilities may be completed by Chernoff's bounding:

$$\mathbb{P}\left[Z - \mathbb{E}\left[Z\right] \geq t\right] \leq \exp\left[-\sup_{s>0}\left(ts - \mathbb{E}Z\psi(s)\right)\right]$$

and

$$\mathbb{P}\left[Z - \mathbb{E}\left[Z\right] \leq -t\right] \leq \exp\left[-\sup_{s<0}\left(-ts - \mathbb{E}Z\psi(s)\right)\right].$$

The proof is now completed by using the easy-to-check (and well-known) relations

$$\sup_{s>0}\left[ts - \mathbb{E}Z\psi(s)\right] = \mathbb{E}Zh(t/\mathbb{E}Z) \quad \text{for } t > 0$$
$$\sup_{s<0}\left[-ts - \mathbb{E}Z\psi(s)\right] = \mathbb{E}Zh(-t/\mathbb{E}Z) \quad \text{for } 0 < t \leq \mathbb{E}Z.$$

$\square$

3.6   VC Entropy

Theorems 2 and 13 provide concentration inequalities for functions having the self-bounding property. In Section 2.2 several examples of such functions are discussed. The purpose of this section is to show that the so-called VC entropy is a self-bounding function.

The Vapnik-Chervonenkis (or VC) entropy is closely related to the VC dimension discussed in Section 2.2. Let $\mathcal{A}$ be an arbitrary collection of subsets of $\mathcal{X}$, and let $x_1^n = (x_1, \ldots, x_n)$ be a vector of n points of $\mathcal{X}$. Recall that the *shatter coefficient* is defined as the size of the trace of $\mathcal{A}$ on x_1^n, that is,

$$T(x_1^n) = |\text{tr}(x_1^n)| = |\{A \cap \{x_1, \ldots, x_n\} : A \in \mathcal{A}\}| \ .$$

The VC *entropy* is defined as the logarithm of the shatter coefficient, that is,

$$h(x_1^n) = \log_2 T(x_1^n) \ .$$

Lemma 3. *The VC entropy has the self-bounding property.*

Proof. We need to show that there exists a function h' of $n - 1$ variables such that for all $i = 1, \ldots, n$, writing $x^{(i)} = (x_1, \ldots, x_{i-1}, x_{i+1}, \ldots, x_n)$, $0 \le h(x_1^n) - h'(x^{(i)}) \le 1$ and

$$\sum_{i=1}^n \left(h(x_1^n) - h'(x^{(i)}) \right) \le h(x_1^n).$$

We define h' the natural way, that is, as the entropy based on the $n-1$ points in its arguments. Then clearly, for any i, $h'(x^{(i)}) \le h(x_1^n)$, and the difference cannot be more than one. The nontrivial part of the proof is to show the second property. We do this using Han's inequality (Theorem 7).

Consider the uniform distribution over the set $\text{tr}(x_1^n)$. This defines a random vector $Y = (Y_1, \ldots, Y_n) \in \mathcal{Y}^n$. Then clearly,

$$h(x_1^n) = \log_2 |\text{tr}(x_1^n)(x)| = \frac{1}{\ln 2} H(Y_1, \ldots, Y_n)$$

where $H(Y_1, \ldots, Y_n)$ is the (joint) entropy of $Y_1, \ldots, Y_n$. Since the uniform distribution maximizes the entropy, we also have, for all $i \le n$, that

$$h'(x^{(i)}) \ge \frac{1}{\ln 2} H(Y_1, \ldots, Y_{i-1}, Y_{i+1}, \ldots, Y_n).$$

Since by Han's inequality

$$H(Y_1, \ldots, Y_n) \le \frac{1}{n-1} \sum_{i=1}^n H(Y_1, \ldots, Y_{i-1}, Y_{i+1}, \ldots, Y_n),$$

we have

$$\sum_{i=1}^n \left(h(x_1^n) - h'(x^{(i)}) \right) \le h(x_1^n)$$

as desired. ☐

The above lemma, together with Theorems 2 and 12 immediately implies the following:

Corollary 5. *Let $X_1, \ldots, X_n$ be independent random variables taking their values in $\mathcal{X}$ and let $Z = h(X_1^n)$ denote the random VC entropy. Then $\text{Var}(Z) \le \mathbb{E}[Z]$, for $t > 0$*

$$\mathbb{P}\left[Z \ge \mathbb{E}Z + t\right] \le \exp\left[-\frac{t^2}{2\mathbb{E}Z + 2t/3}\right],$$

and for every $0 < t \le \mathbb{E}Z$,

$$\mathbb{P}\left[Z \le \mathbb{E}Z - t\right] \le \exp\left[-\frac{t^2}{2\mathbb{E}Z}\right] .$$

Moreover, for the random shatter coefficient $T(X_1^n)$, we have

$$\mathbb{E}\log_2 T(X_1^n) \le \log_2 \mathbb{E}T(X_1^n) \le \log_2 e\mathbb{E}\log_2 T(X_1^n) .$$

Note that the left-hand side of the last statement follows from Jensen's inequality, while the right-hand side by taking $s = \ln 2$ in the first inequality of Theorem 13. This last statement shows that the expected VC entropy $\mathbb{E}\log_2 T(X_1^n)$ and the *annealed* VC entropy are tightly connected, regardless of the class of sets $\mathcal{A}$ and the distribution of the X_i's. We note here that this fact answers, in a positive way, an open question raised by Vapnik [69, pages 53–54]: the empirical risk minimization procedure is *non-trivially consistent* and *rapidly convergent* if and only if the annealed entropy rate $(1/n)\log_2 \mathbb{E}[T(X)]$ converges to zero. For the definitions and discussion we refer to [69].

3.7   Variations on the Theme

In this section we show how the techniques of the entropy method for proving concentration inequalities may be used in various situations not considered so far. The versions differ in the assumptions on how $\sum_{i=1}^{n}(Z - Z_i')^2$ is controlled by different functions of Z. For various other versions with applications we refer to Boucheron, Lugosi, and Massart [26]. In all cases the upper bound is roughly of the form e^{-t^2/σ^2} where σ^2 is the corresponding Efron-Stein upper bound on $\mathrm{Var}(Z)$. The first inequality may be regarded as a generalization of the upper tail inequality in Theorem 13.

Theorem 14. *Assume that there exist positive constants a and b such that*

$$\sum_{i=1}^{n}(Z - Z_i')^2 \mathbb{1}_{Z>Z_i'} \le aZ + b .$$

Then for $s \in (0, 1/a)$,

$$\log \mathbb{E}[\exp(s(Z - \mathbb{E}[Z]))] \le \frac{s^2}{1 - as}(a\mathbb{E}Z + b)$$

and for all $t > 0$,

$$\mathbb{P}\{Z > \mathbb{E}Z + t\} \le \exp\left(\frac{-t^2}{4a\mathbb{E}Z + 4b + 2at}\right) .$$

Proof. Let $s > 0$. Just like in the first steps of the proof of Theorem 12, we use the fact that for $x > 0$, $\tau(-x) \le x^2$, and therefore, by Theorem 11 we have

$$s\mathbb{E}\left[Ze^{sZ}\right] - \mathbb{E}\left[e^{sZ}\right]\log\mathbb{E}\left[e^{sZ}\right] \le \mathbb{E}\left[e^{sZ}\sum_{i=1}^{n}(Z - Z_i')^2\mathbb{1}_{Z>Z_i'}\right]$$

$$\le s^2\left(a\mathbb{E}\left[Ze^{sZ}\right] + b\mathbb{E}\left[e^{sZ}\right]\right) ,$$

where at the last step we used the assumption of theorem.

Denoting, once again, $F(s) = \mathbb{E}\left[e^{sZ}\right]$, the above inequality becomes

$$sF'(s) - F(s)\log F(s) \le as^2 F'(s) + bs^2 F(s) \ .$$

After dividing both sides by $s^2 F(s)$, once again we see that the left-hand side is just the derivative of $H(s) = s^{-1}\log F(s)$, so we obtain

$$H'(s) \le a(\log F(s))' + b \ .$$

Using the fact that $\lim_{s \to 0} H(s) = F'(0)/F(0) = \mathbb{E}Z$ and $\log F(0) = 0$, and integrating the inequality, we obtain

$$H(s) \le \mathbb{E}Z + a\log F(s) + bs \ ,$$

or, if $s < 1/a$,

$$\log \mathbb{E}[s(Z - \mathbb{E}[Z])] \le \frac{s^2}{1 - as}(a\mathbb{E}Z + b) \ ,$$

proving the first inequality. The inequality for the upper tail now follows by Markov's inequality and the following technical lemma whose proof is left as an exercise.   □

Lemma 4. *Let C and a denote two positive real numbers and denote $h_1(x) = 1 + x - \sqrt{1 + 2x}$. Then*

$$\sup_{\lambda \in [0,1/a)} \left(\lambda t - \frac{C\lambda^2}{1 - a\lambda}\right) = \frac{2C}{a^2} h_1\left(\frac{at}{2C}\right) \ge \frac{t^2}{2(2C + at)}$$

and the supremum is attained at

$$\lambda = \frac{1}{a}\left(1 - \left(1 + \frac{at}{C}\right)^{-1/2}\right) \ .$$

Also,

$$\sup_{\lambda \in [0,\infty)} \left(\lambda t - \frac{C\lambda^2}{1 + a\lambda}\right) = \frac{2C}{a^2} h_1\left(\frac{-at}{2C}\right) \ge \frac{t^2}{4C}$$

if $t < C/a$ and the supremum is attained at

$$\lambda = \frac{1}{a}\left(\left(1 - \frac{at}{C}\right)^{-1/2} - 1\right) \ .$$

There is a subtle difference between upper and lower tail bounds. Bounds for the lower tail $\mathbb{P}\{Z < \mathbb{E}Z - t\}$ may be easily derived, due to *Chebyshev's association inequality* which states that if X is a real-valued random variable and f is a nonincreasing and g is a nondecreasing function, then

$$\mathbb{E}[f(X)g(X)] \le \mathbb{E}[f(X)]\mathbb{E}[g(X)]\| \ .$$

Theorem 15. *Assume that for some nondecreasing function g,*

$$\sum_{i=1}^{n}(Z - Z_i')^2 \mathbb{1}_{Z<Z_i'} \le g(Z) \ .$$

Then for all $t > 0$,

$$\mathbb{P}\left[Z < \mathbb{E}Z - t\right] \le \exp\left(\frac{-t^2}{4\mathbb{E}[g(Z)]}\right) \ .$$

Proof. To prove lower-tail inequalities we obtain upper bounds for $F(s) = \mathbb{E}[\exp(sZ)]$ with $s < 0$. By the third inequality of Theorem 11,

$$s\mathbb{E}\left[Ze^{sZ}\right] - \mathbb{E}\left[e^{sZ}\right]\log\mathbb{E}\left[e^{sZ}\right]$$

$$\le \sum_{i=1}^{n}\mathbb{E}\left[e^{sZ}\tau(s(Z_i' - Z))\mathbb{1}_{Z<Z_i'}\right]$$

$$\le \sum_{i=1}^{n}\mathbb{E}\left[e^{sZ}s^2(Z_i' - Z)^2\mathbb{1}_{Z<Z_i'}\right]$$

(using $s < 0$ and that $\tau(-x) \le x^2$ for $x > 0$)

$$= s^2\mathbb{E}\left[e^{sZ}\sum_{i=1}^{n}(Z - Z_i')^2\mathbb{1}_{Z<Z_i'}\right]$$

$$\le s^2\mathbb{E}\left[e^{sZ}g(Z)\right] \ .$$

Since $g(Z)$ is a nondecreasing and e^{sZ} is a decreasing function of Z, Chebyshev's association inequality implies that

$$\mathbb{E}\left[e^{sZ}g(Z)\right] \le \mathbb{E}\left[e^{sZ}\right]\mathbb{E}[g(Z)] \ .$$

Thus, dividing both sides of the obtained inequality by $s^2F(s)$ and writing $H(s) = (1/s)\log F(s)$, we obtain

$$H'(s) \le \mathbb{E}[g(Z)] \ .$$

Integrating the inequality in the interval $[s, 0)$ we obtain

$$F(s) \le \exp(s^2\mathbb{E}[g(Z)] + s\mathbb{E}[Z]) \ .$$

Markov's inequality and optimizing in s now implies the theorem.   □

The next result is useful when one is interested in lower-tail bounds but $\sum_{i=1}^{n}(Z - Z_i')^2\mathbb{1}_{Z<Z_i'}$ is difficult to handle. In some cases $\sum_{i=1}^{n}(Z - Z_i')^2\mathbb{1}_{Z>Z_i'}$ is easier to bound. In such a situation we need the additional guarantee that $|Z - Z_i'|$ remains bounded. Without loss of generality, we assume that the bound is 1.

Theorem 16. *Assume that there exists a nondecreasing function g such that $\sum_{i=1}^{n}(Z - Z_i')^2 \mathbb{1}_{Z > Z_i'} \le g(Z)$ and for any value of X_1^n and X_i', $|Z - Z_i'| \le 1$. Then for all $K > 0$, $s \in [0, 1/K]$*

$$\log \mathbb{E}\left[\exp(-s(Z - \mathbb{E}[Z]))\right] \le s^2 \frac{\tau(K)}{K^2} \mathbb{E}[g(Z)] \ ,$$

and for all $t > 0$, with $t \le (e-1)\mathbb{E}[g(Z)]$ we have

$$\mathbb{P}\left[Z < \mathbb{E}Z - t\right] \le \exp\left(-\frac{t^2}{4(e-1)\mathbb{E}[g(Z)]}\right) \ .$$

Proof. The key observation is that the function $\tau(x)/x^2 = (e^x - 1)/x$ is increasing if $x > 0$. Choose $K > 0$. Thus, for $s \in (-1/K, 0)$, the second inequality of Theorem 11 implies that

$$s\mathbb{E}\left[Ze^{sZ}\right] - \mathbb{E}\left[e^{sZ}\right]\log\mathbb{E}\left[e^{sZ}\right] \le \sum_{i=1}^{n}\mathbb{E}\left[e^{sZ}\tau(-s(Z - Z^{(i)}))\mathbb{1}_{Z > Z_i'}\right]$$

$$\le s^2\frac{\tau(K)}{K^2}\mathbb{E}\left[e^{sZ}\sum_{i=1}^{n}(Z - Z^{(i)})^2\mathbb{1}_{Z > Z_i'}\right]$$

$$\le s^2\frac{\tau(K)}{K^2}\mathbb{E}\left[g(Z)e^{sZ}\right],$$

where at the last step we used the assumption of the theorem.

Just like in the proof of Theorem 15, we bound $\mathbb{E}\left[g(Z)e^{sZ}\right]$ by $\mathbb{E}[g(Z)]\mathbb{E}\left[e^{sZ}\right]$. The rest of the proof is identical to that of Theorem 15. Here we took $K = 1$. $\square$

Finally we give, without proof, an inequality (due to Bousquet [28]) for functions satisfying conditions similar but weaker than the self-bounding conditions. This is very useful for suprema of empirical processes for which the non-negativity assumption does not hold.

Theorem 17. *Assume Z satisfies $\sum_{i=1}^{n} Z - Z_i \le Z$, and there exist random variables Y_i such that for all $i = 1, \ldots, n$, $Y_i \le Z - Z_i \le 1$, $Y_i \le a$ for some $a > 0$ and $\mathbb{E}_i Y_i \ge 0$. Also, let σ^2 be a real number such that*

$$\sigma^2 \ge \frac{1}{n}\sum_{i=1}^{n}\mathbb{E}_i[Y_i^2].$$

We obtain for all $t > 0$,

$$\mathbb{P}\{Z \ge \mathbb{E}Z + t\} \le \exp\left(-vh\left(\frac{t}{v}\right)\right),$$

where $v = (1 + a)\mathbb{E}Z + n\sigma^2$.

An important application of the above theorem is the following version of Talagrand's concentration inequality for empirical processes. The constants appearing here were obtained by Bousquet [27].

Corollary 6. *Let $\mathcal{F}$ be a set of functions that satisfy $\mathbb{E}f(X_i) = 0$ and $\sup_{f\in\mathcal{F}} \sup f \leq 1$. We denote*

$$Z = \sup_{f\in\mathcal{F}} \sum_{i=1}^{n} f(X_i).$$

Let σ be a positive real number such that $n\sigma^2 \geq \sum_{i=1}^{n} \sup_{f\in\mathcal{F}} \mathbb{E}[f^2(X_i)]$, then for all $t \geq 0$, we have

$$\mathbb{P}\{Z \geq \mathbb{E}Z + t\} \leq \exp\left(-vh\left(\frac{t}{v}\right)\right),$$

with $v = n\sigma^2 + 2\mathbb{E}Z$.

References

1. Milman, V., Schechman, G.: Asymptotic theory of finite-dimensional normed spaces. Springer-Verlag, New York (1986)
2. McDiarmid, C.: On the method of bounded differences. In: Surveys in Combinatorics 1989, Cambridge University Press, Cambridge (1989) 148–188
3. McDiarmid, C.: Concentration. In Habib, M., McDiarmid, C., Ramirez-Alfonsin, J., Reed, B., eds.: Probabilistic Methods for Algorithmic Discrete Mathematics, Springer, New York (1998) 195–248
4. Ahlswede, R., Gács, P., Körner, J.: Bounds on conditional probabilities with applications in multi-user communication. Zeitschrift für Wahrscheinlichkeitstheorie und verwandte Gebiete **34** (1976) 157–177 (correction in 39:353–354,1977).
5. Marton, K.: A simple proof of the blowing-up lemma. IEEE Transactions on Information Theory **32** (1986) 445–446
6. Marton, K.: Bounding $\bar{d}$-distance by informational divergence: a way to prove measure concentration. Annals of Probability **24** (1996) 857–866
7. Marton, K.: A measure concentration inequality for contracting Markov chains. Geometric and Functional Analysis **6** (1996) 556–571 Erratum: 7:609–613, 1997.
8. Dembo, A.: Information inequalities and concentration of measure. Annals of Probability **25** (1997) 927–939
9. Massart, P.: Optimal constants for Hoeffding type inequalities. Technical report, Mathematiques, Université de Paris-Sud, Report 98.86 (1998)
10. Rio, E.: Inégalités de concentration pour les processus empiriques de classes de parties. Probability Theory and Related Fields **119** (2001) 163–175
11. Talagrand, M.: Concentration of measure and isoperimetric inequalities in product spaces. Publications Mathématiques de l'I.H.E.S. **81** (1995) 73–205
12. Talagrand, M.: New concentration inequalities in product spaces. Inventiones Mathematicae **126** (1996) 505–563
13. Talagrand, M.: A new look at independence. Annals of Probability **24** (1996) 1–34 (Special Invited Paper).
14. Luczak, M.J., McDiarmid, C.: Concentration for locally acting permutations. Discrete Mathematics (2003) to appear
15. McDiarmid, C.: Concentration for independent permutations. Combinatorics, Probability, and Computing **2** (2002) 163–178

16. Panchenko, D.: A note on Talagrand's concentration inequality. Electronic Communications in Probability **6** (2001)
17. Panchenko, D.: Some extensions of an inequality of Vapnik and Chervonenkis. Electronic Communications in Probability **7** (2002)
18. Panchenko, D.: Symmetrization approach to concentration inequalities for empirical processes. Annals of Probability **to appear** (2003)
19. de la Peña, V., Giné, E.: Decoupling: from Dependence to Independence. Springer, New York (1999)
20. Ledoux, M.: On Talagrand's deviation inequalities for product measures. ESAIM: Probability and Statistics **1** (1997) 63–87 http://www.emath.fr/ps/.
21. Ledoux, M.: Isoperimetry and Gaussian analysis. In Bernard, P., ed.: Lectures on Probability Theory and Statistics, Ecole d'Eté de Probabilités de St-Flour XXIV-1994 (1996) 165–294
22. Bobkov, S., Ledoux, M.: Poincaré's inequalities and Talagrands's concentration phenomenon for the exponential distribution. Probability Theory and Related Fields **107** (1997) 383–400
23. Massart, P.: About the constants in Talagrand's concentration inequalities for empirical processes. Annals of Probability **28** (2000) 863–884
24. Klein, T.: Une inégalité de concentration à gauche pour les processus empiriques. C. R. Math. Acad. Sci. Paris **334** (2002) 501–504
25. Boucheron, S., Lugosi, G., Massart, P.: A sharp concentration inequality with applications. Random Structures and Algorithms **16** (2000) 277–292
26. Boucheron, S., Lugosi, G., Massart, P.: Concentration inequalities using the entropy method. The Annals of Probability **31** (2003) 1583–1614
27. Bousquet, O.: A Bennett concentration inequality and its application to suprema of empirical processes. C. R. Acad. Sci. Paris **334** (2002) 495–500
28. Bousquet, O.: Concentration inequalities for sub-additive functions using the entropy method. In Giné, E., C.H., Nualart, D., eds.: Stochastic Inequalities and Applications. Volume 56 of Progress in Probability. Birkhauser (2003) 213–247
29. Boucheron, S., Bousquet, O., Lugosi, G., Massart, P.: Moment inequalities for functions of independent random variables. The Annals of Probability (2004) to appear.
30. Janson, S., Łuczak, T., Ruciński, A.: Random graphs. John Wiley, New York (2000)
31. Hoeffding, W.: Probability inequalities for sums of bounded random variables. Journal of the American Statistical Association **58** (1963) 13–30
32. Chernoff, H.: A measure of asymptotic efficiency of tests of a hypothesis based on the sum of observations. Annals of Mathematical Statistics **23** (1952) 493–507
33. Okamoto, M.: Some inequalities relating to the partial sum of binomial probabilities. Annals of the Institute of Statistical Mathematics **10** (1958) 29–35
34. Bennett, G.: Probability inequalities for the sum of independent random variables. Journal of the American Statistical Association **57** (1962) 33–45
35. Bernstein, S.: The Theory of Probabilities. Gastehizdat Publishing House, Moscow (1946)
36. Efron, B., Stein, C.: The jackknife estimate of variance. Annals of Statistics **9** (1981) 586–596
37. Steele, J.: An Efron-Stein inequality for nonsymmetric statistics. Annals of Statistics **14** (1986) 753–758
38. Vapnik, V., Chervonenkis, A.: On the uniform convergence of relative frequencies of events to their probabilities. Theory of Probability and its Applications **16** (1971) 264–280

Concentration Inequalities   239

39. Devroye, L., Györfi, L., Lugosi, G.: A Probabilistic Theory of Pattern Recognition. Springer-Verlag, New York (1996)
40. Vapnik, V.: Statistical Learning Theory. John Wiley, New York (1998)
41. van der Waart, A., Wellner, J.:   Weak convergence and empirical processes. Springer-Verlag, New York (1996)
42. Dudley, R.: Uniform Central Limit Theorems. Cambridge University Press, Cambridge (1999)
43. Koltchinskii, V., Panchenko, D.: Empirical margin distributions and bounding the generalization error of combined classifiers. Annals of Statistics **30** (2002)
44. Massart, P.: Some applications of concentration inequalities to statistics. Annales de la Faculté des Sciencies de Toulouse **IX** (2000) 245–303
45. Bartlett, P., Boucheron, S., Lugosi, G.:   Model selection and error estimation. Machine Learning **48** (2001) 85–113
46. Lugosi, G., Wegkamp, M.: Complexity regularization via localized random penalties. submitted (2003)
47. Bousquet, O.: New approaches to statistical learning theory. Annals of the Institute of Statistical Mathematics **55** (2003) 371–389
48. Lugosi, G.: Pattern classification and learning theory. In Györfi, L., ed.: Principles of Nonparametric Learning, Springer, Viena (2002) 5–62
49. Devroye, L., Györfi, L.: Nonparametric Density Estimation: The L_1 View. John Wiley, New York (1985)
50. Devroye, L.:   The kernel estimate is relatively stable.   Probability Theory and Related Fields **77** (1988) 521–536
51. Devroye, L.: Exponential inequalities in nonparametric estimation. In Roussas, G., ed.: Nonparametric Functional Estimation and Related Topics, NATO ASI Series, Kluwer Academic Publishers, Dordrecht (1991) 31–44
52. Devroye, L., Lugosi, G.: Combinatorial Methods in Density Estimation. Springer-Verlag, New York (2000)
53. Koltchinskii, V.: Rademacher penalties and structural risk minimization. IEEE Transactions on Information Theory **47** (2001) 1902–1914
54. Bartlett, P., Mendelson, S.: Rademacher and Gaussian complexities: risk bounds and structural results. Journal of Machine Learning Research **3** (2002) 463–482
55. Bartlett, P., Bousquet, O., Mendelson, S.:   Localized Rademacher complexities. In: Proceedings of the 15th annual conference on Computational Learning Theory. (2002) 44–48
56. Vapnik, V., Chervonenkis, A.: Theory of Pattern Recognition. Nauka, Moscow (1974) (in Russian); German translation: *Theorie der Zeichenerkennung*, Akademie Verlag, Berlin, 1979.
57. Blumer, A., Ehrenfeucht, A., Haussler, D., Warmuth, M.: Learnability and the Vapnik-Chervonenkis dimension. Journal of the ACM **36** (1989) 929–965
58. Anthony, M., Bartlett, P.L.: Neural Network Learning: Theoretical Foundations. Cambridge University Press, Cambridge (1999)
59. Rhee, W., Talagrand, M.: Martingales, inequalities, and NP-complete problems. Mathematics of Operations Research **12** (1987) 177–181
60. Shamir, E., Spencer, J.: Sharp concentration of the chromatic number on random graphs $g_{n,p}$. Combinatorica **7** (1987) 374–384
61. Samson, P.M.: Concentration of measure inequalities for Markov chains and ϕ-mixing processes. Annals of Probability **28** (2000) 416–461
62. Cover, T., Thomas, J.: Elements of Information Theory. John Wiley, New York (1991)

63. Han, T.: Nonnegative entropy measures of multivariate symmetric correlations. Information and Control **36** (1978)
64. Beckner, W.: A generalized Poincaré inequality for Gaussian measures. Proceedings of the American Mathematical Society **105** (1989) 397–400
65. Latała, R., Oleszkiewicz, C.: Between Sobolev and Poincaré. In: Geometric Aspects of Functional Analysis, Israel Seminar (GAFA), 1996-2000, Springer (2000) 147–168 Lecture Notes in Mathematics, 1745.
66. Chafaï, D.: On ϕ-entropies and ϕ-Sobolev inequalities. Technical report, arXiv.math.PR/0211103 (2002)
67. Ledoux, M.: Concentration of measure and logarithmic sobolev inequalities. In: Séminaire de Probabilités XXXIII. Lecture Notes in Mathematics 1709, Springer (1999) 120–216
68. Ledoux, M.: The concentration of measure phenomenon. American Mathematical Society, Providence, RI (2001)
69. Vapnik, V.: The Nature of Statistical Learning Theory. Springer-Verlag, New York (1995)

Author Index

Lecture Notes in Artificial Intelligence (LNAI)

Vol. 2934: G. Lindemann, D. Moldt, M. Paolucci (Eds.), Regulated Agent-Based Social Systems. X, 301 pages. 2004.

Vol. 2930: F. Winkler (Ed.), Automated Deduction in Geometry. VII, 231 pages. 2004.

Vol. 2926: L. van Elst, V. Dignum, A. Abecker (Eds.), Agent-Mediated Knowledge Management. XI, 428 pages. 2004.

Vol. 2923: V. Lifschitz, I. Niemelä (Eds.), Logic Programming and Nonmonotonic Reasoning. IX, 365 pages. 2004.

Vol. 2915: A. Camurri, G. Volpe (Eds.), Gesture-Based Communication in Human-Computer Interaction. XIII, 558 pages. 2004.

Vol. 2913: T.M. Pinkston, V.K. Prasanna (Eds.), High Performance Computing - HiPC 2003. XX, 512 pages. 2003.

Vol. 2903: T.D. Gedeon, L.C.C. Fung (Eds.), AI 2003: Advances in Artificial Intelligence. XVI, 1075 pages. 2003.

Vol. 2902: F.M. Pires, S.P. Abreu (Eds.), Progress in Artificial Intelligence. XV, 504 pages. 2003.

Vol. 2892: F. Dau, The Logic System of Concept Graphs with Negation. XI, 213 pages. 2003.

Vol. 2891: J. Lee, M. Barley (Eds.), Intelligent Agents and Multi-Agent Systems. X, 215 pages. 2003.

Vol. 2882: D. Veit, Matchmaking in Electronic Markets. XV, 180 pages. 2003.

Vol. 2871: N. Zhong, Z.W. Raś, S. Tsumoto, E. Suzuki (Eds.), Foundations of Intelligent Systems. XV, 697 pages. 2003.

Vol. 2854: J. Hoffmann, Utilizing Problem Structure in Planing. XIII, 251 pages. 2003.

Vol. 2843: G. Grieser, Y. Tanaka, A. Yamamoto (Eds.), Discovery Science. XII, 504 pages. 2003.

Vol. 2842: R. Gavaldá, K.P. Jantke, E. Takimoto (Eds.), Algorithmic Learning Theory. XI, 313 pages. 2003.

Vol. 2838: N. Lavrač, D. Gamberger, L. Todorovski, H. Blockeel (Eds.), Knowledge Discovery in Databases: PKDD 2003. XVI, 508 pages. 2003.

Vol. 2837: N. Lavrač, D. Gamberger, L. Todorovski, H. Blockeel (Eds.), Machine Learning: ECML 2003. XVI, 504 pages. 2003.

Vol. 2835: T. Horváth, A. Yamamoto (Eds.), Inductive Logic Programming. X, 401 pages. 2003.

Vol. 2821: A. Günter, R. Kruse, B. Neumann (Eds.), KI 2003: Advances in Artificial Intelligence. XII, 662 pages. 2003.

Vol. 2807: V. Matoušek, P. Mautner (Eds.), Text, Speech and Dialogue. XIII, 426 pages. 2003.

Vol. 2801: W. Banzhaf, J. Ziegler, T. Christaller, P. Dittrich, J.T. Kim (Eds.), Advances in Artificial Life. XVI, 905 pages. 2003.

Vol. 2797: O.R. Zaïane, S.J. Simoff, C. Djeraba (Eds.), Mining Multimedia and Complex Data. XII, 281 pages. 2003.

Vol. 2792: T. Rist, R.S. Aylett, D. Ballin, J. Rickel (Eds.), Intelligent Virtual Agents. XV, 364 pages. 2003.

Vol. 2782: M. Klusch, A. Omicini, S. Ossowski, H. Laamanen (Eds.), Cooperative Information Agents VII. XI, 345 pages. 2003.

Vol. 2780: M. Dojat, E. Keravnou, P. Barahona (Eds.), Artificial Intelligence in Medicine. XIII, 388 pages. 2003.

Vol. 2777: B. Schölkopf, M.K. Warmuth (Eds.), Learning Theory and Kernel Machines. XIV, 746 pages. 2003.

Vol. 2752: G.A. Kaminka, P.U. Lima, R. Rojas (Eds.), RoboCup 2002: Robot Soccer World Cup VI. XVI, 498 pages. 2003.

Vol. 2741: F. Baader (Ed.), Automated Deduction – CADE-19. XII, 503 pages. 2003.

Vol. 2705: S. Renals, G. Grefenstette (Eds.), Text- and Speech-Triggered Information Access. VII, 197 pages. 2003.

Vol. 2703: O.R. Zaïane, J. Srivastava, M. Spiliopoulou, B. Masand (Eds.), WEBKDD 2002 - MiningWeb Data for Discovering Usage Patterns and Profiles. IX, 181 pages. 2003.

Vol. 2700: M.T. Pazienza (Ed.), Extraction in the Web Era. XIII, 163 pages. 2003.

Vol. 2699: M.G. Hinchey, J.L. Rash, W.F. Truszkowski, C.A. Rouff, D.F. Gordon-Spears (Eds.), Formal Approaches to Agent-Based Systems. IX, 297 pages. 2002.

Vol. 2691: V. Mařík, J.P. Müller, M. Pechoucek (Eds.), Multi-Agent Systems and Applications III. XIV, 660 pages. 2003.

Vol. 2684: M.V. Butz, O. Sigaud, P. Gérard (Eds.), Anticipatory Behavior in Adaptive Learning Systems. X, 303 pages. 2003.

Vol. 2682: R. Meo, P.L. Lanzi, M. Klemettinen (Eds.), Database Support for Data Mining Applications. XII, 325 pages. 2004.

Vol. 2671: Y. Xiang, B. Chaib-draa (Eds.), Advances in Artificial Intelligence. XIV, 642 pages. 2003.

Vol. 2663: E. Menasalvas, J. Segovia, P.S. Szczepaniak (Eds.), Advances in Web Intelligence. XII, 350 pages. 2003.

Vol. 2661: P.L. Lanzi, W. Stolzmann, S.W. Wilson (Eds.), Learning Classifier Systems. VII, 231 pages. 2003.

Vol. 2654: U. Schmid, Inductive Synthesis of Functional Programs. XXII, 398 pages. 2003.

Vol. 2650: M.-P. Huget (Ed.), Communications in Multi-agent Systems. VIII, 323 pages. 2003.

Vol. 2645: M.A. Wimmer (Ed.), Knowledge Management in Electronic Government. XI, 320 pages. 2003.

Vol. 2639: G. Wang, Q. Liu, Y. Yao, A. Skowron (Eds.), Rough Sets, Fuzzy Sets, Data Mining, and Granular Computing. XVII, 741 pages. 2003.

Vol. 2637: K.-Y. Whang, J. Jeon, K. Shim, J. Srivastava, Advances in Knowledge Discovery and Data Mining. XVIII, 610 pages. 2003.

Vol. 2636: E. Alonso, D. Kudenko, D. Kazakov (Eds.), Adaptive Agents and Multi-Agent Systems. XIV, 323 pages. 2003.

Vol. 2627: B. O'Sullivan (Ed.), Recent Advances in Constraints. X, 201 pages. 2003.

Vol. 2600: S. Mendelson, A.J. Smola (Eds.), Advanced Lectures on Machine Learning. IX, 259 pages. 2003.

Vol. 2592: R. Kowalczyk, J.P. Müller, H. Tianfield, R. Unland (Eds.), Agent Technologies, Infrastructures, Tools, and Applications for E-Services. XVII, 371 pages. 2003.